Armand Gatti in the Theatre

Frontispiece: Gatti reading *La Passion du Général Franco* at the TNP (1968). Photo Chaussat

Armand Gatti in the Theatre

Wild Duck Against the Wind

DOROTHY KNOWLES

The Athlone Press
London
•
Fairleigh Dickinson University Press
Rutherford · Madison · Teaneck

First published 1989 by The Athlone Press Ltd
44 Bedford Row, London WC1R 4LY

© Dorothy Knowles 1989

British Library Cataloguing in Publication Data
Knowles, Dorothy, *1906–*
   Armand Gatti in the theatre: wild duck against the wind.
   1. France. Theatre. Gatti, Armand, 1924–
   I. Title
   792'.092'4

ISBN 0–485–11364–3

All rights reserved. No part of this publication may be reproduced, stored in a retrieval system, or transmitted in any form or by any means, electronic, mechanical, photocopying or otherwise, without prior permission in writing from the publisher.

Library of Congress Cataloging-in-Publication Data

Knowles, Dorothy, 1906–
   Armand Gatti in the Theatre: Wild Duck against the Wind
   / Dorothy Knowles.
      p.   cm.
   Bibliography: p.
   Includes index.
   ISBN 0-8386-3371-4 (alk. paper)
   1. Gatti, Armand—Criticism and interpretation.   2. Theater-
-France—History—20th century.   I. Title.
PQ2667.A8Z73   1989   88-28744
842'.914—dc19   CIP

Associated University Presses
440 Forsgate Drive
Cranbury, NJ 08512

The paper used in this publication meets the requirements of the American National Standard for Permanence of Paper for Printed Library Materials Z39.48–1984.

Typeset by J&L Composition Ltd, Filey, North Yorkshire
Printed in the United States of America

Contents

List of Illustrations	vii
Acknowledgements	ix
Foreword	x
Introduction: Armand Gatti, the Wild Duck Flying Against the Wind	1
1 A Journalist-Dramatist in Guatemala	18
I *Le Quetzal. Le Crapaud buffle*	
II *La Naissance*	
2 China: the Discovery of a Country, a Revolution, a Theatre	42
I *Le Poisson noir*	
II *Un Homme seul*	
3 Armchair Theatre as an Interlude: a Cat's-Eye View of the Establishment	62
Le Voyage du Grand Tchou	
4 Nazi Camps: Drama as an Escape from an Obsession	67
I *L'Enfant rat. La Deuxième Existence du Camp de Tatenberg*	
II *Chroniques d'une planète provisoire. L'Enclos*	
5 The Caribbean: Aggression and Resistance	93
El Otro Cristobal. Notre Tranchée de chaque jour	
6 Rebuttal as the Good Fight	107
I *La Vie imaginaire d'Auguste Geai. Chant public devant deux chaises électriques*	
II *La Cigogne*	
7 Two Plays for Special Occasions	137
I *V comme Vietnam*	
II *Les Treize Soleils de la rue Saint-Blaise*	

8 Spain: a Constant Preoccupation   157
   *La Passion du Général Franco. La Passion du Général Franco
   par les émigrés eux-mêmes*

9 Facets of Rosa Luxemburg: a Dramatic Character?   173
   Rosaspartakus prend le pouvoir. Rosa Collective

10 May 1968 and the Mini-Plays   189
   *Petit Manuel de guérilla urbaine.
   Interdit à plus de trente ans. Le Chat sauvage*

11 Belgium–Germany: Not a Theatre but a Human
   Community   201
   I   *La Colonne Durruti. L'Arche d'Adelin*
   II *Quatre schizophrénies à la recherche d'un pays dont
       l'existence est contestée. La Moitié du Ciel et nous*

12 France: an Official Challenge   220
   Avignon – *La Tribu des Carcana en guerre contre quoi?*

13 In Search of a New Creative 'Language'   226
   I   Montbéliard – *Le Lion, sa cage et ses ailes*
   II Ris-Orangis – *Le Joint*
   III Saint-Nazaire – *Le Canard sauvage*
   IV Avignon – *Le Cheval qui se suicide par le feu*
   V   L'Isle d'Abeau – *La Première Lettre*

14 Northern Ireland: a Blind Imperative Rendezvous   256
   Nous étions tous des noms d'arbres.   Le Labyrinthe

15 Toulouse: the Archaeopteryx: the Wild Duck
   Continues its Flight Against the Wind   275

   The Nomad Moves On   287

   Selective Bibliography   291

   Index   296

List of Illustrations

Copyright *La Parole Errante*

Frontispiece: Gatti reading *La Passion du Général Franco* at the TNP (1968). Photo Chaussat

Gatti preparing *La Cage aux fauves* (1954). Photo *Le Parisien Libéré*

Le Crapaud buffle, TNP (Jean Vilar, 1959). Execution of Atahualpa by Pizarre/Tiburcio. Photo Bernand

La Naissance, Villejuif Théâtre Romain-Rolland (1968). Production Roland Monod, décor, Hubert Monloup. Photo Bernand

La Naissance (Die Geburt), Kassel, Staatstheater (1969). Directed by Gatti, décor Hubert Monloup. Photo Kaspar Seiffert

Un Homme seul, Comédie de Saint-Étienne (1966). Directed by Gatti, décor Hubert Monloup. Photo Chaussat

Chroniques d'une planète provisoire, Grenier de Toulouse (1967). The new Nazi 'religion'. Photo Chaussat

Chroniques d'une planète provisoire, Grenier de Toulouse (1967). Directed by Gatti, décor Hubert Monloup with the astronauts' space-cabin projecting into the auditorium. Photo Chaussat

Chroniques d'une planète provisoire, Grenier de Toulouse (1967). Shertoc in the concentration camp with the memory of Pepi-(Parachronique). Photo Chaussat.

L'Enclos (film 1960). Mauthausen Concentration Camp, 'prisoners' working. Photo Chaussat

L'Enclos (1960) the Concentration Camp orchestra playing a Resistance song. Photo Chaussat

El otro Cristobal (film 1962). Directed by Gatti, décor Hubert Monloup. Photo Gasparini

La Vie imaginaire de l'éboueur Auguste Geai, Villeurbanne (1962). Directed by Jacques Rosner, décor René Allio. Photo Roget Pic

Chant public devant deux chaises électriques, TNP (1966). Venturelli in Uncle Sam's hat. Photo Chaussat

Chant public devant deux chaises électriques, TNP (1966) by Gatti, décor Hubert Monloup. Photo Chaussat

Armand Gatti in the Theatre

La Cigogne, Nanterre, Théâtre des Amandiers (1971). Directed by Pierre Debauche, décor Yannis Kokos and Danièle Rosier. Photo Chaussat

V comme Vietnam, Grenier de Toulouse (1967). Directed by Gatti, décor Hubert Monloup. Photo Chaussat

V comme Vietnam, Grenier de Toulouse (1967). Final scene in front of 'The Chestnut' with multiple megasheriffs. Photo Chaussat

Les Treize Soleils, TEP (1968). Directed by Guy Rétoré, décor Hubert Monloup. Varlin's watch. Photo Bernand

La Passion du Général Franco par les émigrés eux-mêmes, Ney Calberson lorry depot (1976). Directed by Gatti, décor Gilles Lacombe, with actors and standing audience. Photo Rajak Ohanian

Rosa Kollektiv, Kassel, Staatstheater (1970). Directed by Gatti, décor Hubert Monloup. Photo Seiffert

La Colonne Durruti (IAD) Brussels, Rasquinet factory in Schaerbeek (1972). Written and directed by Gatti with actors, puppets, audience. Photo Chaussat

L'Arche d'Adelin (IAD) in Brabant-Wallon (1973). Written, co-ordinated and produced by Gatti. Photo Rajak Ohanian

La Tribu des Carcana en guerre contre quoi?, Theatre Festival of Avignon (1974): the square in front of the Chapelle des Pénitents blancs. Photo René Jacques

La Tribu des Carcana en guerre contre quoi?, Theatre Festival of Avignon (1974): inside the Chapelle des Pénitents blancs. Photo René Jacques

La Première Lettre (films) 1978 L'Isle d'Abeau (St Quentin-Fallavier) Author, Gatti; filmed and edited by Stéphane Gatti, Hélène Chatelain, Claude Mourieras. Arrival of the wedding cake. Photo J.-J. Hocquard

La Première Lettre (films) 1978, L'Isle d'Abeau (L'Abbaye de Tamié). Monks singing. Photo J.-J. Hocquard

Nous étions tous des noms d'arbres (film) 1982 (Londonderry, the Workshop scholars). Youth actors of the Workshop and the Graffiti. Photo Paolo Gasparini

Le Labyrinthe, Theatre Festival of Avignon, 1982, le Cloître des Carmes. Directed by Gatti, décor Stéphane Gatti. Photo Vaucluse-Matin

L'Émission de Pierre Meynard Toulouse, Archéoptéryx, first *'stage de réinsertion'*, theme Nestor Makhno (1984). Directed by Gatti, décor Stéphane Gatti. Photo J.-J. Hocquard

Opéra avec Titre long, Montreal, Théâtre du Monument National (1986). Directed by Gatti. Production of the École Nationale de Théâtre du Canada. Photo Julien Bassouls

Acknowledgements

I wish to thank:

Armand Gatti for days of enlightening conversation.

Jean-Jacques Hocquard, his friend and administrator, for opening up to me Gatti's archives.

Dr K. L. Schaefer, director of performances at the Staatstheater in Kassel, Germany, for loaning documents from the theatre's archives on its production of three Gatti plays.

Mr Rubén Medina of the Cuban Institute of Art and the Cinematographic Industry in Havana, for a private viewing of Gatti's film *El otro Cristobal* and further documentation.

The monks of the Abbey of Tamié.

Mrs Silvia Earl, who delved energetically for me in various collections of press cuttings.

Professor J. S. Spink, my late husband, without whose help and co-operation in following Gatti productions and Gatti himself, this book could not have been written.

The British Academy for its contribution towards the publication of my manuscript.

'La Parole Errante' for contributing the Illustrations.

Foreword

The purpose of this book is to present in its full force the work of a thinker who has an avowed political stance, and this will be a challenge to the open-mindedness of readers who do not share this stance. Gatti's political formation was decided from the outset by his origins – his father, an anarchist, was an Italian immigrant worker in the USA, then in France – and by his own experience of life: his *vécu*, as he referred to it. What this *vécu* is was made clear by the 'grand reporteur' Marc Kravetz in his description of Gatti as 'historiographer of the century, the real century, our century'.[1] Kravetz defines at one and the same time the field in which Gatti works and Gatti's particular approach to historical events. Like his compatriot Michèle Firk, who refused to be 'objectively informed' and died in Guatemala, Gatti too has preferred, often at risk to himself, to become involved and so be in a position to give an inside view of 'the real century, our century'. Having no parallel experience myself, it would seem to be preferable in this study to let Gatti speak for himself.

Notes

1. *Libération*, 16 July 1979.

I need first to germinate my plays,
incubate them a hundred times, and,
over time, have them live through and
nurture each other.

Introduction:
Armand Gatti, the Wild Duck Flying Against the Wind

Armand Gatti is a poet. It is true that all his activity has been devoted to the theatre; not the theatre as an imitative art but the theatre as a creative activity. Gatti does not propose to imitate the real world; he proposes to create a parallel world of the same substance but submitted to the rhythms of creativity, not imitation. Gatti looks upon theatre as a parallel reality, but composed of the same substance. There is for Gatti one world only. The reality he creates is contemporary. Theatrical activity does not attempt to represent this contemporary reality, but *be* it in parallel with it. The contemporary reality that composes the substance of his world is multifarious, covering wide tracts of our contemporary experience, and in that it is essentially poetic and guided by the rhythms of creativity. It is also essentially critical. The poetic world is never a mere photograph, and Gatti's theatre is in no sense a mimetic art. His activities are the centre of great interest in the French theatre world under all its aspects: acting, staging, creation of texts, creation of themes; and it is doubtless as a great innovator in all theatre arts that his name will be heard more and more frequently in the future.

These positions of Gatti's were not reached by an *a priori* abstract theorizing; they emerged as the fruit of what must surely be one of the most varied experiences in the war-torn world we are living in. In the Resistance, as a concentration-camp inmate, as an escapee, as a member of the British SAS during the war, he knew the difference between an identity and a cover-story. But it was as correspondent for such papers as *Le Parisien Libéré*, or reviews like *Esprit*, travelling the world over, that he came to realize the difference between the 'facts' of an episode and the innumerable possible approaches to those 'facts', or awareness of those 'facts'. The facts themselves are not many-faceted, but the possible appreciations thereof are. Who, for instance, can claim to know anything about Patricia Hearst after her presentation by the media? Gatti's efforts have been concentrated on finding a method of reliving the facts, not attempting to observe them objectively or to piece together an objective account from witnesses' stories. Drama thus becomes a reliving of the 'act' and not a plausible representation of the 'act' as Aristotle would have it. Gatti is anti-classical, inchoative, open-ended.

It would be idle at the present time to attempt a critical biography of Armand Gatti. Perhaps in the future university researchers will constitute dossiers and card indexes full of references and cross-references, but as things are, little fruit would come from research in military records, concentration-camp files and police card indexes. Armand Gatti's biography is the sum of its possibilities, and I shall make no attempt to sort out the possibles from the probables in the life of this poet, playwright, patriot and political rebel who has lived like a salamander in all the fires of our times. He has often been accused of being a Herostratus; he has in fact always been an Æmelius Paulus. Gatti's *vécu*, his 'lived experience', forms an integral part of his work, and I shall attempt to adopt a method like his own in trying to recount the progress of his experience and activities as they are reflected in his works.

Gatti should have been born in Chicago, where his father Auguste, an Italian anarchist, had sought work immediately after the First World War, taking with him his wife Letizia Luzana. Unfortunately for Auguste his 'subversive activities' during a strike drew down upon him the wrath of the Pinkertons at the slaughter-house where he worked. He had to be got rid of; so they tied him in a sack, stabbed him repeatedly and threw him into Lake Calumet, south of Chicago. Auguste managed to escape through the lacerations in the sack, and was found badly wounded on the lakeside by an Italian who cared for him until fellow-workers helped him to get back to Europe. Meanwhile his unborn son had made the journey to Piedmont through the kindness of immigrant workers who paid his 'widow's' fare.

When Letizia heard that Auguste had survived and was living in Monaco with one of his sisters – as a known anarchist he could not return to Mussolini's Italy – she set off on foot from Piedmont for Monaco. For four days she was held up at the frontier because she had no visa; finally a compassionate guard quietly let her through and she arrived, still on foot, just in time to give birth to her son in hospital in Monaco on 26 January 1924, during the noisy festival of Sainte-Dévote. According to the legend of Sainte-Dévote the martyr's body was brought to Monaco from Corsica by two fugitive priests and a boatman, guided only by the Saint's soul in the form of a dove. To commemorate the legendary event a boat is burned on that date to the accompaniment of a cannonade. When Letizia heard the cannonade she murmured, 'That's Auguste up to his tricks again'. At that moment her son was born. This is how Gatti told me the story of his beginnings.

Gatti's father would seem to have been as vivid a story-teller as his son who lived, as it were by proxy, through the 'White Terror' of the 1920s

Introduction: Armand Gatti, the Wild Duck Flying Against the Wind

in the United States and made it the subject of a play on the fate of Sacco and Vanzetti. The story of his father Auguste was a story of poverty and hunger. He was one of twenty-one children of whom six died in early childhood; 'all those mouths to feed'. At the age of thirteen he was hired out as watchman in Saint-Laurent-du-Var, and slept in the kennel with the guard dog which he used to hold tight in his arms to stop it barking, he was so afraid. Three years later, back in Italy, he helped his father to work the village priest's plot of land, but whenever there was a nice fat chicken which 'could have been shared among the family', 'grandmother' took it to the priest. For Letizia, a distant cousin of Auguste's and partly Slav like him, life had been as hard. She was in fact born in Marseille, but on the death of her father, who fell from roof-scaffolding when she was two, her mother took her to Italy. There she worked as a farm hand until she was thirteen, when she was sent to Turin with a placard round her neck: 'I am looking for work'.

Seven of Auguste's brothers were killed in the 1914–18 War. Auguste himself was one of thirty survivors of the Italian Brigade that fought at the Chemin des Dames. Later, on the Italian front, he was buried in a bomb explosion but managed to escape. He finished up seriously wounded in a Milan hospital where his father, who did the 120 kilometres there on foot, sat by his son's side for three days and nights, 'holding his hand; he would not let him die'.

When Auguste and Letizia went to the United States after the war it was at the invitation of Auguste's brother Angelo, who had made a good living there as a baker, but before they arrived Angelo had committed suicide because of a 'blonde' who had robbed him of all he possessed. The incident, like the sorry lot of immigrant workers, was grist to Gatti's dramatic mill, and Gatti himself, much impressed by the story of the 'blonde' told so frequently by his father, professes to have had ever since an 'ambivalent attitude to blondes'.

Gatti's Christian name is really Dante – Dante, Sauveur. During the war his father had learnt to read and write and wanted to call his son Giotto, but the French registrar would have none of it; so Dante it was. When Dante became a journalist he took the name of his uncle in Monaco, Armand. As a child he lived in Tonkin, Monaco's *bidonville* for immigrant workers consisting of 'Poles, Neapolitans, Arabs, Bretons, people from Savoy and Calabria'. This shanty town has long since been cleared away, but Gatti paints a vivid picture of it and the seamy side of life there in his key work *La Vie imaginaire de l'éboueur Auguste Geai*, dedicated to the memory of his father.

A subsequent move took the family across the frontier to Saint Joseph, the working-class quarter of Beausoleil. School provided the only escape from the humiliations of the life of an immigrant, although Gatti, naturalized French in 1956, used proudly to claim as his 'nationality':

'being an immigrant's son'. All the way to school, little Dante drank in his father's lurid tales of war, his endless talk of class confrontation and of the impending 'Revolution'. Every morning on waking the child, under the strong influence of his very Catholic mother, used to pray to Christ to ask him to hold back the Revolution that his father was always announcing: 'I could not do anything. I was too little.' But 'Auguste', the playwright's dying dustman, was impatient: 'What about the Revolution? When is it coming?' These early influences went a long way towards determining the political stance Gatti was to take up for the rest of his life.

At school Dante worked hard to learn to speak French 'like the others' – the French children – and proudly beat them on their home ground by coming first in French in the class. The French language became 'one of the greatest loves of his life', 'his very existence even', and continues so today. Gatti is not a poet only when composing his own texts, but also in his manifold activities in the worlds of the theatre and film.

At eleven Gatti had to leave school. At twelve he worked as a furniture remover. At fourteen he got 'piecework' with an undertaker. He was paid per burial: 'People had to die for me to eat.' When his father was killed in 1939 in a brush with the police, his mother sent him to the small seminary of Saint Paul in Super-Cannes, where he went through a mystical crisis. Out of term, when the seminary was shut, Gatti became a voracious reader in the Monaco town library, from which he appropriated Rimbaud's works before returning to the seminary. But Rimbaud was on the Index, and the scandal of the discovery of the books in the boy's possession led to his expulsion. Several of Gatti's works bear the mark of his stay in the seminary and he has explained certain reactions of his with this remark: 'Je suis un peu curé'.

Gatti's next vital experience was of Nazi concentration camps. He was sixteen when Hitler's war began, and France had become an occupied country. In 1942 he joined the maquis and explained his decision to Marc Kravetz later in 1979, saying that after the Spanish Civil War all the working-class movement had known was a 'series of burials', and this doubtless explained why everything he had done and written thus far, apart from his 'reflection on the Soviet dissidence' in 1976–7, constituted a series of *chants funèbres*. In 1942, however, at the age of eighteen, he still believed that the Revolution was 'for tomorrow' and that the Resistance movement was the eve of that tomorrow. He made his appearance on the Plateau de Millevaches in the Corrèze looking 'just like an artiste, wearing a cloak and floppy bow tie', and carrying a box of books like one of his characters – Ma, a Kuomintang officer who had defected to the Partisans in the 1930s. But the books Gatti carried were by Henri Michaux, Hölderlin, Mallarmé and, of course, Rimbaud. Gatti's particular maquis consisted of four men with a single revolver, a

Introduction: Armand Gatti, the Wild Duck Flying Against the Wind

6.35, and they spent the terrible winter of 1942 in a hole in the frozen ground of the Corrèze. This hole on two levels in the form of a T was to become a whole play, *Les Hauts Plateaux*. When in the hole, Gatti passed the time 'settling an account with God, a very abstract god who had nothing to do with the God of the Catholics or any other god'. Eventually Gatti and his companions were tracked down by gendarmes and the Gardes Mobiles Républicaines: the riot police, forerunners of the post-war Compagnie Républicaine de Sécurité.

By a miracle Gatti survived the attack by three hand grenades; the following machine-gun fire tore his clothes to shreds but left him unscathed. In Tarnac, brutal interrogations about his reasons for joining the maquis drew from him the unexpected reply: 'To make the infinitely good and infinitely perfect God in his heaven understand something of man's experience on earth'. In Ussel torture was more sophisticated, and in the prison in Tulles – where the men were so tightly chained together in twos in cages meant for a single drunk that they had to lie on top of each other and, in the cold, distressingly soaked each other with urine – Gatti followed during interrogations the disconcerting line he had taken at Tarnac, answering with verses from Gérard de Nerval, improvisations on Pierre Louÿs and improvisations of his own. The torturers laughed, thinking him weak in the head, but an army doctor at Ussel who had taken part in the torture pointed to Gatti, shouting: 'Take care, the maquis is becoming intellectual'.

From then onwards Gatti knew how to defend himself, how to distance himself from the torturers. It was to be by literature, by the need to invent. In this way he came out of the ordeal 'relatively intact, unlike many of the prisoners'. He had built up a defensive linguistic barrier round himself just like the prisoners in Long Kesh who, as he was to learn during his stay in Derry in 1981, used Gaelic as an 'escape route' from their English-speaking gaolers. It was after a round of torture that the four maquisards, Joseph, Marcel, Georges and Donqui (in the maquis Gatti was officially known as Don Quixote), admitted to each other that 'if it was still to be done, they would do it again'. The tremendous feeling of 'liberation' that came over them at that moment told them they had found 'the right word' [*le mot juste*] at 'the right time' in 'the right place'. Ever since Gatti has sought *le mot juste*, with literature and the event nurturing each other. This is what Gatti calls 'l'aventure de la parole errante', and he insists that 'the whole of [his] political activity can be summed up in this search for *la parole errante* in all places and at all times'. His plays and films are there to bear out his claim.

The tribunal in Limoges sentenced the four men to death. The agony of mind which must follow such a sentence finds very personal expression in a poem of 1978, 'La Dernière Nuit', which features in the final telling episode of a video film, *La Première Lettre*, on the execution of

Armand Gatti in the Theatre

Roger Rouxel at the age of eighteen (Gatti's own age then) by the Nazis on Mont Valérien. Gatti was spared, doubtless because of his powerful physique, and despatched instead as Number 171173, in a cattle truck, to the Neuengamme camp, where the Lindermann organization selected him for work on the construction of underwater submarine shelters at Hamburg, 200 metres down. There he became Number 713. The fact that these numbers were passed on from those who had died in the work served to camouflage the real death toll.

Gatti complained that in the diving-bells he could never get used to 'bleeding from the nose and ears. Like my father twenty years before, I was haunted by visions of the end of the world, and by death which I saw all around me'. Poetry was his refuge. Composing it helped him to keep a grip on his mind and since he had no writing material, he counted the alexandrines on his ribs and the rhymes on his fingers and toes in a sort of 'experimental writing', as he put it. This prevented him from sinking into the fatal indifference that claimed so many of his fellow-deportees.

One day the brutal killing by a Kapo of Vladimir, a Russian who worked with him in the diving-bell, followed by an ominous turn of events on the Appelplatz after his rash request for the return of his blue exercise book, made it clear that certain death or escape were the only alternatives before him. He decided on escape, despite the haunting image of former attempted escapees changed into ice statues by a hosepipe in the winter cold, and left standing on the Appelplatz as a warning before being finally thrown into the sea. When an accident to a diving-bell momentarily diverted the guards' attention Gatti took a chance and walked out of the camp, a grotesque figure in a shabby Russian army coat with a partly shaven head, carrying a shovel as if engaged in work. He began on an unprepared marathon trek via Bordeaux, where he had the address of a Resistance fighter's family. It could not risk taking him in.

Gatti's trek took him three months and he ended up in the same maquis where he had been caught, as he had nowhere else to go. All skin and bone and at the end of his tether, he staggered towards old Élie's farm, eight kilometres from Tarnac, where he was warmly welcomed. By then the plateau was a reception area for parachuted 'missions' from England. It was also a centre for SAS landings, and Gatti served as a link between the SAS and the local population. He finally flew back with the missions to England, where he joined the French unit of the 4th SAS division and was subsequently dropped near Arnhem.

This unfortunate episode having scattered the units, Gatti found himself alone in the Netherlands countryside and decided to try to get to Monaco to see his mother, who had had no news of him since he joined the maquis. It appears that this never occurred to him as being an act of desertion, and doubtless his SAS uniform made him acceptable along

Introduction: Armand Gatti, the Wild Duck Flying Against the Wind

the route, but the local authorities took a different view, and after an unfortunate altercation in a police station where his mother, being an Italian, had been taken in, he was arrested and handed over to the British, who sent him to London. He was not court-martialled as he agreed to join a French airborne unit which landed several times in Normandy. It was in this situation that he was finally demobilized with medals which he has never worn, but with no gratuity.

Gatti's next problem was to get a job. He went to Paris in 1945 with a thousand francs from his mother's savings and a letter of introduction from a friend in Monaco who, since the Resistance was then 'fashionable', also provided him with a naval officer's uniform – too big for him. He presented himself to Jacques Rebeyrol, a director of *Le Parisien Libéré*, a product of the Resistance movement along with *Franc Tireur*, *Libération* and *Combat*. His career as a journalist began then and was to last for fourteen years: journalism could provide a living which poetry, Gatti's real bent, could not. But Gatti was not to be sidetracked; he sought straight away to get in touch with the Surrealist poets because of their revolutionary approach to language. Surrealism – defined by André Breton in his *Manifeste* as pure psychic automatism through which it was intended to express, verbally or in writing, the true function of thought, thought uncontrolled by reason or aesthetic or moral preoccupations, together with Breton's belief in the future resolution of the two states of dream and reality into some kind of absolute reality, a *surreality* – had a certain appeal for Gatti – Gérard de Nerval had already taken him some way along this path. The subsequent extension of the Surrealists' revolutionary activity from the world of art to the political arena was also in line with the thinking of this young revolutionary poet.

Of the Surrealists, Robert Desnos, perhaps the closest in spirit to Gatti, had just died in an international ghetto set up by the Germans at Terezin in Czechoslovakia. André Breton, who had gone in 1941 to America, where he worked as a radio announcer for the Voice of America, had not yet returned to France, but Philippe Soupault, co-founder of the Surrealist movement with André Breton, was in Paris and received Gatti with open arms, and it is to Soupault that we owe the first portrait of Gatti, a young man who called on him, somewhat embarrassed but nevertheless determined to read his poems to him. During the visit Soupault got him to talk of his life since 1942. 'I know,' Soupault writes in *Journal d'un fantôme* (1946):

> I who listened to him, I know he was not lying. You don't talk of hunger and the pangs of hunger as he did unless you have experienced them, and above all of the joy which, several months after he had felt it, lit up his face when he described to me his delight at having drunk milk, 'at the very least half a litre!' after three days trekking without food.

Armand Gatti in the Theatre

Given what Gatti had been through, Soupault predicted that

> no new struggle would hold any terrors for him, and nothing, not even success, would spoil him or come between poetry and him .... This young man may perhaps know what Rimbaud had lived through. But he still knows nothing of the literary circles which Rimbaud found so distasteful. It is strange that he wants to get to know them. If he is disappointed, which is very likely (I feel already that he is worried about the attitude of certain poets) how will he react? Will he once again strike out on his own?

Clearly Soupault had understood his visitor.

Gatti's overriding desire, however, was to meet William Faulkner and the poet and painter Henri Michaux, whose books had provided him with 'fundamental reading' in the maquis and in his several prisons. He failed to meet Faulkner, but met Michaux through the musician Pierre Boulez who, together with the 'non-formal' painter Bernard Saby and himself, formed a close-knit trio. The meeting with Michaux took place at a concert, arranged by Boulez, at which the American musician John Cage was to play some of his *Sonates et Interludes* on his 'prepared pianos' – pianos specially 'doctored' to produce particular effects. Michaux, who spent so much of his time exploring 'L'Espace du Dedans', to quote the title of a work of his, quickly understood Gatti and christened him the 'Monégasque Kafka', a 'twenty-year-long parachutist', but 'where the devil did he fall from?'

Saby (non-representative, non-geometrical) was in full activity when Gatti attempted, somewhat adventurously, an analysis – or rather, a 'read-in' – of an unfinished canvas responding to the impression of clanging bells it produced on him at first sight. The bells were neither the tocsin nor the death knell. The bells he 'heard' were for him those of the Sicilian Vespers (so he told me), and he called Saby's canvas by that name. When he published his 'read-in' under the significant title *Les Analogues du réel*, in 1974, 'analogues' replaces the word 'parallel', which he normally uses. They are parallel paradigms. The mark of Surrealism has remained permanently in Gatti.

Almost immediately journalism became for Gatti a kind of creative writing, and remained so even when he moved over to legal correspondent and specialized for nine years in civil and criminal cases, including trials of wartime collaborators. At the trial of the German military who had murdered all the inhabitants of Oradour-sur-Glane in June 1944, he startled the court by his cry of dismay on seeing the editor's 'correction' of the line he had quoted from Hugo's *Booz endormi* to describe the somnolence of one of the accused. His reports on social political problems left no doubts about his own political stance, formed as it had been by his origins and his early experience of life; this is well

Introduction: Armand Gatti, the Wild Duck Flying Against the Wind

illustrated by his despatch of August 1951 on the death of a planter in Martinique during a revolt of the workers. The despatch turned the accusation levelled against sixteen of the men into a blistering attack on racial harassment and class confrontation in the 'overseas departments' of France.

1953 was a turning point in Gatti's career. In collaboration with Pierre Joffroy and – in the first stages – the dramatist Kateb Yacine, whom he had met in Algeria in 1950, Gatti wrote *La Vie de Churchill* (Seuil, 1954) rather unwillingly, as he was intent on his own literary research at the time. After finishing the book he embarked on a provisional career as amateur animal tamer of panthers, wolves and Marcello the bear, under the watchful eye of Paul Le Royer, so determined was he to get away from the routine reporting of legal proceedings. He was twice mauled, and after eight weeks *Le Parisien Libéré* refused to continue payment of the insurance premium. The despatch, *Envoyé spécial dans la cage aux fauves*, was, however, finished. It appeared in January–February 1954 and won for Gatti the coveted Albert Londres Prize for journalism. Seuil then published it in book form.

Journalism, considered so far by Gatti merely as a livelihood, was now to help him 'acquire a conception of the world on a planetary scale', and 'haunt the corridors of an event, in contact with very different peoples'.[1] The weeks and months spent in far-flung parts – China, Korea, Latin America – collecting data and observing social and political struggles at close quarters, even taking part in them at his peril, gave Gatti an insight into the ideas and ways of life of these peoples quite different from the 'folkloric notions' (to use Gatti's own term) often entertained about them. 'One gets a much broader view of man', he said. His experience as a journalist was in fact one of the most decisive factors in the development of Gatti as creator, whatever the field of his creation, and he readily acknowledged his debt.

The literary journalist reasserted himself in the fascinating volume *Sibérie – zéro + l'Infini*, published by Seuil in 1958, in which the despatches to *France-Soir, Libération, Les Lettres Françaises* ('Le Théâtre Yakoute renaît', 21 December) are taken up again and developed. Gatti went to Siberia in 1957 as a member of a delegation which André Pierrard, the director of the revue *France-URSS*, organized for 'sympathizers' as distinct from Party members. They were to make a film with Chris Marker on the legendary hero Niorgoun Bootour. In his book Gatti describes the making of the film. He also produces, off the cuff so to speak, an amazing evocation of the immensity of the Siberian space and the intensity of its cold, together with an appreciation of the herculean efforts of the still relatively small body of men who – because they were natives of the place, or because they had volunteered, or because they were exiled to Siberia – built great

Armand Gatti in the Theatre

cities and laid the foundation of industrialization beyond the Urals. The possibility of war on two fronts had accelerated the 'progressive movement' in all walks of life, a film producer at Krasnoyarsk proudly told Gatti. Tomsk, seen by Gatti as a big, clay 'Negro' village when he passed through in 1955 on his way to China, had become a town which could well be 'twinned with Chicago'. After this second – and this time lengthy – visit to Siberia, he was wont to say to those tourists normally 'limited to the Leningrad, Moscow, Odessa triangle': 'You don't know the USSR. The USSR is Siberia first and foremost' (p. 8). He ends his book on Siberia not with the word FIN, but with the word COMMENCEMENT, the only 'suitable' word.

When discussing the different peoples in Siberia 'the Western conditioned reflex', Gatti writes, comes out in the inevitable question: 'What about the deportations?' Gatti does not avoid the political question. He refers to the Khrushchev report at the Twentieth Congress in 1956 which, for the preceding twenty months, had spread alarm and despondency throughout that vast movement of progressive opinion that had looked towards the Soviet Union for better standards than heretofore in public and international relations. What was unacceptable to the whole of progressive opinion was that the man to whom they had looked to correct all the bad that had bedevilled human relations in the past should turn out, like so many other great men, to have stooped to assassination and other atrocious means in order to free himself from the rivalry of close friends and colleagues. Gatti did not, however, allow these considerations to dominate his description of the country and its peoples. He did not, like so many of his journalist colleagues, move over to the Right, contribute to *L'Aurore* and *Figaro*, and publish books with desolating titles. His enthusiasm for the country remained undiminished. The account he gives in *Sibérie* demonstrates this, and so does the text he wrote for Chris Marker's very successful film *Lettres de Sibérie*. However, certain remarks concerning Stalin and an implied preference for a more moderate policy are significant.

When the delegation moved on to North Korea, Gatti gravitated actively towards cinema and called on Jean-Claude Bonnardot to direct a film for which he had himself written the script. *Morambong* begins in Kaesong, just south of the 38th Parallel, with the outbreak of the Korean War in June 1950 and tells of the separation of the lovers Yang Nan, an opera singer, and the joiner Tong-Il, who had volunteered for the North Korean Army. In a makeshift underground opera house in Morambong, after the opera house itself had been flattened by US bombers, a story of legendary lovers whom nothing can separate is presented in counterpart, with Yang Nan singing the role of the heroine. She 'lives' the role intensely, just as Tong-Il in real life 'lives' the legendary lover's role. Real life enriches the legend, and the legend enriches real life.

Introduction: Armand Gatti, the Wild Duck Flying Against the Wind

The opera sequences so impressed Jean Cocteau that he recommended the film for the Vigo Prize in 1960, but the sequences from newsreels highlighting the havoc wrought by the war, in counterpoint with the operatic sequences, were doubtless behind the prompt banning of the film in France as 'likely to be deleterious to the well-being of French policy, particularly in relation to Korea'. The ban was maintained for five years; even then the film was shown only in small specialized cinemas, such as the Ursulines in rue d'Ulm in Paris.

From Korea Gatti went on to China at the personal invitation of the Foreign Minister. It was his second visit, the first being in 1955. Instead of writing a dramatic text on an epic event in Chinese history, as was suggested to him, he felt drawn towards a defeated leader of the Partisans in the Kwansi province who was completely autonomous in his decisions. He made him the hero of a play and finally this *homme seul*, in the play of that name, reaches a position which is in accordance with the Party but does so independently of the Party, a wild duck flying against the wind.

In 1958, in the meantime, Seuil had published Gatti's 'literary' play, *Le Poisson noir*. It was met with silence by the critics. Gatti was restless. For fifteen years he had gone the rounds of the French newspapers – *Paris-Match, Le Parisien Libéré, L'Express, France-Observateur, France-Soir, Libération* – and found himself 'at home' in none. A wire from Raymond Cartier of *Paris-Match* to the prize-winning journalist about a despatch of his from Guatemala, 'I thought I was reading *L'Humanité* this morning', makes this clear; also Gatti's political stance. In October 1959, therefore, Jean Vilar's production in Paris of *Le Crapaud buffle* presented a possible new outlet for Gatti's activity, and despite the critics' attempted 'kill' of a disquieting young dramatist, Gatti did not hesitate to abandon the world of journalism for this new world of the theatre. His final contribution to journalism was an article written in December 1959 in homage to a great actor, *La France pleure son Gérard Philipe*. Soupault was not wrong in his judgement of Gatti's character.

Gatti's real start in the theatre came two years later when Roger Planchon produced his key work *La Vie imaginaire de l'éboueur Auguste Geai* in his much-talked-of theatrical enterprise in Villeurbanne. During the following six years Gatti's plays figured almost as prominently in number as Brecht's on the programmes of the Centres Dramatiques in the provinces where the Popular Theatre Movement, a striking feature of French culture, was developed in the post-war years. Gatti's play of 1967 on the Vietnam War was not restricted to these Centres and was seen in many other theatres and halls throughout the country, also outside France. It originated nevertheless in the Centre at Toulouse, the Grenier, where Gatti had become an almost resident dramatist at the invitation of Maurice Sarrazin, its director. Sarrazin felt convinced, after seeing Gatti's film *L'Enclos* on the concentration camp at Mauthausen, that any play by Gatti would be 'just what he was looking for'. And so it turned out: Gatti figured four times on his playbills between 1963 and 1967. In 1968 a second billing of a Gatti play at the Paris Théâtre National Populaire incurred a government ban on the production for convenient diplomatic reasons, not only at the TNP but in all government subsidized theatres – the only ones, in fact, which had the resources to stage a Gatti play, given the large casts always required. In consequence Gatti, like the exiles from Franco's Spain who figure in his play, became himself an exile, an artistic exile from France.

During his life Gatti has been everywhere, seen everything and done everything, and for him the material of drama is that contemporary reality of which he has such vast first-hand experience. He did not depart from this view when in exile, although once again he characteristically struck a new line.

The Italy of Fascism and the 'White Terror' of the United States – these he had, as it were, lived through by proxy; but the France of the Resistance and the France of the immigrant workers had come within his own personal experience, as had Guatemala after the fall of Arbenz, the Nicaragua of the hated Anastasio Somoza, the Germany of the war, the concentration camps, the Displaced Persons' camps and of the Baader-Meinhof activities, war-torn Korea, the 'birth' of Mao Tse-tung's China, and also Cuba of the Revolution ('before' and 'after'), the Nagasaki of the Bomb, the Spain of Franco and the exiles; also the dissidents of the USSR, self-acknowledged 'wild ducks'. A 'wild duck' himself, Gatti admits to having 'lost a few feathers' in this particular 'theatrical' venture.

Although he has always aimed at taking contemporary reality into the theatre, Gatti cannot be classed as a realist. It is the very substance of our political, social and ideological reality which is for him the subject and matter of valid theatre. He openly stated this in 1963, thereby distancing himself from the current theatrical vogue of the 'Absurdists' while, however, recognizing the special qualities of their plays. He accepted the validity of Ionesco's exploration of the particular problems of particular people, but saw his own work as being diametrically opposed to such a conception. He belonged to a new generation of playwrights who were turning away from metaphysical allegorizing on the human predicament towards the concrete *hic et nunc*, the *Ici et Maintenant* (1964) of Arthur Adamov, already applied by him in his play *Paolo Paoli*, which Planchon staged in 1957 at his small Théâtre de la Comédie in Lyon in the face of veiled threats, financial and other.

In the view of this generation, plays on topical subjects could perfectly well be heuristic and exploratory. They were not necessarily didactic. Didactic theatre was not in his line, Gatti said, and in this he differed

Introduction: Armand Gatti, the Wild Duck Flying Against the Wind

from Brecht. His subject matter is man in relation to events; he had no thought of carrying out the 'Revolution' on the stage. It is indeed to Gatti himself that we owe the best analysis of his dramatic work and intention up to 1967:

> I am not interested in writing plays, in becoming a professional PLAYWRIGHT in capital letters. I am not interested in having people make studies of my plays and decorticate them as they would a lobster. Theatre is a medium; its business is not to provide answers, or say 'this is what you must do when you leave the theatre'. Its business is to put the issues squarely before the spectator for him to question, because when a man starts asking questions he is beginning to change, and he could one day want to change the world. (Programme note, 'Grenier de Toulouse' No. 4, February 1967)

For this reason Gatti has always intended his theatre to divide his audience, not to unite them in a reassuring unified image.

With regard to Gatti's dramatic technique, his experience of theatre in China would seem to have been behind his desire to free the theatre from all confining limits and create an action situated on several planes and in different time-scales, with characters revealed in their multiple aspects.

This experience reinforced his experience of the Liberation, when – in contrast to life in concentration camps, where an individual no longer had a past or a future but only 'an undernourished present' – all possible pasts and futures, and conditionals of the present, could be conjured up. It was experiences such as these which dictated the form of theatre, *théâtre éclaté* (exploded or destructured theatre), *l'écriture du possible*, developed by Gatti. Such theatre offers neither a unified plot nor a unified setting. Its subject is fragmented in the sense that parts of it may be performed with no reference to the whole; nor is the subject presented as existing in the consciousness of the playwright or his public. The happening may be viewed from many different angles or reflected in several different consciences. Sometimes they are united by the action. In Gatti's later theatrical activities, the act of creation by the actors is a search for the subject itself. In this case the actors are not actors in the usual sense: they do not embody characters. The act of composition, together with the theatrical presentation of that composition, constitutes for Gatti the total act of creation.

Gatti's preference for *théâtre éclaté*, and his rejection of the 'Italian' stage with its fixed locations, firmly establish his relationship with the modern theatre movement both in France and outside, although one would not be justified in alleging direct influences but only, to use a Gatti image, what one might call 'parallel thinking'.

Modern theatre movements in other countries were introduced to the

French theatrical world of the 1960s mainly through theatre festivals in Nancy, Cassis, Bordeaux, Avignon and the 'Théâtre des Nations' in Paris. The high spot of the Paris festival of 1965 was the visit of the Peking Opera. In 1966 there were two high spots: the visit of Jerzy Growtowski, the director of the Wroclaw Laboratory Theatre, who sought to exploit to the full the possibilities of bodily expression; and the visit of the Living Theatre of Judith Malina and Julien Beck.

The Living Theatre's earlier visit in 1961 to the 'Théâtre des Nations', when it performed *The Connection*, Jack Gelber's play on drugs (for the French not then a very familiar world), had made no great impact, but in 1966 the company was enthusiastically welcomed as a nomadic tribe in exile after the closure of its theatre in New York in 1964 by the tax authorities, and the exception taken to the group's apparently deliberate provocation of opinion by its production of *The Brig*, presenting a disciplinary prison for marines on the island of Okinawa, by one of the marines himself, Kenneth Brown. The Living Theatre followed up this production in Paris with *Mysteries and Smaller Pieces*, in which actors sought to bring the stage and spectators together by going to 'die' alongside the spectators in their seats, while other actors on stage continued with 'scenic gymnastics' in line with the training given them by Joseph Chaikin before he left the company to form the Open Theatre of New York. Chaikin took the Open Theatre to the Cité Universitaire in Paris in 1969 with *Terminal*, a collective creation on the phenomena of death, with actors making vain forays into the auditorium to persuade the 'living' to participate in this dialogue with death. On the same occasion the Cité invited from Scandinavia the Odin Teater of Eugenio Barba – reputed to be the most gifted of Grotowski's pupils – who, like Grotowski, saw theatre in terms of the actor.

The Nancy Festival of May 1968 introduced into France Peter Schumann's Bread and Puppet Theatre. With its masks and puppets of all sizes, its response to the system or to particular historical events such as the Vietnam War was not political; rather it was an emotional response, albeit wholly committed. The group also performed in the street, and in New York in 1963 was practically the only one to do so. Gatti was actually set, quite independently, to use both these techniques during the student troubles in Paris later that same month.

The following year Nancy welcomed back the Bread and Puppet Theatre and also presented the Teatro Campesino, which had been created at Delano in California in response to the agricultural workers' strike against important wine-growers in 1965. For two years the chosen place of performance of their *actos* (collective improvisations) was the field and work camps, and as they played themselves in their own particular circumstances – Gatti was to use this technique in 1974 – their performances were a political action, not 'theatre'. But from pure

Introduction: Armand Gatti, the Wild Duck Flying Against the Wind

agitprop the movement developed in the hands of its director, Luis Valdez, into broadly popular and 'professional' theatre. The rudimentary *acto*, *La Conscience du 'jaune'* (seen in France), moved on to the more complex *Vietnam Campesino* (1970). Valdez had defined the intent of the *acto* as being to incite the public to social action, to elucidate particular points in the field of social problems, satirize the opposition, point to or suggest a solution, and express the people's feelings.

All these visiting companies gave Frenchmen of the theatre plenty of food for thought, but the fact remains that as far as Gatti is concerned, the only masters he has ever recognized are Piscator and his first producer Jean Vilar who, like Gatti himself, was intent on 'situating the theatre in the social history of his time'. There is, however, evidence of 'parallel thinking', and Julian Beck summed up some of this 'parallel thinking' after the Living Theatre's expulsion from the Avignon Festival in 1968 because of *Paradise Now*, part of which they had performed *gratuitously* in the street and with some actors in slips; also after further trouble in Rome and elsewhere:

> At the end of *Paradise* we say we must 'liberate the theatre', 'free the streets', 'take the theatre on to the streets'. We have also decided no longer to perform bourgeois theatre in bourgeois theatres, in places where art exists as a consumer article, but to make of theatre a new revolutionary weapon, and take it to those who have no access to culture and who are almost always the economically and socially deprived.[2]

They would perform in the streets, factories and other places of work. None of this is foreign to Gatti's thinking or practice over the years.

After his exclusion from the theatre in France in 1969 Gatti went to Belgium, and the work he undertook there confirmed the development already in germination in his mini-plays, his agitprop plays, which the disturbances of May 1968 in France had led him to write. With facilities afforded by the University of Louvain in 1971–3, Gatti set out to help people 'speak for themselves': invent their own form of expression, their 'own language'. In a first experiment in collective theatre, the students were encouraged to write a dramatic text on a given theme by themselves and produce it under Gatti's guidance. The final goal of a second experiment was a 'show without spectators', as all would themselves be the creators of the show. To this end the students toured the countryside helping the countryfolk to put on performances which had a direct bearing on the difficulties that confronted them in their everyday lives.

In Germany in 1974 two equally collective experiments were run on a rather different line. They bring us back to the wild duck flying against the wind, but as the experience of the wild duck can be shared by the many, Gatti chose from his own experience two wild ducks, Michèle Firk and Ulrike Meinhof. In the first experiment Gatti organized a theatrical event in which the cast of a Berlin theatre played – or rather lived, – parallel existences, their own and that of the real person of the Michèle Firk drama. In the second experiment the unutterably tragic figure of Ulrike Meinhof made her personal contribution to the theatrical event despite her imprisonment, assuring in this way the complete integration of drama and life.

In France this was the time when serious attempts were being made to stimulate local artistic activity, and Gatti lent himself during the next four years to various schemes. At the Peugeot car works in Montbéliard he encouraged workers, mainly immigrants, to write for him scenarios about their lives in their own countries and at Peugeot's. It was at Montbéliard that he discovered that he was fulfilling the function of public scribe. The immigrants came to him, one after another, saying: 'You must put this or that in the film'. Gatti asked why, and during the discussions which followed took copious notes. The final scenarios took shape gradually out of these notes and were written by him.

Gatti continued this line of work in the various communities in which he was successively 'implanted'. His ill-starred venture at Saint-Nazaire was intended to fit into this context. Unfortunately he had imagined that the plight of Soviet dissidents would provide a theme acceptable to the workers of that area, but the wild ducks who came to him from the USSR proved a great disappointment to him, particularly when the Voice of America sent a team to record a message from him to be relayed to the Soviet Union. This set back, however, was followed by a triumph in that the subject he chose, the story of a French Resistance youth who was executed on Mont Valérien, produced one supremely beautiful episode that was made in Upper Savoy in the Cistercian Abbaye de Tamié. It was shown on French television in 1979. The story of the youth had been worked out in several French localities with uneven success, but there is no doubt that the Upper Savoy episode, which is available on video tape, is a masterpiece.

The importance and originality of the Toulouse venture, the Archéoptéryx, which ran from 1983 to September 1985 is that it was largely remedial. *Le Monde* (1 July 1986) called Gatti's special work there 'une expérience sociale époustouflante', an astounding social experiment. It was carried out in part of the beautiful old building of the former Faculty in the rue des Lois, le Cloître des Cordeliers, which the University placed at Gatti's disposal. The wild ducks of the marshes have no wish to be socialized, but the poor and rejected in our society, and particularly the immigrant population of Toulouse, are outside society because they were never allowed in. Collective creation offers a way in. Gatti used it. He suggested to the group of ex-delinquents, unemployed,

Introduction: Armand Gatti, the Wild Duck Flying Against the Wind

drug addicts, young prostitutes, immigrants who came spontaneously to him that they should write a play on the Ukrainian Anarchist Makhno.

This suggestion, hotly disputed at first, provided them finally with a possible meeting-place with a man who, as one of society's rejects, had much in common with them. The fact that towards the end of the experiment the group firmly refused to accept the historical fate of Makhno in their play *La Colonne Makhno: La Rencontre historique*, and insisted instead on his being assassinated by thugs, is indicative of the path it had trod during the remedial exercise: 'Makhno is in his coffin in Le Père Lachaise,' they said, 'but *we* are not dead ... Tonight we tried to enter the real grown-up world. We'll try again tomorrow.' Gatti made no objection because, to his way of thinking, it was the creative activity that was to be liberating, not any moral story. 'Thank you, Monsieur Gatti, for saving me', one of the group said. 'I did not save you, you saved yourself', was his reply.

The two sides of Gatti came together perfectly in his Toulouse venture. Gatti is a wild duck, and Gatti is intensely social. Any attempt to make of him an egoist would be ludicrous. He is neither an egoist like Barrès or Valéry, nor an egoist like our modern neo-liberals. The real prophet of our modern neo-liberals is the eighteenth-century writer Bernard Mandeville, author of *The Fable of the Bees*. Gatti has never had any truck with such thinking.

Notes

Unless otherwise indicated the quotations are taken from my conversations with Gatti, or from Marc Kravetz's six lengthy interviews with Gatti published in *Libération* 1979, 16–22 July, under the collective title *L'Aventure de la Parole errante*:

16 July	Le fils du balayeur
17 July	Le mot juste au moment juste
18 July	Profession: écrivain public
19 July	L'Homme crucifié
20 July	Dans le maquis de l'espace utopique
21–22 July	Les écritures plurielles

L'Aventure de la Parole errante (subtitled 'Multilogues avec Armand Gatti'), published by Marc Kravetz in 1987, draws extensively on the above six interviews, but develops them and takes them up to 1986. In the preface Kravetz writes, justifiably, 'The miracle of the interview is the presence of Gatti'.

1. 'Théâtre d'aujourd'hui', TV française. 16 June 1967.
2. *Le Monde*, 11–12 January, 1970: 'Scindé en groupuscules, Le Living veut faire du "théâtre de guérilla"'.

1
A Journalist-Dramatist in Guatemala: Resistance is Drama

I Le Quetzal. Le Crapaud buffle
II La Naissance

As 'Journalist of the Year', after his award of the Albert Londres Prize in May 1954, Gatti was sent by *Le Parisien Libéré* and *Esprit* to Guatemala in June to cover events at the time of the overthrow of the progressive government of Jacobo Arbenz Guzmán by the Guatemalan *émigré* Colonel Castillo Armas, with troops trained in Honduras. Armas was backed by the CIA in the interests of American big business and stage-managed by the American ambassador, John Peurifoy. He also had the backing of the papal nuncio. The rigging of Armas's 'election' as President, and his subsequent attack on the achievements of the Revolution made under President Arevalo and Arbenz, were also observed by Gatti. Unlike his fellow-journalists, who were happy to look on from a safe distance, Gatti joined a group of insurgent Indians so as to see the situation from the inside. He spent twenty-six days amongst them in the Zacatepec maquis in the mountains. There he met an 'Argentinian doctor', Che Guevara, and made friends with Felipe, a nineteen-year-old Maya Indian, the only one of the group to speak Spanish.

Felipe told Gatti the story of the attempted mass suicide of the Maya people after the invasion of their country by the Conquistadors. As Felipe saw it, the oppression to which they were then being subjected in the new times was a continuation of the oppression suffered in the past. Six hours after he had told Gatti the story, Felipe was no more than a skeleton stripped bare by a flock of urubus. A detachment of Armas's troops armed with automatic weapons had surrounded the Indians, whose only weapons were machetes, and all were shot in front of Gatti. Gatti himself owed his life to his French press card. He was none the less marched off to prison in Escuintla, where he was to witness further executions.

On his arrival back in Guatemala City Gatti felt completely alienated

A Journalist-Dramatist in Guatemala: Resistance is Drama

from his fellow-journalists, who were drinking to Arbenz's fall: their work was over; they could return home. Amid the jollification Gatti was ironically toasted as 'the journalist who had turned guerrilla'. The proposer of the toast was an American journalist, but Gatti felt that the irony was no longer of any account; he had made his choice. The life he had shared with Felipe in the maquis had revealed a different way of life which had enriched his own. To accept the world of Guatemala City – the world of intellectuals, of journalists like himself – would be to side with the very people who had killed Felipe. He sent his despatch from Guatemala and then wrote a poetic oratorio, *Le Quetzal*, to 'clarify his ideas'. But above all, his first definitive dramatic text, which was published only in June 1960 (*Europe*), was intended to do homage to the memory of the Indian peasants of San Juan Zacatepec who had perished at the hands of Armas's troops, and also to retell the sad tale told him by Felipe.

I Le Quetzal

Le Quetzal, based on a Maya legend, is the first panel of Gatti's 'Indian Trilogy' which includes the unpublished *La Montagne Ixtaccyhuatl*, based on an Aztec legend, and *Le Crapaud buffle*, which recounts an Inca legend. In *Le Quetzal* two time-cycles, one in the early sixteenth century and the other in the mid-twentieth, are linked at the outset by a Maya drum-roll, at one and the same time recalling the fall of the capital Iximche to the Conquistadors and announcing the forthcoming public speech of General Elfego Castigo Ubi, President elected 'not by the grace of God or man, but by his own prowess', to quote from the General's proclamation. The two periods are not intricately interwoven as themes in the dramatic action, but allusions are made and parallels drawn.

In the lyrical scenes based on Felipe's story of the Conquistadors, the destruction of the baby expected by Tulan's wife, Juilin, is demanded by the grandfather as an ultimate gesture of defiance. He argues that after the heroic death of the Maya leader, Tecun Uman, in single combat against Pedro de Alvarado – during which, as legend had it, an encircling quetzal had tried vainly to protect him by attacking his adversary – the birth of a child meant the birth of a slave. To allow a child to live was to *accept* slavery and humiliation. For Tulan and Juilin this was a defeatist attitude: children must be allowed to live to carry on the fight. Tulan himself attempts to step into the breach left by Tecun Uman's death, but succumbs in his turn. In her despair Juilin sacrifices her newborn son.

The play ends as it begins with the triumphal appearance of General Ubi, and a parallel is drawn between the Conquistadors of old, who had 'two lumps of gold in their eyes', and General Ubi, who equates the quetzal, the bird that cannot live in captivity and which has been from time immemorial the emblem of a people struggling for freedom, with the vulgar image of the quetzal on the country's banknotes. 'A quetzal is worth a dollar', is the lesson he cynically teaches the terrorized children, adding that 'to observe traditions by adapting them to the march of history' is a 'subtle achievement'.

The three names of the *général-dictateur* contain clear allusions to Colonels Elfego Monzon and Castillo Armas implicated in the overthrow of Arbenz, and to the infamous Jorge Ubico, the dictator in Guatemala from 1931 to 1944. All the scenes in which Gatti's general appears are deliberately burlesqued. An Ubu-roi figure, somewhat similar to Don Tiburcio in *Le Crapaud buffle* which he was to write next, emerges. Ubi arrives on stage in a motorcar carried on the shoulders of four Indians. For this apparent eccentricity there is a factual basis, just as there is for the chain-gangs of Indian labour used in road construction by order of Ubi, as they had been by his historic namesake Ubico. When Ubi finds that his car has flat tyres and faulty headlights he upbraids his porters and says his message is 'technique liberates man', so drawing a parallel with the inscription on the entrance to Nazi concentration camps, 'Arbeit macht frei'.

Trigger-happy, as the dictator in *Le Crapaud buffle* was to be, Ubi keeps firing into the air as if he were in a Western, but he also shoots to kill. He even shoots his car-bearers when they set the car down on the ground, unable to carry it any further. 'What!' he exclaims, 'a rebellion, banditry against the Chief of State! The Constitution is violated!' This so-called rebellion gives him his cue for posing as the 'Saviour of the Constitution'. He also cynically claims to have done his bearers a service by liberating them from the mediocrity and tribulations of their existence. When faced with the continued cult of Tecun Uman, he equally cynically decides on a policy of domestication of the legendary hero in order to discredit him. The Indians refuse, however, to accept the humiliation. Their refusal goes back in time to the past, and is represented visually on stage by the 'backward march' of the resuscitated car-bearers, in which they are joined by the Mayas of the sixteenth century. Together they recall their long history of covert protest and reaffirm their faith in the uncaged quetzal bird.

These burlesque historical scenes interrupt the *lament* and its scenes of ceremonial, such as the preparation of the 'meal of the defeat', or the sacrifice of Juilin's child, or the circling movement of his child held high in the air by Juilin during Tulan's mortal combat to simulate the protective hovering of the quetzal over the head of Tecun Uman. Had this short act reached the stage at the time it was written, it would have appeared very novel with its rich mixture of dramatic action, oratorio, ritual and burlesqued satirical scenes. By the time it was produced on 5 April 1974, by the Théâtre-Action de Lyon under the title *L'Oiseau-dollar*, this kind of dramatic composition had come into its own with such plays as *Gesang vom lusitanishen Popanz (Le Chant du fantoche lusitanien)* by Peter Weiss (1969), *Orden* by Pierre Bourgeade (1969) or the work of André Bendetto in Avignon or Gérard Gelas with Le Théâtre du Chêne noir.

With *Le Quetzal* and *Le Crapaud buffle* which followed it, Gatti freed himself from the constraints of journalistic despatches, while at the same time drawing his subjects from his experiences as a reporter. It was a pattern he was to follow on his return from China when he wrote *Le Poisson noir*. This was considered, at least at first, as a literary not a dramatic text, and it was not until 1959, when Jean Vilar staged *Le Crapaud buffle*, that the experience of theatrical production began for Gatti. Vilar had already declared his interest in 'political' plays, not 'political' in a party political sense, but 'political' in the sense used by Plato when he wrote *Politeia*. 'Politique ... polis ... cité ... problèmes qui concernent tous les hommes' – such was Vilar's oft-repeated definition of the theatre he sought to serve. *Le Crapaud buffle* was such a play, and Vilar decided to inaugurate the experimental Petit TNP in the Théâtre Récamier with it. His statement of intent was that the plays staged there would disregard technical norms and would present deliberately topical subjects of concern to all sections of the public, even though some might consider them as provocative. Spectators and critics were warned of what to expect.

Le Crapaud buffle

Le Crapaud buffle was written in 1954–5, when Gatti, on his own admission, was still struggling to exorcize memories of his experience of Nazi concentration camps by giving them verbal expression in dramatic form. The camps as such do not figure in *Le Crapaud buffle*, but the society pictured in this dialogued satire is a 'parallel' society barely distinguishable from that of the camps. Jean Cayol made this point in a round-table discussion after Vilar's production, when he referred to it as the first *pièce concentrationnaire* to reach the French theatre.[1]

Like *Le Quetzal*, the play describes Gatti's experience of Central American dictatorships supported and exploited by American trading companies such as the United Fruit Company, which in Guatemala formed almost a state within the state, and also of US State Department intervention in pursuit of American interests beyond the American frontiers, as the principle of American foreign policy requires. Theodore Roosevelt's 'big stick' or *gran garrote* policy is the subject of an early table-turning sequence with loud knockings from the Beyond – answers being given on the dictator's 'cosmic telephone': that is to say the table. Gatti writes in his despatch *La Libération du Guatémala*, published in *Esprit*, November 1954, that policy was still being pursued despite Franklin D. Roosevelt's preference for *buena vecidad*. Much of the material in the play is taken from Gatti's despatches from Central America, such as *Petit portrait d'un petit dictateur*,[2] which is an open attack on the 'strong man' of Nicaragua, Anastasio Somoza, who had put Gatti in prison because he complained too loudly about the loss of his luggage, or his interview in El Salvador with Guatemala's ex-ambassador, Miguel Angel Asturias, dismissed with opprobrium by Castillo Armas.[3]

La Libération du Guatémala provides a well-documented account of the situation in the country from the time of the 1944 October Revolution, when President Arévala 'made the mistake' of attempting to establish a democratic regime, and in 1950, when Arbenz similarly 'erred' in introducing a four-year plan for road developments, agrarian reforms, etc., thereby prejudicing American interests. It also paints the portrait of the United States ambassador, John Peurifoy, the 'Number-One Eliminator of Reds' who 'after distinguishing himself in Greece was sent on to Guatemala'. This 'grand impresario of the show' in Guatemala becomes Mullifoy, 'Ambassador of the United Nations' (read United States) in *Le Crapaud buffle*. Further documentation on the reality behind the farcical dramatic action of the play is to be found in the lengthy quotations from less accessible despatches by Gatti given in their book by Gozlan and Pays. In no sense, however, is *Le Crapaud buffle* a 'documentary' on Central or South American dictatorships, Central and South American being blended together in the action. Gatti's aim, as he told the press before the production, was to criticize a 'certain form of power, not specifically South American' – namely, the absolute power that corrupts the human mind, not the absolute power of a madman when he seizes power.[4]

The action is set in the imaginary dictatorial state of Cuzcatlan, the name used by Indians for the Republic of El Salvador. Don Tiburcio, a former dealer in motorcars, has the quirks and vices of a number of dictators of the Americas both past and present. For the spectator's information some of these were recalled in the TNP programme: they include General Maximiliano Hernandez Martínez, known as *el téosofo ametrallador*, who ruled El Salvador from 1932 to 1944 and 'liberated spiritually' (with machine-guns) some twenty thousand Indian peasants. Martínez declared, as Tiburcio does in the play, 'It is a greater crime to kill an ant than a man, because man is reincarnated after his death, whereas the ant dies once and for all.' Also, as in the play, he refused his dying child proper medical care, preferring to treat him with blue water of his own concoction.

A Journalist-Dramatist in Guatemala: Resistance is Drama

The dictators include also Anastasio Somoza, Don 'Tacho', the 'strong man' of Nicaragua (1937–56) who put a Renault 4 CV in prison because it was 'Communist-made' (Renault is nationalized) and then had it shot for 'high treason'. Gatti shared his cell with the Renault car when in prison in Managua, and says that the car had been put there because the American ambassador was annoyed at Somoza's preference for the small Renault, which he took an almost childish delight in driving about, rather than for his big American car. Another dictator mentioned is General Trujillo of the Dominican Republic (1952–61), who had declared: 'Trujillo and God require ...', in that order! Because, after all, 'who is in command in Santo Domingo?' This grotesque declaration provides Tiburcio with the opening line for his numerous proclamations, many of which are taken from speeches by Central American dictators, and Tiburcio Carias Andino of Honduras (1933–49) provided a name for Gatti's dictator.

All this creates a weird Latin American environment, though it is not the atmosphere of light opera. Over the Ubu-roi figure of the dictator, addicted to his 'cosmic telephone' which puts him into communication with History and not the Beyond, preoccupied with his 'magic pendulum', and accompanied by a standard bearing the nation's emblem 'La Rana-Toro', or bullfrog, there hangs for every reader or spectator the dark shadow of the mythomaniac Hitler with his occultism and his magic Swastika. Both had a sinister scarecrow quality. Gatti refers to Tiburcio as a 'publicity marionette worked by the real politicians, the USA ambassador and the archbishop'.

The opening scene of the play is a visual representation of a dream by Tiburcio, in bed in his palace (upstage) with his pyjamas hung around with hand grenades. The action which follows illustrates the horrible authenticity of the dream. Bound and blindfold figures of condemned opponents are wheeled across the front stage, one by one, to be executed in the presidential chair so that Tiburcio can remain in contact with them in the Beyond; meanwhile, in middle stage, their future widows chant the Inca legend of the 'song' of the *'crapaud buffle'*, although here its croaking begins to sound like machine-gun fire. The sleeping dictator is awakened by a gust of wind which carries away the standard; he leaps to his feet brandishing a revolver – a favourite gesture of his. 'Order' has not been maintained. His machine-guns, his proclamations, his slogans, his theosophy – the sole means of government at his command – are not sufficient.

To consolidate his position he decides to identify himself with some great figure of the past. Given his belief in man's reincarnation, he can take his choice of the great names of History. With the help of his Capuchin friar, his choice falls not on Caesar, Bolivar, Goering(!) or others, but on Francisco Pizarro, one of the 'black-bearded white gods' who were guided through the Peruvian mountains by the bullfrog's 'song'. Everything actually points to the choice of Pizarro, so, the better to establish the authenticity of his 'reincarnation', Tiburcio orders his entourage to re-enact the Pizarro saga. This begins with the execution of a dissenting colonel who had been 'metamorphosed' by Tiburcio into Pizarro's enemy, Atahualpa, the Inca Emperor who was defeated by Pizarro in the Battle of Sacsahuamán, then publicly strangled by him at Cajamarca in 1533. For the part of Pizarro's brother Juan, who was killed in the battle, Tiburcio nominates the chief of police.

A new and 'final' version of this battle is to be a revolt deliberately fomented by the police among the lower classes, then mercilessly suppressed in order to 'reassure the better-class districts'. The chief of police, however, prefers a less illustrious fate and flees. For his part, the 'United Nations' ambassador, Mullifoy, invested by Tiburcio with the role of another of Pizarro's brothers, Fernand, plots Tiburcio's overthrow in the interests of his country and his replacement by his more amenable counsellor, Huacarimac. To compensate for these defections and betrayals – and also for the accidental death of the bullfrog, promoted to Mullifoy's role – Tiburcio decides to 'multiply his presence' by making a 'gift of his person to the nation' in the literal sense of the term: first his legs, then his arms. He ends up a limbless trunk on a bullet-scarred throne. He has been converted to the Indian belief that the 'song', the croaking of the bullfrog, separates heads and limbs from the living body and gives them an autonomous existence. He is also firmly convinced that he will grow other limbs to replace those he has had chopped off and paraded among the people.

His wife begs him to relinquish power and, when he refuses, stabs him to death with his own dagger. He sees it as the dagger with which Almagro's son had stabbed Pizarro on 'Sunday the 26th of June 1541'. The illusion is complete. Tiburcio's successor enters wearing two heads, his own and Tiburcio's. Clearly nothing has changed in the 'new democracy'. Like Tiburcio before him, he draws his revolver at the slightest alert. With the firing squad that had served Tiburcio so well, he 'puts an end to the Marxist terror', as he sees fit to call the preceding dictatorship. The laws he promulgates are as repressive, and feudal forced labour, introduced under the previous dictatorship, remains the order of the day. The same corruption is practised. The same deals are made with foreign powers for personal profit.

These final scenes are played in a dual set: in the background a palace indicated by Tiburcio's presidential chair and by two big commemorative tablets bearing the names of Pizarro's brothers; in the foreground a cemetery where Tiburcio's head, resting on his anonymous grave watched over only by his widow, gives vent to his spleen at the complete takeover of his policies by the usurper: 'He robs me of everything'.

Tiburcio, still a prey to his delusion has 'lost his head': it bounces away to the palace proclaiming that all nature is in need of 'Don Tiburcio François Pizarre'.

The play is an allegory rich enough to be approached on three different levels: legendary, historical and political. Huacarimac, Tiburcio's Indian counsellor, and the tragic widows of the victims of the Tiburcian terror, introduce the spectator to the Inca legend of the *crapaud buffle*. Not that the play is a piece of folklore. The legend is used like filigree work in the composition of the play. On the historical level the two threads of the sixteenth and twentieth centuries, closely interwoven to form the web of the dramatic action, are disentangled for the spectator by the friar who reads out to Tiburcio the saga of the Conquistador, leaving him to adapt Pizarro's feats to his own circumstances.

On the political level, the attitude of Gatti as a professional journalist in Central America is left in no doubt, and it was on political rather than artistic grounds that the play – and through the play, its disquieting young author – came under intentionally crippling fire from the press. The 'howls of indignation' that went up from certain papers when faced with a play on 'dictatorship pushed to the absurd', with an action entirely carried along by the 'logic of the absurd', were commented on by Raymond Lavigne in his penetrating review of the production for *L'Humanité* (10 November 1959). Gatti himself considered the political import to be paramount and, in his own comments before the production, insisted that both he and his producer had sought to underline it by minimizing the legendary element. He had even thought of subtitling the play 'the History of France told to adults'.

In the bulletin-programme, *Bref* (No. 29, October 1959), a similar caption, 'Histoires d'ailleurs et d'ici', by Pierre Joffroy, moved Gabriel Marcel to contribute a grossly offensive review headed 'Un CRAPAUD qui se veut aussi gros qu'un BUFFLE' – with obvious reference to a La Fontaine fable.[5] In it he expressed, 'along with other spectators', his 'indignation' at the play's burlesque of the recent 'atrocious drama' in France from which so many had 'not emerged unscathed'. Scenes of police brutality, cruel interrogations, prison torture, denunciations and the official placarding of death sentences, all unpleasantly reminiscent of the atrocities and the 'Affiche rouge' of the Occupation years and all heavily satirized, shocked. Marcel was especially indignant at the burlesque of 'a certain personage in recent French history'. That personage was obviously Marshal Pétain, the Chief of State who had 'made a gift of his person to the nation' in 1946.

To those who preferred to see in his burlesque *général-président* a more contemporary reference, Gatti replied that the play had been written in 1954, even though it only reached the stage in 1959; it therefore could not refer to May 1958, when de Gaulle became President. This *général-président*, a blood-bespattered puppet some way between Jarry's King Ubu and Charlie Chaplin's Dictator, is not as such the sole butt of Gatti's satire; he is a tool of the established order for which the enemies are 'the poor, the envious, the *sans-chemise*'. It is moreover in the interest of the rich that the 'anti-inflationist President' presses for a deliberately depressed wage rate. Meanwhile the President prepares his defences against the 'red and yellow' perils that threaten the 'free world', along with possible *coups d'état* from rivals on the Right, the 'blue peril'. Pierre Joffroy said of the play that it arose from the marriage of a poet and a journalist, and that it is journalism with the force of poetry.

There was obviously plenty in the play to bemuse the 'first night' critics who came along to pass judgement on one of the earliest products of the newest *avant-garde*. They had been schooled by a long familiarity with Claudel, Pirandello, Anouilh, and had a growing familiarity with the recently emerged 'Absurdists', but Gatti belonged to neither tradition. The critics had, in fact, been summoned to review, on two successive nights, Claudel's *Tête d'or*, with which Jean-Louis Barrault inaugurated the Odéon-Théâtre de France in front of a number of state dignitaries, and *Le Crapaud buffle*, likewise in a state theatre but unattended by any such dignitaries. They gave the royal treatment to *Tête d'or*, after some sixty years a well-digested classic, commending the magnificent orchestration of the theme of personal power in its unalarming epico-biblical setting. If they admitted to any incoherence in *Tête d'or*, they saw this incoherence as shot through with brilliant flashes.

The unredeemedly 'incoherent' *Crapaud buffle* was said to flounder in the 'Cuzcatlan marshes'. Such an assessment was vigorously contested by Georges Auclair at the round-table discussion already mentioned. The system which required official theatre critics to make a judgement after a single viewing, particularly in the case of unfamiliar works, was to be deplored, he said. It was easier to demolish them than to seek to shed light on them, and as Gatti's text was available before the production, a better understanding of what the new generation of playwrights, represented here by Gatti, was attempting to do, would have been arrived at had the critics consulted it beforehand.

Technically this first play already showed that Gatti was unlikely to make use of any of the current types of dramatic composition. He presents a series of tableaux, some realistic, some lyrical, but all are set in a 'concertina-d' time-scheme. He groups the tableaux into five 'acts' but they are not acts in the usual sense; their titles indicate different levels on which they are to be approached: 'Acte Officiel', 'Acte Intime', 'Acte Transitoire', 'Acte Historique', 'Acte Légendaire'. These are preceded by the dream sequence under the title 'Amorce' – that is to say, the fuse or priming which introduces the spectator into the oneiric world of theatrical representation.

The day then begins, and in the 'Acte Officiel' the characters move around a significantly empty throne, the dictator being so far only a voice offstage. His official *persona*, which is 'multiple', is the creation of the politicians around him; he himself is nonexistent as a real man. A frame containing a life-size 'portrait' of the dictator comes down at the back of the stage. The 'portrait' postures and talks, examining the ambassador's credentials – that is to say, his hat – with a grotesque 'magic pendulum'. But the official character which Tiburcio is expected to assume is not grandiose enough for him; he feels the urge to 'metamorphose' himself into some great figure from the past. This scene is logically constructed but the overall construction of the play is less rigorous, being a series of loosely linked burlesqued tableaux, as in Jarry's *Ubu roi*. One of these is a banquet – reminiscent of one given by Ubu roi – in which supposedly poisoned dishes are rejected one after the other because the swing of the magic pendulum condemns them.

With this production Vilar moved away to some extent from the austere 'Jansenistic' staging, in the manner of Jacques Copeau, which he used to great effect on the vast stage of the Palais de Chaillot. He made extensive use of scenic means to convey the complexity of the modern world, essential to Gatti, but by shying away from the deliberate grossness of Gatti's farce he composed a show that retained the polish of a classical production, and this proved a sterilizing astringency. The staging was too stylized and did not adequately translate the atmosphere of overripeness that permeates the play. Instead of a cemetery packed full of crosses on the graves of 'traitors', as required in the text, Vilar put up only two crosses, Tiburcio's and his child's. Instead of boldly outlined figures, grossly but firmly set in contemporary reality, the characters, equally stylized by Vilar, were puppet-like creatures living in a world apart.

Despite this toning-down of an obviously explosive text, the production caused a storm to break over Jean Vilar's head as well as that of Gatti, whose social and political opinions clashed radically with the accepted norm. There were demands for Vilar's instant dismissal from the directorship of the state-subsidized TNP. A similar demand had been made in 1952 after Vilar's production of Brecht's *Mother Courage* in the Palais de Chaillot, but happily it was not heeded by the Minister. On this second occasion Jean-Jacques Gautier went so far as to demand Vilar's arrest, along with Gatti's, for 'wasting public funds'. One or two less antagonistic critics regretted that Vilar had not chosen to introduce the new author to the Paris theatre-going public with his poetic play *Le Poisson noir*, on which the seal of respectability had been set by the award of the Fénéon literary prize that same year.

Armand Gatti in the Theatre

Thrown to the wolves as he was, Gatti began to fear that he was not made for this new profession, but Vilar's insistence that he should return from Italy, where he had taken refuge, and face up to the critics, restored his confidence. Apart from Claude Olivier, Paul Morelle and Raymond Lavigne, who had sought seriously to evaluate this new dramatic development, the critics boycotted the public debate with Gatti organized by Vilar. The public, however, came and was enthusiastic; 11,554 of them attended the fifty-eight performances in the small Récamier Theatre. So Gatti continued to write for the stage and became, alongside Brecht and O'Casey, one of the leading figures of the rapidly developing decentralized theatre movement.

In *Le Crapaud buffle*, as in *Le Quetzal*, submission or death are presented as the dark perspectives always open to the restive Latin American peoples under the heel of ruthless oppressors, whether Spanish Conquistadors in the sixteenth century or petty dictators bolstered up nowadays by foreign commercial interests. Both plays recount a story of oppression that gives no sign of coming to an end. In both plays Gatti's sympathies are as firmly on the side of the victims as they were during his hazardous experience in Guatemala. Nevertheless, the plays are not museum pieces of past Central American history. They are as historically and politically relevant today as when they were written in 1954–5.

Gatti had confirmation of this conviction of his in 1968 in Kassel in West Germany, where he was producing a further play on Guatemala, *La Naissance*. He received the unexpected visit of a university teacher from Guatemala who was a member of a guerrilla group and had translated *Le Crapaud buffle* whilst in prison, because it 'corresponded exactly to what was happening in his country'. Despite the danger, the translation was performed by the students behind locked doors in the University of Guatemala City, to the discomfiture of the forces of law and order. Gatti said he was greatly encouraged to learn that the play had subsequently become part of the Theatre of Opposition in Latin America, in Managua, Tegucigalpa, Lima and particularly in Guatemala, where he had emerged as a political dramatist. Ten years after the play was written, events in Guatemala brought Gatti back in spirit to that country and he wrote *La Naissance* as the third panel of a Central American triptych.

In the meantime he had written his concentration-camp triptych which, like the first two panels of the Central American triptych, concentrates on the victims. He had, however, also written *La Vie imaginaire de l'éboueur Auguste Geai* and *Chant public devant deux chaises électriques*, in which the emphasis shifts from the victims to the revolutionaries. *La Naissance* follows in this tradition. The very title indicates the theme – recurrent in Gatti's theatre – of birth. Here it is 'the birth of a continent'. In the earlier *Le Poisson noir* it is the birth of a nation, China. Among the prisoners in the concentration camps, or among the enslaved people of Central America, it is the birth of a collective conscience. Gatti sees revolution not as the triumph of violence, but as the birth of a new conscience in each and every one.

II La Naissance

La Naissance is the direct expression of this idea. This intensely dramatic play was written in 1966 for the Spectacles de l'Étang de Berre, directed by Alain Rais and centred on Martigues. Between 1962, the date of its formation, and 1966 this company had performed works by such playwrights as Brecht and Charles Prost throughout the region, before audiences from the petrol refineries, metal and chemical works and market gardens. It was, so Gatti told J.-P. Leonardini of *L'Humanité* (15 November 1966), the only company in France to champion 'a truly militant theatre', a form of theatre after his own heart. L'Étang de Berre was not, however, an area where the theatrical fortunes could be made, and in June 1966 the company was forced to move to Nîmes, where it was to open with *La Naissance* in a production by the author. Rehearsals were under way with the company's actors working alongside the group that had formed round Gatti in Cuba in 1962, but the state's failure to settle the company's preceding liabilities led to the production being abandoned and the company itself being disbanded. That was in December 1966.

Two years later (8–30 October 1968) the play was put on in a new version at the Théâtre Romain-Rolland in Villejuif by Roland Monod in conjunction with actors from the Paris company Productions d'aujourd'hui, but before that, on 18 September, the production group inaugurated the 27th International Theatre Festival in Venice with this play, and then went on to perform it at the Berlin Festival. On 5 and 6 October Monod's production of *La Naissance* was the final 'event' of a 'Gatti week' with which Marcel Maréchal inaugurated the Théâtre du 8ᵉ in Lyon, with the express purpose – bearing in mind the social and university upheaval of May 1968 – of opening up the theatre to problems of general topical concern in the world.

Since Gatti's theatre is so inextricably bound up with his personal experiences, Maréchal looked forward to the rewarding experience that a week-long dialogue with this author would be for his public (*Approches*, June–August 1966, No. 1). He invited the public to 'live' with Gatti – a complete Gatti, Gatti recounting his life story, giving a reading of *La Passion du Général Franco* billed by the TNP for the following February, showing his Cuban film *El otro Cristobal*, and discussing *La Naissance* before its performance at the end of the week. Maréchal described the dialogue – with students, schoolchildren, and working men mainly from the Rhône-Poulenc and Berliet factories – as enthralling. There, as J.-J. Lerrant wrote, Gatti expounded his ideas on new forms of theatre; he saw each play inventing its particular space in a bare hall so that the actors could be at the very heart of the theatrical ferment. The production toured many other Centres Dramatiques and Maisons de la Culture, and this was possible because of the all-round economy of the means employed. Instead of the large cast and complicated sets usually needed for a Gatti play, there were only fourteen actors and one multiple set.

The dramatic structure is simple, almost classical, despite the grouping of the scenes into seven 'Instantanés', ten 'Trajectoires', and a final group entitled 'Bouclier, poème arrêté'. The linear action moves to its conclusion without any of the *éclatement* or fragmentation of the time factor usual in Gatti's plays and takes place in a strictly delimited space, consisting of three sites in an insect-ridden Guatemalan forest, all represented on the stage at the same time.

When Gatti agreed to write a play for the Spectacles de l'Étang de Berre, his intention had been to study the reactions of a couple caught up in a revolutionary movement but on different sides, and needing at the same time to sort out their personal problems. *La Naissance* is one of only two love dramas by Gatti, but as he himself said, 'with age everything is possible'. *Notre Tranchée de chaque jour* is the other, and in both Gatti goes back in spirit to Spanish America. He first tried to picture a French couple and set it in present-day society, but the attempt turned into comedy which, Gatti admitted, is not his forte. Subsequent attempts to situate the couple in relation to the Resistance movement or to Vietnam were equally unsuccessful because of Gatti's dislike of reaching outside the scope of his personal experience.

While searching for a suitable dramatic action, Gatti was brought back to the reassuring realm of his own experience by the story of the true adventure of a number of Green Berets in Guatemala in 1963. Latin America, which he saw as the *continent-type* of revolutionary action, was a conscious obsession with him. The unusual adventure of the group of Green Berets raised the question of armed commitment to the cause of freedom and concerned the men of the maquis, regular government troops, and the uncommitted who were plunged willy-nilly into the struggle and forced by circumstances to take sides.

These particular Green Berets were five Guatemalan officers who had undergone, along with other members of the 'Special Forces', anti-guerrilla training at the Polytechnic in Panama and then in Georgia with the Rangers at Fort Benning. On their return to Guatemala they joined the men of the maquis instead of fighting against them. They declared themselves to be the Edgar Ibarra National Liberation Movement. The leader, Turcios Lima, had likewise been through an American military school in 1959–60 and boasted of his 'excellent military training' in Fort Benning. An American–Guatemalan mission, acting for United Fruit, mounted a clearing-up operation so radical that not a soul was left alive in the area between the Motagua and Polochic rivers.

Gatti worked the adventure of the deserting Green Berets into his own personal experience of the country, and the 'couple', the original starting point of the play, became Juilin and Osmany. Juilin is closely modelled on a woman Gatti had known in Guatemala – he even retains her very gestures and words. Osmany has in him something of Gatti himself at the age of twenty – the text gives this information. He is modelled also to a large extent on Osmany Cienfuegos, whom Gatti met in Cuba in 1962 when making the film *El otro Cristobal*. Osmany was the brother of Camillo Cienfuegos, a companion of Castro's who became a national figure. Gatti considered Osmany to be a fine man whose heart was in the revolutionary movement in his country. Osmany also had a sentimental problem, and it was partly this, Gatti said, that inspired his creation of the character Osmany, one of the deserting Green Berets.

Another of Gatti's friends to appear in this third panel of the Central American triptych is the Indian Felipe who had been killed before Gatti's eyes in the Guatemalan maquis. He reappears as the young guerrilla fighter Ierba Buena, who loses his life in the Turcios maquis. Gatti's personal knowledge of these people and his up-to-the-minute familiarity with the Latin American situation, on the government side as well as on the revolutionaries', was brought to bear on the writing of *La Naissance*. He had himself been caught up in skirmishes between Nicaragua and Costa Rica, and was in Guatemala when Castillo Armas, with whom the Americans had replaced Arbenz, was assassinated on 22 July 1957.

There are three distinct groups of people in the play: the government army group of five, officially commanded by Captain Lopez but commanded in reality by Lieutenant Butch, a Negro dubbed by Lopez a 'superman of the American military school'; the maquis group of three 'deserter' lieutenants, together with Sombreron, a black schoolteacher, and the apprentice blacksmith Ierba Buena; and between them the uncommitted group consisting of Juilin, the wife of Professor Cootel, a well-known entomologist and specialist in butterflies, and Mario, a Mexican journalist on the lookout for a scoop for his paper. Armed with his war-correspondent's card, like the press card that had saved Gatti's life in the Guatemalan maquis in 1954, Mario is guided into the maquis by Juilin, who acts as a link with the city. Two outsiders – Pijje, a peasant who is looking for his lost hen, and Twenty-five, a scapegrace villager caught in the zone – are finally integrated into the third group by force of circumstances.

The structure of the play seems to reflect Gatti's work in films, particularly the use of the word 'Instantanés' and the composition of these sequences, which suggest 'stills' from a film. In the 'Instantanés' the characters are presented with their individual history, their social and political background and their particular reasons for being in the forest. Each character is a main character and is there in his own right. The course their individual lives take is described in the 'Trajectoires' when the characters are brought together, paths cross and contacts are established. These sequences describe in concrete terms the military encounter between the two opposing sides, ending with the guerrilla fighters and the uncommitted all being taken prisoner. The aftermath of the engagement, 'Bouclier, poème arrêté', with the government soldiers awaiting further orders and the immobilized captives singing their defiant lament, not only brings the action to a close but marks the *real* 'birth' of the various characters.

In a Postscript to the published edition the director, Roland Monod, referring back to *Un Homme seul* (p. 25), where one of the characters remarks: 'The birth and death of a man have no connection with the dates entered about him in the civil register', writes that 'birth' is the moment when a man awakens to consciousness of his existence amongst others, and in that context decides what course his life should take, and that many 'die' well before the time for them to be officially mourned. This is in line with Gatti's insistence that the subject of the play lies beyond the military struggle in the characters themselves, and in the way they are modified by their contact with each other. This is their 'trajectory'. Under the collective heading to the seven opening 'stills', 'sept instantanés de l'aigle qui, peint sur un bouclier, voulait s'envoler', Gatti likens the characters to the captive eagle, the quetzal, painted on the Cakchiquel warriors' shields. In the final sequence of the 'Bouclier, poème arrêté', while some of the characters are seen to soar like the quetzal to freedom, others remain in 'captivity' and die, as does the quetzal when kept in captivity.

The characters sporadically interrogate the theatre. On neither side are they mere 'compensatory figures': Lopez, for example, reproaches the invisible 'Author' for wanting to make of him just a government army officer. They frequently refer to the technique of 'character–author relationship' and insist that they are characters in their own right, not just combatants on one side or the other, and that each is himself a sufficient subject for a whole play. Not that they are characters in search of an author. Rather are they characters in revolt against their author whose concern, according to Lopez in the third 'Instantané pour rappeler à l'Auteur ses partis pris', is with the guerrilla movement and not, as Lopez considers it ought to be, with his – Lopez's – life story: that is to say, with his search for his true identity in the context of the ancestral struggle between Indian and Spaniard in Guatemala. He accuses the 'Author' of not being interested in the story.

In the play which they are performing, the characters define themselves in relation both to the theatre and to life. The extra dimension this technique gives to the play is already indicated by Juilin in the opening lines of the first 'Instantané du décor qui doit signifier la forêt': as she leads Mario on to the stage she says: 'We are in a forest (at least that is what this place is meant to signify)' – and indeed, any stage set belongs to the world of 'signs': that is to say, art. It is not reality: in Hubert Monloup's set for this production, the forest was suggested by an entanglement of tropical creepers hanging from the flies and on a back curtain of string netting. Photographs of the production appear in *Avant-Scène*, No. 417, 1 January 1969.

A clear definition of the extra dimension is given in the fourth 'still' when Ierba Buena says straight out that he is 'in the theatre'. Other characters refer to the personal prejudices of the 'Author' and to the 'big or little parts' he gives them each to play. Choco – or, to give him his 'stage' name, Twenty-five (the name by which he was generally known) – states that within the space of a few hours and a few square metres (obviously the stage), they are going to pour out a part of the story of their lives in front of people they do not know, but 'our shortcomings are none of their business. Let them settle their scores over other heads than ours.'

There is no theatrical 'illusion'; no realistic reconstruction of the conflict, nor any identification of stage time, place, or happenings with those of the real experience. The use of character-to-'Author' apostrophies is designed to underline the fact that the real struggle does not take place in a theatre building; that the spectator cannot partake in the struggle as it were by proxy. All a play can do is to bring the spectator face to face with a concrete situation, albeit in a different context, and suggest that there are equivalents everywhere.

A particularly striking use of the technique of character–author relationship occurs in the sequence entitled 'La Révolte du Capitaine Lopez'. The two characters Lopez and his prisoner Juilin both consider themselves to be 'victims' of the 'Author's' prejudices, and apostrophize him on the stage. Lopez concentrates not on the military situation but on what he considers should have been the subject of the play, his life story – despite the 'Author's' apparent lack of interest in it. He seeks to elucidate the absorbing problem of his own birth and his father's mysterious death by means of a psychodrama which implicates Juilin and, later on, Butch – there is a clear reference here to the suicide of Gatti's uncle, Armand, in America because of a blonde woman. In the context of the concrete military situation in which the 'Author' has placed him, Lopez proposes to assert his personal freedom by a purely 'gratuitous act' which is the freeing of men whom, as an army officer, it is his duty to keep captive. Juilin considers him incapable of such an action and events prove her to be right: he is the eternal 'prisoner of his uniform'. She, he retorts, is a prisoner of a uniform she does not even wear: the uniform of a petrified middle-class society.

Juilin, however, refuses to live according to the code of others, even that of her husband, despite her real affection for him. This is her 'woman's revolt'. She also rejects the 'regeneration' the 'Author' plans for her through involvement in the cause of the deserting lieutenants. Only after sharing their perils – she is wounded alongside Ierba Buena and Osmany, with whom she has fallen in love – can she commit herself fully to their cause and become 'the real equal' of Osmany. This is the moment of 'rebirth' that the 'Author', Gatti himself, it would seem, had desired for Juilin.

Juilin is the most truly human of female characters to figure in Gatti's theatre, doubtless because she comes from his personal experience. On this point Gatti once remarked that he was not prepared to commit himself more fully. A personal note is also to be heard in Osmany's preoccupation with the revolutionary ideals of his dead father, an immigrant worker who tramped from place to place in search of a job with his bag on his back, and died in an accident at work. His story is that of Gatti's father, and his childhood, like Gatti's own, 'was the country called Social Revolution and it had to be reached' (p. 35). Those who had given their lives for it must not have done so in vain. Echoes of Gatti's key work, *Auguste Geai*, itself very personal, ring through these sequences.

Butch, for his part, does not believe in the possibility or even advisability of social revolution, since it would lead to the collapse of the existing social structure in which he, as a Negro, had achieved promotion only after a long struggle. Like Lopez he is obsessed by the memory of his early beginnings, by the drug-peddling, the violence and the squalor of the Negro ghetto of Harlem. He is haunted by the image of childhood companions who had ended up in Woodburn prison or on the electric chair in Sing Sing. By joining the 'forces of order' in the American Army he had obtained social advancement; but by carrying out his duties as an American soldier in Vietnam for eighteen months, then in Guatemala, he had protected the very 'order' of which he had been born a victim. Whereas Butch equates happiness with the full performance of duty, Lopez equates it with winning freedom.

In Guatemala Butch could have joined the guerrilla force, as the Negro schoolteacher had done. Instead he berates the Negro, whom he sees as a living accusation of himself. He beats him up, showing that his struggle is not against the 'Author', as was Lopez's, but against himself and his own guilty conscience. When he finally kills the Negro this does not signify, as he thinks it does, his liberation from all the black ghettos of America, but his moral suicide – 'the amputation of his whole being', as the Negro teacher had put it earlier. Clad in the uniform of the 'superman of the American military school', Butch stands petrified in his social function just like the policeman in *Auguste Geai*, and just as solitary: 'A cop is always a man on his own, it's not fair'.

The sergeant and the private, whose mental horizons are limited to the hierarchical succession of army ranks, each with additional responsibility and pay, are equally petrified. As soldiers they are ready to kill – even each other, should the need arise. On the other hand, self-sacrifice and the spirit of solidarity and fraternity, born of years of oppression, characterize the men of the maquis who seek to create a better life for all. Their spirit is caught by the hitherto uncommitted who have been captured alongside the guerrilla fighters and suffered the same treatment. All except Juilin and the Negro teacher, who are kept prisoner by Lopez and Butch, have been buried up to their shoulders in the earth to prevent their escape before they can be identified. To survive the fatal onslaught of red ants and vultures in these conditions, they must not fall asleep. They must keep on talking, and what they say reveals the change that comes about in them through their contact with each other. For example, Mario, who has worked for newspapers whose policies he disagreed with in order to support his wife and family, is now tortured by the thought of the sensational and dishonest reports he had written in the past, and by the fear of dying before he can write a true account of the maquis. He struggles to frame his report in his mind, despite the delirium brought on by the blazing sun.

During the half-sane, half-delirious discussions of the prisoners, Gallo Giro, one of the so far unidentified 'deserters', puts his American anti-guerrilla training to good use and introduces positive action. By seemingly betraying his fellow-prisoners, he tricks his captors into digging him out, then kills the guard and makes off to warn the other guerrillas. To avoid being shot at by them, those who are still half buried indicate their whereabouts by intoning the 'Twenty-Five Cents Opera'. Twenty-five sings of his theft of a coffin which he used as a bed; the others, in chorus, sing the refrains.

During the 'opera' Ierba Buena dies of his wounds, though not before managing to sing 'Le Chant de la Naissance' which Gatti wrote in Guatemala and had put into the mouth of Juilin in *Le Quetzal* at the birth of her son. In Buena's mouth it no longer celebrates the birth of a single warrior-child but the birth of a new race of men ready to fight oppression. The final words of this later version are: 'tracer bullets will write the name of the new man, Tecun Uman', the legendary hero who led the fight against the Spaniards centuries before, the 'Joan of Arc of the continent', as Gatti called him. The link between *Le Quetzal* and *La Naissance* is further underlined in the discussion between Butch and his

Armand Gatti in the Theatre

Negro captive, who tells him that the name Tecun Uman, which Butch has to look up in his Soldier's Manual, 'signifies the zero year' of a resistance that he and the other guerrilla fighters are still pursuing today and to which Butch, as the underdog of American society, should belong if he were true to himself.

In a later sequence, entitled 'We shall overcome', the two Negros and Lopez discuss the value of human life. In Butch and even Lopez, who at one time would have been concerned about whether prisoners lived or died, humanity and moral values have been replaced by an unquestioning acceptance of the principle of obedience to orders. Butch even goes so far as to say that were they to carry out the order to execute the prisoners, it would be a just revenge for the indifference shown to them by men and society – 'Each for himself' was a trustworthy motto. Later when the situation becomes critical for the two of them, Butch proposes to 'put an end to the suffering' of the three surviving prisoners – Osmany and Xahil, two of the 'deserter' lieutenants, and the villager Twenty-five – and make a getaway themselves. But Gallo Giro returns and shoots them both dead, then, seizing his victims' water bottles, pours the water over the delirious prisoners' heads, saying, as Xahil struggles to sing 'Le Chant de la Naissance', 'Wake up, it is already the baptism' – the baptism of the 'newborn man'.

Gatti does not give a single definition of this second birth because it is different for each individual. For Butch the rebirth is an 'amputation of his whole being', a 'suicide', the deliberate choice of a vegetative existence. For Sombreron it is a sort of Camusian 'superior suicide', death knowingly courted in an attempt to convert Butch to the maquis. For the romantic Lopez it is the quixotic acceptance of death at one's post, and of the ultimate disappearance of the feudal society of Guatemala of which he is himself a representative. For Juilin it is the cutting of the cord which has bound her to her previous bourgeois existence. For Osmany and the other 'deserters' it is the 'desertion' that is the truly creative act: they risk their lives to 'change man', to create new moral values – though to believe in such a possibility one must be 'pretty naive', according to the 'superman of the American military school'.

Of the many themes woven into the web of this play, one that is treated at length is the practice of torture, and it is viewed differently by those it concerns according to their circumstances. During the discussion on the tortures practised in Guatemala all the characters are present on stage, grouped separately in simultaneous sets. The discussion rebounds like a ball from set to set, from group to group. In the army observation post, where preparations are under way to film the encounter between the troops and the guerrillas, Butch declares that everything need not be filmed or told. Lopez prefers to have the tortures filmed, as this would ease his conscience. Both confess to drowning the memory of the tortures afterwards in drink. When discussing the subject with the guerrilla fighters, the journalist Mario maintains that the general public should be informed about the tortures. Sombreron objects, saying that torture is contagious and that to show torture is to give a blueprint to those who have not so far practised it. Later, when Mario has fallen into the hands of the government troops and declares that he is a journalist, Butch denounces a number of American newspapers by name for publishing what he calls highly coloured reports on the subject.

In sequences such as those in which the characters opt out of normal conversation and turn in on themselves for a brief moment, their diction, according to the stage directions, becomes 'non-realistic', and lighting plays an active part in creating, as it were, a 'close-up' of the speaker who is thinking his thoughts out loud. The technique is particularly effective in the two sequences in which Juilin, inside the army post with Lopez and Butch, and Osmany, still in the general 'burial-ground' some distance away, bid farewell to each other. Each, framed in an isolating spotlight, monologizes, but a real dialogue results from the questions and answers rebounding across the space which separates them. When the spotlight fades on Juilin, the gradual broadening of the spot on Osmany to take in all the prisoners – living, dead and dying – leads back to the concrete situation and to normal conversation at the same time as Osmany's voice rises in a delirious cry to Juilin.

By the use of such techniques Gatti creates characters in depth, torn between their hopes and their fears, their weaknesses and their strength. According to Roland Monod, who appears to have had access to four versions the play had been through since 1966, the characters had become more independent of their creator with each version. He presented the play, however, mainly as the drama of revolutionary forces in Central American countries which repressive governments, created and supported by America in American interests, sought with American help to exterminate. The production was put on a few months after the events of May 1968 when battle was joined in France in the streets and when, as Monod put it, 'theatre suddenly went out on to the street'. During these events Gatti himself had taken to the streets to project a rapid montage of the Commune on street walls or, in the absence of a suitable wall, on the back of a burly militant friend six foot eleven tall, until the friend was run in by the police.

Whatever his reasons, Monod played down the human drama, particularly the drama of the couple which Gatti intended as the essential element of the play. He went so far as to cut a number of Juilin's lines, including the passage in which Juilin and Lopez passionately proclaim, in identical words, their love: Juilin for Osmany, Lopez for 'the creature' who had cost his father his life. In Monod's production the characters tended to be reduced to the 'compensatory figures' that Lopez had accused the 'Author' of wishing to make of them. Besides detracting from the human dimension of the play, this procedure somewhat obscured Gatti's thesis indicated in the title: that Revolution is more than military triumph; it is the birth of a 'new man' in each and all.

Despite any criticism of this kind that could be levelled against Monod's production, *La Naissance* got a warm reception from both public and press. Philippe Madral summed it up when he wrote of the performance at Villejuif:

> One would like those who consider that this theatre is too 'difficult' for a popular public (it is generally the intellectuals who say this), to be in the auditorium packed to the doors by this famous public, and see the triumphal reception it gave to *La Naissance*. (*L'Humanité*, 9 October 1968.)

One wonders whether in fact Gatti was out to prove with this play that he *was* able to treat ordinary classical themes, using all the techniques of ultra-modern French drama. With *La Naissance* no drama critic could take offence. By contrast, even in earlier plays such as *L'Enfant rat*, which has no forerunners, Gatti's own creativity soars above this, and is like a violin coming into a concerto.

Some nine months after Monod's production of *La Naissance* in France, the play was staged at the Staatstheater in Kassel (26 May 1969) under the title *Die Geburt*, and was directed by Gatti. It was an entirely new version, written for a German audience. It was written, furthermore, with Michèle Firk in mind. The news of her suicide in Guatemala, where she had gone as a 'revolutionary fighter' (she described herself as such in her last letter sent to France) prepared to fight to the death for the 'ideas of Che, Fidel and the Vietnamese people', was announced in September 1968, when Gatti was planning his production for Kassel. The event which led to her preferring suicide to capture and torture is referred to in the opening moments of this version: it was the death of the American ambassador, killed by FAR (the Armed Revolutionary Forces of Guatemala), of which Michèle was by then a fully fledged member. On her previous visit in 1967 (May-September) she wrote, under the pseudonym of Francisco Coban,

> 'It is difficult to find words to describe the corruption of the situation in Guatemala, or the day-long terror in which the people live ... Never perhaps has the country been plunged in such a blood bath since the revolution was crushed in 1954 and systematic repression was organized by Castillo Armas. With this difference however, that the present regime was democratically elected'.

This, of course, was not news to Gatti. It is one of the main themes of the version performed in France.

A Journalist-Dramatist in Guatemala: Resistance is Drama

In the new version the technique of a play-within-a-play, which is only hinted at in the French version, is made explicit. The elusive 'Author' becomes a dramatic character on stage. It is Sophie, a West-German woman who is writing a play on Guatemala. The stage set in Kassel, which Gatti considers to be one of the most remarkable ever designed for a play of his, provided a striking visual presentation of this particular aspect. Sophie is on stage throughout, and has at hand all the accessories needed for her work: a real writing table front-stage at one side, a selection of newspaper articles and reviews on a side-table at the other. These real accessories in duplicate formed the set, but were all outsize. An outsize desktop stood on its side backstage, and ten huge screens carrying outsize reviews were set diagonally on the stage. When Sophie consulted a review, the duplicate screen glided away to reveal the object of her search. On the floor lay huge sheets of discarded writing paper which had missed the monumental waste-paper basket which was moved about on the set and from which characters could emerge. Outsize pencils, with coloured points uppermost, protruded from between the discarded sheets of paper, suggesting a forest, the site of the play's action. This made it clear at the same time that within the play was 'a play in the making'.

The first screen to move away revealed a Mexican journalist, Maya Aleman, the author of an article on Guatemala which Sophie dictates into a tape recorder, adding that the journalist is a possible character for her play. An entomological review on Central America has an article on a woman who gave her name, Juilin, to a butterfly in Guatemala. Juilin is of West German stock, and in Sophie's mind that should help her future spectators to a better understanding of Guatemalan reality. Guatemala is a place of tombs, a Golgotha, but without the resurrection. One of Sophie's characters, a lieutenant who has deserted from the Guatemalan Army, emerges from behind a screen and describes it as such.

Sophie has misgivings about having the 'butterfly woman' (who is seen wearing wings when the screen moves away) as the guerrillas' liaison agent. She toys with the idea of creating a 'militant modelled on Michèle Firk', and perhaps even of keeping the two possible Juilins. Two actresses are needed for the parts and are called Juilin I and Juilin II. Outside the theatre Juilin II hands out to the arriving audience copies of Michèle's tracts and of her letter written after the killing of the ambassador. She argues that to follow the logic of the guerrillas they should take the theatre out on to the streets, and in the closing moments of the play attempts to do this. Juilin I is a middle-class woman, but not a die hard bourgeoise. She suggests transposing the action into the Maya era as being better-known and another character considers this to be less dangerous as a subject.

Sophie's indecision creates difficulties for the other characters; they are amused at her subsequent attempt to reconcile the two Juilins in a romantic portrait of a woman breaking with her middle-class past and risking her life to join the man she loves. They are amused too at the idea of someone so totally ignorant of guerrilla life attempting to describe it. When the Vietnam War (or, says Gatti, any other struggle taking place at the time when the play may be put into production) and also the horrible death of the Guatemalan poet Otto René Costello and of his wife at the hands of government troops are called to Sophie's mind by Juilin II, Sophie concludes that the only suitable liaison agent for the guerrillas must be a 'clandestine militant'.

The plot of the play-within-the-play follows much the same lines as in the original version, but alongside it Sophie keeps up a running dialogue with her characters. Towards the end of the play Juilin II climbs back on to the stage to interrupt the action and read out Michèle's 'last letter', which carries a reproof of those who are happy to be 'objectively informed' without themselves engaging in any action. For her part, Juilin II declares that in a play which is a fictional composition, the revolutionary fighter she sees herself to be has no place. To follow logically on from this idea of herself, she invites the audience to go on from the performance to a meeting to be held immediately afterwards in the Kassel Technical College. According to Gatti, this provided the pretext for an important political movement. On stage the play closes with the 'baptism' of the survivors, as in the previous version, watched by Juilin II, who has joined the spectators in the auditorium before the move to the Technical College.

Already, however, in this version the greater development given to the 'interrogation of the theatre' by the characters in the play provides for a more vigorous expression of the theme hinted at in the earlier version: that the theatre is not a place where battles are joined and spectators can act by proxy. Action can be taken only by people themselves. As there is discussion in the play between government troops and guerrilla fighters, some members of the audience – including, says Gatti, the comfortably off manager of a brewery – protested during the meeting that it was anti-revolutionary. Gatti replied that a number of the rehearsals were in fact directed by a guerrilla fighter from Guatemala – the same guerrilla who had translated *Le Crapaud buffle* while in prison and had since died in the revolutionary cause, just as Michèle Firk, from whom he had started in this version, had died not long before.

Notes

1. *Arts*, 4–10 November 1959.
2. *Esprit*, No. 12, December 1954.
3. 'Sur la route de l'exile', *Lettres Françaises*, 3, November 1954.
4. 'Le Mythe de la Grandeur au petit T.N.P.' by Jacqueline Autrusseau, *Les Lettres Françaises*, 15–21 October 1959.
5. *Les Nouvelles Littéraires*, 6 November 1959.

2
China: The Discovery of a Country, A Revolution, a Theatre

I Le Poisson noir

II Un Homme seul

When Gatti first went to China in September 1955 it was as a member of a Franco-Chinese Friendship Society delegation invited by the Chinese Association for Cultural Relations with Foreign Countries. The delegation returned to France at the end of a month, but Gatti extended his stay to two-and-a-half months, travelling about, discovering a country, a revolution and a theatre. 'China is a vast country', he explained. His three-page lyrical history of Peking, entitled *Prose pour Pékin*, figures in *Esprit* (January 1956) alongside Paul Ricoeur's political comments on the revolution, René Dumont's on China's agrarian reform, and Chris Marker's plates 'Clair de Chine'.

Chris Marker was making a 'short', *Dimanche à Pékin*, and from him Gatti had his first lessons in the use of the cine camera. At Marker's request, he wrote *Chine* for his *Petite Planète* collection. It is Number 12 of the series and was published the same year, 1956. In this booklet Gatti gives a colourful account of the country, its history and civilization. His chapter on Chinese theatre ranges from the Peking Opera to performances of the fourteenth-century writer Kouan Han-chin in which social and political themes were combined with striking verbal imagery: 'Only Shakespeare in the Western theatre can be compared with him' (p. 160). In a subsequent article entitled 'Kouan Han-chin, Le Shakespeare chinois', published in *Les Lettres Françaises* (6 August 1959), Gatti describes his first contact with the plays of Kouan Han-chin through an unforgettable performance of his *The Butterfly's Dream*. His analysis of the playwright's themes, language and dramatic structure gives a foretaste of what was to be seen later in Gatti's own plays and in his production method, even to his use of the 'selmaire' (p. 119 explanation), though the word itself is used neither here nor in *Chine*.

Gatti confesses to have learnt in China that theatre as an art form closely related to contemporary reality in its revolutionary aspect was not an unrealizable dream. The visual eloquence of Chinese theatre, through which he could understand the plays even though he did not speak the language, particularly impressed him. He admired the art of the actors who created the time and place of a dramatic action on a bare stage with the help of simple, significant accessories. The actors made of the audience a 'co-producer or co-creator' of the action. Gatti quotes as an example a boatman ferrying a fastidious general across the lake of Hang-Tchéou using a long pole as his only accessory: 'The boat nearly capsizes. Its balance is restored. The audience, who have held their breath, breathe a sigh of relief'. (p. 162). Gatti's experience of Chinese theatre has left its mark on his work as a 'man of the theatre'. How strong its influence was to be became immediately clear in his production of his own play, *Le Poisson noir*. The play itself is the fruit of his experience in China, just as *Le Crapaud buffle* is the fruit of his experience in Central America. The two plays have in common the character of the dictator, but in the context of ancient China, which is the context of *Le Poisson noir*, the dictator is not a crazed tyrant; he takes on the dimensions of an empire-builder – cruel, but far-seeing.

I *Le Poisson noir*

Le Poisson noir was published in September 1958 and, in the words of Philippe Sollers,[1] met with a scandalous silence on the part of the critics until it was awarded the Fenéon Prize eight months later. Sollers urged the public to read this 'unforgettable work' while waiting hopefully to see it performed on the stage. Six years later it was put on at the Grenier de Toulouse whose director, Maurice Sarrazin, had introduced his public to Gatti with a production of *Chroniques d'une planète provisoire* twelve months before. For the occasion, Gatti wrote a second version – 'to limit the disaster', said hostile critics who considered the highly imaginative *Le Poisson noir* to be unplayable. This stage version is described scene by scene in the Grenier's bulletin-programme, Number 2, November 1964, headed 'Naissance d'une Nation'. Gatti had cut his published text to measure for the stage, just as he had watched Jacques Rosner cut the published text of *La Vie imaginaire de l'éboueux Auguste Geai* two years earlier at the Théâtre de la Cité in Villeurbanne. This version of *Le Poisson noir* is more direct, but loses much of the poetry of the original. It also reflects a certain change of outlook in Gatti since he first wrote the play; this was brought about by the unexpected developments of 1956 on the Soviet political scene.

In the introduction to the published text, Gatti names as sources of an ancient chronicle, *La Chronique des Royaumes Combattants*, and some prints entitled 'Attentat de King K'o contre Ts'in che Houan-ti'. The Grenier's bulletin mentions in addition the history of Ts'in according to Se-ma Ts'een,[2] and a short outline of the historical situation on which the play is based is also to be found in Gatti's essay *Chine*. Le Père Léon Wieger, Gatti tells me, was one of his main sources.

This is the only play by Gatti in which the action is set in the past. The story told is that of Ts'in Che Houng-ti, the 'First Emperor', who lived two hundred years before the Christian era and who, in the space of the eleven years from 221 to 210 B.C., conquered and unified six warring principalities and imposed on them, for the first time in their history, a centralized administration which determined the structure of the country for the next twenty centuries. This is stated in the closing lines of the stage version when the Sage of Prince Tan, Kao Tsoun Li, who made the fifty-fourth abortive attempt on the life of Ts'in but, unlike the other fifty-three would-be assassins, was spared to write up the story as he saw it, describes it as the story of 'the birth of a nation which will henceforth be called China'. He ponders over the event and concludes that his reflections will serve as a preface for a book to be entitled 'Mémoires d'un lettré sans mérite pour éclairer les hommes de notre temps' – an oblique reference, perhaps, to Gatti himself.

The story of Ts'in is not entirely historical. It is bound up with the legend of the Black Fish said to be able to confer immortality on its captor. Gatti retains both aspects of the story, historical and legendary, but despite the historical background, *Le Poisson noir* is a concourse of resonances of contemporary events and preoccupations, at times even consciously elicited, and not the mere dramatization of a page of ancient history. Gatti admitted this to the present author. The central character, however, is the Emperor Ts'in. He caught Gatti's imagination because Ts'in was the only Chinese emperor to arrest the attention of Mao Tse-tung, and this struck Gatti as all the more curious because Ts'in had been detested for centuries as a ruthless tyrant and still was, in contemporary Chinese opinion. How could Mao's regard for such an unpopular figure be explained, unless it was as the only Chinese emperor who had shown himself to be a political thinker? Gatti decided to get to know the emperor, to 'live with him' just as he had 'lived' with the 'abominable dictator' of *Le Crapaud buffle*. There was a certain danger in this, Gatti realized, when he did not think like his subject.

The bombshell of Khrushchev's denunciation of Stalin's crimes at the Twentieth Congress came in February 1956, when Gatti was busy writing *Le Poisson noir*. He could not remain indifferent to the denunciation. Moreover, it created a number of problems for him, including the very practical one of writing at the time about the Chinese Emperor Ts'in, who was a despot, albeit a progressive one. Parallels with modern historical figures were inevitably drawn, and when the play reached the stage certain critics and some members of the audiences in post-performance debates identified Ts'in with Stalin, Mao or even Hitler.[3]

Gatti dismisses the parallel with Hitler as sheer stupidity, but agrees that in Ts'in there are 'echoes' of Stalin and also of Mao. He does not, however, accept that there is any 'amalgamation' of Ts'in with the one or the other.

Gatti is no writer of parables. In fact it can be said that here he worked from the other end, since he admits to having sought what was 'Stalinian' in Ts'in, the bad as well as the good, and what there was of Mao in the progressive dictator. He fully supported Mao's outlook, but saw Mao as caught up in the contradictions of the times, contradictions which have still not been resolved, such as that of a revolutionary movement keeping an unblemished character when it is attacked on all sides; for a revolution not to defend itself when it is attacked, is, of course, to accept defeat in advance. Ts'in the progressive ruler consolidated China. To do so he brooked no opposition. Stalin consolidated the gains of the Revolution, similarly brooking no opposition. Mao, to quote his obituary notice in *The Times* 10 September 1976, was the 'revolutionary leader who inspired the regeneration of China and was instrumental in bringing about the birth of the Popular Republic of China in 1949'. There were similarities with both, Gatti admits, even influences, but he 'kept close to Ts'in', and when he was writing of Ts'in, he was writing of Ts'in. That was his intention.

Just before the production, in a conversation with Maurice Sarrazin about the current vogue of productions of former masterpieces in which directors sought to bring out their continued immediacy, Gatti expressed the opinion that masterpieces of the past are a precise expression of a particular period and as such are not suitable for interpretation in terms of the present. He specifically rejects this 'drama of allusions' appealing to current preconceptions. Instead he seeks a *théâtre de rupture* which will break with the preconceived ideas of the spectator and stimulate in him a new awareness.

Gatti met Chou En-lai on his first visit to China, and met Mao only on his second. Had he met Mao before writing *Le Poisson noir* he would, he said to me, have worked into his text Mao's revealing words of warning to the young:'Remember, men are not leeks. Cut off a leek's head and it grows again. It does not grow again on a man.' Ts'in had not hesitated to cut off thousands of men's heads. The Great Wall built by him is reputed to be the longest cemetery in the world. As against Ts'in's 'necessary' cruelty, Gatti insists on the 'humanity' of the Chinese leader as he saw him in the 1950s, and he told the present author of a parade where Mao was taking the salute. A group of children filed past carrying flowers, which they threw at him. Mao took off his cap and, smiling, bent forward to hold out his hands to them. Gatti was so moved by the gesture that he

Armand Gatti in the Theatre

joined in the cheering of the crowd with the only words of Chinese he knew: 'Mao, Mao, Mao'.

The play turns on Ts'in, but it was not Ts'in's China that Gatti had before his eyes in 1955; it was a China dominated by the figure of Mao Tse-tung. What Gatti was witnessing was not the first but the second birth of the country with all its attendant problems, and as Gatti always works on his own 'lived experiences', his *vécu*, this, it must be insisted upon, covers the years 1955 to 1958. Furthermore, given his view of history – that it is not what is written but what is lived – Gatti's attention could not be focused exclusively on an emperor who reigned two hundred years before Christ. What was of concern to him was the relevance to our own times of the problems behind the emperor's story: for example the problem of dictatorship, reactionary or progressive; the problem of reconciling moral values and political necessity; the problematic justification of the means by the end; the question of state at the service of the people or the people at the service of the state; the intractable problem of the treatment of dissidence.

As played at the Grenier, *Le Poisson noir* begins with a dialogue of the dead in an imaginary cemetery. The voices of the characters describing the part they are about to *replay* in the drama set the story of Ts'in in its historical context but do not limit its importance to that context. The final statement by Ts'in's general's son, whom he had executed, is that although the story of Ts'in goes back two thousand years there has been no escaping from it; it forms part of a 'continuous present'. The same argument appears in the Grenier's bulletin-programme of October 1964, Number 1:

> It is as if, over the last two thousand years, mankind has gone on re-enacting, time and time again, the tragedy of Ts'in with all its attendant contradictions and terrible necessities. Ideas, passions, ways of life have continued to clash according to the same inexorable laws, as if history were bent on unravelling a single skein.

Nevertheless, despite pessimistic references to a 'continuous present' or a 'single skein', or to the birth pangs of China highlighted in the action of the play, Gatti does not meditate on the inevitable inhumanity of history. Such a notion is a comfortable alibi and Gatti has constantly refused alibis insisting instead on facing up to conflicts.

The Emperor Ts'in, who has adopted the name of the principality where he was born, and Tan, Prince of Yen, are the two main characters of *Le Poisson noir*. The war between Ts'in and Tan is the concrete expression of the opposition of two political and philosophical systems. Ts'in is a disciple of the Legalist School: efficiency is his guiding principle. He considers government from the point of view of those who govern, not of the governed. He is not concerned with what would bring

China: The Discovery of a Country, a Revolution, a Theatre

the greatest happiness to his subjects but with what would ensure efficient rule, namely self-interest and fear.

His purpose is to establish a model autocracy on the rotting remains of a corrupt feudal system. He will build with the blood, sweat and tears of others and his logic leads to the burning of all books, including those of Confucius and Lao-tseu, in order to make a clear break with the past. He savagely represses the ensuing revolt of the literati and even deports his own son to the Great Wall for opposition to his policy. He uses art in the interests of propaganda; his fairground actors proclaim 'inherited knowledge' to be a 'lame tortoise', a confining 'prison', a rope around one's neck which allows one to die 'peacefully'. These measures were intended to make any return to the old order impossible.

So new laws are promulgated and a new style of government created. A new art of warfare entailing thousands of executions is devised. New plans for industrial development are drawn up and everything is placed under the sign of 'efficiency'. Mountains are blasted to change the course of rivers, a canal is dug to irrigate a desert, trees are planted, land is distributed to the peasants, because 'There is no worse evil than to die of hunger. Now the peasant eats better and the state's granaries are full. What is wrong with that?' Ts'in enquires. His General, Fang, objects: 'It is achieved by bloodshed'.

To protect his expanding empire from ravaging hordes from the north and west, Ts'in builds the Great Wall, readily sacrificing three hundred thousand men to the future of the country: soldiers, peasants and intractable literati. For the wretches who toil to build the wall, dying in their thousands in freezing cold or under a blistering sun, their sole recompense is to hear the Emperor's voice proclaim, albeit through 'loudspeakers' (the first form under which Ts'in manifests himself in the play), 'Your day of suffering is your greatness for ten thousand years [the Chinese term for 'eternity']. Because of you, birth leads to maturity.' A note in the Grenier bulletin 'Naissance d'une Nation' reads that to be successful:

> every birth must bear at the outset the stamp of an unshakeable determination, of logic and firmness in the aims and means, of a harsh rejection of compromise or of bargaining. Two hundred and twenty years before our era the Emperor Ts'in understood this [...] And every birth that does not aim at appeasing the hunger of men is useless. That is what history teaches. Armand Gatti is there to remind us of it.

Prince Tan, the ruler of Yen, is presented, on the other hand, as the embodiment of the teaching of Confucius and Lao-tseu – the teaching that Ts'in has been at pains to eradicate in his country as an obstacle to progress. But whereas Ts'in seeks to inaugurate an age of 'miracles' so as not to sink into the 'fascinating mediocrity of man', Tan's sole concern is the maintenance of the *status quo* in his conservative, etiquette-ridden principality, where religion offers a splendid alibi, privilege is jealously guarded, and lip service alone is paid to the miserable plight of the people. He calls on his Sages to justify and defend his regime.

When the army of Ts'in (after the disappearance of Ts'in) seeks to annex the country of Yen, the struggle is presented in a balletic 'Mimodrama' in which the influence of the visual aspect of the Peking Opera is clearly visible. The accompanying dialogue reveals that the combat is in fact not real but a symbolic combat whose purpose is to illustrate the clash of the political and philosophical systems of the two sides. In annexing Yen, Ts'in's army offers Yen the 'Great Peace', not as a 'shroud' but as 'swaddling clothes' indicative of a birth – that is to say, of a new awareness. It attacks the blind observance of outmoded traditions and God-given values as providing a useful alibi. It also attacks the privileged classes in whose hands the means of production are concentrated.

Tan, for his part, claims, hypocritically, to be defending the cause of liberty while liberally shedding the blood of his least-favoured subjects to prepare the way for his serfs to fight for the privilege of the landowners and, ironically, to perpetuate at the same time their own slavery. When they are besieged in their capital, they do not die of hunger but feed on their dead – that is to say, on the lessons of their ancestors since their minds are closed to all other arguments. They are the first victims of the ideology of which they have long been the willing prisoners. Since war has nothing to do with the decisions of the heavens, as Tan believed, nor is it a 'gesture of culture', all are massacred by Ts'in's army: 'Kill, the destruction of the enemy alone counts', is Ts'in's command. Only Tan and his Sage, Kao Tsoun Li, survive.

A third important figure is the antihero, King K'o. He is the second Sage called upon by Tan to assassinate Ts'in to save the country. But the Sage is not a man of action; he meditates on the relative merits and demerits of the systems of Tan and Ts'in and sees Tan's conformism as a curse which hangs over the whole country and undermines every aspect of life, while Ts'in appears as a progressive ruler, although his rule entails the suppression of freedom and the death of thousands. How is one to choose between the two? King K'o chooses both; the dramatic structure of the play is based on this conflict between the two systems.

When at last King K'o presents himself at Ts'in's court and is admitted to the presence of the emperor who appears on stage for the first time, he sees him seated on his throne; he has a black fish-head. While this association of Ts'in with the Black Fish is in accordance with the myth, the fish-head materializes in Ts'in's appearance his overriding will to immortality. King K'o attempts and fails to kill Ts'in, and is himself mortally wounded in the struggle. As he lies dying, Ts'in discusses with him systems of government. He sees King K'o as a sentimentalist who subconsciously refuses to kill him because the death of a man 'seems scandalous to him'. But this is an error of judgement on Ts'in's part. In an earlier scene using the imagery of the river which symbolizes the domain of man's imagination, King K'o has been seen as a blind fish which constantly blunders into the two river banks, Ts'in's and Tan's. Murder is a pointless act for a man who refuses to make a choice – Gatti changes the myth here to suit his dramatic purpose and makes King Ko's gesture that of a desperate man caught up in the cogwheels of fate. Ts'in's defecting General Fang, on the contrary, has enough hatred in his own heart to plunge a dagger into the heart of a man, so he readily agrees when called upon to give his own head to serve King K'o as a passport to Ts'in's presence.

The climax of the play is the conversation between the dying Sage and his intended victim. It ends with the Sage's triumphal cry: 'Ts'in, the attempt has succeeded'. The sword may have failed, but the Sage has come upon a more deadly weapon as he watches the ritual duel between Ts'in and his Prime Minister, accused by Ts'in of 'prevarication', of complicity in the plot on his life. The ritual duel, with Ts'in attired as a tiger and his Prime Minister as a monkey, is in the tradition of Western trials by jousting and duelling in the Middle Ages, but here the different phases of the fight are accompanied, on loudspeakers, by the dialogue the combatants would have had in the absence of a physical fight.

The Monkey is seriously wounded and, as a last thrust, predicts the disappearance of Ts'in and his palace: 'Grandeur is a firework which burns itself out [...] The fire at Tchang N'g'ann will be total.' The prediction of Ts'in's death catches the emperor off his guard, and King K'o seizes the opportunity to throw down a challenge to Ts'in: 'I recognize you [...] You are the Black Fish.' Since Ts'in's magicians have failed to secure for him the immortality-giving drug, King K'o invokes the Black Fish, with its promise of immortality for its captor. 'What is a fish compared to Ts'in's power? It is enough for Ts'in to want to find it for that to be', Ts'in says. Gatti transforms passive reliance on magic into a school of human endeavour: 'Ts'in will not need his Kingly power to capture the Black Fish; he will do it himself.' Well may King K'o claim victory and Tan say, 'Ts'in will certainly be eaten up by his victory.'

This so far is *l'endroit de l'histoire*; The spectator is told this. What follows is *l'envers de l'histoire*: its reverse side. The story is the same, but there is 'a difference of appreciation'. On *l'endroit* King K'o's attempt on Ts'in has failed: Ts'in is still alive, King K'o dies and the country of Yen is annexed. But on *l'envers* King K'o has succeeded: the story is that of Ts'in's quest of the Black Fish and of his death which, as an absolute prince, he alone has the right to decide on for himself. Whether, as in the published version of the play, Ts'in disappears in the river while searching for the Fish, his imaginative double, or, as in the stage version and the original chronicle, he kills the Fish with an arrow and dies forthwith, he is immortalized by his achievement, 'the birth of a country which will henceforth be called [by his name] China'. More mundanely, Ts'in's courtiers have a vested interest in the survival of the myth of Ts'in. For order to prevail, Ts'in must not disappear; he must continue to sit on his throne; he cannot be replaced by his son; so when Ts'in's fifty-fourth would-be assassin, Kao Tsoun Li, the third Sage of the now-defeated country of Yen, enters the presence of Ts'in, he stabs a dummy which has a black fish-head. 'The Emperor's robes are torn, change them', Ts'in's magician coldly orders the impassive courtiers.

Le Poisson noir presents, in addition to *l'envers* of Ts'in's personal career, *l'envers* of his successful and fruitful system of government. Without this the play would appear as the complete acceptance of the negative as well as the constructive aspects of total dictatorship, which for Gatti would be unthinkable.

The first manifestation of *l'envers* is the prayer addressed to Ts'in by the deportees as they die in their thousands on the Great Wall which, besides being a grandiose achievement, is also a symbol of the emperor's oppressive regime: 'Put an end to your daily miracle, Ts'in.' 'Miracles are not for men. They are too heavy a burden to bear.' When they rebel and execution follows execution, Fang stands inattentive, musing on the execution of his infant son and on the seven hundred castrated tradesmen he has seen toiling in the desert – 'parasites of the state', Ts'in's voice explains. 'New men have been made of them, who will complain of that?'

Throughout the play the cost in terms of human life and human suffering of each of Ts'in's great exploits is counted. 'Your methods may be necessary, but they are not always valid.' These words of King K'o could well represent Gatti's personal assessment of a monarch who has arrogated to himself the power to destroy whatever and whomsoever may stand in his way. The point was taken up in the theatre during one of the post-performance debates by a charge-hand who said that the question of the 'necessary' association of violence with efficiency posed in the play was a question one might have reflected on before seeing the performance, but the lesson to be learnt from *Le Poisson noir* was that if violence was necessary in the past, in the present times one may look forward to the creation of a new world in which violence need have no part. For Maurice Sarrazin, who chaired the debate, this crystallization of a spectator's ideas was 'the highest praise' that could be given to a play.

Contemporary events and haunting contemporary preoccupations reverberate throughout the play. They clearly awakened Gatti's own memories of Hitler's camps; these colour his picture of the deportees working on the Great Wall, and hint at the discouragement of the French Resistance at the 'much-heralded journey' of the general who twice (the text is specific) at the head of the armed forces could have taken power had he so wished. As for the duel between the Tiger and the Monkey, it could contain a hint of the Sino-Soviet rift and the accusation of 'revisionism' made by Mao against the USSR in the 1950s; he saw this as a dangerous step towards complete capitulation to capitalism. The Monkey questions whether the palace of Tchang N'g'ann can stand up to incendiarism on all sides and, answering 'No', predicts the total destruction of the palace.

The dissension between the Tiger and the Monkey who 'together had defended the cause' – the Marxist-Leninist cause – plays into the hands of the West, the 'ten thousand cranes' waiting with folded wings for the pickings. Support of Chiang Kai-shek by Stalin in 1945–6 may well be aired in the accusation of 'prevarication' levelled in the play by the Tiger against the Monkey for affording the 'enemy' an entry into his palace, and so becoming a party to the assassination plot. No 'amalgamation' of the two dramatic figures with the two historical figures is, however, intended. Gatti's own position seems to be defined by the words of the Emperor's son: 'as long as the Great Wall continues to wind through the clouds, the Tiger and the Monkey will have a rendezvous'.

As for the picture painted by Gatti of the country of Ts'in, it differs little from the 'folklore' picture (to use Gatti's term) of the socialist democracies of the East commonly presented in the West. Gatti's intention in painting such a picture could well be summed up in the words used by Chris Marker in his introduction to his film *Cuba si*, made in January 1961 during the first invasion alert in Cuba. Marker intended his film to counter the 'monstrous wave of MISINFORMATION indulged in at the time by the French press, which mocked Fidel Castro's 'paranoiac belief' in a coming invasion of his country. Marker uses the English word 'misinformation,' saying it would become part of the French language just as the phenomenon itself was now part of ordinary life.

The lurid picture is of a police state with loudspeakers (Ts'in's voice) pouring out incessant propaganda, where intellectuals are mercilessly persecuted, dissident subjects are deported to inclement regions, and life is held cheap. Because of his ingrained prejudices King K'o expects to see police everywhere and feels uneasy at the absence of any sign of them: 'They must be hiding behind the tree or lying flat in the fields.' 'What would they be doing in a sweet-potato field?' 'You have obviously had no dealings with the police', his bandit-protector replies.

The first image actually projected in the play is that of the ragged deportees on the Great Wall, but they themselves cast doubt on the authenticity of such a picture in the 1950s; they are, they say, just 'pulverized images'. Towards the end of the play they recognize themselves as actors and bid the spectators whom the play has set thinking 'Good Day', and bid 'Good Night' to those who, prisoners of their prejudices, have stopped short at the performance that ends when the curtain drops.

Fixed ideas, against which Gatti campaigns incessantly, account for Tan's surprise at finding that Ts'in's defecting General Fang is not the 'monster' he had expected him to be. The question consequently arises: What of Ts'in himself? Does he really exist in some point in space? But Tan concludes that since everything happens *as though* he exists, that is good enough. Ts'in could therefore be a *creation* of Yen, a figment of the imagination of each and all. So, if we accept the existence of contemporary echoes in the play, Tan's view of the country of Ts'in could well be an image of the socialist democracies of the East such as the West has created for itself in an effort to stop the spread of 'dangerous' new ideas. This is one of the several ironic passages that give the text its depth and distance.

In the face of deeply rooted prejudice, Ts'in's final desperate attempt to divest himself of his caricatural image as a 'creator of corpses and garrotter of liberties', and become the man he really is, *l'homme vrai*, is doomed to failure: 'I remain a prisoner of the emperor's throne'. The image Kao Tsoun Li seeks to destroy with his dagger is a false image. Others, like Ts'in's courtiers, carefully cultivate this false image for their own benefit. For 'order' to be maintained, Ts'in 'the terrible' must be felt to be everywhere. His 'omnipresence is his greatest achievement [...] without him the country would fall a prey to anarchy and disorder' (Enchaînement VI). Others, like Fang's daughter-in-law, 'secure' in their fixed ideas, *need* to create for themselves the threat of a bogeyman, here the bloodthirsty Tiger. Tan alone finally 'sees the light'; it is time to recognize his error. He tells Kao Tsoun Li that he has become a 'tree' – Gatti's image of *l'homme vrai* – upright and not alienated from himself. Others would follow, to be useful to men.

During public discussions of the play, a certain disquiet was expressed concerning the difficulty of identifying with any of the characters. For which of the two systems – the one violent and progressive, the other non-violent and reactionary – should they opt? Wherein lay the play's commitment? But Gatti's aim was not to point in a particular direction; it was to promote a new awareness through the examination of the issues presented by the historical event, because without awareness there can be no creative action. Opinion as to the general accessibility of *Le Poisson noir* was divided. According to Maurice Sarrazin it was the working-class members of the audience who had shown themselves to be most appreciative of the play and most in sympathy with its general sense.

In Gatti's hands the production of *Le Poisson noir* became the materialization of a fantastic dream involving a keen awareness of

China: The Discovery of a Country, a Revolution, a Theatre

contemporary issues. The miming, the acrobatic feats, the sabre dancers, a festival dragon seeking to link together its various parts and, above all, the Monkey skipping and pirouetting about on the stage, all recalled the Peking Opera. But the Monkey is both Tan's and Ts'in's Prime Minister, and as such makes his contribution to the political argument of the play. He confesses that, at each retelling of the story, he cannot remember whose Prime Minister he had been, nor which of the two he should follow.

The set was 'structured', consisting of two massive blocks, one black (Ts'in's colour) and one green (Tan's colour). Light streaming between the two masses conjured up the image of the river whenever the river was the location. The incessant crossing of the river in both directions by the characters gave a visual representation of the fundamental opposition of the two political systems proposed for the spectator to reflect upon. It underlined that opposition even more effectively than the balletic battle between the armies of Ts'in and Tan.

The whole dramatic action takes place within this structure and on three screens, one backstage and one at each side where live actors join with moving and talking images of themselves: as when, for example, a picture of the Great Wall appears on a screen, deportees are chained to it, some literally; it is not just a backcloth. The screens fulfil a further function when the characters on stage depart from the historical context: the context is taken up by filmed images of the same characters in close-ups. In one striking sequence, two fish (the imaginative doubles of King K'o and his companion Chang Nien in flight) swim about in the river and engage in a conversation in counterpoint to the main theme, which is stated on two film screens in close-ups of King K'o and Prince Tan. *Exposés* and *enchaînements* are used instead of acts and scenes, enabling the action to proceed, as Maurice Sarrazin put it, 'with the rhythm of a television news programme'.

Le Poisson noir is rich in ideas, theme and technique, possibly overrich for stage presentation. Nevertheless the novelty of Gatti's contribution to the contemporary theatre aroused critical interest and approval. Imagination and ideas: these are the two elements which men of the theatre in France dream of uniting perfectly on the stage.

II Un Homme Seul

Un Homme seul is Gatti's play on China just as *La Naissance* is his play on Guatemala, so he told me, but it is 'socialist China in the future'. The starting point of the dramatic action is the defeat of the Communists by the Kuomintang in the Battle of Seven Days and Seven Nights before the epic Long March to Yenan in 1934–5, but Gatti makes the defeat contemporary with the Long March out of which came, in 1949, the Popular Republic of China with its seat in Peking and Mao Tse-tung as its chairman, so bringing to an end the thirty-three year civil war which began in 1916. The Long March is not part of the play's action, but it is always in the background. So too is the figure of Mao Tse-tung. Like *Le Poisson noir*, *Un Homme seul* is enriched by its contemporary 'resonances'.

The play is the fruit of Gatti's second visit to China, of six months' duration, in 1959. It was undertaken at the invitation of the Chinese Minister for Foreign Affairs through the intermediary of the Chinese ambassador in Korea, where Gatti was making the film *Morambong*. 'China needs men like you', the Minister told him. He had been impressed by Gatti's book *Chine* which, like *Prose pour Pékin*, contains the reflections of a privileged bystander watching the revolutionary action of a whole people transforming a tottering imperialism. The transformation was noted in the Grenier's bulletin-programme 'Naissance d'une Nation' where Ts'in's words in *Le Poisson noir*, 'I shall measure myself against the skies', are quoted. The bulletin goes on:

> Two thousand and two hundred years later the voice of Mao Tse-tung rejoins that of Ts'in I, Ts'in the Great. It is the same birth all over again on a gigantic scale, the scale of a country of more than four hundred million people. The conquest of Yen by Ts'in's armies has many points in common with the Long March; the incredible work of construction of the Great Wall (which covers more than five thousand kilometres) has its counterpart in the huge building yard that China is today.

On his arrival in the country Gatti was urged to write a play on the suppression of the Tai-Ping insurrection of 1864, for which the generals themselves were responsible because of their untimely rivalry when they were already master of three-quarters of the country. The play would be widely performed as a warning to officials and people alike of the dangers still ahead, just as the story had been recalled as a warning to the Red Army six months before it entered Peking. As it was, Gatti's attention was diverted from the Tai-Ping revolt by his own experience in the Kwansi province where he heard the story of Wei-Pa-tchoun, the defeated leader of the Partisans. The man fascinated him. He questioned everybody about him wherever he went in the province.

The stories he heard were legion. Wei was clearly not *l'homme disponible*, the uncommitted man of Gide, nor the Goetz of Sartre, whose choice was centred on himself; nor was he the militant convinced from the outset, for whom the Party's 'truth' was gospel truth, as it is for the son in Brecht's *The Mother*. Under the name Li Tche-liou, Wei became the hero of Gatti's play *Un Homme seul*. Li Tche-liou is a militant who fights for the Party, but does not follow the Party line on a grave issue of

China: The Discovery of a Country, a Revolution, a Theatre

strategy. The play itself, with man in relation to the event as its basic theme, is a combination and confrontation of the different versions of Wei's story, written up just as Gatti heard them.

Gatti began on his play in Peking in 1959. Events in neighbouring Vietnam brought him back to his script in 1964, and only then did he think of an 'imaginary tribunal' as offering the best analysis of his hero's predicament. The 'imaginary tribunal' is the tribunal of the future (China as it was before 1965, when the script was completed). It would be called into being by Li Tche-liou, and would give its verdict on the Partisans' defeat in the Kwansi. Had the defeat been a 'victory in the future' or had it not? Did it, or did it not, justify Li Tche-liou's conduct of the campaign?

In speaking of his play Gatti says: *'le futur enfante tout'*, – the future gives the past its history, the past exists in a function of the future; the future decides Li Tche-liou's way of life and the time and manner of his death. From the 'real' present of the dramatic action situated in the cave in the Long-Chen mountain where Li Tche-liou has taken refuge after defeat in the Battle of Seven Days and Seven Nights by Pai Tchoun-shi, at that time governor of the Kwansi province, his imaginary tribunal offers a number of flashbacks into the past and projections into the future. The projections establish a link with the spectator, who knows that the 'future' is the existence of the Popular Republic of China, while the Nationalist China of Chiang Kai-shek exists only in Formosa under American protection.

This dramatic procedure, Gatti told Gérard Guillot, runs contrary to the procedure he had adopted so far.[4] Whereas in the earlier *L'Enfant rat* and *La Deuxième Existence du Camp de Tatenberg* the future is blocked for the characters by their memory of their concentration-camp past, here, in this play, Gatti 'sought to throw into high relief the historical potential represented by the soldiers of the Long March, the Robin Hoods of the Kwansi, on the frontiers of North Vietnam'.

In the cave with Li Tche-liou is Tsoun-jen, the only remaining partisan who has not been killed or abandoned the apparently lost cause. They are hunted by Chiang Kai-shek's men, and a price is set on Li Tche-liou's head, as it had been set on the head of Mao Tse-tung by Chiang, and later by the Japanese. The only *real* place represented in the play is the cave, and the two men are the only *real* characters. The action involving the two is the only *real* action and it ends with the murder, still in the cave, of Li Tche-liou by his one companion, whom the strain of waiting and the solitude of the snow-covered mountain has made mentally ill, and a self-inflicted wound physically ill.

The *real* action forms a framework for a parallel action conducted by Li Tche-liou's imaginary tribunal composed of members of his family, all of whom have been sacrificed to the Revolution, of fellow-combatants for the most part already dead, and members of the enemy Kuomintang alive in Formosa. The 'future', the creation of the two Chinas, although already known to the spectator, is not known to Li Tche-liou, who meets his death long before it comes about. It can therefore only be a 'possible' future, and it is one in which his companion fails to believe, given their desperate situation.

During Li Tche-liou's incessant questioning of the imaginary tribunal the action moves swiftly from place to place according to where the events referred to actually occur. It also moves freely backwards and forwards in time between the real present, which is in the cave, and the past or the future, which are not always a factual past or a factual future but a 'possible' past and a 'possible' future, depending on how they are seen or imagined by one or other member of the imaginary tribunal. Although the tribunal is a figment of Li Tche-liou's imagination it is independent of it; its members give their own versions of the events, and these do not always coincide with Li Tche-liou's. Some versions are even completely new to him. That is because the imaginary tribunal, which is the tribunal of history, continues to function after Li Tche-liou's death *because* it is the tribunal of history.

On its first appearance, immediately after the *real* scene in the cave, the tribunal introduces a concrete vision of the future, which is the existence of a Nationalist China in Formosa. There, Pao Tchoun-shi, now a high official of Chiang Kai-shek's, is busy establishing his own version of events in Kwansi in Li Tche-liou's time. For Li Tche-liou this 'future' can be only a 'visionary future' since he has not lived to see it. He greets it with the triumphant cry: 'China is ours'. The defeat in the Battle of Seven Days and Seven Nights, to which Pao Tchoun-shi refers, is therefore in Li Tche-liou's eyes the first step towards ultimate victory, the founding of the Popular Republic of China, and historically speaking this is so.

His companion, Tsoun-jen, cannot see the imaginary tribunal; he has no intuition of possible historical developments. He lives in the present and replies despondently: 'For the moment things are in a bad way, but one must hope against hope.' It is only at the end of the play, when he has cut off Li Tche-liou's head, that he sees the imaginary tribunal. Its members, Communists and Nationalists, dead and alive alike, all crowd on to the stage and the spectator learns that this is the 'third' head of Li Tche-liou's to be brought in. Earlier in their 'enquiry' the Nationalists had set the count of heads as 'some thirty' during the 'ten years' following Li Tche-liou's murder. The count of thirty confirms Li Tche-liou's hope that the idea for which he has sacrificed his whole life has triumphed in the end. The Republican victory of 1949 is therefore to be inscribed in Li Tche-liou's future without his having lived it, except in imagination.

China: The Discovery of a Country, a Revolution, a Theatre

The permanence in time of the historical event once it has taken place is fundamental to the construction of *Un Homme seul*. As Gatti sees it, when theatre seeks to present a historical event, the dramatic future of that event must be implicit in the dramatic event, itself merely a particular phase of history. Here the dramatic present is the lost battle, the Long March, the internal dissentions in the Communist Party, the exclusion of Mao Tse-tung from the Party for deviationism in 1928, the Third International in Moscow. The dramatic future is the appearance of the two Chinas. The whole is, of course, in the past with regard to the spectators' present.

Elements of the event all figure in the play, but Li Tche-liou's imagination frees itself from them in order to reconstruct them according to his own inner logic. In the opening scene set in the *real* present in the cave after the lost battle, Li Tche-liou gives a 'history lesson' to his 'ignorant' companion, Tsoun-jen, using a log of firewood as a history book. In its rings he reads the story of the struggle from the time of the Tai-Ping insurrection up to their own lost battle and the epic Long March, in which he perceives the seed of the future Republican victory, just as the seed is the tree 'in the future': 'The fate of battles is decided over many years, even centuries. Why are we both here? To prove it was not lost.' A graphic day-by-day description of the lost battle is given by the Partisans, one of whom insists that if the Long March is successful, it will be due partly to the lost battle which had diverted two thousand enemy troops away from the march.

This scene in the *real* present of the two men in the cave is followed by the sittings of the imaginary tribunal through which the different versions of the story of the militant, as heard by Gatti during his stay in the Kwansi, are presented. Those concerning the relationship between Li Tche-liou and his wife Yi-hua give a human dimension to the life of a militant. They end with the final encounter of the couple in Li Tche-liou's hideout, to which Yi-hua has come on hearing that it has been betrayed.

The encounter is replayed by the imaginary tribunal in which Yi-hua now has a place, since in real life she was caught by Kuomintang soldiers when leaving the hideout, and torn limb from limb. In the run-up to the encounter, during a search of her house by the soldiers, she describes the lonely life of the wife of a militant by referring to her usually absent husband as a puff of wind, *un courant d'air*. In the replay in the hideout she tells him, as she runs her fingers through his hair, what she had left unsaid on that fatal night there. It was that the very probable sacrifice of her own life had not been envisaged as a romantic gesture but as the act of a fellow-combatant, seeing that, in accordance with Party discipline which he closely observes, the Revolution had to come first, even before wife and family. Mao's first wife had been garrotted before his own eyes by Chiang Kai-shek's men. He himself escaped to form the Red Army.

Li Tche-liou's amorous adventures are numerous, but they draw the women in to work for the Revolution for love of him. Yi-hua's sister 'married the Revolution', as she put it, because she could not marry Li Tche-liou himself. She appears as a worker for socialism in the People's Republic, and the tasks she has to perform, such as teaching people not to bind the feet of baby girls, add to the picture of the new China that emerges during the course of the play. At the same time she shares the Partisans' view that Li Tche-liou is *un homme seul* with an ever-mounting number of dead around him. His unshakeable determination to take up the fight again from his mountain refuge, alone if need be, is denounced as 'grotesque' by the few survivors of the Battle of Seven Days and Seven Nights. Some of them hold him responsible for their defeat in the battle and call him an 'adventurist'. They vote his exclusion from the Party. A song improvised by the unwilling bearer of the news to Li Tche-liou draws a parallel with Mao Tse-tung's one-time exclusion for deviationism. As for Pao Tchoun-shi, he maintains that there is no such person as Li Tche-liou, that Li Tche-liou is the generic name of a long line of brigands who had devastated the country for centuries and had to be suppressed if an end was to be put to the myth. Pao Tchoun-shi is here the mouthpiece of Chiang Kai-shek, who in 1946 broke the truce with Mao and began on his 'final campaign to rid China of the red bandits'.

Where does the truth lie amid such contrasting evaluations? A contradiction in the character of Li Tche-liou – which, according to Gatti, is behind the whole action of the play – is put by him into the mouth of Lieutenant Ma Young-su, a welcome deserter from the Kuomintang to the Communist Partisans: 'Brother Tche-liou, who seeks to embrace the whole world (and who does perhaps embrace it), is a lone wolf, whatever he may do.' Cannot the militant, whom Gatti describes as the salt of the earth, serve his cause without sacrificing everything, and without finding himself isolated after making life insufferably hard for those who fight alongside him?

At the head of the third section of the play Gatti specifies that he is no longer concerned with a version of an event by someone in a privileged position but with contradictory versions existing quite apart from those who lived the events. In the three versions of the death of Li Tche-liou's small son, sentenced by Pai Tchoun-shi to progressive strangulation on the public square with the aim of trapping his father, the child does die, and the father does not appear. But had Li Tche-liou put the Party's requirement, the 'Revolution before everything else', first? Or had he been physically restrained by his men? Or, even, had restraint been faked? 'What does history become, if those who write it are not those who make it?' The question is Li Tche-liou's. A bonze who is later mistaken for Li Tche-liou, and tortured to death, says in reply:

> History is made of the majority opinion of a number of people who have been associated more or less closely with an event. Subsequently (whatever the compromises reached for it to become majority opinion) interpretations filter through it. What is left is history. (p. 19).

In *Un Homme seul*, as in *Le Poisson noir*, history as such is not, however, Gatti's prime concern. His concern is with a problem of universal application raised by a particular chapter of history: the problem of commitment – whether to adapt oneself to the situation and live with a comfortable conscience, or to act. To be a man *in abstracto*, without social responsibility, is an impossibility. We exist only in the world of others. One's commitment depends on the context of one's life, but commitment there must be. This is Gatti's firm belief and he states it clearly at the end of the play when Li Tche-liou, now dead, joins the Partisans on the imaginary tribunal to sing with them the words of the 'Chant fleuri de la Montagne en hiver': 'In the future of men, who are we? Where are we going? Where shall we go?' Coming at the end of the militant's vision of the future this justifies the title, *Un Homme seul*.

Un Homme seul was staged on 11 May 1966 at the Comédie de Saint-Étienne in the midst of a crisis over the relationship between the Centres Dramatiques and the more prestigious and costly Maisons de la Culture – that is, between a creative centre such as that of Jean Dasté at the Comédie, or a 'garage' at a Maison de la Culture for money-spinners or touring companies. A pamphlet on the problem written by Jean Dasté, who founded the Comédie in 1947, was handed out to the critics at the first night of *Un Homme seul*.

The very large cast needed for the production consisted of the members of Jean Dasté's company, actors from Roger Planchon's theatre at Villeurbanne and still others from Gatti's own company formed in Cuba by him for the film *El otro Cristobal*. These had already taken part in *Le Poisson noir* in Toulouse and in *Chant public* at the TNP. It was an experience to watch, as I did, this relative newcomer to the theatre, and still newcomer to the task of directing plays, everywhere at once on the stage as he brought his text to life. Over and over again he acted their different parts for the cast, reproducing with meticulous care the gestures and movements of Chinese actors on their own stages. It was quite an experience too to watch Jean Dasté, son-in-law of Jacques Copeau, who had himself worked with Copeau and was a lifelong man of the theatre, happily accepting the direction of this newcomer in his part as Li Tche-liou's father.

Gatti expressed his delight at the company's readiness to fall in with the theatrical procedures, new to them, which he employed in his play.

Armand Gatti in the Theatre

The actors were required to perform in three dimensions at once: in the past, present and future, which intertwined and took them through some eighteen locations in a destructured time-scale. The text was put on the stage by Gatti in its original form without any rewriting to adapt it for production or to suit it to a particular purpose for which production was being undertaken.

On this occasion, as on others, some critics accused the author of not being able to stand far enough back from his text as director to handle it to the best advantage. Piscator would have given an interesting answer to the critics, but the attitude adopted by his theatre's Dramaturg over a play in which the hero was a militant Chinese at the time of the Long March made it clear that even a Piscator was not free to do as he wished at the Freievolksbühne.[5] Author and director would have had to compromise by generalizing the theme in some way or other. Neither was prepared to do so. That was the last Gatti was to see of Piscator, who died the following year, but he says he has never forgotten Piscator's comment on *l'Homme seul* and the other heroes of his plays: what difference was there between his (Gatti's) heroes and Jesus Christ? He was always the same idealist, abandoned by all, betrayed by his own; it was the same story as Jesus Christ's. It was easy to argue with the dead. To try to argue with the living was to lose grandeur but gain truth. As it was, Hannes Rajum produced the play at the Schloss theatre in Celle in West Germany in 1968, under the title *Die Schlacht der Sieben Tage und der Sieben Nächte*.

For Gatti's production, the stage designer was once again Hubert Monloup. He distinguished clearly in the overall design the two planes on which the action takes place. The only set representing a really existing site – the mountain cave – was arranged on the apron of the stage. It had a lookout post, a camp fire, logs and an arm-rack, roughly star-shaped and camouflaged with a net. This rack served as a motif for the rest of the set. A tree on the other side of the apron symbolized the strength of mind and rectitude of the militant. Further back, the stage proper, in the shape of a horizontally fragmented five-pointed star lit from beneath, provided a poetic space for the imaginary tribunal. There the various members of the imaginary tribunal – whether dead or alive, and often including Li Tche-liou himself – re-enacted their own versions of the past or of the future, factual or 'possible'. The fragmented star was itself reproduced on the 'flies'; these sloped down to meet the stage, which sloped upwards, forming a kind of open cockleshell. This second star, with its 'boîtes à lumière', used lighting, in each sequence, to provide an indication in Chinese and French of the time and place where the events were being re-enacted. This visual presentation of parallel actions underlined the fundamental structure of the play and was not just an adjunct to the text. As always with Gatti, it was an integral part of the 'dramatic writing'.

China: The Discovery of a Country, a Revolution, a Theatre

The critic Émile Copfermann[6] did not, however, consider the 'occupation' of the theatre space to be completely satisfactory, and there are admittedly some indecisive moments. He also decried the 'abusive' use of luminous flashes to pinpoint the various sites in the action: it caused visual fatigue and verged on 'system'. He nevertheless accepted that 'with all its shortcomings', Gatti's work for the theatre was the most promising of his time and that in choosing to put on Gatti's play, Jean Dasté gave a clear demonstration of the real role of a Centre Dramatique: to 'create theatre for an audience coming into being, which in turn creates the theatre'. This, I think, underestimates the significance of the play and of its production at the Comédie. I did not see the production itself, only rehearsals, but would consider Tania Saintova's broader evaluation of the event to be nearer the mark. She wrote:

> I was present at an important event in the history of the theatre (visual, literary, physical, human) [...] Any theatre bold enough to invite the *Homme seul* to Paris will be able to boast of helping to make of this play an event that will have wide repercussions.[7]

The challenge was not taken up. The Paris theatres continued in the 1960s to remain largely the fief of 'boulevard' and 'Absurdist' drama, of Feydeau and Jean Anouilh, of Beckett and Ionesco.

Notes

1. *Arts*, 13 May 1959.
2. See *Les Mémoires historiques de Se-ma Ts'een*, by Édouard Chavannes.
3. 'Les Chemins du Dialogue', in the *Grenier* bulletin No. 4, January 1965.
4. *Lettres Françaises*, 'Gatti à la Comédie de Saint-Étienne', 19 May 1966.
5. M. Kravetz, *L'Aventure de la parole errante*, Multilogues, p. 94.
6. *La Mise en crise théâtrale* (Paris, Maspero, 1972), p. 182.
7. *Combat*, 25 May 1966.

3
Armchair Theatre as an Interlude: A Cat's-Eye View of the Establishment

Le Voyage du Grand Tchou

Le Voyage du Grand Tchou owes its existence to Gatti's frustration at seeing his prize-winning play *Le Poisson noir* ignored by theatre directors and his earlier text, *Le Crapaud buffle*, lambasted by the main body of Paris critics. He decided to write, for his own pleasure, a play that would defy theatrical performance. Seuil published the text in 1960 along with *L'Enfant rat*, and 1962 saw a production of it by the Théâtre Quotidien de Marseilles in its pocket theatre in Montgrand Street, very like Planchon's pocket theatre in Lyon, and built by the actors in a disused warehouse.

The Théâtre Quotidien de Marseille was founded by Michel Fontayne, a young Paris actor. His director, Roland Monod, had been a journalist in Paris with Gatti, and saw the play as a challenge he wanted to take up. The cast was diffident about the idea of staging such a play, and Michel Fontayne feared a complete flop, but finally agreed because he was hoping to move into a large theatre in order to build up really 'popular' theatre, as was being done at the time in the provinces. *Le Grand Tchou* would therefore be the company's adieu to their theatre-workshop; they would also have the satisfaction of knowing that they would be staging a play which could not be put on in a 'popular' theatre.

Le Grand Tchou was staged on 6 October and ran for fifty-one nights to audiences of about fifty in a capacity hall of 135 seats. On the artistic level, the TQM proved that a limited public did exist for works of this kind and that the play could be stage despite Gatti's intention when writing it. The production was highly praised by the critics, although their opinion was that this sort of play was incomprehensible to people with no experience of the new dramatic techniques. Unfortunately the TQM's financial position was worsened by the venture, and the new production announced for the followng season had to be abandoned. Gabriel Cousin's successful *L'Aboyeuse et l'automate* was revived instead but drew in only forty spectators at each of its eighteen performances, as against seventy at each of the previous seventy-five performances.

Armchair Theatre as an Interlude: A Cat's-Eye View of the Establishment

The initial inspiration for *Le Voyage du Grand Tchou* came from Gatti's home life in 1959 when a 'republic of cats' existed in the family flat. A she-cat, Placente, ruled the 'republic', and Chris Marker had a particular affection for her until the day she turned on him and scratched his face badly. From then on she became 'the cruel cat' – 'Cruelle' in the play. Another of the cats, Tchouta, fell some sixty feet from a window and was none the worse for it. He was rechristened Le Grand Tchou. One day he disappeared and 'the cruel cat' awaited his return in vain. In his play, Gatti imagines that before her demise Cruelle dreamed that the Grand Tchou had gone on a long journey to America to 'discover the New World'. When the curtain rises she is seen asleep. She is, of course, of human size.

In spite of its title the only Chinese thing about the play is the type of acting required for the optional final monologue by Cruelle, which is an 'attempt at a bridge' between Cruelle's dream world and reality. The subject of the play could be that of any French farce featuring the problems and conflicts of a small provincial town with the mayor and the *curé* as the central figures of fun. But Gatti's approach is neither farcical nor realistic. Gatti himself suggested as a possible subtitle: 'How the real world is integrated into the imaginary world'. This gives the reader a lead: it is theatre of fantasy.

The characters are of two kinds: those who 'play parts and appear on stage' – Cruelle the resident Town Hall cat, Colin the dead mayor, his widow and the town councillors – and those who 'play parts but never appear'; these are purely animal-characters. Apart from the absent Grand Tchou, whom Cruelle sees in the person of Colin, to whom she is particularly attached, they are imagined by Cruelle as dead and buried in the 'executed criminals' patch' (executed doubtless by her as rats, birds, etc.) with crosses marking their graves. These are the defunct members of the opposition.

The action is sparked off by the real burial of the mayor, and from time to time the ceremony intrudes into the world as imagined by the Town Hall cat. Cruelle sees the world in terms of her own animal world, and disfigures and transfigures the human world in strip-cartoon fashion – the comparison is Gatti's. In the eyes of the cat the mayor's widow, for example, appears hung about with pots and pans, bottles and beauty aids. She is the object of the cat's intense dislike. Cruelle insinuates that she is part of the 'clandestine' opposition, and even connives at her murder by the mayor. The cat's view of the happenings in the Council Chamber provides an amusing satire on local government, with its mayor stricken by an official disease, 'municipal sickness', thought up by Cruelle to help the mayor 'gain time and save appearances' after a particularly difficult Council meeting which would seem joyously to smack of the 'theatre of the absurd', were it possible to see Gatti as following in the footsteps of Ionesco.

Armand Gatti in the Theatre

With this 'municipal sickness' Gatti anticipates, by some twenty-three years, the thinking of Jean-Marie Colombani writing in *Le Monde* (23 January 1985) when he uses the term *la maladie de l'Élysée* and describes its symptoms as it affects 'the behaviour of the then Head of State (President François Mitterrand) and perhaps, and chiefly, his entourage', halfway through their term of office.

People always revere a 'martyr to the municipal cause', so the 'municipal sickness' must not be allowed to escape from the Town Hall if any resurgence of the defunct opposition under the leadership of the 'gros rat oppositionnel', done to death by its natural enemy the Establishment's cat, is to be prevented. A mausoleum must be erected to the sickness. It takes the form of a cat basket big enough to house the mayor. The pomp and circumstance of the funeral in the real world – according to Rufus, the keeper of the cemetery – is a political operation designed to bring the opposition back to life, the better finally to crush it. With his gun nervously at the ready, he takes aim at the cross of the 'gros rat oppositionnel' in accordance with Establishment policy of shooting the dead to prevent them from working on the living. He is a firm believer in the 'wisdom of the municipality' but, finally believing no longer, commits suicide.

The Establishment comes in for a good and joyous drubbing, but nothing is gratuitous. The cat's world has its own logic. Cruelle imagines Pilet, the official winder of the Council Chamber's grandfather clock as altering the time to suit the needs of the Council. When he is accused of joining the opposition and ordered to resign he refuses, and locks himself inside the clock to make himself the Master of Time. 'From now onwards it will always be midday, the hour of justice', he retorts with reference to Valéry's 'midi le juste'. When sentenced by the mayor to be buried in the clock in the 'patch of the executed criminals' he escapes, flapping his arms like a duck in flight (he was the 'only duck to have agreed to take a seat on the Council after his demise'). He decides to cause a scandal at the Town Hall by committing suicide in the clock duck-pond, by then in the middle of the 'executed criminals patch'. 'The very existence that a duck-pond gives to ducks, a clock gives to man', are his last words.

The two worlds, human and animal, are superimposed one on the other from the outset by the cat Cruelle when, in her imagination, she persuades the mayor that he *is* the Grand Tchou, and the councillors accept her as the mayoress in spite of the bigamous situation this creates. As the play proceeds the two worlds gradually merge, as in the case of the councillor-duck and in the closing scene when the *curé*, who has given a colourful account of how 'little cock, the unbeliever' defied him in the Confessional, ends up himself with 'wings' outstretched as if crucified on the cross above the little cock's grave, madly cock-a-doodle-doo-ing – causing day, which had not dawned since little cock's demise, to break and flood the world with light.

The scenic presentation as imagined by Gatti is an essential element of the play's structure. The two parallel worlds which come into conflict are separated from each other by a transparent screen. 'The *real* world, at least as the inhabitants of the Commune see it, appears as a shadow-play on the screen, whereas the same world, as *imagined* by the cat, is represented on the stage' where the cat was seen dreaming at the rise of the curtain (opening stage direction). The picture of real life as it appears inside the cat's brain is enacted on stage. What takes place behind the transparent screen is the mayor's funeral, with the procession and the committal to earth of the coffin in its reality. Only towards the end does the transparent curtain open for the mayor's widow (as she really is, without the pots and pans) and for the mourners at the funeral to come on to the stage. As they do so the cat backs towards the front stage, with her eyes fixed on them: 'It is the intrusion of the real world into the imaginary world'. This stage direction follows Cruelle's tearing of the corner of the screen beneath the mysterious shadow that she has mistakenly believed to be the Grand Tchou's. But there is nothing there, until the feet of the characters of the *real* world returning from the funeral come into view.

Towards the end of the action there are some over-long monologues but this armchair play offers many excellent theatrical moments such as the scenes in the Council Chamber of wordy parody of stereotyped civil and religious phraseology, or of the councillors' shambling address to an invisible barking, quacking, cheering, howling crowd. Satirical too is this picture of the small-time town with its nucleus of gutter-cats, the Grand Tchou, Cruelle and the crippled, one-eyed Gougou with its crutch – all happy to roam on the rooftops under the light of the moon – and its municipal menagerie busy with crazy problems. It is a menagerie with the individual on the borderline with some animal or other offering a glimpse of the animal behind the human gesture, before that individual is suddenly transformed into cat, rat, duck, cock, faithful poodle, to confound the actor, almost, in his interpretation, particularly in the case of the less sharply defined transformations. One thinks inevitably of Edmond Rostand's *Chantecler*, but there is a world of difference between Rostand's pedestrian farmyard and Gatti's flight of fantasy – so close, he believed, to Henri Michaux's heart, to the poetic magic of Michaux's descriptions of real and imaginary journeys, written, like his own play, without reference to anyone or anything and carried along uniquely by their own momentum.

With its animals and humanized animals, *Le Grand Tchou* has a special place in Gatti's 'bestiary' to which he frequently refers and in which figure the *enfant rat, crapaud buffle*, quetzal, cat, dog, horse, stork, wild duck, wild cat, fishes, and 'all the birds of the air', as a follow-up to the live tigers, panthers, bear, that Gatti had set out to tame in the *cage aux fauves* in 1954.

The play links up with the tradition of escapist theatre, but its originality lies in the direction of the escapism: into ordinary everyday life, with ordinary everyday characters transformed by the imagination of a poet in a highly inventive text. It also has an importance for the study of Gatti's dramatic technique, since it foreshadows that of *La Vie imaginaire de l'éboueur Auguste Geai*, where the fusion of the real and the imaginary was to be used so powerfully.

As for the 'voyage' of the Grand Tchou, imagined by Cruelle as begun in the mayor's coffin – which was to serve as Tchou's 'place of retreat' in his campaign – the Grand Tchou, she says, had confided in her on the eve of his departure his fears about the mysterious consequences of the adventure ahead, yet his need to escape from the existing 'edifying system', he was caught up in, so as to be always ready to face the demands of 'midday, the hour of justice'. America as his destination was, he said, the 'trivial version' of his journey meant for the consumption of others, but they could not contest it since he was in fact setting out to 'conquer the New World', there to face, in Cruelle's words, 'l'ensemble des différentes lumières de Midi', of 'midday, the hour of justice'. This 'voyage of the Grand Tchou' may it not foreshadow Gatti's own 'voyage' which was to have no fixed itinerary, no final destination, only a number of stop-offs: in the Guatemalan maquis, in the labour camps of Germany, in the bombed city of Hiroshima – a voyage which was a continual pressing ahead in the *aventure de la parole errante*, as if just to go on going on was the goal to aim for?

4
Nazi Camps: Drama as an Escape from an Obsession

I l'Enfant rat. La Deuxième Existence du Camp de Tatenberg
II Chroniques d'une planète provisoire. l'Enclos

> Ne dormez pas auprès des déportés ... La Nuit, ces hommes qui marchent libres, qui parlent, qui mangent, qui rient, retournent aux camps. Leurs masques plombés par la peur réapparaissent, ils courent, ils se débattent. Les fours fument éternellement. Cinq années à revivre ... Ils ont le temps. Et quand ce sera fini, ils recommenceront. Combien d'années de camps cela fera-t-il à la fin de leurs jours? On les entend aussi crier. Hurler parfois. Ne dormez pas auprès des déportés. Anna Langfus, déportée à Auschwitz; *Le Sel et le souffre* (Gallimard, 1960)[1]

The testimony of Anna Langfus squares with that of Gatti, who still comes back to his experience of concentration camps in conversations and interviews. He confesses that he has never been able to rid himself of the haunting memory. No wonder, then, that it is the substance of two plays completed in the late 1950s, *l'Enfant rat* and *La Deuxième Existence du Camp de Tatenberg*. But already at the Liberation in 1945 Gatti had sought to write a play, *Le Nombre ci-gît*, based on his experience as a deportee. He however declared this first attempt to be nothing more than a 'verbal exercise with almost nonexistent characters'.[2] Each morning a man is executed by others who hope to prove to themselves by this act that they are themselves truly alive. But each morning the man they execute is one and the same man, so in their frenzy they proceed to execute him twice, three times, ten times a day, only to find the man alive next time. As the memory of their act becomes more obsessive, its repetition becomes more frequent. Although Gatti discarded this first attempt to dramatize obscure memories of concentration-camp life, the theme remains central in the action of *L'Enfant rat*. It is stated in the opening scene, where the 'victim' says to the former camp guard:

> When the war was over you used to execute me once a month. It seemed to me that you must have felt very uncertain that you had survived, if only in that way could you convince yourself of your existence. Now you execute me every week, is it because you are even more uncertain?

The camp chaplain replies: 'Survivors of a war never stop killing the dead. How else can they prove that they themselves have survived?'

From the failure of this first attempt to make a play on the camps, Gatti concluded that the experience was incommunicable, unless the obstacle lay not in the experience but in drama itself because the 'code-language' of the 'civilized' world had no co-ordination with the 'parallel' world of deportees, nor could the terrible reality of the camps be contained within the language and forms of traditional theatre. Nevertheless the image of the camps continued to haunt him and for seven years, while earning his daily bread as a journalist, he worked at night on a script describing the camps. This began as *La Traque des assis* then became *Bas-relief pour un décapité*: its subject was the execution in Plötzensee prison of a childhood friend, Lino. How could he, Gatti, dismiss the execution and give his friend the life that had been taken from him? The script ran through forty-nine versions before being finally discarded after Gatti's return from Guatemala in 1954. He had come to realize that this nightly rendezvous with his script was *his* way of returning to the camp and of being again in the company of those, now dead, whom he had known in the camp when he was twenty years of age.

In 1956, determined to exorcize the persistent nightmare, he wrote a scenario which was later to become the prize-winning film *L'Enclos*. He also returned to the problem of finding a suitable dramatic form for this 'capital experience of the century'. This time, however, he had not only his lived experience of the camps to draw upon but also his experience of theatre in China. *L'Enfant rat* is the first of a cycle of finished works on the Nazi concentration camps. The film, *L'Enclos*, brings the cycle to a close. The second play of the series is *La Deuxième Existence du camp de Tatenberg* which, like *L'Enfant rat*, is also set in the years following the war and turns on the ex-deportees' obsessive memories of life in the camps, and their inability to live a new life other than in terms of their experience of the camps. Gatti had already developed this theme in a despatch to *Le Parisien Libéré* (7–25 July 1955), *Malheur aux sans-patrie. Le Drame des personnes déplacées à vie*, during his visit to a number of 'Displaced Persons' camps in Europe. One such camp – set up by the Displaced Persons themselves in the Mauthausen Concentration Camp where Gatti, along with some others, spent several nights round fires in the camp huts after watching the grim reminders of its past history being cleared away during the day – provided the starting point of the

Tatenberg play and accounts for the claustrophobic atmosphere which pervades it. 'Tatenberg' becomes 'a camp on the Danube – like Mauthausen'. 'Why?,' as Gatti explained to Marc Kravetz, 'Once the gates were shut, the camp began its second existence with me always locked up inside' (*Multilogues*, p. 73).

The third play in the series, *Chroniques d'une planète provisoire*, is less introspective and is more directly concerned with the politico-social aspects of the concentration camps and the real nature of the Nazi philosophy which made the creation of such camps possible. The action is presented in a series of 'chronicles', with science fiction playing a colourful and amusing role. The satirical portraits of Hitler and his minions which it presents precedes by some months the satirical portraits of the egregious Central American dictator of *Le Crapaud buffle* and his equally outrageous entourage. In both plays the ludicrous details are based on solid fact and both, despite the difference of geographical siting, present a picture of the 'concentration-camp universe' in a broader sense than David Rousset used the expression in his book *L'Univers concentrationnaire* (1946). For Gatti the concentration camp is not just a historical accident. It is a persistent reality, and is shown as such in *L'Enfant rat*. One of the characters remarks that it is because it has existed – and still exists – that the story of the murder in the mine calls for so many different versions. It has nothing in common with those places of violent death which have been turned into green parks, not to blot out the horror! but to make it digestible (p. 86). The remark makes one think of Dachau.

I *L'Enfant rat*

In *L'Enfant rat* the post-Liberation civil status and way of life of each of five ex-deportees is established at the beginning, and their past in the camps is resurrected in terms of their present situation. They appear first in a life-size 'Photograph' taken at a post-Liberation reunion party in Aubervilliers. This photograph bears the inscription 'Former deportees of the salt-mine'. The five men step out of the frame in turn to reveal their identify and give some hint of their memories of life in the mine and the effect they continue to have on their everyday existence. Auguste, who had become an agricultural worker in Italy, declares that behind the photo which unites the deportees, even though they are now widely dispersed, there lies the story of a murder committed in the mine just before the Liberation. It is on this murder that the dramatic action turns, and all five remain as much its prisoners as they were of the trusty and guards in the mine.

The play is very unusual in its form. Instead of scenes or acts there is a series of sections which take no account of chronology and do not even tell a coherent story. An announcement, 'The Old Testament', made by the ex-trusty with an added comment, 'It is we who wrote it', opens the play and reveals the influence of the Catholic seminary on Gatti's thought. The ex-chaplain then carries on stage a huge 'Bible' of which the title, 'L'Enfant rat', is plainly visible. He announces 'Genèse' and, as the action proceeds, names other books of the Bible, including 'Psaumes des survivants' which, along with 'Genèse', tell of the horrors of life in the salt-mine. In the section 'Les Prophètes Antérieurs' the four ex-deportees give different versions of the original crime, varying from a claim to have saved the life of one of their number whose head had been split open by a blow from a trusty's spade to a confession of deliberate murder of the wounded man in order to stifle his cries and save their own lives. In 'L'Ecclésiaste', Pétrus, now a police superintendent in post-war Monte Carlo, relives the murder in the mine in every murder he has to investigate. He sees the trusty in his police informer, and a fellow-deportee in his Chief Inspector. In 'Exode' this fellow-deportee, now M. Loyal, a travelling circus manager who was in Berlin at the time, confesses to having got the idea of a circus act in which the tamer is 'mauled to death' by the tigress from the incident in the mine.

The story of the mine as it affects the present lives of the former prisoners is taken up in three 'Gospels according to ...' Pétrus, M. Loyal and Joseph Claravel, a workman in Aubervilliers. A further 'Gospel' is that of a fringe character, the washerwoman 'Adelaïde the poisoner'. She is the protagonist only in so far as she is involved in a childhood experience of her son, Auguste, which he carries with him into the mine. What he has experienced as a deportee is a repetition of the humiliation and persecution he suffered as a child when he was brutally 'taken into care' because his mother, Adelaïde, was sentenced to hard labour for life for having allegedly poisoned her husband. Besides being the story of the mine as seen through Auguste's eyes, this 'Gospel' carries a clear statement of the main burden of the play, which is the persistence of oppression all the world over, the permanence of the 'concentration-camp universe'.

The theme is further illustrated in this 'Gospel' by the story of Adelaïde's mental torture in the dock, told through a superimposition of images as though in a film. Her story echoes the case of Pauline Dubuisson on which Gatti, as a journalist for *Esprit*, reported in January 1954. Like Pauline, Adelaïde was a 'convicted murderess even before the trial'. An excited public demanded for Adelaïde a 'pickaxe and shovel for life', just as it had clamoured for the public execution of Pauline. One vote saved Pauline from death, and she was given hard labour for life. Like Pauline, Adelaïde was the 'creation' of the public who all lent her a 'thousand different faces'. Adelaïde lost her identity. Everyone had his own Adelaïde to fling in the faces of other people. There were twenty Adelaïdes struggling with each other at every court sitting, which she likens to the slaughter of the bull in the bull ring.

The permanence of the concentration-camp universe in the post-Liberation period is the subject of the 'Gospel according to Joseph',[3] the machinist who has spent six months in prison for sabotaging his machine in an effort to prevent it from being taken over by blacklegs during a lock-out. The method he instinctively used was that used by the deportees in the mine, but on his release he has found himself expelled from his trade union for the trouble he had caused with the firm by his action. The shock of his expulsion parallels the emotional shock of finding that his wife has gone off with a fellow-deportee. The emotional and professional experiences are superimposed one upon the other by the very words Joseph uses: 'Pascale and the grinding machine – how ironical! I sabotaged them both the same day' (p. 29).

These events are not recounted in chronological order. The 'Gospel' begins with Joseph's emotional shock at discovering his wife's desertion, and only towards its end are the events leading to his imprisonment revealed. Joseph's story is unravelled in a major 'flashback'. Within it is a minor 'flashback' expressing Joseph's pride in the new machine he had been supplied and his instinctive proprietorship of it, which led to his sabotaging it. On this emotion is grafted his feelings for his wife: 'I thought one could mistake one's wife for one's machine, whereas they were already one and the same thing.'

Homeless, jobless, penniless, unable even to buy a rope to hang himself that the cynical receiver offers to sell him, Joseph has also seen the failure of the political revolution on which he and the other Resistance fighters in the camp had pinned their hopes for the future of France. The human appeal is strong in this 'Gospel', much more so than in the parody of the police investigation with Pétrus in the fairy-tale Principality of Monte Carlo, or the bustle and glitter of the circus with M. Loyal. Technically also this 'Gospel' is the most interesting.

The action of the play consists of the musings and reminiscences of the characters in turn. There is no setting. A few essential accessories locate the destructured [*éclaté*] action, such as the tip-truck which symbolizes the mine and serves as the tigress's cage, and as the dock for Adelaïde. Time is as destructured as place, chronology counts for nothing, since the order in which events are related is dictated by the experiences and memory of the characters. Both are entirely mental.

The characterization is as unusual as the dramatic form. The *dramatis personae* are designated by numbers, whether they be officials of the camp or deportees – in the camps a man was a number not an individual. Here the designation by numbers is intended to ensure the permanence of the identity of each person in whatever different situation he may figure in the four 'Gospels'. In each of these, the 'Evangelist' becomes, in his own mind, the main character, with the others as secondary characters. He is the 'sun-character' with attendant 'satellite' characters, each of whom retains his identity by means of his number. For example Number 10, the ex-camp warden, reappears first as a bouncer at a sleazy nightclub, then as a ringside spectator looking for thrills, a gendarme, and finally a cynical official receiver.

The aim of this 'theatrical experiment' is to show that there is a real person behind the number, but that everyone in whose life we are not personally involved is an abstraction in our minds. Gatti does not admit the possibility of confusion arising from this designation by numbers because the roles are played by flesh-and-blood actors. To give the characters names would have blunted the point of the play. When Gatti does give the ex-deportees in their post-Liberation existence a name and civil status, they are generally circus names such as Pétrus, M. Loyal and Auguste, or Joseph, a name to recall the 'New Testament'. Such names are as general as numbers.

Since Gatti considers that to be valid a dramatic work should stir the spectator to action, he fixes attention in a 'sub-gospel' between the 'Old' and 'New' Testaments, on 'the spectator with conventional views [*emmétrope*]' in order to secure his 'redemption'. In this 'sub-gospel' the camp is mentally re-created by the characters, all of whom are present in their original roles as prisoners, etc. They offer the spectator a 'replay' of camp life in terms of currently held illusions, seeing that no 'privileged' (objective) witness ever managed to penetrate into the camps. This unauthenticated testimony is therefore a 'sub-gospel' painting popular mental pictures of a camp with searchlights sweeping across the hutments, warders nervously cracking their switches against their jackboots, dogs barking, men working frantically to the crisp commands of the trusty, the frequent rattle of rifle fire by execution squads, the order to strip for 'selection', heroic attitudes struck by deportees on their way to the gas chambers and the cringing cowardice of a trusty faced with the same fate so that his tattooed skin might make an interesting lamp-shade for an officer's wife.

All this presents a very different picture from the one drawn from the memories of the authentic inmates of the camp in the opening moments of the play. In it a trusty counts them in sevens and eights as they enter the cage to be lowered down the salt-mine, all scared lest the worn cables should break, all dreading the cold, the mud, the dark of the dank tunnels, their tattered clothes soaked with icy water, the rock salt eating into their hands, their arms, their legs. After the 'replay' in conventional terms, the ex-chaplain, who is the mouthpiece of the 'conventionally minded' spectator, advances book in hand towards the audience to address it with the statement: 'Good and evil! Misfortune befalling the innocent, punishment coming to the wicked, that is the normal order of things for the conventionally minded spectator'.

The last section of *L'Enfant rat*, 'The New Testament', is full of echoes of the story of the 'Child-King'. A child is born in the mine to Number 4, Pascale Claraval, and is not the child of her husband, Joseph. It is a horrible enfant rat 'fathered', says Number 1, Pétrus, 'by the irresponsible century in which we live'. It is the image of man born of an inhuman society. But one will soon get used to a 'rat-child'. It is already 'adapted to circumstances – a rat can live anywhere, and it is a stroke of genius that a child born in deportation should resemble one', says Number 2. The hope of the birth of *a new man* from the suffering which humanity has brought upon itself would seem to be a vain hope and, given the society into which *the new man* has been born, he is as like as not to be the exact image of former man. The action itself ends with a crib-like tableau lit by a lamp, with a shade made from the skin of Number 9, the trusty.

There follows a direct appeal from the ex-deportees to the spectator. They beg for understanding, not judgement; for remembrance, not for a date in the calendar of festivals. In fighting the 'trusty that is latent in each of us' they had tried to uphold the dignity of man, and they issue a challenge to the spectator to form a new 'brotherhood' with them and not remain indifferent bystanders. Gatti spells out here the relationship he wishes to establish between the spectator and the dramatic subject, which in this case is the general problem of the permanence of the 'concentration-camp universe' and the repercussions of the concentration-camp phenomenon on individuals, as on society. The subject of the camps, set in a biblical framework, made no appeal to producers in France, but H. Wochunz staged it in Vienna in 1961, and it was staged later in Montreal. Gatti himself confesses to having a certain affection for the play.

La Deuxième Existence du Camp de Tatenberg

La Deuxième Existence du Camp de Tatenberg, a more direct and more intimate drama than *L'Enfant rat*, is a subtle piece of psychological drama based entirely on the play of the separate memories of two very human characters. It draws little on the actual personal memories of Gatti, nor does it juxtapose several witnesses' memories in order to establish a fact or situation as is done when one investigates a crime. It is an artistic composition which explores in depth two totally different memories, travelling moreover in diametrically opposite directions: the memory of the Baltic Jew Ilya Moïssevitch, a survivor of the concentration camps, and that of Hildegarde Frölick, a German war widow who attempts to visualize the circumstances of her husband's death. Moïssevitch's memories, as Gatti explains in the Preface, are concrete, being memories of his lived experience of the Tatenberg camp, and they constantly erupt, spontaneously and automatically, into his daily life. The memories of Hildegarde Frölick, on the contrary, are imagined 'memories' because she was not present when her husband was summarily executed as a deserter on the Eastern front. It is out of the images of war within her personal experience that she seeks to reconstruct his end by means of her life-size puppet theatre. Since 'the past constitutes the present with Moïssevitch, whereas with Madame Frölick the present reconstitutes the past', any understanding between the two characters, any meeting of minds, is fragile and transient.

To be dramatic the encounter between the two different mental processes must necessarily be dialectical, not converging, and must be pursued over a period of time to constitute an action. Gatti makes of Moïssevitch and of Hildegarde showpeople in a travelling fair, a situation by its very nature already once removed from common reality. Their story is summed up by the subtitle of the prologue (*Présentation Aide-Mémoire*), the 'Ballade of the Man and Woman who seek to come together along the banks of the Danube'.

The action begins on the fairground of Grein, a small town on the Danube, and moves along the river at carnival time to the Prater in Vienna, the 'city of illusion', as the Viennese themselves call it. It turns on Hildegarde, who still runs the puppet theatre for which she and her husband were known in Austria before the war, and on Moïssevitch with his fake musical robot which re-echoes the last songs of those who ended their existence as smoke rising from the crematoria.

The prologue is visual and contains in essence all the elements of confrontation between the two memories of Moïssevitch and Hildegarde. This confrontation is the matter of the play. In a muted evocation of the Grein fairground, with its flashing coloured lights and confusion of sounds on the banks of the Danube, represented by a blue ribbon stretching across the stage, the task of the *dramatis personae*, according to a stage direction, 'is to situate themselves in the spectators' memory'. 'Present there', says Guinguin, the crippled boy who works Moïssevitch's robot, 'were the ghosts of Ilya Moïssevitch's past, and in a certain sense those of Hildegarde Frölick's past.'

Those which haunt Moïssevitch's memory glide across the stage on a moving belt behind the blue ribbon as they tell who they are. Those whom Hildegarde conjures up with her puppets, Corporal Frölick and his two companions-at-arms, emerge from the puppet theatre to cover the blue ribbon of the Danube with the white ribbon of the snowstorm which dispersed the German troops in front of the 'wall of the Tartars' and led to the execution of the three men for 'desertion', when,

Nazi Camps: Drama as an Escape From an Obsession

half-crazed with hunger, they had gone hunting a snow hare. The prologue closes on these invented memories of Madame Frölick and the recital of the 'Lament of three soldiers buried in the Steppe of the Kalmucks' by the puppets as they mime their last offensive. The fact that the prologue is designed as a play-within-a-play is further demonstrated by the reappearance on stage of the puppets and ex-deportees, come to dismantle the 'set'.

'Tatenberg', situated not far from Grein where the notorious Mauthausen camp once stood, is not Mauthausen reconstituted. Rather, it is a synthesis of many camps. It has a station which could be that of the infamous station at Birkenau. The Ukrainian ex-deportee, Gregori Kravchenko, remarks that the station, with its cynical Welcome Committee, was built 'solely to reassure' the long convoys of deportees arriving for 'selection' for the gas chambers (p. 261). It is on this station with its mock ticket office, mock buffets, mock waiting-rooms, now derelict, that Gatti's characters – Moïssevitch and other homeless survivors of the camp: Kravchenko, Abel Antokokoletz, a Polish Jew, and Manuel Rodriguez, a Spanish revolutionary – had found an uncomfortable refuge for four years. 'For me, on the day of Liberation, a camp gaped open in front of me. It never closed again', Moïssevitch says.

This 'second existence' of the Tatenberg camp is visually recalled in four flashbacks [*retours en arrière*] featuring Moïssevitch's memories. They alternate with four 'Actualités' located on the Grein fairground featuring the daily life of the two main characters, Moïssevitch and Hildegarde, and of Guinguin. The crippled boy had been dragged by his mother through all the Displaced Persons' camps in Europe in search of his two brothers lost in their deportation. They finally arrived at the Tatenberg 'station', where his mother died. On the fairground with them is a fire-eater, Reuter, an impenitent Nazi, incongruously boastful of his three war wounds and his decoration won on the Moscow river. On the fairground Moïssevitch relives the life of the camp in all its degradation and amid the hostility and suspicions of its inmates. He relives it not directly but through the prism of his experiences on the camp's fake railway station. His recollections are tantalizingly uncertain and become confused with his recollections of the four severe winters spent on the site as a Displaced Person and in much the same company as when he was an inmate of the camp itself. He can no longer be sure of anything. Was Abel, the Cracow Jew then living on the 'station', the former trusty? Or was he his double? Was Abel a hero and a saint? Or was he the traitor to his fellow-prisoners whom Moïssevitch had helped to suppress? Perhaps Abel was still there beside him because he had failed to suppress him in the camp? Will he ever know?

The atmosphere of unreality which permeates the flashback scenes is the intentional result of memory being taken as the force generating the action. In following the trail of memory in his characters, Gatti claims to have traced a path parallel with 'reality' but bearing on it only incidentally. 'Reality' itself also serves as a screen on which memory projects a shadow-play of its own making. This occurs in the sequence of events on the Prater. In an attempt to destroy the past, Moïssevitch 'shoots' Hildegarde's metal marionettes as they are about to replay the scene of their execution. He then turns the gun on the really live persons, Antokokoletz, Kravchenko and Rodriguez, and also on Guinguin in the mistaken belief that he is ridding himself of ghosts from his own past. He is no longer able to distinguish between the living and the dead. 'We are in the city of illusion – alas! – get up and go, the pair of you', he shouts to the corpses of Rodriguez and Guinguin.

The final phase of the action, 'Retour en avant', is projected into an unrealized future and contains an indirect plea to humanity to react against the bondage of the past and adopt a constructive attitude to the future. Moïssevitch had hoped to start life afresh with Hildegarde after the destruction of her marionettes and the memories they embodied. But in losing the marionettes she has 'lost the reasons which give her the impression of being alive', and she refuses Moïssevitch the 'place on the Kalmuck Steppe' which he had begged her to give him.

In a last highly dramatic scene Moïssevitch finally capitulates to the phantoms of the past. He dons a German helmet and shouts 'I am your enemy', but he is completely encircled by the ghosts of all the people he had known as a deportee and in the camps. Hildegarde tries to reach him crying out: 'Come back among the living, Ilya – I am waiting for you', but in vain. A solution had seemed possible. Transcendence almost surmounts confrontation but at the last moment fails to be realized.

Between the scenes on the fairground in Grein and those on the fairground in the Prater, Gatti intercalates the highly imaginative sequence of the 'Ballade des Processions parallèles' marking the showmen's entry into the 'Imperial and Royal city of illusion'. As they arrive they meet a number of curious processions moving in the opposite direction. By means of these 'parallel' processions, the sequence, by telescoping time so to speak, leads the spectator through the history of Vienna from the fire that destroyed the cathedral in 1285 and the mammoth shinbone, 'Saint Stephen's leg' that was hung on the sole remaining door, the Giant's Doorway, on through the reigns of numerous emperors and empresses – history reduced to the vowels AEIOU (*A*ustria *E*rit *i*n *O*rbe *U*ltima) – and up to the destruction of the Franz-Josef Embankment during the Soviet offensive of 1945. With the familiar procession of footballers on their way to the stadium in the Prater, contemporary Vienna exists side by side with historical Vienna and gives a further dimension to Gatti's picture.

Gatti plays on the word 'parallel' throughout the scene and Antokokoletz calls the Vienna police 'the most parallel police he had known'. This might seem a snide reference to de Gaulle's unsavoury 'police parallèle'. Richard N. Coe[4] suggests Robert Musil's satirical novel *Der Mann ohne Eisenchaften,* published in French in 1957 under the title *L'Homme sans qualités,* as the likely inspiration of the notion of 'parallelism' in the sequence. But Gatti's sources, he has often said, are rarely literary; his sources are his own experience. He tells me that finding himself in Vienna without a passport he went to report to the police. The police told him that he was living illegally in the country, that it was their duty to arrest illegal immigrants, so he had better leave the police station quickly and continue to live illegally. Musil's character, Diotima, calls for 'parallel action' to spread the world with the spirit of 'our grand old Austrian Culture', the Good, the True, the Beautiful, to mark the Austrian Emperor's seventieth birthday and counter the campaign for efficiency and progressiveness of the materialistic Prussia-Germany of William II. 'Parallelism' would seem to be synonymous, for Musil, with escapism, but Gatti sees parallel situations as a means of bringing light to bear on the theme. Any event or situation has its particular significance, but a number of events or situations must be juxtaposed to ensure enlightenment.

The concept of parallels occurs frequently in Gatti's dramatic writing. So too does the concept of the 'imaginary' as a part of the total reality of life and of an individual's world; the title of the play *La Vie imaginaire de l'éboueur Auguste Geai,* as well as its content, illustrates this. The imaginary provides the ground in which man's possibilities can take root and grow. The imaginary presents alternatives to existence. The imaginary is a project. So Vienna is not just a geographical location, a capital city; it is a nexus of perspectives. 'With the Viennese everything is possible', Antokokoletz concludes as he gazes on the strange processions.

La Deuxième Existence du Camp de Tatenberg was produced in Lyon on 13 April 1962, by Gisèle Tavet at the Théâtre des Célestins with the group Théâtre actuel, formed specifically to serve a 'living theatre which bore witness to the times'. It was considered a masterly production which Paris would be well advised to see – but did not. In Lyon it had to be accommodated in a theatre with an Italianate stage, but in 1967 (22 February), when it was produced by Jean Hustel at the Institute of Theatrical Research at Strasbourg University, the experimental studio in which it was performed allowed the play, according to Gatti, to develop its potentialities to the full. On 3 July 1971 the text was broadcast by France Culture in a production by Jean-Pierre Colas. Outside France, Joachim Fontheim staged the play at Essen on 9 January 1965, and in December 1967 in Bradford, England, it reached the final of the National Union of Students' Drama Festival organized by *The Sunday*

Armand Gatti in the Theatre

Times. It was performed by students of Liverpool University in an English version (unpublished) prepared by its student producer J.K. Robinson, and it provoked keen discussion among the participants in the competition because of its original features.

Hubert Monloup designed the set in Lyon: it provided for two scenic areas, the front stage with the Danube running alongside for the realistic action of everyday life on the fairground, the backstage for the imaginary action of the camp. Behind, on a cyclorama (replacing the three large screens indicated in the text), shadowy shapes and coloured lights were projected in rapid succession. Between the two areas ran a zone of shadow, a zone of half-consciousness: the dividing line, and also the link, between dream and reality; it had to be crossed whenever the live characters capitulated to the ghosts of the past or reacted against them. At such moments the projections on the cyclorama provided a counterpart to the dramatic action; graffiti were briefly illuminated reproducing the names of widely scattered concentration camps and Displaced Persons' camps that Moïssevitch had known. Acting styles were devised to suit the different types of memory in play, jerky for the puppets, smooth and gliding for the camp ghosts: this also obviated the need for the moving belt suggested by Gatti for the presentation of the ghost characters in the opening scene.

In the 'spatial theatre' in Strasbourg, raised acting areas set up throughout the hall were linked by crisscross gangways, themselves acting areas. The light of three projectors played on them. Another gangway ran round the wall of the theatre behind the spectators, who sat where they could between the various acting areas and so were drawn physically into the dramatic action, the underlying theme of which is the condemnation of war and of the worldwide phenomenon of the concentration camp. The lyrical incantations of the characters also help to create in the spectators' minds a new awareness leading to a positive stand.

Such has always been Gatti's goal. He has no desire to please the indifferent spectator who merely buys a ticket and watches a dramatic action taking place beyond the footlights as just 'entertainment' for an idle evening. The theatre must be more serious than that.

II *Chroniques d'une planète provisoire*

When writing his plays, Gatti, on his own admission took no account of the production element but subordinated everything to the logic of the characters and the situation. A second stage in the creative process came later with the rehearsals, which gave a new look and new life to the written text, often changing it radically. The 'work of re-imagination' which Gatti, as a newcomer to the theatre, had watched Jean Vilar carry out on the script of *Le Crapaud buffle* in 1959 actually led him to deny the existence of the 'dramatic text' as a 'work of art', and indeed the only text of *Le Crapaud buffle* which has come into public hands is Vilar's acting text published in the TNP collection. Then three years later (1962) Gatti was to watch another of his 'dramatic texts', *La Vie imaginaire de l'éboueur Auguste Geai*, being prepared for the stage.

Both these experiences stood Gatti in good stead the following year (1963) when, together with Maurice Sarrazin of the Grenier de Toulouse, he staged the *Chroniques d'une planète provisoire* on 3, 4 and 5 October as part of a dramatic festival at the Théâtre du Capitole, and again in 1967, when he undertook to direct the play himself for twenty-eight performances in the Grenier's new premises, the Théâtre Daniel-Sorano. Because of the considerable lapse of time between composition and production, Gatti completely revised the text. When it was written in the early 1950s, Nazism and the concentration camps were still part of the lived experience of the general public, so a theatrical retracing of a lived historical reality seemed to him a pointless exercise, all the more so as it would necessarily be incomplete and no longer topical. On the other hand, by combining history with science fiction in a drama showing astronauts from this earth setting out in their space rocket to get pictures of a Provisional Planet (provisional since it lasts only the space of a performance) and of the life of the people on that planet, he could make an artistic transcription of recent historical events on our own planet using Brechtian 'distancing' of those events to avert identification or purely emotional involvement on the part of the spectator. Such emotion is easily shrugged off at the theatre's exit door, so Gatti puts the spectator in the position of judge and jury instead. This is indicated by a kind of Nuremberg trial conducted by the space rocket's crew towards the end of the play.

One of the countries on the Provisional Planet is obviously Germany. It is renamed Barberoussie, after Barbarossa and 'Operation Barbarossa', Hitler's code name for the invasion of the Soviet Union, here called Tolstoïevski. The others are Ongrille, Les États Étoilés, the Rousseauist Republic, and Picadilicircus. Hitler appears as *Premier Grand Chef*, Himmler as *Second Petit-Rat*, Eichmann, organizer of the 'final solution' of the Jewish problem, as *Ange Stagiaire*, Colonel Berner, in charge of the million Hungarian Jews destined for the gas chambers, as *Colonel Bonbon*, and the Hungarian Jew, Joël Brand the intermediary, as *Juri*. The German characters are, for the most part, Ubuesque figures. Not so the Jews; they remain Jews with a thousand different faces – defiant, resigned, cowardly or even brutal. When the play was first produced in 1963, the 'distancing' proved disconcerting. The subject was clearly no longer part of the lived experience of the general spectator. What had

Armand Gatti in the Theatre

been his 'youth' for Gatti and his generation was ancient history for postwar generations and of no personal concern, as Bertrand Blier's documentary film on the preoccupations of the young, *Hitler? Connais pas!*, bore out that same year.[5] But Gatti refused to see the Nazis and their extermination camps as a page of past history. Deportations and exterminations are part of a permanent drama in which we are all implicated, he said to Henry Lhong, editor of the *Bulletin du Grenier* (No. 4, 1967) at the time of the second production of the play. Men were still being put to death and children tortured. Tomorrow the Nazis could be us.

The revision of the play included the individualizing of the 'earth-dwellers', the astronauts, hitherto designated only by their functions such as *Chef de Bord*, and the reduction of their number to the essential three who were given names and nationalities. The *Chef de Bord*, now named Souvtchinski, has to decide whether they are in fact in contact with a parallel world, or whether Wolfgang (formerly 'Radio Operator'), in an attempt to fight against his own German guilt complex, has himself dreamed up the 'reassuring' images of Pepi, a German woman who has fled Nazi Germany and dared to fall in love with a Russian Jew, Shertoc; and whether Gold (formerly 'Photographer'), obsessed by the guilt of not having shared the fate of his family in the camps, is himself the source of the images of the camp massacres picked up on their television screen? In this new 'psychological' version it is Gold, and not just 'un homme', who vainly seeks to shut these obsessive images out of his mind. This mental theme is presented scenically by figures from the past breaking down the wall that Gold has built from the ruined walls of the ghetto in order to shut them out. The invaders trample over his body as they bear down towards the auditorium. Meanwhile Pepi's voice is heard calling to the survivors – that is to say, to us as spectators – not to forget, and not to be smugly satisfied with our own 'clear' consciences. A 'clear' conscience can kill as effectively as napalm or the atomic bomb and this, Gatti says, is the central theme of his play.

The link between the spectators in the auditorium and the astronaut-spectators of the Provisional Planet was given material form in the two productions by setting the space cabin in the orchestra pit. It projected into the auditorium where the astronauts, equipped with 'instruments', picked up the pictures of the Provisional Planet on a huge 'television screen' for which the whole stage set in a frame (the proscenium arch) did duty.

Events on the planet are presented in some thirty historical 'Chroniques' which recount authentic incidents of the concentration-camp saga. They also outline the 'philosophy' that gave rise to such incidents. So incredible are they that Gatti felt the need to begin by convincing his actors that the horrific events evoked in the play were not a mere

Nazi Camps: Drama as an Escape From an Obsession

figment of his imagination. To do this he showed them every film he could find on the Nazis and their extermination camps. The actors confessed that they had had no idea that such things could ever have happened. Today the *reader* can turn for corroboration to the testimony of survivors from the camps, published in Paris in 1975–6 by the Fédération Nationale des Déportés et Internés, Résistants et Patriotes, in five volumes abundantly illustrated by telling photographs. Interspersed among the 'Chroniques', a number of 'Parachroniques' tell the story of a single detainee (K.Z.): that is, the story of the individual as against that of the nameless masses, arithmetically calculated in convoys or camps. In the production the deportees, faceless men, wore masks to underline their anonymity.

The first image picked up by the space rocket's crew on the 'screen' – which, in this particular context, Gatti described as the 'wall of memory' – is a close-up of the single Jewish detainee, Shertoc, awaiting his turn for extermination behind barbed wire. Superimposed on this image of his present is the photo of Pepi, whom he loves, together with a picture of the ticket for the boat to America that they did not manage to catch. The flash illustrates his memories of the past, which he speaks aloud. In subsequent flashes in the 'Parachroniques', Shertoc or Pepi, in close-up, continues to reminisce without knowing whether the other is alive or dead. These are lyrical scenes and are placed in counterpoint with the burlesque extravagances of the 'Chroniques'. When recalling the circumstances of Shertoc's arrest and deportation in one of them, the 'camera' moves backwards to give a full-length image of Shertoc arguing in the Malkine ghetto with a Jewish leader who is present in person on stage. Shertoc hopes to persuade him to organize an escape route for the community instead of passively waiting for the Almighty to come to their rescue, or accepting death as His will. The flash ends with Shertoc alone, still an image on the 'screen', murmuring: 'They denounced me [...] so that no one should disturb, at the last moment, the terrible rendezvous they had with the promises of their prayers.'

The first of the images of the 'Chroniques' to be picked up is a misty image of a stretch of yellow, barren earth and large sky-blue and field-grey insects 'marinating' in muddy trenches; it is accompanied by the sound of explosions. The image needs no explanation. As it gradually clears, a group of crippled and be-medalled ex-servicemen of fifty and over are seen in a beer-cellar fighting over and over again the battles of 'Bouaumont', 'Bourbille', 'Fort de Veaux', and 'Merdun', on a model of the river 'La Gueuse', with toy soldiers and toy cannons. In the first performance the toy soldiers were replaced by ninepins! The game is interrupted by a radio announcement concerning the front at 'Gavrograd', where Barberoussian soldiers are dying in their thousands in a battle against the Tolstoïevskians. The two 'chroniques' are linked by a communiqué. Breaking as it does into the middle of the older men's war game, it incites them to refight the battle of 'Merdun'; meanwhile, in the nightmarish makeshift hospital at 'Gavrograd' (the *locus* of the second 'Chronique'), a speech by *Petit-Rat* follows the communiqué. It extols the herculanean achievement of *Premier Chef* in 'creating out of a shapeless mass of men a nation as hard as steel' (illustrated in the 1963 programme by a vast cemetery of crosses). The communiqué is drowned by the cries and protests of the crazed, wounded and dying, who defy the order to listen to the speeches of the leaders. The identity of the Provisional Planet is made clearer still when the astronauts discover the presence of Jews: 'At last we have a means of comparison with what is happening on our earth', the Captain says. The first reference to Hörbiger's theory of the history of the universe as being 'a continuous struggle between ice and fire', and its link with the 'philosophy' of the Nazi movement, is also made in this context. The link is developed in subsequent 'chroniques'.

The fourth 'Chronique' – into which the third has 'dissolved', as in a film – reveals *Petit-Rat* clutching the microphone to his chest and trying to make his speech as he rolls about on the floor with stomach pains, a sorry specimen of the Master Race. He orders the doctor to find a cure for his ills by experimenting on the detainees, and a number of 'chroniques' detail the appalling experiments carried out on the prisoners in the camps 'KLA' and 'KLB' (Auschwitz and Buchenwald) by doctors who inject carbolic, prussic acid, phenol and the syphilis virus into their human guinea pigs. A cure is being sought for *Premier Chef*, who is said to be suffering from syphilis. In tests for air-sickness of flight crews, prisoners are subjected to different pressures under a glass bell until they die. The plentiful supply of soap (made from human bodies at the Anatomical Institute in Danzig) is referred to by *Ange Stagiaire*.

The tests of amounts of Zyklon B crystals required for the speedy elimination of the detainees amid the horrors of the gas chambers are described by the chemical expert *SS Lieutenant Quatrain*, whose special province this is. He is called to book by the camp commander because he has not been able to bring himself to order the shooting of the Tolstoïevskian prisoners who have survived the experiment. He is told to 'treat them with prussic acid'. The allusion is to the 850 Russian prisoners of war gassed at Auschwitz on 3 September 1941. *Quatrain* is next seen trying to persuade various Embassy and Church officials, even the 'Holy Father, the Protopope himself', to denounce to the whole world the horrors being perpetrated at Pitchepoî (the name used by Central European Jews for a distant unknown place – the concentration camps): 'It is monstrous to think that He has blessed the Barberoussian troops and their allies a second time'. All, however, send him about his business (and their refusal of any commitment was underlined in the production by their wearing masks). *Quatrain* ends by taking his own life in despair in front of the screen on which flash the images which haunt him.

Quatrain's story is that of a real person, Kurt Gerstein, who joined the SS in order to 'get an insight into this whole machine and then shout it out to the whole world'. But no one would listen to him. As Colonel in the SS Institute of Hygiene, Gerstein was concerned with the supplies of Zyklon B gas to the camps, and had to watch a day's extermination in the Polish camp of Belzek. His attempt to sabotage the destruction process failed and finally, on 26 July 1945, he is presumed to have hanged himself in the Cherche-Midi prison in Paris, where he was held along with other German soldiers. His letters and papers, which came to light after his death, provide the only eye-witness account of Nazi atrocities in the camps written by a member of the SS. In Gatti's play *Quatrain*'s story is run through rapidly, and being 'distanced' avoids the accusation of 'provocation' levelled against Rolf Hochhuth's romantic-historical drama *Der Stellvertreter*, which was being performed at the same time (1963) in Paris under the title *Le Vicaire*, in a production by Peter Brook and François Darbon. Gerstein figures in this play under his own name, but Riccardo, who pleads with Pope Pius XII in the Vatican and ends by denouncing his diplomatic silence over the Nazi massacres of Jews, is a fictitious character.

Further authentic events make their way into Gatti's 'history' of the Provisional Planet. They include the story – declared 'incomprehensible' by the astronauts, and by extension incomprehensible to 'all on this earth' – of the despatch to the gas chambers of four hundred small children orphaned in the destruction of the Warsaw ghetto, who were being cared for by a teacher called Januz Korczak. He voluntarily accompanied them on their journey right into the gas chamber, telling them stories the while. This incident is related shortly and simply by a chorus chanting 'Le Dit du ghetto vide', but Liliane Atlan makes a full-length play on the incident, calling it *Monsieur Fugue ou le mal de terre* (staged by Jean Dasté on 28 April 1967 at the Centre Dramatique in Saint-Étienne).

The main action of Gatti's play concerns Himmler's incredible proposal in April, 1944 for a million Hungarian Jews due for the gas chambers on Hitler's orders – 'perishable merchandise', in Eichmann's language – to be exchanged for 10,000 British and American army trucks for use on the Russian front. Heinar Kipphardt's strictly 'documentary drama' on the subject, *Joel Brand, die Geschichte eines Geschäfts* (1965) presents the proposal as an attempt to drive a wedge between the Allies, and details in realistic fashion the various stages of the negotiations between Eichmann and Himmler on the one hand, the Central Jewish Committee in Istanbul together with the English and

American authorities on the other, and Joel Brand, a member of Waada, the clandestine Jewish organization for mutual aid, as negotiator.

The dramatic interest of Kipphardt's play suffers from the weight of documentation. Not so Gatti's transposition of the event, with its emphasis on the fears and scheming of some Barberoussian leaders faced with the precarious state of the various fronts, particularly the Tolstoïevskian front. In the hope of saving something in case of a final collapse, *Petit-Rat* and *Bonbon* play the humanitarian card and offer the Allies a million *Ongrillois* Jews due for extermination on the order of *Premier Chef*. In exchange they ask for a thousand 'carnivorous plants' in the hope of convincing *Premier Chef* that they are obtaining 'natural secret weapons' – Gatti plays here on Hitler's mystical approach to the conduct of the war. The deal never comes to anything because it is soon apparent that the one point on which all are agreed – the Jewish negotiators, the Nazis, the Allies, the neutrals and the Churches – is that the million Jews shall disappear, in smoke if a deal cannot be made. No one feels responsible for them. All have 'clear' consciences.

The play moves to a climax with the news of the Allies' advance on all fronts. Confusion reigns. 'We are losing the war on the Eastern and Western fronts; so much more reason for winning it in the camps. From tomorrow 35,000 must be exterminated each day' – such is *Petit-Rat*'s order. How the quota is fulfilled, is the burden of several grotesque 'Chroniques'. In one a Jewish policeman in a deserted ghetto complains: 'Now they know they are being arrested to be sent to their death, they are making difficulties'. *Ange Stagiaire*, the arch 'eliminator', gives orders at the KLA for the numbers to be made up from workers (those who had escaped 'selection' for the gas chambers and had been sent to work at the Buna-Monowitz factories run by I.G. Farben). But the gas ovens, he is told, have been blown up by the detainees (this happened at Auschwitz in October 1944 with seventy SS losing their lives as well as 853 gas-chamber Kommandos who revolted against their own future extermination).

In reprisal *Ange Stagiaire* orders the mass shooting of detainees and their common grave to be dug by the remainder. Shertoc is amongst those to face the firing squad, and as he waits his turn the image of Pepi's face, which is ever before his mind, appears on the screen. *Bonbon*, for his part, considers it prudent to obliterate all evidence of the camps' existence, and orders the destruction of the crematoria (in the extermination camp at Birkenau this was done by the SS in January 1945). He also attempts to countermand the order concerning the prisoners in the KLM (Mauthausen; it was in fact Neuengamme), who were to be put in ships to be sunk at sea. In half a dozen lines Gatti evokes the incident at Lübeck complying with an order from Berlin on 24 April

1945, to all camp commanders: 'No prisoners must fall into enemy hands'. Prisoners evacuated from the camps at Neuengamme, and also Dora, were herded into the *Athena*, the *Deutschland*, the *Cap Arcona* and the *Thielbek*, which after ten days without any supplies of food or water, were towed out to sea, with the exception of the *Athena*, and scuttled with all on board. A French detainee who survived is known to the present writer.

Horrified by the spectacle of the holocaust on the Provisional Planet, the space rocket's crew set up a tribunal to try those responsible. Gold acts as Prosecutor, and Wolfgang as Counsel for the Defence. The Captain asks *Ange Stagiaire*: 'What about your gas ovens?', and elicits the reply: 'What about your "clear" conscience – which of the two has caused the most deaths, your "clear" conscience or our crematoria?' This raises the uncomfortable problem of general responsibility. Gatti takes issue with the 'parasitical' clear conscience affected by some in order to justify personal refusal to take action, and in a conversation with Francis Gendron (*Lettres Françaises*, 3–8 October 1963), declared that the number-one criminal is the man with a 'clear' conscience, the gentleman with 'clean hands'. The issue of clean or dirty hands was, he also said, the subject of his play *Sacco and Vanzetti* (as it was then called) which both Piscator and Planchon were planning to stage. In the meantime he hoped that the impact of the *Chroniques* would alert the spectator to the fact that there is an assassin in each of us: 'Beware! don't say that the assassin is someone else, that you have nothing to do with the matter, that your hands are clean.' These words re-echo those of one of his characters in *L'Enfant rat*: 'A Kapo is not a different person from us [...] he is deep down in every one of us.'

The trial scenes which conclude the play – like certain seances of the Nuremberg trial in which Nazi leaders were judged as 'international criminals' – present a real dialogue of the deaf, the two sides belonging, as it were, to two totally different planets, the judges being ordinary mortals, and the accused leaders of a 'spiritual' war to 'regenerate the human race'. This notion is given a scenic dimension in the play when *Petit-Rat* comes face to face with the astronauts: he has a wing on one shoulder and another tucked under an arm and replies scornfully to the suggestion that he has disguised himself as a dove of peace: 'You fool – the superman is amongst you and you take him for a bird.' He shoots himself, and his Archangel double rises slowly up to the heavens, announcing as he goes the imminent arrival of the 'fourth moon'. The reference, like the earlier reference by *Petit-Rat* to the 'third moon', is to the conception of the cosmos of the 'twentieth-century Copernicus', Hörbiger, which formed the cornerstone of Hitler's 'anthropology'.

When Gatti wrote his play he was, so he told me, familiar with the

Hörbigerian cosmogony, whereas the general public in France was not. He had also heard German political prisoners in the Neuengamme camp talk of it. For the guidance of the spectator a short abstract of Hörbiger's theories was included in the programmes of the two productions at the Grenier under the heading 'Philosophie du National-socialisme'. The 1967 programme welcomes the publication in French in 1961 of *Le Matin des Magiciens* by Louis Pauwels and Jacques Bergier as helping to acquaint the general public with the links between Nazism and the Hörbigerian cosmogony and also with the mystical illuminations of Hitler, whose 'spiritual formation' had been undertaken by the Thule group, which was in communication with occult Powers.

It acquainted the public too with the occult and Satanistic aspect of Himmler's SS, with the expeditions to Tibet right up to 1943 to secure 'Aryan' animals for scientific experiment, and with the theory of the 'concave earth' of which Gatti had also heard in the camp. In April 1942 an unwilling Dr Heinz Fischer was forced to work on this theory on the island of Rügen with the idea of obtaining, by reflection from the supposed concave curvature of our world, images of the movements of the English fleet in Scapa Flow. The theory of 'la planète creuse' comes up for discussion between *Petit-Rat*, two alchemists and the 'plénipotentiaire des mathématiques de l'astronomie et de la physique', the title given by Hitler to his personal astrologer, by name Führer.

According to Hörbiger the moon, a block of ice, descends towards the earth and its increased attraction causes a mutation productive of a race of giants, the 'Lords of tomorrow', whereas in the intervening moonless millenia only dwarfed crawling races, gypsies, Jews, Negroes, emerge. In his conversation with his doctor, *Petit-Rat* says that this 'derisory hiatus', the Jews, must not be allowed to contaminate the Master Race. Regeneration by fire was the only service one could render such human larva.

The theatre programme also mentions Hermann Rauschning's *Hitler m'a dit* (1939), which relates Hitler's confidences to Rauschning in 1933–4. Hitler spoke of working for the development of the 'God-man' by a process of selection, which could result in the elimination of the 'Mass-animal':

> Now do you understand the fundamental meaning of our national-socialist movement? [...] He who understands national-socialism only as a political movement understands little. National-socialism is more than a religion; it is the determination to create the superman' (p. 273).

Ange Stagiaire, the *'avant-garde* moralist of the new religion', recalls that *Premier Chef* had declared the creation to be still incomplete, and the stakes of their struggle to be the 'Advent of the sons of God' (Hitler's

Nazi Camps: Drama as an Escape From an Obsession

words). So, given the imminent arrival of the fourth moon, they had to prepare themselves for the future mutations which would endow them with powers such as the Ancients attributed to the gods. How this is to be done is contained in the 'Preface to the new religion' prepared by *Petit-Rat*:

> To pile up a hundred, a thousand, ten thousand corpses – to have been able to do this and, at the same time, in so far as human weakness allowed, to have remained correct and dignified, that is our pride and glory. It is a grandiose page of our history that has never been written. (XXII).

There is therefore the SS which is 'correct' and the SS which kills. In this context the concentration camps must be seen as the logical outcome of the new 'philosophy', and in the light of this 'philosophy' one must interpret *Petit-Rat*'s words on learning that 'the front has cracked': 'Do you realize that it is a whole way of thinking, a whole conception of the universe that has suffered defeat? The spiritual forces are going to be crushed. The hour of judgement approaches.' Gatti is using Goebbels's words after the defeat at Stalingrad. Hitler was no longer a prophet.

In the play one never sees the face of *Premier Chef Suprême* because he is God, *le dieu caché* (the hidden God), but God with the face and thoughts of Hitler. *Ange Stagiaire*, an angel serving his apprenticeship as an exterminator on the Provisional Planet, takes his orders from God. These he receives through an electric bell on his head. In other circumstances the orders are 'barked', because *Premier Chef* has achieved a dizzy degree of mutation as yet unattained by his followers: he is completely dehumanized; he has taken a 'great leap backward' to 'attain' the status of animal. He believes he is a dog, and a 'phototachyscope' worked by *Boulingrin* presents the scientifically processed and illusionary image of a dog running hard – such is the dehumanized *Premier Chef*. At the end the machine is 'dead' (so too the Nazi myth machine which had created Hitler); the *Premier Chef* has 'flown from it, disappeared'. The machine is last seen riding on a cloud with *Boulingrin* alongside the archangel *Petit-Rat*, both of whom have committed suicide.

The text is written as though it were a film scenario. It consists of short scenes which follow each other rapidly and move in space from the ghettos to *Petit-Rat*'s office. In 1967 these places were localized for the spectator on small 'TV screens' fixed around the frame of the main 'TV' screen for which the stage does duty. The country called Picadilicircus, for example, was localized by a film slide of Tower Bridge. In this production Gatti, by now a director in his own right, moved deliberately towards a filmic presentation of his text, using the techniques of cutting, montage, fade-in, close-up, mid-shot, panoramic shot and superimposition. He applied these techniques to stage scenes with live actors, not just to film strips, as when telling Shertoc's story. Gatti envisaged the whole production in terms of a cinematographic *fondu enchaîné* or continuous fade-in and fade-out, with lighting as the basic tool. The use of the fade-in and fade-out allowed successive scenes to merge into each other, and similarly the lateral panoramic movement of actors from out of the semi-darkness into sharp focus and out again. Lighting also added a further dimension to certain scenes, as when *Petit-Rat* made his broadcast to the country under a concentrated beam from a projector, while in the surrounding penumbra could be distinguished the movements of the wounded and dying as they were being carried into the hospital at 'Gavrograd'. Full lighting was used afterwards for the scene inside the hospital. *Ange Stagiaire*'s appearance before the tribunal provided another example of an additional dimension accruing from the use of lighting. All that could be seen of him were his hands caught in a beam from a projector and the enormous shadow cast by them on the 'wall of memory'. These shadows completely dwarfed the judges, who had been 'beamed' on to the planet in the guise of dark silhouettes.

Sound is also used to merge one scene into another, as when the harmless firing of the toy cannons in the battle of 'Merdun' develops into the roar of dangerous exploding bombs at 'Gavrograd'. The superimposition of scenes with live actors was arranged during rehearsals, and Gatti described one to Francis Gendron:

> You are simultaneously in a nightclub in Hungary where the Jewish Mutual Assistance Committee is discussing ways and means of getting in touch with the ghetto through agents of the counter-espionage, in a train carrying deportees which makes its way through the nightclub, and in the concentration camp where Shertoc is about to be shot; this is set in the middle of the train.

The mental and physical torture suffered by the deportees during their long train journey to the gaschambers is described the while by the deportees speaking in chorus, with Shertoc adding his voice to theirs.

With the earth as its starting point and the discovery by the 'earth-dwellers' of the parallel world of the planet, the play ends with the mental superimposition of the one world on the other carried to the point where the 'earth-dwellers' do not know whether they are on the earth, on the Provisional Planet, or on the two at once. History repeats itself, and *Petit-Rat*'s final words, 'A show that has come to an end is always a show that is beginning', warn the spectator of this. For his part Gatti said in 1963 that if the *Chroniques* were still to be written – that is, in Toulouse, where he was at the time – his mind would turn to the resistance put up in the past against the Dominican order by the Albigenses of Languedoc. Hitler would be Louis IX, Himmler Saint Dominic and the Nazis the Dominicans, and soon there would be a million dead. Sadly, history teems with analogies of this kind.

L'Enclos

The public acclaim which Gatti had not obtained with his newspaper articles, his poems or his plays was suddenly secured for him by his first solo venture into the field of the cinema with *L'Enclos*. In 1961 the film won a prize at the Cannes Festival. At Mannheim it obtained a special commendation outside the festival programme. At the ceremony in Moscow, where the film received an award, Gatti was suddenly too overcome with emotion to speak. His mind went back to the diving-bells in the Baltic, and to Vladimir who had given him a rendezvous in Moscow after the war. He finally managed to say: 'He is not here because he died in the diving-bell at the bottom of the Baltic Sea'. At that moment 'the bell clamped down hard on me as in the days when I dug the sand at the bottom of the sea with a triangular shovel'.[6]

L'Enclos[7], which Gatti again sets in the imaginary Konzentrationslager Tatenberg in March 1944, is not the expression of his own experience of a single camp, but a synthesis of the Lindermann camps, Mauthausen, Buchenwald and Dachau. All the camps, Gatti said, had certain traits in common, such as fear. It was fear, first of all, of the man above one in the prison hierarchy, up to Himmler at the top of the pyramid. An incident in his own camp involving an Italian and a Spaniard who though friends – a rare phenomenon in a camp – had come seriously to blows over a matter of national pride, provided the inspiration for the first draft of his film, but he soon realized that even though the incident was real, an Italian and a Spaniard could not give an adequate idea of the reality of a concentration camp. Jews were a fundamental element, and moreover, against a Jew could be set not a Nazi, nor a camp commander, nor an SS, but only a political prisoner, an anti-Nazi. So he created the characters David Stein, a Jewish watchmaker from Belleville in Paris, deportee Number 73421, and Karl Schongauer, prisoner Number 24, a rebellious sailor in the German navy turned turbulent trade unionist, imprisoned in 1933 in the first concentration camp at Oranienburg. But no film company would have accepted a scenario with a German Communist as one of the chief characters in a concentration camp.

An opportunity nevertheless arose in 1960 for Gatti to make the film. He was finishing a scenario on Kafka's *The Castle* for Clavis Film when the rights for the film lapsed. The company needed to make a film there and then, so Gatti proposed *L'Enclos*. The directors, Mr and Mrs Ulrych, had themselves been victims of Nazi oppression. They decided to produce *l'Enclos* with Gatti as its director. Finance was the problem, but after an advance of 250,000 francs from the Centre National du Cinéma, the film was made in co-production with Triglav Film in Yugoslavia, not far from Lubliana. Apart from Jean Negroni, an actor from the Théâtre National Populaire, as David, Hans-Kristian Blech of the Berliner Ensemble as Karl and one or two others, those appearing in the film were not professionals. Some three-quarters of them were former deportees or partisans – French, German, Yugoslav, Czech and Spanish – all speaking their own language in the film. Many had worked in camps in the region, and the opening shots show over two hundred of them, 'Kommandos of Paradise' ('Paradise' being their destination sooner or later) at work in the film's quarry, just as they had worked at Mauthausen and elsewhere, hewing blocks of stone weighing thirty kilos out of the colossal face of the quarry and carrying them up to the top on their backs like lines of ants. The illusion was perfect.

It was not, however, Gatti's intention to dwell on the spectacular horror of the camps: this had been done in other films, and horror becomes 'digestible' in the end. His interest explores the human dimension of those living in the 'parallel' world of the camps, which like the real one has its hierarchy of prisoners, kapos, then SS guards. In this 'parallel' world a man could be slave-driven and humiliated without losing his dignity, but only within limits. What happens when a man is obliged by his torturers to kill a fellow-prisoner or be killed himself?

The film presents two such incidents. The first is one of the daily occurrences in the quarry, but it suggests to the SS lieutenant a convenient way of disposing of Karl, who knows of his misappropriation of stocks and could well denounce him to the Gestapo during their impending visit. Karl is put into an enclosure together with the last remaining Jew of the January convoy, David. David has been told that Karl is there to kill him, but should he succeed in killing Karl within twenty-four hours he can go back to repairing watches in the camp.

The film is based on the strengthening of awareness in David's mind of his dignity as a man, and on his victory over fear. Sequences which reveal the growing understanding between the two men alternate with sequences depicting the activities of the camp's clandestine international resistance organization, of which Karl has been the moving spirit. At the risk of their own lives, those in the organization arrange to substitute for Karl the mangled body of the Czech who has that day been brutally killed by the SS in the quarry. These sequences involve prisoners from the prison kitchens, hospital and brothel, and they incorporate the daily life of the camp into the dramatic action, particularly in the lavatories, the general meeting-place where plans are made and various objects passed from one to another.

At the outset of the 'experiment', as they call it, the camp colonel and his lieutenant each cynically bets a horse on the one he thinks will be killed, the 'subhuman Jew' or the Aryan, and they climb into the mirador to view the progress of the 'gladiators' in the 'arena'. At dawn, the sight of David seated beside the mangled body, calmly smoking, leads them to think that the 'subhuman Jew' has won the fight. But the Jew has 'shed Aryan blood' and must pay with his life. When his number is called, David, his head held high, walks of his own accord out of the enclosure towards the vans waiting to take the daily quota of men to the gas chamber. He goes not as a victim but as a man who has accomplished an act of resistance, knowing that by his silence he has saved the underground organization. 'What matters is not the man but the struggle' – so Karl had said to him during the night. The film ends on a very near close-up of Karl's eyes, which open wide when he hears the camp's orchestra daring to play 'Fallen in the fateful fight', and they remain wide open to the end.

When the film was shown in the Lenin Stadium Gatti was criticized for giving only some five minutes at the beginning of the film to showing the violence of Fascism and the horrors of the camps and for insisting, during the remaining one-and-three-quarter hours, on the spirit of solidarity amongst the detainees – a rare phenomenon in their eyes. Gatti's reply was that he was not interested in what made man smaller than man – in his degradation, in the collapse of human values – but in man's power to stand up against all odds – to be larger than life. This was the reality that mattered to him.

In making this film Gatti managed to free himself, at least temporarily, from the obsession of the camps, though he was to come back to it in 1987 with his *Opéra avec Titre long* on the execution of 117 anti-Nazi Germans in a German prison camp in Berlin in 1943 where man smaller than man was transformed by a new-found spirit of solidarity into man larger than man. With regard to *L'Enclos* Gatti insisted on the topicality of the film because he sees the predicament it describes as present at all times, in all societies.

When Gatti started making *L'Enclos* he did not know, he admits, the first thing about using a cine camera. He had, however, very definite ideas about film 'language'. It includes constant variations on the theme of the human body which is shot in part or in whole, in close-up, mid-shot, long-shot, etc. Should the image not be actually that of the human body, the presence of the human being should none the less be felt; what is seen must always be seen in relation with the human body. The way in which the shots are made to relate to each other by means of the cutting and mounting of the film is the grammar of the filmic language. A film is written in images. Cinema is the art of writing in images.

Notes

1. 'Do not sleep near deportees ... These men who walk about freely, who talk, eat, laugh, go back to the camps at night. Once again their features become livid with fear, they run, they struggle. The gas ovens smoke unceasingly. Five years to be relived ... They have the time to do it. And when it is all over, they will begin again. How many camp years will that make up by the end of their lives? We also hear them cry out, and sometimes scream. Do not sleep near deportees.'
2. *Arts*, 23 August 1959. Interview with Jacques Boussac.
3. The story of a workman from Saint-Nazaire who lost everything after a series of strikes was told to Gatti by Simone de Beauvoir. 'I have given a whole "gospel" to this story. It is one of my favourite compositions, and I have not yet staged it,' says Gatti.
4. 'Armand Gatti's carnival of compassion: La Deuxième Existence du Camp de Tatenberg': *Yale French Studies*, 'From stage to street', No. 46, 1971.
5. See *Les Lettres Françaises*, 2–8 May 1963: 'Hitler? Connais pas!' onze jeunes Français devant la caméra-question de Bertrand Blier', by Maurice Martin; and 1–7 August 1963: 'Autoportrait par "copains" interposés', by Georges Sadoul.
6. Kravetz, *Multilogues*, p. 78.
7. Jean Michaud published the text of *L'Enclos* in 1962, (Fayard), but instead of illustrating it with stills from the film he presents on the opposite pages relevant passages from Gatti's writings so far: *L'Enfant rat*, *Chroniques d'une planète provisoire* and the lost text of *Bas-relief pour un décapité*, and from books such as *L'Univers concentrationnaire* by David Rousset.

References

Pierre Joffroy, *L'Espion de Dieu; La Passion de Kurt Gerstein* (Paris: Grasset, 1970).
Bruno Bettelheim, *Surviving and other Essays* (London: Thames & Hudson, 1979).
– *The Informed Heart. Autonomy in a Mass Age.* (Thames & Hudson, 1960).

5
The Caribbean: Aggression and Resistance

El otro Cristobal. Notre Tranchée de chaque jour

Edouardo Manet, a Cuban who spent ten years (1950–60) in Europe working in the theatre and cinema, happened to be in Paris in 1959 when Jean Vilar staged Gatti's *Le Crapaud buffle* at the Récamier Theatre. He was so impressed by the play that after his return in 1960 to Cuba, where he became director and producer at the National Theatre and also a film director, he invited Gatti to make a film in Havana for the Cuban Institute of Art and the Cinematographic Industry. The film was to be *El otro Cristobal* or 'Les Tambours d'Ogoum'. Shooting began on 22 September 1962 and finished on 31 January 1963. The first version ran for four-and-a-half hours but was cut to two hours for the commercial cinema circuit. It was awarded the Critics' prize at the 1963 Cannes Film Festival but was never put into the commercial circuit in Europe. Mr Rubén Medina of the Institute in Havana kindly arranged a private viewing of the two-hour version for the present writer. The film is listed in the *Filmografia del cine cubano* 1959–80 as follows: 'A través de una sátira de fantásticos símbolos, se muestra la rebelión de un pueblo sojuzgado por una dictadura de un país imaginario de América ('By means of a satire based on expressive symbolism, we are shown the revolt of a people living under the yoke of a dictatorship in an imaginary Latin American country'. When he explained the subject of the film to his cast Gatti said that in ten years' time when the history of Cuba 1962 was written, with its blockades and threats of annihilation, the fact that Cuba had produced a comic film in which a sailor launched an attack on heaven would be seen as a remarkable achievement. It was in that context that the actors should view their artistic responsibility.

The inspiration for the film came from Fidel Castro's words after his failed attack on the Moncada barracks in Santiago on 26 July 1953, with only 160 men at his command: 'We attacked heaven itself'. In Gatti's film the attack on 'heaven' is led by 'the other Christopher Columbus' in a story full of fantasy. The film in no way observes the canons of socialist realism. Gatti admitted the interest socialist realism can have, but believed that as soon as one begins to glorify a situation or enlarge on it one is engaged in a 'flight from the real'. *Notre tranchée de chaque jour*, written immediately after the film was made, illustrates this point using dramatic form. The five-page synopsis of the film which Gatti submitted to the Institute created some disquiet, though it received the support of Osmany Cienfuegos, who took the matter to Fidel Castro. Castro pointed out to the Institute that its role was to support inventiveness, not to repress it, so Gatti was given the go-ahead with his project, which came to be known as 'la película del loco', the crazy fellow's film.

For someone like Gatti, who had not known the 1917 Revolution and had been too young to take part in the Spanish War, the invitation to make a film in Cuba was, he says, a rare opportunity to play a part, albeit very small, in a revolution, namely that of Cuba. With the brigades of builders, etc., in the USSR and the international brigades in Spain as his inspiration, he set to work to form an international film brigade to express solidarity with the Cuban revolutionaries. He returned to France in 1962 after his fact-finding trip to Cuba, in order to recruit Jean Bouise for the part of Cristobal following his triumph in the role of Auguste in the Villeurbanne production of *Auguste Geai* earlier that year; also Jean Michaud, with whom he had worked in the film *L'Enclos*, and Hubert Monloup, stage designer for *La Deuxième Existence du Camp de Tatenberg* when it was produced in Lyon (April 1962). Jean Vilar, who was to have played the dictator, had to withdraw.

These men formed the nucleus of Gatti's 'brigade'. They were joined by Manet, some well-known Cuban actors, the Cuban actress Bertina Acevedo, and Terluniano Izaguire, a 'superb' Negro waiter in the Havana Libre Hotel whom Gatti cast in the role of Olofi, that is to say God the Father. Almost immediately 'God' disappeared into the trenches somewhere on the coast to face the American threat. A week before he began to shoot the film, Gatti received a card from the missing Olofi: 'Con el otro Cristobal tambien venceremos!' ('With the other Cristobal we shall also win through'). Three days before the sequences in which he was to appear were to be shot, Olofi calmly left the trenches and climbed into his heaven.

The other Cubans engaged in his project gave Gatti equally enthusiastic support, and that included the regular army, without which he might never have solved the many technical problems that beset him because of the lack of materials caused by the American blockade. The army also undertook the assault on heaven. Playing the part of the revolutionary peasant army they marched through thick 'clouds' of insecticide, because they had nothing else to make clouds with. Many times when materials were not forthcoming plans had to be altered or scrapped. At the beginning of a banqueting scene which was being filmed on the twenty-fifth floor of the Havana Libre Hotel in the middle of the 'missile' crisis, the lighting broke down. Gatti thought a moment, then decided to carry on and film the scene 'in silhouette'.

A fascinating account of the ungrudging help received from all quarters appears in the article 'NOUS VAINCRONS, table-ronde avec la "brigade Cristobal"', published in *Miroir du Cinéma* Nos 6–7, 1963. There we learn that the basic principle in making the film was collective responsibility with people of French, Cuban and other nationalities all working together as if they belonged to the same country despite language barriers. All freely took on the necessary tasks. While playing Cristobal Jean Bouise was also assistant stage designer and wardrobe keeper. Manet, who directed some of the shooting, became the back legs of the 'horse' in the bullfight, and also worked the 'snow pistol'. People whom Gatti had looked upon at first as executants became creators in their own right. This, Gatti felt, was a real triumph, and in it can perhaps be seen the seeds of his later work done outside the theatre proper.

Gatti's Cuban assistant, Rogelio Paris, identified Cristobal with Cuba before the Revolution, and Cuba with Latin America. Cristobal was Latin America before the Revolution. Rogelio saw Cuba, Cristobal and Latin America as forming an inseparable historic whole which Gatti was attempting to mould together in his film. Like Columbus who discovered America and changed the course of history, the 'other Christopher Columbus', Cristobal, a shipwrecked mariner from the Mediterranean, discovered America anew in twentieth-century Cuba, where the course of history was again to be changed. For Gatti's French assistant Jean Michaud, the allusion to Columbus stopped at the 'discovery'. Not so for the Cubans: as Mr Medina remarked to me during the viewing of the film, they saw in the 'other Cristobal' a reflection of Henri Christophe, the freed slave who had championed the cause of his fellow-men in Haiti a century and a half before.

Gatti's problem was to create a form of film which 'spoke the language of the Revolution' that was taking place under his eyes, together with all its drama and myths. It should be epic in style, that being the only style suited to the story of a revolution. His film embraces the history and folklore of countries round the Caribbean and is set in an imaginary country of which the name, Tecunuman, has a Guatemalan ring. Its Ubuesque dictator is called Admiral Anastasio in 'homage', Gatti said, albeit ironically, to Anastasio Somoza of Nicaragua, who had had him put in prison some eight years before; and the Black Virgin, who escapes from heaven to earth, is given a truly Mexican-style burial, though according to Mr Medina such a burial was not alien to Cuban tradition.

As the film proceeds, however, it gradually narrows its scope down to Cuba alone, and closes on an impressive travelling vista of Cuba's palm trees filmed from a helicopter flying inwards from the tree-lined coast where the palms mount guard over the island. Cuba's voice swells up from the ground: it is the music of the Manzanillo hurdy-gurdy which had given the signal for the insurrection against the Spaniards in 1895. Gatti sought to make of this symbol a filmic image which would carry the idea of revolution. The hurdy-gurdy is the principal 'character' of the film: revolution in action, not revolution in declarations. It is carted about everywhere in the maquis by Bobadilla, a black Cuban, and his companion Cristobal, who have both escaped from prison with it. It strikes up on its own in unexpected places and at unexpected moments.

The sequences featuring the earth (the country of Tecunuman) were filmed in the natural surroundings of Calmito, whereas for heaven studio sets covering twelve hundred square metres were used. The sets take the form of five mobile spherical cages made of 'whale bones'. They are of different sizes, are hung at different levels and are connected by ladders with circular steps on which intensive human and 'angelic' traffic is to be seen. In the firmament hang equally mobile constellations and planets made of paper, metal or cloth. This heaven which proceeds upwards in stages is in direct contrast with the flat earth of Tecunuman. It is a pedestrian place, littered with rubbish discarded by man in his day-to-day existence. It is devoid of magic or mystery. It is paved with old bones, rags, bits of rope and the like, and not with the gold of good intentions: 'It is we who have created heaven, and to make it convincing we have mutilated the earth [...] In this heaven we have imprisoned our spirit of revolt. We shall liberate our image of heaven' – so sing the 'Combatants who set out to conquer heaven', to quote the song title.

As heaven is a construction of the human mind, it reproduces earth: it has a sports arena, a casino (in the form of a white whale) where the stakes are life's good deeds, a celestial zoo where the whale is a skeleton whale. There Olofi, God the Father, has his luxury flat and his four television sets for watching the goings-on on earth: baseball games, boxing matches, peaceful demonstrations brutally broken up by police with their truncheons, and particularly cockfights.

The fight Olofi is watching at the beginning of the film takes place in Anastasio's prison where political prisoners – and amongst them Cristobal, an enthusiast of cockfights like any true Cuban or Haitian – noisily encourage their fighting cocks, until the prison-guard bursts in and confiscates the birds – to the great annoyance of Olofi, who puts a curse on Anastasio. Anastasio kills himself by shooting at his own image in a mirror, at which he has taken fright. According to popular mythology he then ascends to heaven – or rather heaven's antechamber where, with his ex-chauffeur and other departed cronies, he plots a *coup d'état* against Olofi.

The *coup* takes the form of an impressive 'bullfight' in the heavenly arena, with Anastasio as the bull-dictator and Olofi's administrator the Angel Gabriel as the banderillero. He is attired in a white suit and bowler hat, with two small wings like Mercury's. There is a pantomime horse, and God-Olofi as the matador gets tossed on the 'bull's' horns during the final pass. Having overturned Olofi and proclaimed himself God in his place, Anastasio seeks to take over the earth as well, and attacks it with floods and fires. Cristobal and his freedom-loving companions rise in defence of the Tecunumans and the Black Virgin, who has taken refuge on earth to escape the attentions of Anastasio. They successfully attack Anastasio in his heaven, only to discover the true nature of 'paradise', of the flight-from-the-real that 'heaven' really is, which leads only to acceptance and submission.

Cristobal refuses the Virgin's invitation to remain on in heaven, complete with halo. As a sailor he has no interest in the heavens unless he can study them from beneath, so he returns to earth, taking with him Atelewa, the 'black Jesus' whom his mother, the Virgin, is plotting, in truly earthly fashion, to put on the throne. Like Cristobal, Atelewa dreams of the earth where 'all is true and, at the same time, not true'. A vale of tears it may well be, but, as Cristobal tells him, on earth there are beautiful and wondrous things: frogs that can sing, fighting cocks that are bigger than a halo and can fight three fights a day. 'Mother will scold me', Atelewa says hesitantly, but Cristobal reassures him: 'She has so much to occupy her time: "doing the statue", teaching morals and that sort of thing.'

This vast cinematographic poem contains a wealth of visual imagery from Caribbean folklore and also from Christian mythology and literature. Some images are in counterpart, as when Cristobal speaks to the Madonna of the Seven Sorrows, the familiar household icon of the Black Virgin come to life, down whose cheeks tears freely stream, then her death scene in which he gently closes her eyes as tears well up in his own and a soloist sings: 'She is dead, the Lady of the Camellias', while the chorus concludes: 'Poor, poor mariner, the Earth is round all over, and seeking a home-port you find only a port-of-call.' The action is frequently interrupted by sung poems which Gatti himself translated freely into Spanish. These were put to music by Eriberto Valdés using Afro-Cuban melodies. Some, however, such as 'The song of the rich child who has lost his childhood', are parodies of Hollywood hit songs. The full text of the scenario was written in French and then put into Spanish. This gave the actors a certain latitude and allowed them to speak from the heart, in their own words, while following the general line of the argument.

The positioning of the camera is often striking. In the 'bullfight' it was concealed beneath Olofi's cloak as he manoeuvred in front of the 'bull'. Frames are thrown across each other at angles or inserted into larger frames. Gatti does not admit of an art which is revolutionary in intent without being revolutionary in form. Bourgeois aesthetic norms have to be abandoned, or they end by stifling the revolutionary idea. With this film Gatti aimed at developing an aesthetics in keeping with his theme and as a source of inventiveness and poetry.

The film seeks to interpret a certain moment in the revolutionary experience of the Cuban people; however, in its approach to the subject it ran counter to the realism of the films – mainly high-quality documentaries – then being made on the Revolution, and so did not seem to have any part in the Revolution itself. Even the symbolism of the hurdy-gurdy as the 'Ambassador' of the idea of Revolution was not fully appreciated. The film met with a hostile reception in Cuban cinemas and was quickly withdrawn. At the Cannes Film Festival the press was divided. The Right was hostile, the Left was favourable – both for equally wrong reasons, as Gatti put it.

The press was not concerned with the quality of the film. It was for or against Cuba. Some journalists even insulted Gatti personally, as they had after the performance of *Le Crapaud buffle*, and they barely commented on the film itself. In June 1965 (in *Positif*, No. 70), however, Michèle Firk, a product of the Institut des Hautes Études Cinématographiques, wrote, in her account of the development of the Cuban cinema after the Revolution of 1959, that alongside the disastrous co-productions undertaken with East German, Czechoslovakian and Russian producers, the single success (disputed, however, within the Cuban Cinema Institute itself) was the 'magnificent *El otro Cristobal* of Armand Gatti'.

Courageous but disconcerting, enthusiastic but perplexing, the film is nevertheless an aesthetic achievement which has its place in the history of the Cuban cinema.

Notre Tranchée de chaque jour

Gatti followed up the film with a play, *Notre Tranchée de chaque jour*. It is the fruit of his experience in Cuba in the aftermath of the invasion of the Playa Girón in the Bay of Pigs in April 1961 and during the missile crisis of autumn 1962, when he was making his film. The play has not yet been staged. Even the directors of the Centres Dramatiques failed to take it up. Cuba was then seemingly too remote a subject to attract an audience. Public readings of the play were, however, given by Gatti in 1964 in Paris and at the Maison de la Culture in Caen. Following the success of *Auguste Geai* in 1962 at the Théâtre de la Cité in Villeurbanne plans had, however, been made for it to be staged there by Jacques Rosner, who had directed *Auguste Geai*, and in 1963 Rosner actually went to Cuba to get to know the country, its history and its people, all of which figure in the play. He returned to Villeurbanne with the manuscript only to learn that difficulties had arisen between Planchon and Gatti, and that Gatti had withdrawn the performing rights by telegram to the principal actor, Jean Bouise, but not to Rosner, who had Gatti's confidence. Gatti next saw Rosner in 1985 in Toulouse, where he had succeeded Maurice Sarrazin to the management of the Grenier Theatre. Rosner, it seems, is still tempted by this gripping drama and could well stage it there in the not too distant future.

The text of the play has not been published, and the following analysis is from a typed-copy lent to me by the author. The action covers the first two years of Castro's regime up to and including the Bay of Pigs incident. The historical spectrum, however, is much wider and takes in the Cuban people's struggle against the tyrannical rule of Fulgenio Batista from 26 July 1953, when Castro and his 160 men failed to capture the Moncada barracks at Santiago. The action of the play is centred on two historical events; the abortive attack on the Presidential Palace on 13 March 1957 by the revolutionary Faure Chomon group, no more than ninety strong, and the ill-fated general strike of 9 April 1958 ordered by Fidel Castro, then a guerrilla leader. These events are presented in a massive flashback built around the person of the anarchist Tirso Uriarte, the son of Alfonso Uriarte, an immigrant from Spain and former member of Durutti's anarchist brigade. There is no pretence at historical reconstruction, nor any concern for chronology. Dramatic interest is centred on the repercussions of these historical events on the Cuban people, and in particular on three characters: Silvia Machado, the Communist daughter of a rich bourgeois anti-castrist family; Tirso, her first love, from whom she was separated by their involvement in two different revolutionary groups; and her fiancé Captain Carlos Alberto Baughan, a comrade of Castro and, after 1959, chief of Castro's Security Police.

Historical events are recalled according to the needs of the dramatic action and are presented in flashbacks or by the instant materialization on stage of the characters' thoughts and fears, whether these were experienced in the historical past or arise in the present of the dramatic action. They are often presented in parallel or super-imposed scenes, and at times with a single character acting in them all at once. Events are also recalled during the making of a 'film' in which 'directors from a popular democracy' seek to reconstruct the 1957 attack on the Presidential Palace; also during the preparation of a 'Cuban TV programme' on the uncoordinated April strike of 1958 with its 3,000 dead. By means of the 'film' and the 'TV programme', Gatti makes a criticism in dramatic form of the unreality of the 'realism' of historical reconstructions – his inspiration for this could well have come from the Soviet, Czech and East German directors in Cuba who were busy making films respecting the canons of 'socialist realism'.

Armand Gatti in the Theatre

The posturing and false rhetoric of the 'actor' playing Esteban Delgado, the dictator Batista's Chief of Police in the 'TV sequence', is in telling contrast with Gatti's parallel dramatic action which draws its strength from the repercussions of the historical events on the individual characters. In the 'film', pompously entitled 'La Dictature mourra ce soir', its director seizes upon romantic details 'likely to appeal to the audience', such as the pregnant woman caught up in the storming of the Palace; and he is more concerned to fit into the 'film' a close-up of the newborn babe than to study the important problem of the catastrophic division of opinion amongst the revolutionaries. If the spectators were presented with 'things like that, they would no longer understand the Cuban Revolution', he says. But it was 'things like that' which actually constituted the revolutionary movement. To push them aside is to skirt over fundamental problems in favour of a picture-book presentation of the Revolution.

The first scene of the play is set in a flat in the Calle J – at one time Gatti's own address in Havana. It is the home of the wealthy Machado family. They call on their daughter Silvia to accompany them in their imminent departure for Miami, where a life of 'fewer restrictions' awaits them. She refuses, and in the final scene of the play, a year later, stands, a lone figure, near the funeral parlour in Havana where the coffins of those killed by the mercenaries on the Playa Girón are to be brought. The early scene provides a number of leads on the political and economic situation in Cuba during the first years of Castro's regime. They include the American blockade with the consequent shortage of materials and rationing, the discontent of the peasants in Camaguey who were mistrustful of the new modern houses which replaced their primitive bohios, the important literacy campaign conducted throughout the country by people like Silvia and the threat of invasion by Cuban emigrants in Miami.

Another scene situated in Candelaria del Medio, 'a possible Cuban village in the first years of the Revolution' a hundred kilometres from Havana, raises the matter of the agrarian reform: a young bull is allocated to the village for breeding. 'Fidel even explained on television for three hours how it was to be done', Silvia's grandmother says. The bull is killed in one of the raids by US planes dropping Contras armed with machine guns. This becomes a personal tragedy for the peasant in charge of the bull and the ballade he sings to the dead beast as the carcass is carried away shows how personal his relationship with his charge had been. The scene follows on from one in which the ex-Colonel of Batista's police, Delgado, now an emigrant in Miami, briefs one of the mercenaries for the 1961 attack on the Bay of Pigs.

The scene with the Machado family, whose very name seems to be intended to recall the tyrannical president of the 1920s. also prepares

The Caribbean: Aggression and Resistance

the dramatic action. The family upbraid Silvia for her membership of the Communist Party, for her clandestine activities under the Batista dictatorship – which had resulted in her torture by his police and which they see as a cross *they* have had to bear – and for the intrusion into their flat of Silvia's 'terrorist' friend Tirso, about which they are to be questioned by the revolutionary police. During the interrogation it is learnt that Tirso's unwelcome visit occurred two days after the attack on the Palace and that he was armed and violent. It was with this visit that Tirso's despairing attempt to contact Silvia began, even though he knew he was being trailed by Batista's police. His fruitless search is at the heart of the dramatic action and gives a personal dimension to a drama which might otherwise have been a mere page of history. This personal dimension is heightened by Silvia's enforced renunciation of all contact with Tirso, so as to ensure the safety of the resistance group to which she belongs. She sends him word that she will 'meet him after the victory'. But the meeting is not to be. Tirso is reported to have disappeared the following year, possibly broken down – it is said – by Batista's police.

In the time-scale of the play's action, an enquiry is set up on Tirso's case and is the responsibility of Silvia's fiancé, Captain Baughan. Dramatically, the enquiry binds together the periods 'before' and 'after' – that is before and after Castro's victory of January 1959 – and unravels Tirso's story, in so far as it can be known, to the revolutionaries. At the same time it reveals the inside story of the Revolution because it involves an interrogation of all those who, 'before', had given shelter to Tirso at their own peril and that of their particular resistance group. Tirso had been wounded in the attack on the Palace, as the 'film' which is being made about the attack shows. In the sequences on the attack, scenes of 'real' action in flashback often bestride the 'studio' scenes in a dramatic structure which is as fluid as in a real film using the 'dissolve' technique. An even greater fluidity of structure characterizes the 'TV' sequences on the April strike of 1958.

These sequences add nothing to the Tirso story beyond the fact that Tirso has last been seen talking to Batista's police chief, Delgado, in the street where he, Delgado, was conducting, in person, a raid in the Figuras area. The *theatre* audience, however, learns the final episode of the Tirso story through a 'real' flashback when Ricardo, the 'film actor' playing Delgado, gives place to the 'real' Delgado, who arrives at the rendezvous, 456 Figuras Street, given to him flippantly – or so it seemed – by Tirso. Tirso attempts to shoot him there, but is himself wounded in the attempt. Instead of having his would-be assassin 'finished off', as was his wont, Delgado has him taken prisoner out of curiosity about his identity and his motive for the attempt. Nothing more is heard about Tirso by the revolutionaries, but his disappearance in Delgado's hands makes them fear that he has been made to 'talk'. When Tirso's father and Silvia go to the police station to try to see him, they unwittingly reveal his real identity and at the same time seal his fate as well as their own.

Tirso and Silvia were both tortured but revealed nothing about the anarchist group Action and Sabotage, to which Tirso belonged, nor about the Communists' relationship, if any, with that group. The torture scenes do not figure in the play. Unlike Jean-Paul Sartre, who did not hesitate to put torture into *Morts sans sépulture,* Gatti does not believe that it can be adequately represented on the stage. He uses other means: here a tape recorder records the torture.

Delgado finds torture 'distasteful to witness', so has his victims' reactions put on tape without their knowing. When it suits his whim or purpose, he plays back these tapes. The first occasion is in 1961, when, as ex-Colonel in Miami. he is involved in preparations for the invasion of Cuba and is briefing Father Abreu, a Fascist priest who had emigrated from Spain and then from Cuba, where he denounced Tirso to Batista's police. Delgado plays back part of the Havana tape-recording of the discussion between Tirso, crippled by torture, and his father, who is in chains in the same cell. He hears Tirso's father say that his only remaining joy is the thought of the Fascists who fell before his gun in Spain. Perhaps Uriarte had been among the Republicans who had killed twenty-four members of his family in Spain? The thought made Abreu consider himself a 'crusader'.

On the second occasion a very indifferent Delgado is making love to Silvia's emigrant sister in his office in Miami. By way of distraction he cynically puts on the tape-recording of the appalling sexual torture to which Silvia had been subjected by his police in Havana. At the same time, Father Abreu and the others who had been parachuted into Cuba and captured begin a Way of the Cross in the chapel of the same Havana prison in which Delgado had tortured Silvia. Meanwhile in Candelario del Medio, Silvia herself describes her ordeal to a peasant, Mio Tio, but it is Delgado's tape-recorder that takes over her story with only a few interjections from Silvia.

The tape is thus superimposed on the three parallel scenes. In this scene it reveals that the torture ended with a 'statutory' rape by Sergeant Euterpio, a huge Negro who, Silvia adds, had later been killed by the father of a child he had tortured. It is typical of Gatti that into the story of a past ordeal he introduces the dimension of the present, with the determination to fight on that the present implies. This dimension is supplied by Mio Tio's kindly ironic comment: 'All the same, you are not going to play Sergeant Euterpio's widow all your life'.

There are many other parallel scenes: parallels between the 'film' or 'TV programme' and the 'reality' behind them; parallel interrogations by Batista's police and the Revolutionary Tribunal. They may run side by side, or be interwoven, or even set in different time-scales, as when Delgado's prisoner-henchman, El Tuerco, in a superimposed scene, takes part in the interrogation of Tirso's father by Batista's police in Havana in 1958, and is himself interrogated after the Revolution by Castro's Chief of Police. He implies that Delgado had helped Tirso and his father to escape from Cuba in return for information about the revolutionary cells. Later, when El Tuerco, still in Havana, speaks across space to Delgado in his Miami office, he refers to the Uriartes' true fate, execution and the common grave, about which he had said nothing to the Revolutionary Tribunal as it would have meant the firing squad for him. The film-like structure of the play which ignores the limits of time and space, makes presentation of this kind possible.

The technique of parallelism is not restricted to scenic presentation. It is used thematically as well. Tirso's despairing search for Silvia in all their old haunts is paralleled by that of Baughan, who 'makes Tirso's pilgrimage all over again' as he despairingly works through the police file on Tirso. But just as it was Delgado, not Silvia, whom Tirso had found at the end of his pilgrimage, it is Tirso, not Silvia, whom Baughan finds at the end of his search. In a final dialogue with the materialized image of Tirso, as he bivouacs with the men and women waiting to repulse any attack at the Playa Girón, Baughan comes to understand that his quest for Silvia has, like Tirso's, been more than a personal quest; it has been a 'pre-run' of their quest to maintain the 'integrity of the Revolution'.

Baughan is killed in the attack, and Silvia, waiting at the funeral parlour the return of the bodies from the Cienaga, understands in turn that Tirso too is dead, and that he too has died for the Revolution. The seventh and last name to be read out as the coffins are carried in is Baughan's. 'They died, gun in hand, in the trench we man day and night', the gathered crowd murmurs, bringing the play to a close. Nowadays the hundred and fifty monuments which line the high road behind the Playa Girón bear the names of others who died 'in the trench' there, 'gun in hand'. In 1970, Gozlan and Pays summarized the historical context of the play in these words: 'Today, Cuba, the first people's democracy and the first free territory of America, is no more than a *trench* a few kilometres off the American coast, but a trench manned *each day* by an armed people.' This is as true in the 1980s, when the whole Cuban people is organized in defensive 'block committees' ever on the alert, as it was in the 1960s.

Gatti's experience of Cuba and of the Cuban people, particularly during the missile crisis of autumn 1962 when he was shooting his film *El otro Cristobal*, enabled him to recapture the enthusiasm and determination of the Cuban citizen army as it prepared to resist attack. 'Cubans have never been keen on working every day,' Mio Tio remarks, 'but they have never been backward in facing death' – and they had to face it with unfamiliar weapons in their hands, weapons which the play shows them as even then just learning to handle. To quote Fidel Castro's words at a commemorative celebration which I attended in 1981, just twenty years after the event:

> Our army was beginning to learn how to handle modern weapons [...] When our tanks reached Girón and took up their positions there, face to face with the Yankee warships and aircraft carriers, everybody was very calm and every gun was loaded ready to fire [...] Whereas our people were strong in the days of Girón, today they are a hundred times stronger and better prepared militarily, politically and psychologically.

His concluding words, 'Patria o muerte! Venceremos', form the slogan carried by banners in permanent display on the streets of Havana today.

In his introduction to his play *Chant public devant deux chaises électriques*, written up in Cuba in twelve days during the missile crisis, Gatti describes how every hour of the day the Cubans looked death in the face; how the actors in his film joined their 'trenches' at night and arrived in the morning for the filming so tired that they fell asleep on the ground between shots; and how

> every night there rose up, like a funeral dirge from the heart of Havana, a chant 'Uno – Dos – Tres – Cuatro' by thousands of men and women learning to march together – Atomic death could come – They seemed to have more than guns or cannons to set against it. They had this 'Uno – Dos – Tres – Cuatro', derisory and magnificent at the same time.

This 'Uno – Dos – Tres – Cuatro', which so moved Gatti, finds its way into the last scenes of *Notre Tranchée*.

While refusing to attempt any historical reconstruction, Gatti takes care to implant his dramatic action in Cuban territory and in the life of the Cuban people. He had got to know the country and its people during the preparation of the scenario of his film, so it was quite natural for him to make one of the peasant characters say that if the mercenaries were to land on the Playa Girón they would have to cross the Cienaga and would be bitten by the ferocious marsh mosquitoes there. The pub bar Sloppy Joe's in Havana – part of the 'Ernest Hemingway saga', as tourist guides have it – features in several scenes, and the staging of the attack on the Presidential Palace involves reference to the Palace of Fine Arts, the Tabaccalera and the old graceful Spanish hotel, the Sevilla. Gatti even does a little propaganda for the 'beautiful beach of Varadero' by having a 'commercial' proposing holidays there intercalated in the 'film' by its 'director'. Nor does he forget the annual July carnival at Santiago. It serves as a background for two scenes showing Baughan's distress at the idea of losing Silvia to the 'ghost' of Tirso.

The Caribbean: Aggression and Resistance

There are forty-six short scenes, grouped into what may be considered as five acts. These are prefaced by a few lines of a 'pulverized poem' which, when reconstituted, tells the story of a successful Revolution. There are, however, no stage directions in the typed copy as to who is to speak these lines. A number of songs also feature in the text and provide a commentary on the action. The final song, 'Le Chant des hommes et de la palmeraie', intoned by the Candelarians at the news of the failure of the landing on the Playa Girón, comes back on the story of the Revolution, but in terms of human feelings and effort, not in terms of gunfire power, as in the 'pulverized poem'.

For the forty-six scenes, the basic dramatic technique, Gatti insists, is that of *enchaînement* or the running together of scenes in a continuous, filmic sequence. In such a structure, simplified rapidly changing sets are a prerequisite. Gatti has various solutions. For example, Silvia in Candelario del Medio is telephoning Baughan in Havana. Although she does not move from the spot, she is 'transported' to a clandestine meeting-house in Havana by a screen which slides into place behind her. Next, she is 'transported' to the veranda of her home by another screen which slides into place alongside the first, revealing the 'film director' Ricardo, seated typically in a rocking chair as he questions her about her alleged 'conversion' of the anarchist Tirso to the Communist theory of the necessity of mass support for successful revolutionary action. There are several examples of two straightforward simultaneous sets with the action proceeding in both at the same time, and other examples of superimposed scenes with but the barest indication of the respective *loci*. As with the tape-recordings, these indications may even be purely verbal.

Gatti's approach to the theatre is very visual, and this makes his plays more effective on the stage than in the book, although in the book the stage directions are of considerable help. One such direction concerning the staging, in a flashback, of Tirso in hiding, as recounted by a militant to Silvia's grandmother, defines the technical device used several times by Gatti in this play and in some others as well in order to differentiate between various time-scales:

> All the characters in the play who belong to the past and who come to take part in the action – in this case it is Tirso – are to wear costumes of faded, washed-out colours, in contrast with the normal colouring of costumes worn by characters belonging to the present

(in this case the militant and the grandmother). When characters reappear on the stage in an action in the present, they revert to clothes of normal colour. In Silvia's case the colour of her clothes depends on whether she is figuring in an action in the past, or actively engaged in the present.

A revolutionary technique presenting revolutionary themes, which is the guiding principle of Gatti's dramatic composition, is amply illustrated by this play set in Cuba in the revolutionary years and in the three others set in Central American history. They are the outcome of the personal experience of yesterday of Gatti the 'historiographer' of the region, but they are as topical today as they were at the time when they were written. It might even be said that they are closer to the audience of today than to the audience of yesterday because of the way in which events in Central America and the Caribbean continue to hit the headlines and because, to quote Castro again, after President Reagan's expressed concern to 'contain Communism',

> New aggressive policies against Cuba are being formulated, because the imperialists are talking about a blockade again – and no longer just about economic blockades, but rather about naval, military blockades [...] Hence the similarity between this April 16 (1981) and that April 16 (1961).

Given the continued tenseness of the situation between the two countries, it is interesting to read the short 'History of Cuba' in Paula Diperna's *Complete Travel Guide to Cuba*, published in 1979 in New York by St Martin's Press. The historical survey stops at the missile crisis and so covers the same ground as Gatti's play, which was at least outlined during his stay there. After discussing Batista and his 'brutal regime', Paula Diperna writes:

> What is rarely realized in the United States about the Cuban Revolution is that Fidel Castro did not just drop from the sky with talk of rebellion. He merely culminates [...] a long series of insurrections, protests, and disorders.

She goes on to mention the Cuban exile community's continued attempts to overthrow Castro and the consequent need for the Revolutionary Government to punish the members of Batista's army – as occurs in Gatti's play. She mentions the US total embargo on trade with Cuba announced a week after the Bay of Pigs incident; also the US ban on American travel to Cuba; and she concludes: 'for most US citizens the curtain fell on the Revolution [...] for the most part, Cuba ceased to exist for the average American.' But her last statement is as follows: 'To sift the reality from seventeen years of mystery and mythology is part of the reason to travel to Cuba today.'

6
Rebuttal, as the Good Fight

I La Vie imaginaire de l'éboueur Auguste Geai.
Chant public devant deux chaises électriques
II La Cigogne

I La Vie imaginaire de l'éboueur Auguste Geai

Of the oppression to which the inmates of the concentration camps, himself included, were subjected, Gatti had had a foretaste in his early years as an inmate of an immigrants' shanty town. This oppression remains one of the main themes of the dramatic biography *La Vie imaginaire de l'éboueur Auguste Geai*, which tells of the life of a trade unionist who, like Gatti's own father, was a dustman employed by a private dustbin-collection company, SATOM, the *Société d'assainissement et de transport des ordures ménagères* in Monaco.

Gatti began work on *Auguste Geai* immediately after finishing *Le Quetzal*, which he describes as a re-evaluation of his own culture, a Western culture of which he discovered the relativity only when in contact with the culture of the Indians in Guatemala. The problem was to find a character capable of embodying this reassessment. The character turned out to be Auguste, his own father, who died of hemiplegia during a strike in 1938 after receiving a blow on the head from a riot policeman. Gatti always maintained that in this case *post hoc* means *propter hoc*, and at his father's funeral he vowed that what his father had not lived to say, his son would say for him. This he does in the play *Auguste G.*, G for Gatti, printed 'Geai' for conformity's sake.

Then came the interruption of the years in the maquis and concentration camps. The problems arising in these and subsequent years also find their expression in this play. As regards its form, the juxtaposition of different temporalities was directly inspired by a clandestine performance given in a concentration camp by a group of Lithuanian and Polish Jews. It consisted of a sort of murmured prayer, punctuated at times by the words *Ich bin*. The other prisoners listened in deep silence, but in the discussion which followed the politically minded suggested that the words *Ich bin, Ich war, Ich werde sein*, would express the meaning more clearly. The actors refused to make the change, but Gatti's simultaneous presentation of Auguste in the present, in the past and in the future is directly inspired by this experience, and he acknowledges it.

In his delirium, caused by a blow on the head from a riot policeman's rifle-butt during a demonstration, the dramatic character, Auguste, relives in imagination his life of misfortune and hope. Throughout the play he lies in a hospital bed on stage. Mortally wounded in middle life, he not only relives his past life but re-creates it, and furthermore creates a future he is never to have – whence the title 'La Vie *imaginaire* d'Auguste Geaï'.

In spite of its pathos, the play shows a distinct change of emphasis from that of the concentration-camp plays, in which the characters are victims. Here the main theme is that of working-class contestation, which remains the theme of many of Gatti's subsequent plays. *Auguste Geaï* ends with the significant comment of Perd-Nous the police inspector: 'So also died for the Revolution, in his forty-sixth year, the dustman Auguste Geaï.' With these words the inspector expresses the meaning that Auguste seeks to read into his existence: not to 'die like a dog in bed', but heroically, at the barricades. He had been shot and wounded by riot police in a strike 'at the barricades' at the age of thirty. At the time, it had been rumoured that he had wanted to die because his wife was thought to have a lover. Until his dying day he never knew the truth, but that he was shot in a strike at thirty, and was killed by the riot police at forty-six – this is not imagination. Whatever dreams and suspicions cloud his mind, these are facts which are certain, as is his readiness to die for the Revolution.

As the images pass without any coherent order through his fevered brain, they assume a concrete existence on the stage: the fire that destroyed the shanty town where Auguste lived and which was inhabited by Poles, Italians, Arabs and Savoyards; the kindly grandfather and friendly neighbour, Angelina, who took the place of parents for the little boy orphaned at the age of nine; the construction of barricades for the Revolution of the future; Auguste as a soldier of twenty-one in the First World War in the trenches with his friend, Roger; a messianic tramp, called the 'Black Baron', who terrorizes Auguste as a child; a suave but dictatorial boss, the 'White Baron', who tyrannizes the workers; Pauline, Auguste's young love who wins a dance marathon and leaves the shanty town for finer things, but perishes in a fire at the elegant house with gilded columns – is it a military hospital, or is it a brothel? It is all confused in Auguste's mind, but Gatti makes the social significance clear. Laurence, Pauline's friend, marries Auguste at the age of thirty but dies within the year. Auguste, aged forty-six remembers her funeral, the baby crying alone at home in a basket, the fellow-worker who could have been her lover. In his imagination these people, dead or still alive, come to a final rendezvous with him. He sees them as competing for ten 'gold' francs, to be awarded to the longest-staying couple in the dance marathon organized by the Trafalgar Rat-Poison Company.

In Gatti's play the marathon remains a 'contest'. It never becomes the abominable 'show' that it is in Sydney Pollack's film of 1969, *They Shoot Horses, Don't They?*, based on Horace MacCoy's novel of 1935. In the film, backers and paying spectators loudly urge the poverty-stricken dancers on to dance to their death in a sort of new circus act. This was during the slump years of the 1930s. Many of the same elements are, however, present in both film and play: the numbers on the contestants' backs, the few seconds for resting, the presence of a nurse, collapsed bodies being removed by the forces of law and order. In Gatti's play the marathon is not just a marathon, it is the transposed image of the 'order' of a bourgeois society in which the dice are loaded in favour of the ruling class. It is danced to a tune played by the police band at the command of police whistles, overlaid at times by a peremptory order from the boss to 'get back to work immediately', an order which brings the flagging 'dancers' back on to their feet.

At the same time, in a future which will never be, Auguste sees himself in a nice little cottage, celebrating his retirement with a cake and a bottle of champagne, in the company of his son, Christian, a grown man, even though at the time of his father's death Christian is no more than a boy of fifteen. He also sees him as a director making a film about the Revolution to come. The Revolution is the justification of Auguste's life, the life of an illiterate dustman, which is of 'no less consequence than that of a General or a Cabinet minister'.

The sequence concerning the production of Christian's 'film' are less poetic and more satirical than those of the dance marathon. He who pays the piper calls the tune, and in this case it is the 'White Baron', the director of SATOM, who is prepared to finance a film by Christian, provided it remains within the ideological limits set by him. He favours a vaguely Left cultural policy because this is a useful 'safety valve', likely to take the steam out of any real revolutionary movement. However, Christian makes a film with Revolution as its theme, since such was his father's dream. During a private showing of the film to the 'White Baron', Christian shoots him – at the same moment as the 'Black Baron' is shot on the screen by an unknown hand. In dramatic terms, Auguste can meet a heroic death, in imagination at least.

Such is the drama which, apart from certain 'real' scenes, is played out in Auguste's delirious mind. The mental action takes place in dream settings of which the central point is nevertheless the hospital bed where Auguste really is, because Auguste's comments cut into, or across, the action of every dream sequence. The sequences refer to real incidents which occurred in Auguste's life at different ages: nine, twenty-one, thirty and forty-six. Further sequences centred on Auguste at the age of sixty, an age which he never reaches, are purely imaginary. Five actors are needed to play the single role of Auguste, each set against a determining social and political background but giving a complete all-round picture of Auguste when taken together.

Only Auguste dying at the age of forty-six is a *real* character. The other Augustes are figments of the dying Auguste's imagination and so can be present simultaneously on stage. They present him as he sees himself in the circumstances he is reliving and also re-creating in his mind. It is for this reason that the only *real* settings are the police station, into which the strikers who have been arrested are unceremoniously bundled at the beginning of the play, and the hospital ward where, at certain moments in the action, Auguste is seen in the care of a *real* nurse (who reappears in the dream sequences) and where the *real* police inspector (who also reappears in the dream sequences) comes to enquire whether he is likely to survive. Here, just before the final curtain, Auguste dies, and the inspector orders the attendant *real* policemen to dump his body 'discreetly' in one of the shanty-town streets, so as to make it appear that Auguste has been killed in a common street brawl. But when the curtain comes down, it is on the same inspector's statement that Auguste has died for the Revolution.

Auguste Geai, the second of Gatti's plays to reach the stage, was put on at the Théâtre de la Cité at Villeurbanne on 16 February 1962 by Roger Planchon's assistant director, Jacques Rosner. It was his first production undertaken alone. René Allio was the stage designer. The list of characters and actors in this performance is reproduced on the first page of the original 'literary' text, in Volume 3 of Gatti's *Théâtre*, published shortly *after* the production. The version performed at Villeurbanne appears in *Avant-Scène*, No. 272, September 1962, together with photographs of the production. These show that the stage directions given by Gatti in the original text were completely discarded by Rosner in favour of more dynamic staging. Nor are the two printed texts identical. Changes were made in the interest of the scenic presentation.

Gatti raised no objection to these changes. The only 'dictatorship' he admits to accepting is that of the producer, who must be allowed to develop his particular view of the play he is dealing with. Further changes in both text and production were made before the company took the play to the Théâtre de France in Paris in 1964 (2 May). This text is unpublished, but an actor's typescript of this third version was given to the present author by the principal actor, Jean Bouise, who took the part of Auguste aged forty-six; it was used for a production in the Arts Theatre of Liverpool University in 1966 by the French Department, with the present writer as director. It contains indications concerning the Paris production, made by the actor himself. Changes were also made in the cast although, as was to be expected, the role of Auguste aged forty-six was retained by Bouise because of his success in the part in Villeurbanne.

Rosner also directed a production of the play for the West Berlin Festival of 1963 (2 October) at the Schaubühne am Halleschen Ufer, with Hubert Monloup as stage designer. It was not the success it had been at Villeurbanne partly because, as Rosner says, is is the 'most French' of Gatti's plays, and partly because the German translation did not do justice to the poet that Gatti undoubtedly is. At Villeurbanne, in addition to its appeal as a dramatic work, *Auguste Geai* was seen as highly topical, opening as it did only three days after the disastrous police intervention in Paris at the Métro Charonne. Rosner also tells of his meeting in Berlin with Piscator, who was then working at the Freievolksbühne and had attended the performance. Piscator mistook him for Gatti and, clasping him in his arms, called him 'my son', adding: 'This is the sort of thing I was doing thirty years ago'.

When Planchon accepted *Auguste Geai* for the Théâtre de la Cité, Gatti's involvement in play-production was limited to Vilar's production of *Le Crapaud buffle*. He had, however, reflected at length on the problem of scenic presentation and in his preface to the volume containing *Auguste Geai* states his conviction that the traditional single stage cannot adequately represent a world at several points of time and space. His stage directions which head the original text indicate multiple staging, albeit within the space of a single stage, with each of the 'secondary' spaces differently coloured to represent different periods in Auguste's life – past, present and future – all on stage simultaneously. Movement in both horizontal and vertical directions is ensured by means of a connecting space used in the main by the 'White Baron' and other forces of law and order, and by a stairway leading down to a space for general use. Rosner did not like the idea of the five spaces for Auguste at different ages and so, rather than go through the text with Gatti, asked Gatti, whom he describes as a marvellous story-teller, to recount the play to him. What he staged, he says, was the story as told by Gatti and not the text, with its diagrammatic presentation of the five periods of Auguste's life. It was from Auguste on his deathbed that he (Rosner) started, since that is where the rest of the dramatic action originates.

Rosner's intention was to develop the spectacular and dynamic elements of the play, – the dance marathon, the cinema, the 'Revolution' – utilizing the whole of the scenic space but without precluding the possibility of creating several 'places' simultaneously with sketchy symbolic sets. Instead of the seven spaces indicated by Gatti, Rosner decided on two, with the floor level of both raised to draw attention to the scenes played on them; one ran the width of the stage at the back, the other was a small sloping platform set on one side of the stage and used for most of the main scenes. A very perceptive definition of the performance was given by Jacques Lacarriète when he said that it was 'a kind of uninterrupted symphony in which the episodes and characters intervened from time to time like soloists, without ever destroying the continuity of the whole.' [1] Gatti himself described his play as 'the superimposition of different time-scales on the life of a single individual, each developing along its own particular line within a single framework'.[2]

With regard to the stage decoration at the Théâtre de la Cité, the original idea of the set as designed by Allio was that of a monstrous collection of industrial rubbish such as *bidonvilles* are built of. He discusses this in an article, 'Théâtre, sculpture et déchets', published in the programme at Villeurbanne. At the back of the stage were waste products – tin cans, petrol cans, rags, timber – together with an uneven trelliswork 'ceiling' made of blackened planks nailed together anyhow. This formed a permanent set, designed to keep the background of the action – the depressing shanty town – present in the spectator's mind. As required by the action, various symbolic sets were also lowered from the flies, but never actually came to rest on the stage. Floating, as it were, in midair, they created a dream atmosphere: in one case, the office of the director of SATOM, it was a nightmare atmosphere, because the factory barrier lowered part-way down from the flies was a replica of the 'bars' of the ceiling, implying that there is no escape from the working-class cage. For the brothel, gilded columns and a large scarlet mouth were red-light-district symbols.

All this was set in an inner frame formed by five gigantic photographs of the five Augustes. Rosner told his actors to 'fight the text' and act in a realistic, not lyrical style, as this was the best way to bring out the poetic quality of the work. The accompanying music, written by Claude Lochy, underlined the thematic structure: according to the dictates of Auguste's memory it was elusive, forceful, distorted. The nostalgic waltz tune danced by Pauline and Laurence in the dance marathon turned into a slow march for Laurence's death. The first seven notes of the Marseillaise heralded each entry of the peremptory 'White Baron', but degenerated immediately into a discord. The 'Chant du Refus' which declares the workers' rejection of the conditions imposed on them was a martial air, and, as they sang the striking dustmen waved huge flags, each of a different colour. Music and flags fill the consciousness of the dying Auguste, an apotheosis which supplies the counterpart of the harsh 'Chant des CRS', the riot police, with which the dance marathon opens earlier in the play: 'Les crosses sont faites pour taper' ('Riflebutts are made to bash with') Although the time of the action is 1938–9, Gatti changes the Gardes Mobiles of the time into CRS (Compagnies

Républicaines de Sécurité, created in 1945) in order to underline the continued topicality of his theme. Nearly twenty years later Gatti almost suffered the same fate as his father when reporting on a strike at Saint-Nazaire for *L'Express*. The issue of 31 October 1957 carried a photograph of him with a bandaged head, which had suffered four blows from CRS rifle-butts. A dispassionate account of the 'butchery' and a formal accusation of the police 'desire to kill' is given in his account, *L'Envie de tuer*.

The reaction of public and press to a complex work of this kind must obviously depend to a large extent on the sympathies of the spectator. Those critics who were not in sympathy with Gatti's subject gave the play a rough handling, particularly in Paris, where the yardstick was the aesthetics of the 'Absurdist' *avant-garde*, or else the after-dinner 'digestive' play. For the 'Absurdists', as for the 'Boulevard', politics were unaesthetic, and a complex form such as Gatti had chosen to adopt was 'incomprehensible'. Perhaps the best summary of the arguments used for and against the play came from two spectators themselves during one of the debates in the theatre at Villeurbanne after a performance. One objected: 'What with the action going on all over the place, and five Auguste Geais on the stage at once, how can a worker be expected to understand?' The answer to this came in the local accent: 'We understand probably better than that gentleman over there'. Sympathy was the key.

Gatti himself tells of the reaction of two hundred dustmen who had been invited to the Paris production. They left the theatre in silence after the performance. A week later they asked to discuss the play with him, and by way of thanks for the invitation through which Gatti had offered them a piece of his work, they offered him a piece of theirs, a miniature set of dustmen's equipment. Of the two hundred, only two had been to a theatre before, and these two only twice. In reply to Gatti's question on their attitude to his free use of the time sequence they said, after discussing with each other, 'Some of us have TV sets. In the News they show us things that happened yesterday and things that happened today in Paris, in Moscow, in London. Your use of time is the same, isn't it?' 'That's exactly it', Gatti replied.[3]

The rich stage imagery in Gatti's play was matched by the imaginative work of Jacques Rosner, whose success was admitted even by critics hostile to the play. For Gatti, stage imagery is a dramatic technique by which social confrontations may be given concrete expression.

The protest against the conditions of the lower-paid worker is dramatic material, and *Auguste Geai* is one of the best analyses of these conflicts to reach the stage to date, perhaps because it has as its basis Gatti's personal experience. For most Paris audiences, however, such subjects are taboo, and any presentation of militant trade unionism is 'inartistic' and certainly not 'entertainment'.

Armand Gatti in the Theatre

Gilles Sandier, dramatic critic for *Arts* (14 May 1964), preferred to ignore the issues raised by Gatti and judge the text from the point of view of style – whose merit he considered nonexistent: it was a pity, he thought, that such fine staging should have been wasted on a work which was 'so little worthwhile' and doomed soon to be committed to oblivion. For his part, Gabriel Marcel, the extreme right-wing critic of *Les Nouvelles Littéraires* (14 May 1964), had the grotesque idea of beginning his report on the performance with a lament concerning the attraction of dustbins and their contents for certain *avant-garde* dramatists, and he named Samuel Beckett alongside Gatti! But Gatti's character has nothing in common with those of Beckett: he is a workman, and he happens to be a dustman – like Gatti's own father; he could just as well have been a miner or a bricklayer.

The deliberate injustice of Marcel's remarks, as well as their silliness, can be measured by the irrelevance of his observations on a dustman's pay in Scandinavia and the USSR. When it comes to his final statement about the 'utter boredom' he felt at the performance, and the 'very loud and long applause' of the public, one fails to see how he managed to reconcile the two phenomena. As for the insinuation that this applause could have come only from a 'tiny minority' of the spectators, the present writer can affirm that this 'tiny minority' literally fought for returned tickets at the box-office, night after night, throughout the whole run of the play in Paris.

The privations and humiliations that are the worker's lot to the bitter end constitute one of the play's dominant themes. Through the mouths of his characters Gatti describes the sordid conditions in lower-working-class areas – the squalor, the drunkenness, the fatal brawls – and contrasts them with the luxurious life of the bourgeoisie with its 'fur lined boots and fine silk stockings, its baths, its eau de Cologne, its hairstyles'. He also points to insidious attempts by the bourgeoisie to seduce intelligent young men of working-class origin. 'Are not we two made to understand each other?' the 'White Baron' asks Christian during the making of the 'film'. 'Is not the world one and indivisible?' One can read into Christian's rejection of the 'Baron's' temptation the projection into purely imaginary circumstances of Auguste's firm consciousness of the class to which he belongs. His son cannot possibly sympathize with the class enemy. But Auguste is just as keenly conscious of the divisions within his own class, and the evils which ensue.

Another theme is that of the exploitation of man by man. It is given full voice in the 'Chant du Refus', in which the workers sing their refusal to submit to further humiliation, their refusal to allow 'their hands to be sold any longer'. It is an interesting fact that in the Paris performances, the parts of the revolutionaries were taken by seven men and seven women from the Renault car factory. The counter-theme – that man's activity is a commodity to be bought and sold – is stated during the dance marathon with the arrival of the pimp, Monsieur Jackie, to 'recruit star dancers for the King of Madagascar'. Then there is the moral asphyxia brought about by long hours of routine work, making men incapable of anything other than 'continuing through habit'.

Against this is set the means of escape: commitment and revolt. Bobelin, the trade-union leader, firmly rejects lame excuses, family responsibilities, pleas that life is already difficult enough. Nine out of ten insurrections may fail, says the militant night watchman of SATOM at 'the barricades', but the tenth will succeed. Christian succeeds: he turns on his bourgeois backer and kills him. This action is not a 'real' action in the play; it occurs in a dying man's delirium, but it is the expression of a sympathy, a revolutionary attitude, directed towards the creation of a juster society. In a lyrical passage referring to the dustmen's carts which are locked up in the depot awaiting the hour to go out on to the streets, Bobelin declares: 'Ce sont les balayeurs qui font naître le jour', ('It is the street-sweepers who bring the dawn'). This dawn is also the Revolution. Such is the sense of Gatti's play.

At Villeurbanne it was understood. It is Gatti himself, Jean-Jacques Lerrant wrote after seeing the performance at Villeurbanne,[4] 'who with this play [...] because of its theme and because of its rich and varied form [...], by sweeping away old habits and comfortable positions, makes the day dawn'. Lerrant's judgement was much more perspicacious than that of Gilles Sandier, who wrote two years later that in the light of critical reaction in Paris, *Auguste Geai* could only 'serve as a rod to beat [...] the popular theatre movement, and this was a pity'.

Gatti was to belie the prediction. The popular theatre movement was to continue to flourish throughout the 1960s; on its playbills could be read the names of Roger Planchon, dramatist as well as director, Arthur Adamov, Michel Vinaver, Gabriel Cousin, and even a veteran of the Paris stage, Armand Salacrou, who joined in the movement with *Boulevard Durand* which dates from 1961 and was performed throughout France. It has as its hero a militant docker called Jules Durand who was sentenced to death in 1911 as the result of a scarcely disguised political frame-up in Le Havre, where a street is now called after him. Gatti's name was to be added to these authors'. His plays were soon to be seen in all the popular Centres Dramatiques, at least until the students' revolt of May 1968 made their directors play for safety and their subsidies by putting on innocuous productions. After 1968 Gatti's name disappeared from these Centres' playbills and Gatti himself left France.

Armand Gatti in the Theatre

Chant public devant deux chaises électriques

When the Sacco and Vanzetti affair began Gatti's father was in Chicago, an immigrant worker from Italy, just like the two anarchists. When they were executed he was back in France and his son was three years old. Gatti's memories, as he says, are of the mourning for Sacco and Vanzetti by the workers of the shanty town who were also immigrant workers. That day his father tied a black scarf round his little son's neck. Thirty-five years later in Havana, during the missile crisis. the blockading American fleet, equipped with atomic weapons, clearly visible from his flat near the waterfront, produced in Gatti a 'state of grace' in which he wrote up the play on Sacco and Vanzetti that he had long been turning over in his mind.

This version, *Chant nuptial d'une horloge*, was triggered off by Rogelio Paris, who was helping him to shoot the film *El otro Cristobal*. One night as they stood together waiting in the rain, Paris quoted the Rosenbergs' reply in 1953 to the last minute offer of a reprieve, should they admit to guilt: 'To let us live they want to take away from us the very reason for living. We cannot accept.' It was an echo of similar words by Sacco and Vanzetti, and in turn echoed the nightly marching through the streets of Havana, during the missile crisis, of the Cuban citizen army ready to die with dignity rather than live without it.

The marching feet called to Gatti's imagination Sacco and Vanzetti's pacing of the death row in Charleston prison, and the Rosenbergs' in Sing-Sing, and it reawoke the distressing memory of his own pacing of the death cell in a French prison. For him the parallel was clear between the presence of the American warships round Cuba, and the capitalist regime which persecuted the syndicalists Sacco and Vanzetti. The 'trajectory' of his play, as he told Mireille Boris of *L'Humanité* (16 April 1962), starts in Chicago in 1886 and goes as far as Cuba in the 1960s, even though the events in Cuba do not figure in the text and the play's action turns on Sacco and Vanzetti.

Among the volunteer defenders of Havana who paced the streets and waterfront at night were a number of technicians and others working on Gatti's film. It was on them, and later on French members of the group, that Gatti tried out the first drafts of his play. He noted how each tended to identify himself with one or other of the characters in the real-life drama, according to his personal beliefs or circumstances. Their reactions taken as a whole reconstituted the affair in its entirety. The line Gatti was to adopt in the play was determined in this way. The characters would belong to the present time and be ordinary run-of-the-mill folk. They would assume the drama themselves, and bring it to life as they viewed it through the prism of their own preoccupations.

Such a conception was incompatible with any attempt at a historical

Gatti preparing *La Cage aux fauves* (1954). Photo *Le Parisien Libéré*

Le Crapaud buffle, TNP (Jean Vilar, 1959). Execution of Atahualpa by Pizarre/Tiburcio. Photo Bernand

La Naissance, Villejuif Théâtre Romain-Rolland (1968). Production Roland Monod, décor Hubert Monloup. Photo Bernand

La Naissance (*Die Geburt*), Kassel, Staatstheater (1969). Directed by Gatti, décor Hubert Monloup. Photo Kaspar Seiffert

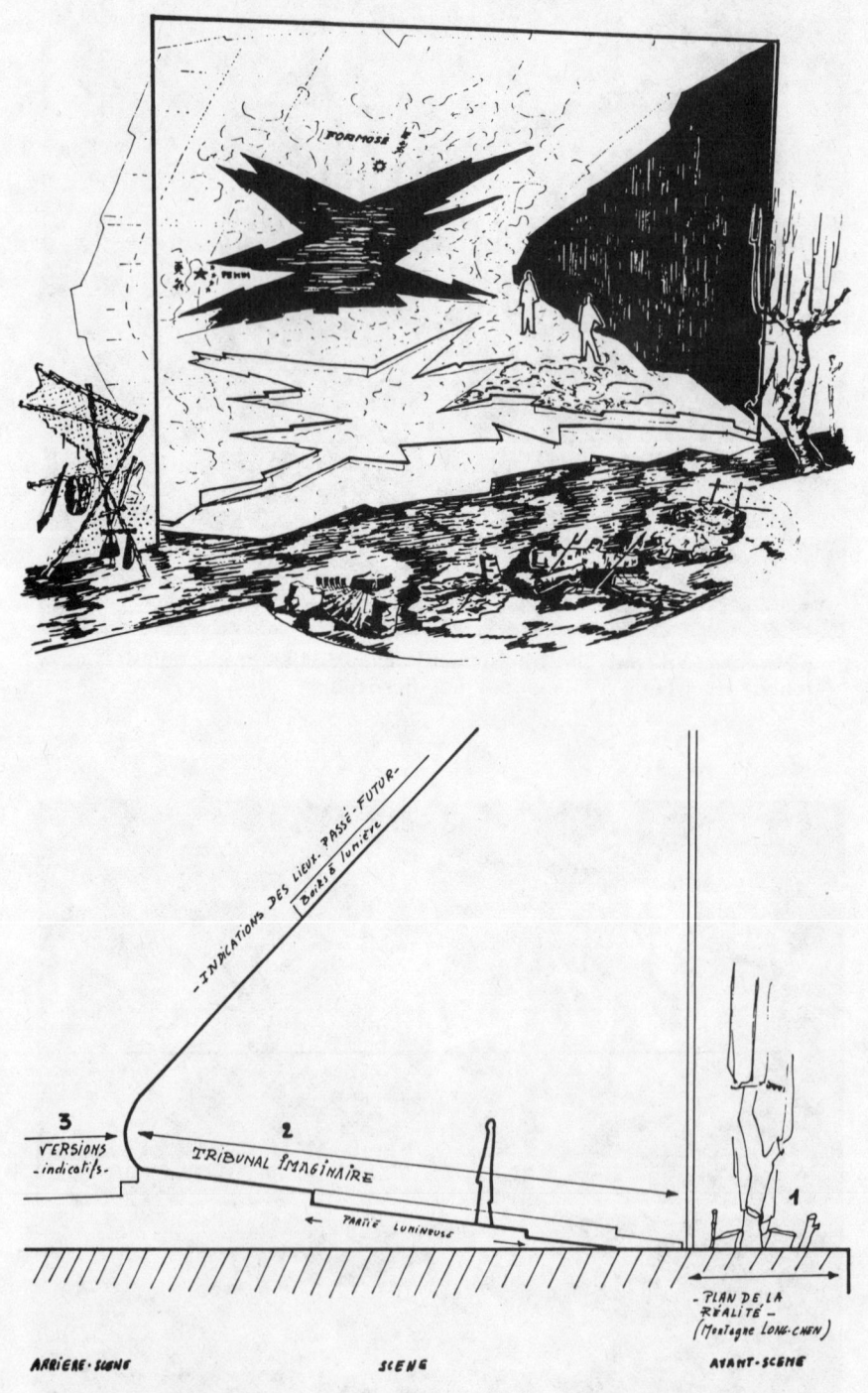

Un Homme seul, Comédie de Saint-Étienne (1966). Directed by Gatti, décor Hubert Monloup.

Un Homme seul, Comédie de Saint-Étienne (1966). Directed by Gatti, décor Hubert Monloup. Photo Chaussat

Chroniques d'une planète provisoire, Grenier de Toulouse (1967). Directed by Gatti, décor Hubert Monloup with the astronauts' space-cabin projecting into the auditorium. Photo Chaussat

Chroniques d'une planète provisoire, Grenier de Toulouse (1967), The new Nazi 'religion'. Photo Chaussat

Chroniques d'une planète provisoire, Grenier de Toulouse (1967). Shertoc in the concentration camp with the memory of Pepi (Parachronique). Photo Chaussat.

L'Enclos (film 1960). Mauthausen Concentration Camp, 'prisoners' working. Photo Chaussat

L'Enclos (1960) the Concentration Camp orchestra playing a Resistance song. Photo Chaussat

El otro Cristobal (film 1962). Directed by Gatti, décor Hubert Monloup. Photo Gasparini

La Vie imaginaire de l'éboueur Auguste Geai, Villeurbanne (1962). Directed by Jacques Rosner, décor René Allio. Photo Roget Pic

Chant public devant deux chaises électriques, TNP (1966). Venturelli in Uncle Sam's hat, Photo Chaussat

Chant public devant deux chaises électriques, TNP (1966) by Gatti, décor Hubert Monloup. Photo Chaussat

La Cigogne, Nanterre, Théâtre des Amandiers (1971). Directed by Pierre Debauche, décor Yannis Kokos and Danièle Rosier. Photo Chaussat

V comme Vietnam, Grenier de Toulouse (1967). Directed by Gatti, décor Hubert Monloup. Photo Chaussat

V comme Vietnam, Grenier de Toulouse (1967). Final scene in front of 'The Chestnut' with multiple megasheriffs. Photo Chaussat

Les Treize Soleils, TEP (1968). Directed by Guy Rétoré, décor Hubert Monloup. Varlin's watch. Photo Bernand.

La Passion du Général Franco par les émigrés eux-mêmes, Ney Calberson lorry depot (1976). Directed by Gatti, décor Gilles Lacombe, with actors and standing audience. Photo Rajak Ohanian

Rosa Kollektiv, Kassel, Staatstheater (1970). Directed by Gatti, décor Hubert Monloup. Photo Seiffert

La Colonne Durruti (IAD) Brussels, Rasquinet factory in Schaerbeek (1972). Written and directed by Gatti with actors, puppets, audience. Photo Chaussat

L'Arche d'Adelin (IAD) in Brabant-Wallon (1973). Written, co-ordinated and produced by Gatti. Photo Rajak Ohanian

La Tribu des Carcana en guerre contre quoi?, Theatre Festival of Avignon (1974): the square in front of the Chapelle des Pénitents blancs. Photo René Jacques

La Tribu des Carcana en guerre contre quoi?, Theatre Festival of Avignon (1974): inside the Chapelle des Pénitents blancs. Photo René Jacques

La Première Lettre (films) 1978 L'Isle d'Abeau (St Quentin-Fallavier) Author, Gatti; filmed and edited by Stéphane Gatti, Hélène Chatelain, Claude Mourieras. Arrival of the wedding cake. Photo J.J. Hocquard

La Première Lettre (films) 1978, L'Isle d'Abeau (L'Abbaye de Tamié). Monks singing. Photo J.J. Hocquard

Nous étions tous des noms d'arbres (film) 1982 (Londonderry, the Workshop scholars). Youth actors of the Workshop and the Graffiti. Photo Paolo Gasparini

Le Labyrinthe, Theatre Festival of Avignon, 1982, le Cloître des Carmes. Directed by Gatti, décor Stéphane Gatti. Photo Vaucluse-Matin

L'Émission de Pierre Meynard Toulouse, Archéoptéryx, first *'stage de réinsertion'*, theme Nestor Makhno (1984). Directed by Gatti, décor Stéphane Gatti. Photo J.J. Hocquard

Opéra avec Titre long, Montreal, Théâtre du Monument National (1986). Directed by Gatti. Production of the École Nationale de Théâtre du Canada. Photo Julien Bassouls

reconstruction as in the chronicle-play *Sacco and Vanzetti*, written by Mino Roli and Luciano Vincenzoni in 1960 and staged by Raymond Gerbal with the Franc Théâtre in a translation by César Gattegno and Eli Marinelli at the Théâtre Récamier in Paris in April 1964, and later in the suburbs. A historical reconstruction of this kind – doubtless also used in the other eighty-five plays on the subject which Gatti seems to have known – tells a story of the past, together with the why and the how those events came to pass and could come to pass again. Roli and Vincenzoni's play remains rooted in the past and is outside the experience of younger generations who knew little or nothing of the events portrayed. Had the Italian play been staged 'red-hot' – that is, at the time of the events in question, as was to be the case with Gatti's play on the Vietnam War – it could have been a 'contestation play', a political act, and not what it was in the 1960s: the dramatization of an 'old truth'.

For Gatti in the 1960s, the Sacco and Vanzetti affair was not just 'folklore'. It was, as he says in his Preface, a kind of rendezvous in time to which he had always been faithful in one way or another. He likewise rejected the idea of a play in which the weight of the action would be carried by a single character. That was the field of psychological drama, and he did not work in that field. When the event is carried by tens, even hundreds of characters, as he told J.-J Lerrant in an interview in *Bref* (No. 91, December 1965), one enters the field of 'sociological' drama. His play was not closed, it was open-ended. Its theme was that the only people who are victims are those who consent to be victims. In this case two men, placed in the worst possible circumstances, with seven agonizing years spent in the deathrow, managed to turn the tables on fate and make of their death their 'triumph'. The last moment of the play, 'Bel Canto', consists of a voice only, repeating in front of two huge cut-out, full size photos of Sacco and Vanzetti, on an empty stage, Vanzetti's defiant statement in the dock, ending with 'our death is our triumph'.

Sacco and Vanzetti never appear on stage, nor do they figure amongst the *dramatis personae*, but they are the heroes of a play which is deemed to be seen by audiences in five different theatres: in Boston (the university theatre of Harvard), in Hamburg (a politically orientated theatre), in Turin (a performance bought out by a trade-union group), in Los Angeles (a Baptist Church for Blacks), and in Lyon, in the 'Jean Moulin' theatre, where a real performance can be seen, in part at least, by the real theatre audience. All the 'theatres' are located on the single stage of the real theatre, and as their supposed audiences arrive, neon tubes light up the various theatre façades.

Once 'inside' the supposed theatres, the supposed spectators take their places in the supposed auditoriums facing the real audience of the real auditorium. Through the reactions of the supposed spectators, necessarily originating in their individual experiences, the real audience follows the course of the play on the imaginary stages. Some of the 'spectators' have a visceral reaction like Muller, the Hamburg barrister who twice had had to appear before a denazification court. He declares the Sacco and Vanzetti trial to be a 'general rehearsal amongst so many others' of the Nuremberg trial, where false evidence was used to convict people who had sought to change the order of the world. Throughout the performance he thinks of how he would plead the case.

Two members of the New York intelligentsia decide to attend the Boston performance *because* it recalls the Rosenberg affair, which had taken place in their time, and Morton Sobell, who was even then in prison. They see the two affairs as bearing on each other, the one even 'repeating the other'. Their attitude underlines the meaning of the whole play, but this was apparently missed by the Special Correspondent of The *Times* in Paris, who wrote: (12 Febuary 1966) 'The violence of American labour relations is historically unchallengeable. But what in the name of common sense have Joe Hill (also mentioned by the New Yorkers) or the Rosenbergs to do with the case?' Gatti's answer is given in a stage direction: 'The spectators reconstitute from one reference to another the different moments of the history of the American working class as being so many prolongations of the show of which they have just seen a part.' Another such reference is the accusation of the Chicago five levelled against the prosecution, which the supposed spectators quote in turn. The trade unionist, Coleone, draws the parallel: 'In the year 1886, in Chicago, already the same words as those of Nicola and Bartolomeo'.

Readers unfamiliar with Gatti's unusual dramatic technique may well find the text of *Chant public* complicated and Gatti himself admits that his plays are not easy to *read*. They need a certain imaginative agility on the part of the reader, but once they take physical shape on the stage they are clarity itself. Gatti has always insisted that his plays do not come alive until they are put on the stage. Writing a play is for him like shooting a film: the process of putting it on stage corresponds with the cutting and montage of a film. For this reason he welcomed the invitation from the director of the Théâtre National Populaire in Paris, Georges Wilson, to direct the play there himself. The performance took place on 17 January 1966, not of the text as published by Seuil in 1964 but of a radically 'edited' version published by the TNP as a programme.

After working with Maurice Sarrazin on the production of *Chroniques d'une planète provisoire* Gatti realized, as he told Mireille Boris (*L'Humanité*, 4 January 1964), that the 1964 text of *Chant public* needed to be cut and restructured to make it suitable for the stage. The stage directions in the Seuil edition are, however, helpful to the reader to locate the various developments of the action, and appreciate the structure of this unusual play. Given the demands of the staging and also the number of actors required – some sixty for the seventy roles – it is unlikely that the play could have been produced elsewhere than at the TNP. Even so the TNP company had to be reinforced with actors from Roger Planchon's company in Villeurbanne, Gabriel Garran's in Aubervilliers, and Gatti's own group.

Information about the Sacco and Vanzetti affair and related cases like the Rosenbergs' is given in three numbers of the TNP magazine *Bref* (Nos 91, December 1965; 92, January 1966; 93, February 1966) together with a discussion of the play's dramatic technique, the style of the production, the reactions of the TNP audiences and those of the theatre critics J.-J. Gauthier of *Le Figaro*, J. Paget of *Combat*, and P. Macabru of *Paris-Press* and *L'Intransigeant*, who insultingly referred to the TNP audiences as 'conditioned'. The statements by Hubert Monloup, who designed the set in collaboration with Gatti, are particularly informative. His problem was how to create an abstract space which would contain the five 'theatres' (entrances, auditoriums, imaginary stages) and also the imaginary spaces in which the 'selmaires' would be enacted.

'Selmaires' are in frequent use in Gatti's later plays. In his 1964 Preface he defines them as a

> parallel creation made by the supposed spectator in accordance with the action that he is [supposed to be] seeing on the imaginary stage. Often the spectator invents, translates or reinvents what he is seeing: this invention, translation or reinvention is a selmaire. Sometimes the reinvention is collective and is therefore a 'general selmaire'.

He later mentions the origin of the word when he says of his play *Le Cheval qui se suicide par le feu* (1977) that it is constructed in 'selmaires', according to the tradition of the Chinese story-tellers who used to go on to the Bridge of the Sky in Peking and tell each his own version of the same event – the four 'Gospels' of *L'Enfant rat* can be seen as a forerunner of this technique. In the *Chant public*, whenever there is a 'parallel creation' by a spectator, the action on stage is 'faded out'. Once the 'creation' comes to an end, the action is 'faded in' again. A stage direction in the 1964 edition (p.50) makes this clear: it states that in spite of the visual presentation of the musings of the various 'spectators', the stage performance goes on. It heads a 'flash' (Gatti himself uses the term) between two 'selmaires' showing Judge Thayer speaking in court and at a public ceremony.

For each 'selmaire' a special set with its own accessories had to be created within or alongside the imaginary auditorium in which the 'spectator' is attending the 'performance'. It had to translate what is passing in his mind. In the TNP version the Negro, Little Ned, imagines the confrontation of Judge Thayer and Sacco and Vanzetti on the day the death sentence was pronounced as 'the boxing match of the century and perhaps also of the next', with Thayer weighing in at 60 kilos and seconded by Dark Angels in bowler hats and with clipped wings, and the acts of the accusation by the State of Massachusetts against Sacco and Vanzetti weighing in at 420 kilos. The match is conducted with all the ceremony of a real boxing match and finishes with a knockout, the death sentence, delivered by Thayer. 'After all, the sentence was pronounced a long time ago – it was already pronounced at Chicago', says Cervi. 'It is the sentence of one class on another, of the rich on the poor. You, Judge, are the oppressor, and you know it.'

The anarchist, Venturelli, whose parents were deported from America for 'anti-constitutional activities' when he was a child, seeks in the first 'selmaire' to reconstitute the American climate, which he considers to be inadequately re-created in the play. In his opinion, publicity is the very breath of life for an American, and the ceremony (as he imagines it) at the Unknown Warrior's tomb for the opening of the 'Massachusetts Laughter Week' makes this cruelly clear. In his provocative 'interview hitherto never obtained' with the Unknown Warrior, a marine (in neon lights crucified on a cross offered by an 'American firm of undertakers') details the business interests behind the American interventions in Haiti, Cuba, Nicaragua, Guatemala, Honduras, etc. He had served them for twenty years 'in virtue of the eleventh commandment – What is good for business is good for the country.' Another set is needed to close the 'selmaire': it takes the form of an enormous figure of Uncle Sam which comes down from the flies to dominate the whole stage. Venturelli climbs into the hat held in the dummy's hand and, as from a balcony, makes a speech laced with words used by President Coolidge, who 'had the honour of crushing the only strike by the police force the world has ever known'.

Early in the play, the action which takes place in the separate theatres is pinpointed by spotlights. As the play proceeds, the action rebounds from one theatre to another as in a film, and lines are taken up from various corners of the stage irrespective of the time or space separating the speakers, causing the theatres to begin to lose their separate identities. They disappear entirely when the prison in Charleston in which Sacco and Vanzetti are finally brought together in the same death row is reconstituted on the central stage by rows of prison cell gates set up during the interval by the 'actors' of the Lyon theatre. The five 'theatres' with their separate auditoriums come into being again towards the end of the play when Celestino Madeiros and Sacco and Vanzetti are executed, as it were by proxy, in the person of three supposed spectators, Vorortzug, Cervi and Vastadour; these have come, in somewhat Pirandellian fashion, to identify themselves with the three invisible victims.

The extras from all the theatres take their places as 'official witnesses' of the executions. The executions are not presented realistically. The bearing of each of the 'victims' is described by a 'witness' as the supposed spectator who had identified himself with him takes his place on the electric chair – a chair in one of the supposed theatres on which all the light is concentrated. The light flickers and goes out. When it comes up again each of the three, divested of the hood, 'has become a spectator like the others'. For the last minutes of Vanzetti, as imagined by the professor of law, Gatti returns to his favourite image of the tree:

> When the door is opened Vanzetti has the dimensions of a tree planted on the hills of Montferrat.[5] Even when he comes down to the dimensions of the death row as he greets his gaolers, he is still a tree [...] Calmly, slowly, once again he declares his innocence. The hatred which kept him going during the last hours [the hatred that is bred by oppression] disappears at this moment. The crackling of the chair and the contortions of his body will not revive it [...] At that moment it was my duty to pronounce him dead. I could not. The words stuck in my throat.

This scene can be compared – and contrasted – with the historical account given by Howard Fast in his novel *The Passion of Sacco and Vanzetti*.

The process of identification of the supposed spectators with individuals in the real-life drama is often only momentary, as when Katz, a Boston businessman, becomes Katzmann, the unscrupulous District Attorney. In the case of Vorortzug in Hamburg, the identification is gradual. Early on, he momentarily identifies himself with Madeiros because his own son is in prison and is about to be brought to trial. The identification becomes complete when, speaking later in the name of Madeiros, he confesses that the sight of Sacco's children visiting him in the death row moved him to provide the evidence that their father was innocent, even though he knew that it would cost him his own life.

The identification is complete also in the case of the anarchist Vastadour, a nickle-plater. He projects himself naturally into the character of Vanzetti. Just as Vanzetti had gone to New York to look for work, Vastadour had gone to Lyon, and had suffered the same rebuffs and humiliations. 'New York is Lyon' for those belonging to the 'world of the deprived and rejected', *le monde humilié*. Cervi, a Fiat worker in Turin and a family man like Sacco, relives in imagination the calvary of Sacco's separation from his family and his distress at their seeing him in the death row. One of the most striking moments of the TNP production was the complete identification of Cervi and Vastadour with Sacco and Vanzetti. It occurred after the stage had been overshadowed for several minutes by the two huge cut-out photographs of Sacco and Vanzetti, which looked far more real than the living actors.

Armand Gatti in the Theatre

The *real* characters in the case – Judge Thayer, Alvin T. Fuller, the Governor of Massachusetts, and the unscrupulous police Inspector, Stewart – created a problem for Gatti. His first listeners in Cuba were clearly reluctant to identify themselves with these men, so he decided to have them played straight by 'actors' in the 'Lyon theatre' – this also gave a certain reality to the supposed play. The 'Lyon stage' was located on the apron of the vast TNP stage with the theatre's 'proscenium arch' turned the wrong way round to simulate, with its footbridges, lighting panels, control platforms, etc., the view from backstage. Scenes between the director of the Lyon theatre and his actors supposedly taking place in the wings, were to be seen in front of the reversed 'proscenium arch' on one side of the TNP stage. In the 'wings' on the other side, the director of the Boston theatre greeted the actresses playing the Boston ladies.

The back wall of the real theatre-stage resembled a perforated sheet of a computer, and in the perforations were to be seen in counterpoint with the 'spectators'' experience of the show, photographs of the historical characters, political slogans, documentary films of events relevant to the case – in short, the historical background *outside* the consciousness of the characters in the play. Gatti said that he sought to go beyond photographs and history. He considered his play to be optimistic and to open out on to life. On this backcloth there were also informative luminous newsbands:

> Two thousand strikers in prison ... twelve newspapers suppressed ... Al Capone condems the extremists ... the law on criminal syndicalism applied in twenty states [...] The Attorney General Palmer decrees the mass deportation of suspects [...] boom in canned fruit juices – execution of Sacco-Vanzetti this evening – zero hour.

With regard to the movement of actors on stage, Gatti's assistant, Pierre Chaussat, stated that the conventional type of entrances and exits was dispensed with; there was no more of a break in the stage action than there is between two shots of a film. Something was always happening on stage, both in the shadows and in the full light. Actors coming on stage in the half-light (visible, however, to the real theatre audience) did so as part of the action. When the full light moved away from them to another part of the action already in progress, they left the stage still playing their parts. Lighting intervened as a factor of choice.[6] Most of the time the stage was crowded, but occasionally and strikingly it cleared, as when Cervi/Sacco and Vastadour/Vanzetti are left alone listening to the song offstage, 'E Lucevano le Stelle', with which the two martyrs greeted each other from their separate cells. 'The song became a duet. None of the prison officers or the other prisoners dared to interrupt; it was the first time that song had ever been heard in the death row on Cherry Hill', the 'Lyon' theatre director explains to his audience.

The richness, variety and extent of the multiple staging (the TNP stage nearly collapsed under the weight of the sets) caused some critics to accuse Gatti of using gimmicks. This criticism is unfounded, because Gatti's intention from the outset was *not* to put everything into the written lines but to use expressive concrete images to carry the action. One such example is that of Fuller in the barber's chair, deciding about the cut of his side whiskers in such a way as to make clear his parallel and irrevocable decision to send Sacco and Vanzetti to the electric chair. The intention of the prosecution to obtain the sentence that suited its political purpose is likewise revealed by the concrete image of the game played on a monumental chessboard by the professor of law and an ecclesiastic in Hamburg. The suggestion is that the defence of Sacco and Vanzetti was as bad as a fool's mate: it implies not incompetence but collusion.

In the face of the Red Bogey that the Spartakist uprising of 1919 had evoked – and, even more so, the triumph of the Russian revolutionaries with their assassination of the Russian Imperial family – it was deemed essential to dispose of Sacco and Vanzetti, all Italians, syndicalists and anarchists, as being a 'threat' to the American Way of Life and to Thayer personally as a member of the privileged classes. What he had to discover was not 'who killed a man, but who is trying to destroy a country', and so he callously brushes aside all proof of the innocence of the two men, including the evidence given by Madeiros. He even uses that evidence to convict Madeiros himself: 'The court is no longer concerned with identifying Sacco and Vanzetti for the purpose of the verdict [...] The only law that matters is the feeling that I, personally, have of their guilt.'

Seeing it as symbolic of capitalist oppression that Sacco and Vanzetti were tried and condemned, Gatti recalls, along with their fate, the fate of others, beginning in 1886 with the hanging of the trade-union delegates in Chicago, and going up to 1953 with the electrocution of the Rosenbergs. In a final updating of the text during rehearsals, Gatti recalls the fate of Morton Sobell, condemned with the Rosenbergs, who had been transferred to prison in Lewisberg in 1965, the sixteenth year of his thirty-year sentence. The intended parallel between the McCarthy terror and the situation in the twenties is underlined by one of the section titles in Scene III, 'Antiphonaire de la Terreur blanche à Palmer-city'.

But as early as in the first explosive moments of the TNP version, the note of terror is struck by the action: the Negro sandwich men advertising the 'Big Show, Sacco and Vanzetti Story' in front of the Baptist Church in Los Angeles, where the 'performance' is due to take place, are subjected to a violent police charge; some are taken into custody – Gatti had substituted Los Angeles for New Orleans (1964 version) because of the outbreak of rioting by unemployed Blacks in Los Angeles in the summer of 1965. Before the 'performance' begins, the Reverend Knight, who is presenting the show in his church at the request of the Almighty to prevent the growing racialism of the Negroes, explains from the 'stage': 'Dear brethren, this is a story about Blacks, although it is told about Whites'. Little Ned subsequently corrects this, saying: 'Told about Whites it is an injustice. Told about Blacks there is nothing unusual in it.' Clearly, for a Black, the story was better understood in terms of the humiliations to which black Americans were exposed than through a story about Whites.

Partway through, the 'performance' is suspended to allow a discussion between officials on the 'stage' and the 'audience' about their reactions to the case as presented in the play, and the way they would like to see it developed. In Boston, Farley asks the producer: 'Judicial error or political persecution?' Both interpretations are correct, is the reply. In Hamburg, the professor of law raises the matter of the periodic return of the 'White Terror' in the United States, saying that it explains the position taken up in the 'play'. When the 'performance' is resumed, various aspects of the case come under review, either by 'spectators' talking among themselves, or in 'selmaires' in which scenic time and space are not identified with real scenic time and space, and the characters may not be fixed entities.

In the section 'Bande-Témoin pour un long métrage policier' the theme is the intimidation, blackmail, ill-treatment of witnesses, even the deliberate use of professional false witnesses. This theme is first stated in the 'selmaire' of the New Yorkers in the Boston theatre; they speak in their own name but quote the evidence actually given by historical witnesses. In 'Bridgewater Parade', concrete imagery is used to show the deliberate twisting and misuse of evidence. The ambitious Chief of Police, Stewart, succumbs to the veiled threats of Thayer and Fuller concerning his career, should he fail to secure the conviction of Sacco and Vanzetti. He is shown soliloquizing amidst sandwich men, each carrying a different picture of him with the notice 'VOTE FOR STEWART'. This TNP version (p.51) is far more pointed than the 1964 version, where an embarrassed Chief of Police, preoccupied with his own image, soliloquizes surrounded by multiple mirrors each reflecting a different image of himself. A prisoner of the contradictory evidence existing on the case, he decided to strike the attitude required by his superiors (p.721).

Another aspect of the case, the worldwide marches, demonstrations and petitions, is referred to, but no mention is made of such incidents as Lindbergh's failure to sign the petition after the American ambassador, Myron T. Herrick, had torn it from his hands. Gatti looks rather to the ineffectiveness of other American protests in face of the organized might of American society, and uses a concrete image: in between two rounds of Thayer's 'boxing match', the mangled body of an Indian leader of the International Workers of the World is carried across the stage to the singing of the 'Muskrat Ramble', which describes his fate during the bloody repression of the protest strike by twelve thousand Colorado miners led by the IWW. The song does not, however, mention the subsequent dismantling of this union, which had tried to save Sacco and Vanzetti by an all-out strike.

An important question is raised in one of the 'selmaires' describing the 'ritual' of the 'toilet' of men being sent to the electric chair. 'How can people turn themselves into officiants of death?' The Boston director in the role of the barber who shaves the heads of the condemned, replies that it is easy: 'some automatically, given their natural bent, others for reasons of class or money' – words to this effect spoken by Vanzetti before the court of 9 April 1927 are retained by Gatti in the text – above all there will be people of passive clear conscience and worthy sentiments: 'us'.

The play is not intended as the simple story of Sacco and Vanzetti. Its purpose is to ask a question, one that could have hinged on the story of the Chicago five, Joe Hill, Tom Mooney or many others, but hinges here on Sacco and Vanzetti. The question is: Would Sacco and Vanzetti, or any of those engaged nowadays in the same struggle against 'the exploitation of man by man', as Vanzetti accusingly said to the court, once again be convicted and executed by us? 'Did Sacco and Vanzetti die for nothing? That is what one needs to know.' The repercussions of an event *outside* the limits of time and place where it occurred is what really matters. In terms of the theatre performance the question is: Would Sacco and Vanzetti be forgotten by the spectator once he had left the theatre? The creation of supposed spectators who – by their differing social status, political views, personal prejudices or preoccupations – have their counterparts in the real audience is intended by Gatti as a means of securing the continued adhesion of the real spectator.

A remark by a 'spectator' in the Hamburg theatre – that a real audience would probably be a replica of the stage audiences and that this would be shown by their reactions to the drama – was borne out by the diversity of opinion in letters sent to the TNP by members of its audience and published in *Bref* (No. 93). When the spectators were not frankly hostile (and fifteen out of fifty-eight were) the letters revealed the strength of the bond forged by Gatti between stage and auditorium:

> To the five different scenic spaces [...] I think Paris could be added. In the auditorium of the TNP, each of us threw aside the role of spectator to assume the role of victim.

Armand Gatti in the Theatre

> Very soon I felt myself caught up in the action that was taking place [...] if that was the intention of the author he has, in my opinion, fully achieved his goal. May he be warmly thanked for creating a collective political awareness [*prise de conscience*].

> You have made an eminent contribution to the mobilization of people's consciences. I was surely not the only one to have a catch in my throat and tears in my eyes for two thirds of the performance.

Gatti *must* be staged.

The letters also revealed that the spectators ranged from young people who had never heard of Sacco and Vanzetti to people who had been personally concerned in the affair. One of these, a man aged sixty-two in 1966, had taken part in the Paris demonstration on the night of 22–23 August 1927, the night of the execution. From the technical point of view, each of the supposed spectators had to be given a different time-scale because of the different relationship in which he stood to the affair, and this did not permit of a dramatic structure based on dramatic time, clock time, or a time continuum [*durée*]. Their involvement in the dramatic action, which led them to discover in themselves so many other 'possible selves', implied a conception of time in the dimension of the possible, not of the real. This *temps-possibilité* embraces the past, present and future, acting the one on the other, and on becoming 'theatrical time' its use leads to the dramatic action being cut up on the principle of 'creations parallel to the given reality', 'selmaires', in which each character is free to indulge.

The structure of the normal theatre building with its Italianate stage had always been a problem for Gatti. He found it constricting, but given the huge size of the TNP stage and the imagination shown by Monloup in his sets, Gatti considered that from the point of view of staging they had almost achieved perfection. Indeed, on this score praise was nearly unanimous, whether by the TNP audience or the press. Some of those hostile to the play itself, normally correspondents of the right-wing press, claimed, however, that Gatti would have done better to call on a professional such as Jacques Rosner, who had done a remarkable job on *Auguste Geai* at Villeurbanne. He would have put some 'order' into the 'confusion' of Gatti's 'pretentious text'. Confusion, pretentiousness – these were the two words with which this section of the press belaboured Gatti. Jean Dutourd of *France-Soir* castigated Gatti for 'out-of-date anti-Americanism', and for 'bad faith' in assimilating the case of two martyrs with that of spies, the Rosenbergs, but hastened to add that he had signed the petition for mercy for the Rosenbergs.

In the face of the chorus of hostile criticism provoked by the subject of the play, Gérard Guillot of *Les Lettres Françaises* (3 February 1966) felt called upon to express his indignation at the injustice to which Gatti was subjected by those 'blinded by their political prejudices'. He termed *Chant public* a masterpiece despite certain shortcomings, and maintained that one would need to go back to 1958 to come across a work of equal importance in the evolution of the contemporary French theatre: *Paolo Paoli*, by Arthur Adamov.

Adamov himself[7] was highly appreciative of the way Gatti showed how the Sacco and Vanzetti affair covered so many others, which brings one back to the title of the opening section of the play, 'Clefs de portée sous forme de spectateurs'. Adamov, however, had some reservations to make about the wide dispersal and number of the 'spectators' and the complete disregard for chronology. He mentioned that he had himself taken part in the demonstration on the night of the execution of Sacco and Vanzetti, and in the Commemorative March for those demonstrators who died at the Charonne métro station on 13 February 1962: 'these were not electrocuted but merely suffocated in the métro station'; and he added sarcastically, 'each country has its own methods'.

Eluard was right when he said that these assassinations are not the outcome of some episodic incident, however appalling, but of a process that goes merrily on. This was also Gatti's opinion, as the quotation from Albert Einstein at the head of the Preface to the 1964 edition makes clear:

> Everything should be done to keep the tragic affair of Sacco and Vanzetti alive in the conscience of mankind. They remind us of the fact that even the most perfectly planned democratic institutions are no better than the people whose instruments they are [...] The fight for the dignity of man is particularly urgent today. May Sacco and Vanzetti continue to live as symbols in all those who strive for a better morality in public affairs.

As was his custom, Gatti gave a reading of the play soon after its completion. It was then entitled *Sacco and Vanzetti*. This was on 22 February 1964 at the Théâtre de la Commune at Aubervilliers under the auspices of Gabriel Garran. On 24 May Roger Planchon's company gave a reading with film sequences by Chris Marker at the Théâtre de L'Est Parisien, under the descriptive title *Chant public devant la chaise électrique*. This reading confirmed the impression Gatti had already formed – at which he hints in the new title – that the work was an 'oratorio' rather than a drama, and was too far removed from day-to-day life to catch the public imagination.

The text as published at the end of 1964, and doubtless revised after the reading, still has this quality. In a number of passages all the 'spectators' who feel they have a common cause with Sacco and Vanzetti form 'Sacco and Vanzetti groups' to act out certain scenes. They also sing in chorus 'The Deportation Round', the 'Ballade of the International Working World' (both omitted in the TNP version) and 'And his five pennies of the New World', sung at the TNP by a Union Maid, one of the three women to become involved in union organizing in Chicago. The songs, particularly in the 1964 version, paint a highly coloured picture of an America in which 'laughter dies in 1921', the year when Sacco and Vanzetti were sent for trial and the 'White Terror' began.

In the TNP version the songs are no longer mere musical interludes in a dramatic text, but are closely integrated into the dramatic action. The pattern is set by the change of role of the very first song. It is a sort of musical curtain-raiser in the 1964 text, where it is presented under the revealing section heading 'Mesure pour rien' and is sung by 'objective-characters': that is to say, the objects of other characters' thoughts. In the TNP version its role is more dramatic because it becomes the reason for the police charge on the sandwich men advertising the Sacco and Vanzetti show. Music for the songs was written by the Czech composer William Bukovi.

By its subject, *Chant public* is in direct line with *La Vie imaginaire de l'éboueur Auguste Geai*, and through it with *L'Enfant rat*. As Gatti saw it, the shanty town of his childhood described in *Auguste Geai* belonged to much the same universe, and so did the concentration camp pictured in *L'Enfant rat*. So also did the wider world of the proletariat, limited in *Chant public* to the American continent with its millions of immigrant workers, victims of unremitting social injustice. The attitude of the protagonists in *Auguste Geai* and *Chant public* is the same. Auguste's hope that his own fight to secure a social revolution may be continued by his son, imagined by him as a film producer – 'You will show me dying for the Revolution, won't you, Christian?' – is the same hope expressed in Sacco's letter to his son, Dante, an authentic letter which Cervi/Sacco reads out as if to Sacco's son in Scene VII, 'Hymne pour un Enfant assassiné'. It concludes with the words: 'They can destroy our bodies but not our ideas, and the young who follow us will continue to defend them [...] It is your father who is calling to you, "Dante! Dante!" It is your comrade Nicola.'

The technique used in both plays is much the same. In *Auguste Geai*, after the single event – the mortal wounding of Auguste in an encounter with the police – the rest of the play, to use the terminology employed by Gatti to describe his technique in *Chant public*, is a single 'selmaire': a creation in an individual's mind which invents, interprets and reinvents in a time-scale in which past, present and imaginary future are all moulded into one. In *Chant public*, the field is widened to include the minds of a number of people directed towards an event which is outside themselves but which is, at the same time, a permanent reality to be faced up to.

This move from the individual conscience to the collective conscience considerably enriches the issue at stake. In *Chant public*, not content with making short shrift of the norms of time, space and even personal identity, as in *Auguste Geai*, Gatti sets going an uninterrupted movement between the real, the historic and the imaginary, and leads the real spectators collectively to reconstruct the course of the tragedy on the lines we, the spectators, would have taken had we been the author. Whatever reservations one may have about the practicalities of the technique, the fact remains that the play opened up perspectives completely unexplored at the time. Here was drama of the collective conscience such as had not been attempted before. Great drama for the Greeks had always been drama of the collective conscience, but Gatti's technical innovations enhanced its possibilities.

II La Cigogne

Acceptance or refusal? The question is also put in *La Cigogne*, but this time it is put outside the context of the working-class struggle. Gatti's concern here is the existence of the atom bomb and the 'inevitability' of a third use of it. When he spoke of *La Cigogne* at a public meeting in Paris at the time it was being performed at the Théâtre Universitaire in Strasbourg (28 March 1968), he seemed to imply that in his estimation it was one of the most important of his plays. Along with critics who saw it in Strasbourg, or three years later on 20 April 1971 in a new version, as I did, at the Théâtre des Amandiers (The Centre Dramatique National in Nanterre), I would not consider the play to be amongst Gatti's most successful dramatic works, but I readily accept that he probably had in mind the urgency of the subject and the need to bring it to the public conscience as some other dramatists had already attempted to do.

Faced with the problem of evoking the 'parallel world' of Hiroshima and Nagasaki after the bomb, a world as far removed from the 'civilized world' as was the 'parallel world' of Auschwitz, Mauthausen or 'Tatenberg', he once again came up against the inadequacy of what he called the 'code-language' of the civilized world and also of traditional dramatic forms. People were no more, but objects which had belonged to them were still there and confronted the survivors every day. Why should not the objects speak in their place? asks one of the characters. They are in themselves a 'language', whether one likes it or not.

With this as his starting point Gatti made use of a technique of extreme *éclatement* involving every single element of dramatic composition – characters, time, space and even the 'plot', which is presented in terms of one of the most difficult 'cases' of the Zen catechism, the 'case' of the stray cat in the temple of Mount Nan-Chuan which gave rise to enormous numbers of bewildered attempts at explanations (Preface). Gatti's characters' attempt to meditate on the 'case' in the light of their experience of the bomb – and conversely, their interpretation of their own situation in terms of the philosophical problem – brings complications which at times overload the play and blur its outline. The spectator does not have time to take in all the arguments put forward.

In Strasbourg *La Cigogne* was produced by Jean Hurstel, who had staged *La Deuxième Existence du Camp de Tatenberg* the year before, and he pointed to the essential difference between the two plays when he said that in the concentration-camp play the characters all have their eyes fixed firmly on the past, and if there is the merest hint of the present in the play there is none at all of the future, whereas in *La Cigogne* there is a clear opening on to the future and the play is the richer for it. The opening comes with the soldier Enemon's return to Nagasaki from the Malayan front. He returns during the commemoration of the day of the dead and finds those still alive 'living off their misfortune', congratulating each other on 'being alive'. 'I reject men', he declares, 'who lie down on the ground and accept the death imposed on them by another. Man must know how to stand on his own two feet.' These words sum up the 'lesson' of the play and Gatti quoted them on various occasions, although they are omitted in the final (published) version. There is no historical reconstruction of the events of 9 August 1945, nor any compilation of testimonies in the manner of the documentary play; rather *La Cigogne* is a parable the burden of which is that however deeply men may be afflicted, they can give a purpose to life and to history through action firmly rooted in the present but directed towards the future.

The starting point of the dramatic action is an old Japanese legend according to which a person who is mortally ill will survive if he succeeds in making a thousand paper storks. The child, Oyanagi, a victim of radiation sickness like all the others who had had the misfortune to be in Nagasaki on 'that fatal day', has completed seven hundred and three when she dies. She had been dragged barely alive from under a pile of disfigured corpses of school children waiting to be cremated, so the paper storks hung around her bed by her fellow-sufferers were symbols of their 'united front against despair' (p.59). To have kept her alive would have been a victory over the bomb, but her death has imprisoned them all in resignation and slammed the door on the future. This is the situation which Enemon finds on his return to Nagasaki. The dramatic conflict is created by Enemon because, unlike those who were in Nagasaki on the day of the explosion, he refuses to consider the future as closed and, despite the 'inevitable' explosion of a third bomb which will be the same for future generations as the first or second bomb was for them, he maintains that one must crawl from under the ruins and slowly but perseveringly set about the invention of a new language.

Rebuttal as the Good Fight

The war from which he has returned is the past. He sees his life as beginning with his arrival in Nagasaki. He rejects the 'sterile visions of horror' which the victims delight in keeping before their eyes, so his action in finally joining a ship as a coal-trimmer is not a flight from horror, but reintegration into life at its most humble level. It is also his interpretation, in a practical form, of the 'case' of the cat of Mount Nan-Chuan which the rival monks of the East and West pavilions sought to adopt, but which the Master, Pou Yuan, decapitated because none could 'say the word' that would have saved it. As the story goes, when the First Disciple returned and learned of the cat's fate, he put his sandals – his most humble possessions – on his head – his most noble possession – and departed, to the distress of the master who said that had he been there, the cat would have been saved.

In the play the ex-engineer Kawaguchi, who was in Hiroshima and in Nagasaki at the time of both explosions, is the first to attempt a solution to the problem. He tries to convince himself that his incurable cancer caused by the radiation, is the 'cat gnawing at his entrails' – an illusion less cruel than the reality, says one of the characters. In his despair he interprets the First Disciple's gesture as 'walling up the prison', with himself inside. No acceptable interpretation is given by the others because, in the situation created by the dropping of the bomb, they have no acceptable interpretation to give to life. Enemon's interpretation is that all the rival monks offered the cat was comfort and ease, a living death in fact, so the Master's action was a practical 'transcription' of their attitude, whereas the First Disciple indicated by his departure that the cat's existence could have no significance except in facing the 'insecurity' of the outside world (p.100). With this interpretation Enemon gives a purpose to living. He obviously has Gatti's sympathy.

The structure of the play follows the different phases of the story. These are indicated in the text by sequences entitled 'Période de ...' with one or other of the characters in the riddle as the centre of gravity. The 'Période du chat' concerns the weeks immediately after the explosion; the 'Période des moines des deux pavillons' the months that followed; the 'Période du Maître' looks backwards over the whole period from the present of the action to the time of the bomb; that of the First Disciple looks forward to a future which is as open and creative as possible. The periods are not discontinuous but arise one out of the other. The sequence headings in the written text obviously escape the *spectator*, but the resulting dramatic structure, which has nothing to do with linear or clock time, creates a time-scale astride past, present and future to give a rounded presentation of the ways of thinking and feeling of the individual concerned.

With the exception of Enemon and Mademoiselle Ayasaki – an American of Japanese origin, likewise newly arrived in Nagasaki – the *dramatis personae* have doubles in the damaged objects which symbolize the role in life of each character before the catastrophe: a teapot for a graduate of the Academy of Cha No Yu and specialist in the tea-drinking ceremony (Tomiko); a sumo belt for an ex-champion wrestler (Tsubakiyama), etc. It is the 'atomized' object which brings back to life, as it were, the person to whom it belonged and with whom it is intimately bound up.

In the version performed at Nanterre and published by Seuil (1971), both objects and owners are played by 'Volunteers' who have been cleaning up the streets of Nagasaki; they attempt no reconstitution of the characters; rather, the characters evolve within the *temps-possibilité* (to quote Gatti) of those who resuscitate them, with their confrontation with the object as their starting point. In consequence the action proceeds on two levels which are given visual representation in the staging. Objects, according to Japanese lore, are credited with a life of their own, so when the Volunteers act as their spokesmen they 'speak from inside the objects' (*programme-dossier* of the Nanterre performance): that is to say from within their separate shöjis or small dwellings which they enter through large cut-outs of the objects in the paper walls.

According to their position inside or outside the shöjis they are objects or characters, and as characters are not subject to the immobility of objects. Although there are a number of allusions in the text to shadows of vaporized people imprinted on walls, and those of cyclists imprinted on the stone of the Yamagawa bridge, Gatti's Preface gives as the source of the idea for the cut-outs the anecdote of an Irishman in a Japanese bar who finds himself inexplicably ignored as if he were not there at all, and so walks out, not through the door but through the paper wall, leaving his silhouette in the wall as proof of his existence.

There is, however, one object with no corresponding cut-out in a shöjis: Enemon's kitbag. Like him, it comes into the stricken city from the outside. The kitbag, says the Trumpet, 'would have us [the atomized objects] believe that the bomb is a mere parenthesis'. 'A parenthesis that Enemon has arrived to close?' the Sumo Belt adds. 'Only parentheses exist, Tragedy does not', is an American comment on the event. The bag disappears during an attempted seduction of Enemon, and an analysis of the reasons that one or the other might have for its theft offers as many incongruous exegeses of the 'case' of the cat of Mount Nan-Chuan.

A demonstration is announced in the opening scene by the Volunteers in the name of the atomized objects against the razzmatazz and 'bad faith' of an American television programme on the bomb. They then introduce themselves and the roles they will play, as these objects and as their one-time owners, to a 'supposed public' of fellow-victims on this third day of the festival of remembrance of the dead. The 'supposed public' is not actually present on stage, as in *Chant public*, but since it is apostrophized two or three times by the Volunteers, who step out of their roles to do so, it forms a link with the real public in the auditorium.

In contrast with the negative image of the Japan of Hiroshima and Nagasaki presented by these objects, that of America is represented by the businesslike desk of the Secretary to the 'Commission d'enquête sur les dégats occasionnés par la bombe atomique', the CEDOBA, 'an organization of which the initials alone are fictitious' (Preface). Mademoiselle Ayasaki is met with hostility by the victims, who accuse the Americans of having prolonged the war in order to try out the bomb and use them as guinea pigs for a study of radiation effects.

Details of such a study appear in the Nanterre *programme-dossier*. Objects as well as people, Mademoiselle Ayasaki says, were examined by scientists in America, but this enquiry – together with the American distribution of television sets, intended to persuade the victims of America's concern for their plight and inform them of the wonders of plastic surgery performed on the disfigured girls flown to Mount Sinai Hospital in New York for treatment – only confirm their suspicions. Mademoiselle Ayasaki finds that despite her unbounded pity for them, she cannot establish any real contact with the victims, nor can she justify the unjustifiable. She is driven to suicide by self-cremation, just as Ayasaki Hiroko (on whom she admits she had been modelled as a dramatic character) had been driven at San Diego on 13 October 1967, as a protest against the war policy of the American government.

The climax of the action is the departure of Enemon's ship in a festive atmosphere, with Nagasaki coming to life again as a port. The example of Enemon, 'the thousandth stork', whom Tomiko comes to love, makes her rebel against the 'suffocating resignation' of her fellow-sufferers and trample underfoot their treasured object-witnesses of the aggression to which they had been subjected. However, the ex-judge Mashimoto (Azebetto in the earlier version) deplores actions of this kind as 'likely to incite quiescent people to revolt'; had not their television sets shown them that peace, as preached by the oppressors, meant non-revolt? Thereupon the objects begin to recite the 'decalogue of resignation', ending: 'You must resign yourselves to the bomb, otherwise a more terrible one still will fall upon you.'

The last word, however, is with Tomiko: 'There are not only storks which fly in the sky. There are also those which fly on the ground – a kind of sky for them. Brought down seven times, they fly up again eight times. That is how these storks fly.' Gatti's vision is clearly not limited to the particular historical event which forms the subject of the play. He is concerned with the general problem of the resistance which should oppose oppression. Humiliation results only when the oppression of one class, race, or nation on another crushes the spirit of revolt in the oppressed.

Despite the obvious political purpose of the play, the human interest is not sacrificed. It is to be found in the interaction of personal relationships between the characters, who are well individualized, and these are presented with the fixed ceremonial that traditionally regulates human and social relationships in Japan. The scenes between Enemon and Tomiko, and between Tomiko and the ex-wrestler, provide particularly expressive moments of such ritual.

Gatti's unusual dramatic technique was underlined by the method of staging adopted by Hurstel in Strasbourg and was in line with the method he had used there for *Tatenberg*. It was also underlined by Pierre Debauche at Nanterre in this, the first appearance of a Gatti work on the playbill of an official theatre in France since the banning of his play on General Franco in 1968. All other Gatti productions, even those directed by the dramatist himself, had been forced into the straitjacket of frontal presentation on the single stage of the traditional theatre. Distressed as he had always been by the limitations imposed by such theatre architecture, Gatti saw Hurstel's presentation as a breakthrough, and this possibly contributed to his personal evaluation of his play.

In 1962, shortly after *Auguste Geai* was put on at Villeurbanne, Gatti saw Jean-Marie Serreau's production of Michel Parent's *Gilda appelle Maë West*[8] on the vast repercussions of the dropping of the first A-bomb on Japan, and he was impressed by the staging. The production was part of an 'experimental theatre series' put on at Dijon during the Burgundy Theatre Festival, not in a theatre but in a rectangular sporting club. The action took place simultaneously or in 'counterpoint' in some dozen localities summarily suggested in the multiple sets which lined the club walls. The public, seated in the centre of the hall and literally hemmed in by the different repercussions of the dropping of the bomb were left to follow them in their entirety by pivoting round on their seats. A similar concern on Gatti's part for the integration of the spectator into the dramatic action by hemming him in physically within the 'ruins of Nagasaki' is revealed in his scenic indications published in the Nanterre *programme-dossier* alongside Danièle Rozier's design for the layout of the acting areas and for the areas occupied by the public, as used at the production.

Gatti's notes stipulated, in addition to the seven shōjis, several other acting areas for scenes such as those between Tomiko and Enemon, or Tomiko and the ex-wrestler. Rozier's design shows these to have been positioned (at Nanterre) alongside, behind, or in front of the blocks of seats reserved for spectators, which in places extended back to the walls of the building. The level of the different acting areas with their adjacent blocks of seats varied, and the impression produced was that of a crater from the edge of which the spectator was looking down on the devastated city. The integration of acting and audience areas curiously foreshadows the new line Gatti was to develop after his ostracism in France in 1969. When he began to work outside the confines of traditional theatre – in Louvain in 1971, and later in France again – he applied his new ideas. His enthusiasm for *La Cigogne* could have originated in the experience of a revelation lighting the way ahead. A revolutionary subject needed a revolutionary technique of presentation.

Gatti and Parent were not alone in their search for a heightened awareness of the ethical and human implications of the bomb, and the subject lent itself to experiment with dramatic form. Pierre Halet's *Little Boy* (1970), like Parent's *Gilda*, focuses the action on the state of mind of the ex-pilot of the plane that delivered the 'little boy' at Hiroshima. By its dramatic technique, however, with its *éclatement* of time, space and even characters, *Little Boy* is reminiscent of Gatti, particularly his *Auguste Geai*. Like *La Cigogne*, *Le Drame du Fukuru-Maru* (1960 and 1964) by Gabriel Cousin concentrates on the physical and psychological effects of radio-active fall-out – in this case on the Japanese fishermen near the Bikini Atoll testing ground in 1954 – but the form is rather that of a dramatic oratorio.

A very different aspect of the bomb came under consideration by Jean Vilar. With the persecution of Dr Oppenheimer for his opposition to the creation of the H-bomb in a 'Cold War' period as the starting point of *Le Dossier Oppenheimer* (1964), Vilar sought to increase his spectators' awareness of the many issues at stake on the nuclear arms race, including the position of the citizen, particularly the scientist, in any confrontation with the political and military authorities. To underline the seriousness of the subject, together with the authenticity of the points made, Vilar tried out a completely new dramatic form and offered his audience not a 'documentary' play but a *pièce-document*, the text of which consists solely of a truncated version of the transcript of the hearing of the case against Dr Oppenheimer. In this particular instance 'document' and 'play' are identical with each other, the exact record of the event being in itself highly dramatic. There was therefore no need for 'poetic invention', and Vilar considered such invention dangerous in matters of serious concern. As always reality is Gatti's starting point, but he is essentially a poet, and in his hands this reality takes the form not of a documentary play but of a highly imaginative work. Imagination does not detract from the matters of serious concern which are Gatti's subjects. It brings them to the forefront of the spectators' conscience.

Notes

1. *Théâtre Populaire*, No. 54, 1964.
2. J.-L. Pays, *Lettres Françaises* 19–25 August 1965.

Armand Gatti in the Theatre

3. Gozlan and Pays, p. 195.
4. *Le Progrès de Lyon*, 24 February 1962.
5. Montferrat = Monferrato, a region to the south-east of Turin with tree-covered hills homeland of the Gatti family (see *Ton Nom était Joie*). For Armand Gatti, his father Auguste was a 'tree'. Villafalleto was the birthplace of Vanzetti, and his ashes are interred there. In this passage the images of Auguste and Vanzetti come together: 'Tous mes personnages avant d'être écrits sont des arbres et c'est à partir de l'arbre qu'ils pourraient être que j'écris un personnage' (*Gatti, Journal illustré d'une écriture*, p. 71).
6. *Lettres Françaises*, 20 January 1966: 'Avant-première sur la Colline aux cerises', Jean-Louis Pays.
7. *Lettres Françaises*. 10–16 June 1965: 'Libérez Sacco-Vanzetti', by Arthur Adamov.
8. 'Michel Parent and Theatrical Experiments in Simultaneity,' by Dorothy Knowles (*Theatre Research [Recherches Théâtrales]*, vol. XI, No. 1, 1971).

7
Two Plays for Special Occasions

I V comme Vietnam
II Les Treize Soleils de la rue Saint-Blaise

Two of Gatti's plays are not the direct product of his personal experience but owe their existence to specific requests from outside bodies. The first is concerned with the conduct of the Vietnam War; the second, written in collaboration with a particular theatre's audience, is centred on subjects of special interest to that audience. Despite the guidelines in each case, the final product bears the unmistakable imprint of Gatti's creative imagination.

I V comme Vietnam (La Nuit des Rois de Shakespeare par les comédiens de Toulouse face aux événements du Sud-Est Asiatique)

V comme Vietnam was commissioned in January 1967 by the Committee of the Association of University Teachers and Scientific Researchers who sought, alongside their American colleagues, to challenge the American 'escalation of the aggression in Vietnam' by stimulating an 'escalation of the general public's knowledge of this aggression'. The Committee's choice of dramatist fell on Gatti because of his known attitude of 'political commitment' – in the sense used by Jean Vilar and already referred to – 'problems of concern to all men'. This had been amply demonstrated by him in Paris at the Théâtre Récamier (the little TNP), in Villeurbanne and in Toulouse. He accepted the challenge and wrote *V comme Vietnam* within twenty-five days at the same time as he was working with Maurice Sarrazin on the new production of *Chroniques d'une planète provisoire*. Without the initiative of the Committee and Sarrazin's immediate offer to produce the play at the Grenier in collaboration with him, Gatti said that it was very doubtful whether he would have thought of writing about Vietnam as he had no personal experience of the country or of the war there, and personal experience

Armand Gatti in the Theatre

was basic to his writing. Sarrazin declared that if he and the Grenier made this 'political gesture', it was because it was also a truly 'theatrical gesture'. There was no question of his putting on just any play about Vietnam.[1]

Some months before this production Peter Brook's 'English Revue', *US*, had sought to bring an apathetic or unenlightened public, 'us', to a clearer understanding of the horrors of the US war in Vietnam, and the consequent need to bring it to an end. Brook was invited to take his production to Paris. He refused, saying that the French should write their own play on the subject. No play was forthcoming. There was only a short 'collage' on the war arranged by José Valverde, the director of the Théâtre Gérard-Philipe, the Centre dramatique in Saint-Denis. It was performed here and there at the request of various unions.

In February 1967 the Théâtre Romain Rolland in the Paris working-class suburb of Villejuif put on Guy Kayat's production of *La Guerre entre parenthèses* by Claire-Lise Charbonnier and Georges Felhandler, on the 'distant war one carefully puts behind one.' It presented the war as a game of chess, with Vietnam as the chessboard. The same month outside Paris saw *Napalm*, a more effective play by André Benedetto staged with his Nouvelle Compagnie d'Avignon. It covers much the same ground as *V comme Vietnam* and is similar in aim and tone. It uses the technique of a play-within-a-play to underscore the horrors of the war, as in *US*, but is more directly concerned with raising issues such as where to look for the responsibility for these horrors, and what effect the relative health or sickness of the moral and social forces at work in both the USA and Vietnam had on the combatants. Benedetto was to return to the subject of the Vietnam War with two shorter plays, *La Chine entre à l'O.N.U.* and *Chant funèbre pour un soldat américain*. Barbara Garson's brilliant satire *Mac Bird* (1966) is the best-known in France of American plays on the Vietnam War, and may well have provided some inspiration for the end of Gatti's play. The Grenier's bulletin-programme (No.5, April 1967) lists it among other suitable reading matter for the event.

V comme Vietnam made theatrical history in France because it was the first time a play was commissioned by an inter-union committee. It was also the first time a tour of a production was arranged by such a committee. Furthermore, the proceeds from the tour were to be donated to the European Universities' fund for providing a library for researchers in the university of the much-bombed city of Hanoi. The action of this committee in arranging the tour proved that it *was* possible to take a play to the country outside the normal circuits, and that a public for such performances *did* exist. Indeed, in the twenty-five towns visited the production achieved not a success but an 'explosion', with spectators supporting or contesting the play and even coming to blows over it. Only in the capital, at the Théâtre de l'Est Parisien, where nevertheless

Two Plays for Special Occasions

every seat was taken up, was the play judged purely as a dramatic composition.

The problem confronting Gatti was whether 'red-hot' topicality could be put on to the stage not as a straight page of history, a document of the times, or piece of propaganda, but be itself a truly 'theatrical gesture'. Furthermore, since to his way of thinking a dramatic performance is by the very nature of things political, crystallizing ideas in the air and stimulating in the spectator a new consciousness, Gatti felt that while exercising his profession of dramatist by writing this play, he was also actively participating in his times.

As he had no personal experience of the Vietnam War he had perforce to rely on vicarious experience: communiqués, despatches, films, photographs, individual accounts and carefully authenticated documents which he 'voraciously devoured' each day in order to follow the course of events. The information so obtained was incorporated into the action of the play, which tells of the senseless maiming and killing that took place, of the strafing of villages and the systematic destruction of countryside and town. The play tells too of massive desertions to the North of South Vietnamese soldiers, often trained by the American Army, and Vietcong penetration into US bases through the very 'strategic hamlets' (hostage hamlets, in fact) set up by the Americans as 'protective shields' for their bases.

Among the sources mentioned in the bulletin-programme is Marcel Giuglaris's 'reportage' *Le Jour de l'Escalade*,[2] and a summary is provided of one of the chapters of the book entitled 'L'Opération Lance d'Argent'. This chapter, which Gatti admits to be the starting point of his play, describes a test manoeuvre alleged (by Giuglaris) to have been conducted in California in February 1965 for the purpose of studying subversive warfare at first hand, and of trying out and perfecting a new global strategy better suited to the modern rocket era. This strategy was designed to enable the United States to intervene anywhere in the world – not only in Vietnam – within the space of a few hours – seven, in fact – by means of mobile bases, namely the fleet, instead of from the cordon of peripheral fixed bases negotiated under Foster Dulles. The new operative factors were to be space, air and the seas.

This book would seem to have provided more than a starting point for the dramatic action of *V comme Vietnam*, possibly even determining the structure of the play together with the stage decoration which consisted of televisers, transmitters, telescriptors, etc. For those, like Gatti himself, far from the scene of action, some idea of the reality of the fighting could only be arrived at through such means of communication, even then it was necessarily a fragmented reality, and Gatti's play shows this clearly.

Faced with the further problem of deciding on his approach to the conflict, Gatti claimed that in the first place it was humanitarian: pity for the plight of the Vietnamese people. His approach changed to a humanistic one as men were involved on both sides and it was too easy, as a mere bystander, to apportion praise or blame. But in the face of the incredible resistance put up by the Vietnamese people, his approach finally became political: what, in fact, was the driving force behind their resistance? His conclusion was that they were defending not an ideology but a conception of man, a human being as against an inhuman robot. The conflict being therefore between two completely opposing conceptions of life, one or the other had to win; compromise was out of the question, and that made the outcome of the struggle a matter of universal concern.

Consequently Gatti set out to present on the stage two totally different civilizations: one the product of thinkers, electronic machines, high finance and nuclear weapons; the other the civilization of a peasant people possessing only their plot of land, their humanity and their human dignity. 'Rag bags in the rice paddies', when they stood upright they killed in self-defence with near-laughable weapons such as the nail-studded plank invented, so Phuong explains, by Trong Truc, a Vietnamese peasant, in 1860. Truc was executed by the French and died crying aloud: 'As long as the grass grows on this earth, there will always be men to resist the invader' (Scene. 18). The plank (the *planche à clous* of Gatti's play) was superseded by the 'shoe mine' made from razor-sharp slivers of bamboo set so as to pierce and infect the feet and legs of the new invaders whom the peasants resisted just as fanatically. In the play they tell stories of their land being bulldozed to make American bases, of the horrors of toxic gases, and of the cold-blooded murder of their families under their very eyes.

As usual with Gatti, there was no question of painting a realistic picture, all the more so as living, historical persons figure in the play. These are caricatured. Nevertheless, it is easy to recognize President Lyndon Johnson in the all-powerful Mégasheriff turned cowboy, nostalgically talking of the prowess of his Texan grandfather against the Indians at the Alamo; the Secretary of Defence McNamara in Quadrature; General Earle G. Wheeler, known as Bus the Mathematician, in his assistant Théo, short for Théorème; Cabot Lodge in the Ambassador Ventriloque, spokesman for the Pentagon; and in Père la Congrégation, Cardinal Spellman, who declared after celebrating Mass on the aerodrome of Saigon-Tan Son Nhut, on Christmas Eve, 1966: 'The Vietnam War is a war for the defence of civilization. It has been forced on us, we cannot give in to tyranny. Any other solution than victory is unthinkable' (Scene 10). The imperturbable commander of the 7th Fleet based at Camp Smith, Admiral Sharp, appears as Admiral Pointu, and the Pentagon's top-ranking expert on counter-guerrilla warfare, General

Two Plays for Special Occasions

Krulak, Commander of the Marines, nicknamed 'the Brute' because of his short stature, appears as General Bulldog. The retired General Ilikike of course needs no introduction, and Scene 8 echoes his statement on 3 October 1966 that, were he still President, he would not have excluded the use of nuclear weapons: 'the main thing is to win the war, everything else is secondary'. There is no caricature of the Vietnamese and the FNL hero Nguyen Hun Tang, Gatti's name for Nguyen Van Troy, who was executed for organizing an attempt on McNamara's life in Saigon in October 1966 (Scene 19 and 25). They are played 'straight'. Their role is to give the lie to the myth of an anonymous and all-powerful American technology.

The Pentagon with the arch-technocrat Quadrature, his band of assistants and a vast electronic brain, 'La Châtaigne' (the Chestnut, representing 'the Walnut', which seems to have been its official name) is at the centre of the play. The action takes place mostly in, or is followed as from the Pentagon, with news arriving from the various fronts and headquarters and by means of the electronic apparatus scattered around on the stage. This audiovisual presentation ensures a certain 'distancing' conducive to critical judgement on the part of the spectator, and avoids emotional involvement through direct representation. The data received are fed into the 'Chestnut', which occupied the back stage at the Grenier, and are analysed by it so as to obtain the information needed for the successful conduct of the test manoeuvre. As the news is relayed by the apparatus to the technocrats in the Pentagon, or is under discussion by them, it is simultaneously enacted by the Vietnamese in a series of flashes on a section of the stage reserved for the purpose. When the play is *performed* the technique of the *éclatement* of time and space is very effective, although a *reader* unfamiliar with dramatic technique of this kind may find it disconcerting.

The play opens with a discussion between the men of the Pentagon and a journalist who has just returned from a long stay in Vietnam. His articles in the '*New York Star*' have been highly critical of American policy towards that country. Quadrature's comment, 'Journalists and the Pentagon are not often in agreement', would appear to be a clear reference to the wide repercussions of Harrison E. Salisbury's critical articles in the *New York Times* of 12–19 January 1967, giving the lie to official communiqués. The discussion in the Pentagon is a prelude to Quadrature's announcement of a new global strategy designed to replace traditional military tactics. With all the sophisticated weapons at their command the United States, he says, would no longer 'be subjected to the laws of history, but to the laws of global geo-history which we shall call hyperhistory. Vietnam will no longer be a war but a problem. We shall not seek to pacify but to strike' – 'strike' in air-force slang meaning 'annihilate' (Scene 11).

Armand Gatti in the Theatre

'To kill abstractly, cleanly, without any morbid or sentimental implications, is the basic concern of the Department of Defence. Because to kill in this way is to create the future, whether one means to or not' (Scene 27). Quadrature echoes here *Petit-Rat*'s (Himmler's) 'preface to the new [Nazi] religion' in *Chroniques d'une planète provisoire*. For the test manoeuvre, which began on 29 February 1967 (according to Giuglaris), specific areas of Lower California and of California did duty for South Vietnam, North Vietnam and China into which Bulldog and the marines dreamed of carrying the war. Here Gatti touches on the problem of the real significance of the Vietnam War. Was it a war to end the conflict in Vietnam? Or was it a war aimed at containing a Communist China? America, so La Congrégation declared, would not be a 'paper tiger' (Scene 1).

To create the subversive element needed for the manoeuvre, 'Vietnamese' villages were built in California and an American commando was detailed to play the part of the Vietcong. They were dressed in black garments and spoke in Spanish in order to confuse 'true' American investigators. The manoeuvre was to continue until all defects had been eradicated through the computer. These details are retained in the play. The actual attack, with massive landings in Vietnam from the sea, took place, according to Giuglaris, on 8 March 1966. 'Lance d'Argent', which had 'proved' that a revolutionary war can be crushed by conventional forces based on the sea (Scene 16) is, in Quadrature's words, 'J. Day minus one of the Escalation'. In the play, the 'real' attack of J. Day is presented in the form of 'an opera' with the officials and the military as soloists and the Pentagon as the chorus. 'Hyperhistory had begun' (Scene 17).

Scenes figuring the Americans consist of discussions and arguments conducted either in person or by means of telephones, televiewers and the like. Democrats and Republicans are at loggerheads over the conduct of the war; so too the military and the technocrats of the Pentagon. The technocrats see the war as a 'problem to be solved' by 'thinkers not gladiators', to use Quadrature's formula: the military see the war in terms of direct and 'epoch-making hecatombs', and do not appreciate being reduced to the rank of mere executive machines in pursuance of a global policy dictated by technocrats.

As General Bulldog sees it, the individual will no longer get recognition for achievements because these will be determined by a computer: 'I am by way of no longer being General Bulldog, nor even a number, but of becoming the 11th degree of latitude North and the 124th degree of longitude East'. (Scene 19). To counter this demotion of the Services he attempts to sabotage the technocrats' test manoeuvre by giving the mock 'Vietcong' expert technical advice on how to wage successful guerrilla warfare. As a result these 'guerrillas' manage to capture a number of marines and even kidnap the Ambassador Ventriloque (Cabot Lodge, who had returned from Saigon to see the manoeuvre).

The final arbitrator between these dissenting factions is Mégasheriff Johnson, but his constant preoccupation with the elections makes him give the go-ahead first to the technocrats, then to the military, in the hope of redressing the balance of his popularity poll. He has a multiple image: he is Mégasheriff 'the Well-Beloved', Mégasheriff 'the Constructor', 'the Good', 'the near-creator of the prosperous Big Society', 'the Liar'. To give concrete expression on stage to these different images which represent 'the whole political career of the President', (stage directions, Scene 14) Gatti had recourse to the technique of *éclatement* used earlier in *Auguste Geai* where several actors together are needed to present a complete image of the single character, Auguste.

The escalation of the war brought problems. The electronic brains, with their unlimited capacity for absorbing objective and statistical data and providing solutions, calculating risks and limits to be observed — calculating even the cost in dollars of killing a single Vietcong — are unable to calculate human reactions; they remain impervious to the strength of feeling that can drive men to subversion, or inspire them to take up their cause, like the bonzes or the Quaker, Norman Morrison, who burned themselves to death in 1965 in protest against the war. Nor do they take account of the ever-growing number of young Americans who refused to serve in it, and readily accepted the consequences. These young men are represented in the play by Stanley Ross, the mock Vietcong whose refusal, at the end of the manoeuvre, is based on 'sentimental reasons' considered by him 'as valid as any other' (Scene 26). His 'sentimental reasons' were the death of Sophie Cunningham, who had worked with Ross as a mock Vietcong and had been captured by 'American' troops. They had interrogated her so brutally that she committed suicide.

In the same scene, even the technocrat Théo begins to have doubts. In all this mechanization he fails to find any meaning to the war. He questions the validity of the purely 'rational' approach: 'Facts and figures are certainly useful, but you should when necessary take some small account of instincts and feelings [...] my instinct tells me that the situation is different from that of the figures given by the computer.' Wrong questions had been put; right answers are elicited only by the right questions. When he says that although plans may be perfect on paper 'there is always a rebellious element in man', Théo puts his finger on the nub. To this Quadrature replies: 'You are mad, Théo! The global strategy is designed to prove that man can no longer rebel', yet as the peasant Tang declares (Scene 6), it is precisely the right of the people to rebel that the Vietnamese are defending.

How the most powerful of war machines can be held in check by a people convinced of their right, is represented scenically by the 'Chestnut' running amok and throwing up indigestible images of the reality of the war such as an American shot by a 'rat of the rice paddies' at the age of twenty-two after a truly American 'preparation for life'; a Negro from Alabama, killed at nineteen and refused burial alongside the Whites – Gatti alludes here to cavalier treatment meted out to the 'second-class citizens' used by the government to fight the Vietnam War (Scene 21 and 27). The computer also throws up groups of Vietnamese who listen to messages, often sad ones, from their families on their portable radios. According to Quadrature the 'Chestnut' has become a propaganda machine for the Vietcong, whereas the head of the psychological services diagnoses a 'neurosis' on the machine's part which makes it present 'an image of things which does not conform to the reality' (Scene 23). Alternatively sabotage is diagnosed, and Stanley Ross is summoned to 'confess' to having thrown a Vietnamese nail-studded plank into the computer's works, but he refuses to go back on his 'subversive' attitude to the war.

The technocrats for their part refuse to admit that they themselves could be wrong, and set about taking the computer to pieces to find out what is blocking its mechanism. The search allows for a 'gigantic kaleidoscopic revue' of the war with all the horrors of napalm, the mutilated bodies of children in a bombed-out school, the suicides of Morrison and of the bonzes, the anti-war marches in the US – a 'nightmare' because, to quote Quadrature, this was the point at which 'history was no longer history, and hyperhistory was not yet hyperhistory' (Scene 27).

To heighten the nightmare, the Johnson-figure comes on stage 'exploded' into five persons: a texan Mégasheriff and four Shakespearian Mégasheriffs, Macbeth and three kings, Richard III, Henry V, and Lear, because whenever the journalists spoke of Johnson at that time, they used the name of a Shakespearian character. The five persons sit enthroned on the wreckage of the 'Chestnut', and their conversation with Quadrature reiterates the main burden of the play: that 'mechanized reason' cannot embrace the total reality of the situation and its contingencies. The Texan Mégasheriff concludes that overwhelming force is the answer to the problem. 'Strike until not a soul is left', he says. Thereupon, not Malcolm but Vietcong guerrillas covered with 'Burnham Wood' foliage erupt from the 'Chestnut' and invade the Pentagon, making the 'invincible' Macbeth exclaim: 'It is like Bill Shakespeare's story. Look, the forest is on the march. The prophecy is being fulfilled.' 'But what are you waiting for?' Quadrature asks. 'The elections', comes the reply from all five. The elections were looming ahead and the Democrats had already lost ground. 'Get the Pentagon here', orders Quadrature.

At this point the theatrical fiction itself 'explodes', and the actor playing Quadrature (Sarrazin himself in this production[3]) steps out of his role to address himself angrily as an ordinary citizen to the men of the Pentagon. These appear on five television screens lowered from the flies, as in the opening scene. 'The whole of humanity', he says,

> is part of each of the rice paddies and jungles of Vietnam [...] There are death-dealing bullets; they are yours. And there are bullets which bring hope. Vietcong will be the name in our language for the man who stands erect under the sun. The forest is on the march – Let the prophecy be fulfilled

– the prophecy that the spirit of revolt in man cannot be indefinitely curbed, as some nations seem to believe.

When Gatti was finishing his play the war in Vietnam was still going on, so any invented dramatic conclusion would have been out of place. He therefore turned to the straightforward technique of anti-theatre to point to action that could be taken *outside* the theatre. This move is foreshadowed in an earlier scene (25) in which the dramatic action is unexpectedly suspended to allow the actors to welcome on stage, as if they were 'the spectators' collective voice', the silent figure of the dead hero Nguyen Van Troy, even though Troy is not a character in the play. For Gatti, Troy was the human element, the historical fact, more important than any dramatic structure: his part was taken by a real Vietnamese, different at every performance.

The main issue was the war and its appalling reality, and to keep it in the forefront of the spectators' mind Gatti had each performance prefaced with a reading of the day's communiqué. He considered the 'reading' to be the first stage of the 'dramatic event', the performance itself being the second. The 'third part of the play', which could go on for two hours, was the debate after the performance in which actors, director and author stepped out as individuals to discuss the play with the audience.

Seated in the auditorium in Toulouse were some Vietnamese soldiers from the Saigon front; also at times some American deserters who had been channelled to the performance under the auspices of the Committee which had commissioned the play. The Americans, whose identity could not be revealed, spoke as 'spectators' and supported the play's contention that the escalation of the invasion had indeed been planned almost entirely with reference to the computer, but their fellow-spectators would have none of it. They claimed to know more about America because they had 'friends and relatives there', and they took no heed of the obvious accent of the American speakers. The Vietnamese fared little better. There were, however, rewarding moments in some of the discussions and Gatti mentions the insight of a woman, 'the ideal spectator',[4] who declared: 'For me the nail-studded plank is the American conscientious objector who says 'no' to the Vietnam War'. Gatti complimented her, saying that these were the words of the true spectator who constructs the play for himself. This led the lady to confess that the play had made her want to be a nail-studded plank herself. In Lausanne, where the company was on tour, one of the actresses saw the plank as the symbol of the growing opposition to the war of Americans for whom the democratic character of their regime was an article of faith.

As often with a Gatti play, more than a single viewing or reading is needed to arrive at a full appreciation, so packed is it with facts and ideas. For example, the question of the validity of humanitarianism raised by Vietnamese peasants who class two Americans of goodwill among the invaders because of their refusal to countenance violence as a means to end violence may easily pass unnoticed, so short is the scene (18). Or one might not immediately relate to the 'Texanization' of the Pentagon, the comico-satirical scene where the Mégasheriff and his entourage, dressed as cowboys as though in a saloon bar in a Western, play poker and draw guns upon each other for a mere word. At a rehearsal Gatti explained this scene as being a scene in the future, yet at the same time a scene in the past: the Johnson story compiled and related in the future by the computer.

There is hardly an aspect of the Vietnam conflict which is not given dramatic expression. The reading of works of Mao Tse-tung and Ngo Dyen Giap by Bulldog and Quadrature, for example, is no fiction but a reference to the study of these and other texts on subversive warfare made by General Karch at the Jungle School in Okinawa. As for the scene about the school teacher, Tran Van Luyen's new Encyclopaedia, Gatti told Robert Bois[5] that it was a sort of guerrilla handbook for the Vietcong compiled with the guile and inventiveness of a determined people fighting their war with, as their weapons, common objects of their daily lives: bamboo slivers, frogs, monkeys, even bees trained to attack (Scene 20). In *Napalm* (Scene 22) André Benedetto writes much the same thing: 'Everything can become a weapon in our expert hands' – bamboo sliver traps, the stretched bow with arrows poisoned, 'fighting bees'.

In Gatti's play the idea of 'fighting bees' is Phuong's contribution to the guerrilla warfare. It is also his contribution, under the letter A [*abeille*], to the Encyclopaedia that the guerrillas are compiling. The last contribution to the Encyclopaedia comes from the peasant Tang and gives the play its title: 'An animal with green hair (like elephant grass), difficult to ensnare, and when he stands upright changes the face of the world. Put that at the letter V (like Vietnam).' Luyen: 'V like Vietnam. Yes, I've put it'. (Scene 18).

Two Plays for Special Occasions

In the Grenier's production, this V was an enormous structure covered with names of American offensives – 1886 Geronimo, 1945 Hiroshima, etc. – and also the slogan 'We shall win through'. At its base was the computer, the 'Chestnut', with numerous screens inset. These, like the television sets which came down from the flies at the beginning and end of the play, were frames with a light at the base that could be switched on by the actors standing behind them whenever they were due to 'appear on the screen'. By modern scientific means, everything that happens in places as far apart as the beaches of California, the Pacific and Vietnam can be seen in the Pentagon, just as in Corneille's *L'Illusion comique* far off events are seen in the grotto through the powers of the magician.

Between this play of 1967 on the Vietnam War and Gatti's play on the Second World War, *Chroniques*, on which he was currently working in Toulouse, there are a number of striking similarities of theme and dramatic technique, particularly in the presentation of contemporary historical figures. In both plays they appear as grotesque, inhuman, puppet-like creations, and stand in strong contrast with the truly human figures of the camp deportees in the one play and the Vietnamese in the other, and with the pair of lovers in both plays.

Whereas in *Chroniques* the Nazi leader is symbolized by a curious machine making sporadic appearances to direct the crazy logic of the action, in *V comme Vietnam* the machine is a real machine, the 'Chestnut', and is present on stage throughout the action. According to a sketch in the Toulouse bulletin-programme, Quadrature's suit, covered with a design of computer parts, clearly relates him to McNamara himself. Later, during the tour of the play, Gatti said in his interview with Robert Bois: 'This man ended up by resembling the machine, by thinking like the machine, by having the same type of intelligence as the machine. It was the machine that did the thinking.' His explanation bears out the stage direction following Mégasheriff's refusal to accept Quadrature's resignation: 'Thereupon, the great computer Quadrature starts to work again with the precision of a machine' (scene 14).

Whether any assimilation of American leaders of the time with Nazi leaders of yesterday was intended or not, the fact remains that each of the two plays presents a fearful image of the dictatorship of absolute logic for which the life of an individual counts for nothing. The role of technical progress in the creation of such a situation is underlined in both, and similarly the 'mission' which Nazi and American leaders would seem to have arrogated to themselves: Scene 6 contains a pointed reference to the periodic appearance throughout the centuries of an elite people who seek to 'hammer the rest of the universe into their own likeness'. The leaders of the *Chroniques* seek 'without hatred' to regenerate the Jewish 'hiatus' by means of gas ovens, and those of *V comme Vietnam* expect to convince the Third World of the benefits of US protectionism through gun-and-bludgeon diplomacy indiscriminately and abstractly employed. 'Were not things so much better in the opposite camp?' they imagine the young Vietcong of the future saying (Scene 27). The 'Jewish problem' has here as its counterpart Vietnam, 'a problem, an operational computation' and not a matter for military tactics.

In both plays the themes of the dehumanization and the enslavement of man by the very machine which could have served as an instrument of liberation are fundamental: Quadrature himself conjures up the image of the sorcerer's apprentice. Gatti does not attack the United States, nor does he, despite his solid documentation, present the spectator with a 'documentary'. Using the facts of history in an imaginative theatrical fiction he seeks to engage the spectator in serious reflection on a conflict, the course of which questions the meaning and value of what is called civilization.

V comme Vietnam was put on at the Grenier on 4 April 1967, with Gatti as director, and ran until 30 April when it went on tour. Its title at the Grenier was *La Nuit des Rois de Shakespeare par les comédiens de Toulouse face aux événements du Sud-Est Asiatique (V comme Vietnam)*, because the production of Shakespeare's *Twelfth Night* (*La Nuit des Rois*) billed by the Grenier for April had been deferred at the request of many of the theatre's season-ticket holders who had asked to see *V comme Vietnam* instead, as its subject was so topical. The theatre's bulletin-programme refers to *V comme Vietnam* as 'a play commissioned of an author by a public' and stresses the importance of live theatre as the 'mutual activity of a public, a company of actors, and a playwright'. The bulletin also juxtaposes two photographs illustrating the 'same universe of violence'. One is from *King Lear* (Act V) and shows a despairing Lear on stage grasping a piece of red-stained rope with which, for our imagination, Cordelia has been strangled. The other is from the reality of the Vietnam War and shows two soldiers actually strangling a Vietnamese woman with a rope which has torn her skin and has become soaked in her blood. The bulletin concludes that when reality resembles fiction to this point it has its place in the theatre, where it can stir the conscience as deeply as any tragedy.

For this production Gatti did not himself choose his actors and according to him they were very much 'right of centre', and more in tune with classical plays than with plays on subjects like the Vietnam War. In addition to feeling some disappointment on this score, he had to face up to 'rather severe' criticism from the French Communist Party, which referred to the current dispute between Peking and Moscow and accused Gatti of favouring China in his play. Gatti replied that he had no intention of adding to the dispute; he was a humble dramatist who had

Two Plays for Special Occasions

tried to write a play on the reality of the Vietnam War, and he countered the Party's objection to Phuong's statement in the last scene that the Vietnamese wanted 'not peace but victory', by saying that 'victory' for the Vietnamese did not mean that Vietnam would carry out a landing in the USA but that a country which had already experienced French colonization, for a long time, would seek to regain its freedom and its identity.

II Les Treize Soleils de la rue Saint-Blaise

The second of Gatti's plays to be written for a special occasion is *Les Treize Soleils de la rue Saint-Blaise*. As a stage play it is the least successful of Gatti's works for the theatre but it is interesting on two accounts: first because it shows a switch of emphasis in Gatti's preoccupation with playwriting as an individual activity to that of play-creating as a collective activity, and secondly because it provides a prophetic glimpse of May 1968, and the role theatre can play.

In July 1967, the bulletin of the Théâtre de l'Est Parisien (The TEP), the Centre Dramatique for the 20e *arrondissement* of Paris, announced a theatrical 'experiment' under the title *Les Treize Soleils de la rue Saint-Blaise*. For this experiment Guy Rétoré, director of the TEP, invited thirty members of his regular audiences to come and discuss with Armand Gatti and himself the problems of their daily life that they would like to see treated in a dramatic work. It was intended that the role of author should devolve on the spectators themselves and live sessions were arranged under the chairmanship of a theatre historian, Émile Copfermann, with a group of theatre-goers which included teachers, trade unionists, two priests and a West Indian immigrant but no representative of manual workers, as it was understood that these did not frequent the theatre.

Discussions ranged over a variety of topics: housing, trade unionism, the exploitation of workers and the soul-destroying 'mechanization' to which they were subjected, working-class militancy, holidays, sport, television, the tote, the insidious advertising of the 'Affluent Society', and finally the situation created by the decision of the Paris Préfecture to demolish the Charonne Quarter of the 20e *arrondissement* to make way for prestige buildings. Notes and recordings taken during the sessions were put at Gatti's disposal. He was to write up the material provided by the group. It would, however, be wrong to see in the final product 'a collective creation', as did a number of critics and possibly Rétoré himself, since such had been his initial intention. The element of 'creation' is to be found in the use made by the artist, Gatti, of the material at hand.

Gatti found the discussions interesting but unrewarding from a dramatic point of view, and admitted that the final text was much more the product of his own imagination than of the imagination of the group. The group realized this on listening to a reading of the text. They saw the material they had provided as being mere grist to Gatti's private mill, and even though they recognized certain ideas and phrases as their own, they felt they had had no part in the authorship of the play.

On the other hand the problem that faced Gatti as a playwright, and which he solved only at a third attempt, was how to create an imaginative work out of the overabundant 'documentation' provided by people whose experience he did not share, any more than they did his. He finally solved the problem during a stroll along the picturesque rue Saint-Blaise in the heart of the condemned Charonne district, where the houses and the little bar, 'Au Soleil levant', were to be replaced by thirty-storey blocks of 'luxury flats' by order of the Paris Préfecture. Some of the group saw in the projected 'decent accommodation' a sign of the 'rise of the working-class'. Others saw the cost of these 'futuristic monuments' as intended to force the existing inhabitants of this patently Red working-class area of Paris out into 'ghettos' in nearby Aubervilliers and Saint-Denis. Echoes of both these arguments are to be heard in the play.

Gatti's walkabout, coupled with the *phrase-miracle* 'I would like to be a sun to light the world' of the West Indian, in reply to the question 'What would you like to be?', sparked off in his mind an idea for a plot: at an evening class in the rue Saint-Blaise, thirteen adult students would be asked to write an essay imagining themselves as suns rising each day over the thoroughfare during its provisional reprieve. Would the suns approve of its destruction, or disapprove? What would they hope to find in its place?

The 'concrete situation' of the impending demolition of the quarter provides the starting point of the play, but the action moves swiftly into the imaginary worlds of the *personnages-soleils*, doubles emanating from the students' imagination, each bearing the name of his 'thinker' [*celui qui le pense*] and speaking and acting on his behalf. Transitions between the real and the imaginary worlds are made with the help of musicians whose theme song, *La Ballade de l'échelle*, begins 'Each is a sun' (actually an oft-repeated profession of faith of Gatti's). The ballade, with its variants, details man's lived experience which gravitates around him in much the same way as the stars and planets gravitate around the authentic sun.

Both worlds, real and imaginary, are present on stage at the same time, the real world on the front stage where the students work silently at their desks under the eye of the teacher, Mlle Blanc, and the world as imagined by the Suns stretching far behind them. In the TEP production the Suns burst through the students' giant copybook pages which formed the wings of the stage, and descended each on his own 'thinker'.

Two Plays for Special Occasions

Indeterminate at first, with no special 'attributes' – that is to say they do not express any individual lived experience – the Suns gradually become more determinate until they finally obtain their autonomy at the cutting of the 'umbilical cords' that bind them to their creators, and go their separate ways in a 'parallel' world.

The Suns vary in character. They are listed in the *dramatis personae* alongside their own separate names and social status: as 'reflective', 'moderate', 'municipal', 'protesting', 'baroque', 'unsatisfied', 'eccentric', 'commemorative', 'subordinate', and in the case of the bill-sticker son of a Catalan anarchist, 'marginal'. Three students have no parallel Suns. Boulise, being unemployed, thinks she has no interest in possible developments in the area and sees herself as a sunflower. The Algerian, Ali Amrani, for whom the fate of the street is a purely French affair, imagines not a sun but a cock-bird, the promise of all dawns to come. Hervé, a West Indian newly arrived in France, finds the subject of the essay too difficult for him.

Despite its pertinence to the problem of the area's future, Gatti clearly did not intend *Les Treize Soleils* to be a treatise on town planning but a dramatic exploration of the dreams and aspirations of the characters he had created out of his discussions with the group. Whatever their political views, all had wanted the 'collective play' to deal with the problems of militancy, but Gatti objected that he had already treated it in *Un Homme seul*, so the debate was directed towards the problems created by the 'Affluent Society' and the pressures it exerts on the individual.

Although this is the basic theme of the play, the theme of the militant worker is carefully fitted into it. The 'Affluent Society' and its effects on the individual are very fully discussed in the 'six days' of Scene 2. Here the Suns, who have gone home to finish their essays, gather on the rooftops to examine the predicament of the men, women and children of this society. The 'Man Commission' finds the concrete definition of 'man' in his pay packet, his tax forms, the tote, sport, or the car seen as a symbol of his virility. The commission on the predicament of women presents a depressing picture of women as slaves to advertisements and the children's commission, which tried to make the cock-bird understand that he is a Sun with a duty to light up the world, discovers that the young have become 'racists' as regards their elders.

The Suns react to their predicament in one of two ways. One group looks back nostalgically to the Commune of 1871, symbolized by a watch presented to Eugène Varlin, hero and martyr of the Commune. Although it had been stolen by the officer in charge of the execution squad, the watch is still felt to beat in the rue Saint-Blaise trod by Varlin on his way to the bloody barricades of Belleville, Menilmontant and Charonne. Rouget, the Commemorative Sun, is a municipal worker and makes it his business to relate the street to one of the glorious moments of the history of the Commune. Was not the heroic *Mur des Fédérés* only a few steps away? Brousse, the Marginal Sun, is of the same political persuasion: 'In the rue Saint-Blaise the Commune hangs like a green fruit. It is up to us to help it ripen' (p. 45).

In contrast to these revolutionary Suns, intent on creating a new society and not merely embellishing the 'Affluent Society' of today, there are those who are only too happy to remain within the gilded prison of existing society, within the 'canary cage'. They are content with holidays which open up the perspective of escape into the world of dreams. But holidays signify capitulation and, says Gatti, these few short weeks of relief from the unpalatable working year are like a bone thrown to a dog. As seaside holidays are the workers' dream, the Eccentric Sun's proposal is to flood the rue Saint-Blaise and line it with beaches. This finds special favour. 'With underwater fishing, monitors and chance encounters, holidays are an unquestionably enriching experience', says the Subordinate Sun. For his part the Municipal Sun maintains that 'in bathing trunks you can't tell a worker from his boss. The rue Saint-Blaise transformed into a seaside resort, there's progress for you' (pp. 67–8). The proposition is so alluring that the ranks of the 'holiday-makers' are soon swollen by defectors from amongst the formerly revolutionary-minded. Barricades carry little weight beside holidays, as Mlle Blanc remarks.

Mlle Blanc, Gatti's newest portrait of authority, finds little to commend in the attitude of the Suns. She considers them to be destructive of society, or else unambitious and inadequate. Whip in hand, this incarnation of elitist culture transforms her class into a real concentration camp. She heaps humiliation after humiliation on her pupils, and even forces Rouget, after his declaration of love to her, to crawl on all fours while she rides astride on his back, both as woman and as teacher, until finally he and the other Suns are driven to rebel and to unhorse her. In a resurgence of the Communard spirit they throw her 'into the 18th of March' the first day of the Commune.

A further challenge to authority comes from the barricades set up by the revolutionary Suns round the two enormous pointers of Varlin's watch which still ticked after he had been shot on the very spot where the Sacré Coeur church now stands. With Varlin dead, that watch, for one of the inhabitants of the rue Saint-Blaise, was the Primordial Sun. That sun alone could shine on the rue Saint-Blaise, and the Suns' action highlights their hostility to the elitist culture embodied in the teacher. According to Brousse, the Marginal Sun, such a culture is no more than 'the warming up of dead festivals of the mind', lifted out of the context which gave them their urgency in the past: in this way great revolutions become 'inhabitable events' with 'hot and cold water laid on and air-conditioning'. What Brousse asks for is a broad human culture, the fruit of one's confrontation with the realities of everyday life: its ambitions, its worries, its violence. He wants a culture pregnant with the realization of his potential, not a referential culture taken from bookshelves, 'the paradise of dead references'.

This, of course, is not in line with Mlle Blanc's notion of culture, and her marking of the students' essays shows it. Three alone get the pass mark and become eligible for 'Higher Spheres'. Top mark goes to Sulviviani, the house-painter who rises to the status of artist. Those below the pass mark are consigned to the waste-paper basket, or rather the 'dustbins of history'. Doussel, with a 'glorious' 0 out of 10, is completely excluded from the teacher's system of references and so remains independent.

When Scene 4 opens, the rejected Suns are on stage in their separate dustbins, each of which bears the distinctive stamp of its occupant's calling – for example that of Mireille Berque, the Moderate Sun (an employee in the clothing trade) is a Monoprix (a Woolworth's) hung with deodorants and sprays of the 'Affluent Society'. However, a curious stage direction at the head of this scene (4) makes it clear that the condemned Suns are not resigned to their lot; it reads: 'The German quarters in Displaced Persons camps should serve here as an indication. A placard states: "An Aim: the primordial Sun".' In the words of two of the condemned Suns, the Primordial sun is 'an image of ourselves which is greater than ourselves'. Such an image offers the only means of escape from the capitalist 'Art of Living' or the capitalist reduction of man to an unthinking machine. To achieve this aim there must be concerted action, but tactical and ideological differences amongst the Suns prevent this. These differences range from Brousse's demand for the 'apocalypse now', which frightens the more timid Suns, to actual collaboration with the 'Affluent Society'. Brousse concludes that the Primordial Sun is obscured by the elitist culture of dead references that they have been taught, and that it can be reached only by starting from Varlin's watch: that is to say, by following an authentically revolutionary path. According to the Eccentric Sun, the solution to the stalemate is not to believe themselves to be Suns but to become authentic Men. Given their combined acceptance of injustice, violence, greed, their delight in the comforts of the 'Affluent Society' and the tote with its weekly escape into dreams, they have finally to admit that they 'have set off on the wrong foot'.

A last attempt by them as Suns to reach the Primordial Sun takes them along the path traced by the West Indian street-sweeper, promoted to Black Sun by the group. In dutifully sweeping straight ahead of him he has prolonged the rue Saint-Blaise beyond all geographical possibility through Paris as far as Orly Airport. The dustbins of history, transformed into cosmic vessels, take off from there. In the TEP production, the flight was depicted by means of film strips projected on to a cyclorama. In front of it the pointers of Varlin's watch racing round anticlockwise took time back through history to the Commune on which the cosmic vessels founder, but as Gatti wrote in the programme, though 'many of these Suns will end their trajectory in the dustbins of history, there will always be one left to say that dawn is near, and to believe in it implicitly.' Standing beneath the pointers of Varlin's watch, two Suns remain firm in their belief: they are Doussel, the Reflective Sun, and Marpeaux, the Unsatisfied Sun. Doussel bows to the great figures of the Commune, gone but still present in the mind, and 'leaving the impression that all has not been said'. It was up to them to invent a new culture, to draw it out of what they were themselves. This too is Marpeaux's belief. The final words of the play are his: 'Beyond the dead suns, there must be a tiny hole through which the rue Saint-Blaise goes on and on.' Gatti himself said that the conception of culture put forward in the play is at complete variance with what is presupposed by the word 'culture' in our 'Affluent Society.'

When the play was performed on the 15 March 1968, the Paris press was even more virulent than they were against *Le Crapaud buffle*, but with a certain justification. What, they asked, was meant by this revolt against scholarship and by barricades in the second third of the twentieth century? As things turned out, the play anticipated the students' revolt and the barricades of the month of May by only a few weeks. During the student demonstrations performances took place in what Gatti describes as an extraordinary atmosphere, with the Confédération Général du Travail and the Communist Party rallying around them. Each night Gatti went to the theatre to discuss with the audience the why and wherefore of the barricades, and whether Varlin's watch had or had not stopped. He also suggested interrupting the performance at some point or other to allow the audience to carry on from there, but with some irredentist claimants demanding to see the whole performance as they had paid for it, the matter often ended in fisticuffs in the auditorium until the day when the CGT, with Rétoré's approval, occupied the theatre. Three attempts by the local inhabitants to get them out failed.

Since then *Les Treize Soleils* has been performed in a number of countries as being representative of May 1968 in France. Gatti made the same point in a discussion with Denis Bablet[6] in 1971 when he said that what occurred in France in May 1968 was already in his play on the level of the imagination with the barricades, the challenge to inherited culture, the demand for new human relations. Without May 1968 he might well have turned his back on the theatre altogether, because he no longer found it possible to continue on the lines he had followed for ten years in the Centres Dramatiques. Not that the events of May solved any problems for him. They did, however, highlight the fact that the theatre itself could not enter directly into the social struggle, and furthermore that the theatre could never be integrated into the 'three-shift system' – that is, into working-class life – despite the efforts made by the Centres Dramatiques to popularize it. If he was to cater for the working-class world, Gatti realized that he would have to make a completely fresh start and it would have to be made outside the constraints of theatre buildings. His mini-plays written later that year and in 1969 – and more conclusively the two experiments at Louvain University, *La Colonne Durruti* (1971–2) and *L'Arche d'Adelin* (1972–3), – testify to this development in his thinking.

As an experiment in an organized reversal of the role of author and spectator, *Les Treize Soleils* cannot be said to have been a success. Nor did it create a truly popular theatre at the TEP, as seems to have been Rétoré's intention. Gatti's earlier play at Villeurbanne, *Auguste Geai*, with Auguste's insistent question: 'Alors cette révolution, elle vient?' that relates it thematically to *Les Treize Soleils*, and with 'Le Chant des CRS' which foreshadows 'La ballade de l'échelle', came much nearer to creating such a theatre, doubtless because it sprang from Gatti's intimate experience of life amongst the lower social classes and had a directness of appeal which the more cerebral approach in *Les Treize Soleils* lacks.

Moreover *Auguste Geai* is not obscured by the proliferation of metaphors, symbols and abstractions that weighs on *Les Treize Soleils* despite its simple starting point. The ordinary daily preoccupations of a group of people of the *20^e arrondissement*, doubtless expressed by them in simple terms, become forbiddingly symbolic in the play. One might even see the *phrase-miracle* which triggered off the idea for the play as a *phrase-catastrophe*. Furthermore, despite a certain didactic intent, *Les Treize Soleils* does not give the workers for whom it was intended any lead as to how to achieve their cultural revolution. There are, notwithstanding, a number of interesting moments in this parable of the Revolution which is treated somewhat in the manner of Brecht, with music, songs, and *tableaux vivants* of fiery figures and working-class profiles. A description of the staging, scene by scene, appears in the theatre's *Documentation No. 9* (19 March, 1968) together with sketches of the set and its varying rearrangements.

Whatever its shortcomings as a play or as a production – it was directed by Rétoré – this Rétoré/Gatti experiment seems to have given an impetus to a movement for 'Collective creations' that many small companies were subsequently to join. One of the most interesting is the Nouvelle Compagnie d'Avignon. Barely three months after the production of *Les Treize Soleils* the company's director, André Benedetto, was invited by the Maison de la Culture in Le Havre to write a play 'in collaboration with the workers of the town'. The resulting work, *Emballage*, described by Benedetto as 'an analysis of merchandise according to the Marxist method', is an interesting piece of work but no more a 'collective creation' than was *Les Treize Soleils*, even though its substance was provided by the discussions Benedetto had had with the workers. Benedetto is as clearly the *author* of *Emballage*, as Gatti is of *Les Treize Soleils*.

In contrast to Gatti's play, which was incorporated into the normal repertory of a Centre Dramatique in a working-class district, Benedetto's had the advantage of being put on at the Labour Exchange in Le Havre, so it became an action not only *for* but *with* the workers who could identify with the main role, with 'Alexandre Zacharie, l'homme qui ne possède rien que lui-même, se vend', to quote the plays's subtitle. The audience of the TEP, which is a more general audience, could not so easily identify with the Suns of Gatti's play, and Rétoré's production, with which Gatti was not in complete agreement, bore some responsibility – though admittedly not all – for this. The production took no account of the black humour which colours the text, nor did it bring out the human dimension which the play actually possesses. The bemused spectator tended to find himself before an unfathomable dramatic event, at least until the events of May 1968 made of it such a topical composition.

Notes

1. *Dépêche du Midi*, 4 April 1967.
2. L'Air du Temps, Gallimard, 1966.
3. Sarrazin confessed to being ill at ease at this point in the play.
4. 'Notes au spectateur idéal, selon Armand Gatti,' interview with Jean Michaud-Maillaud, *Les Lettres Françaises*, 15–21 June 1967.
5. *Réforme*, 17 June, 1967.
6. *Travail Théâtral*, No. 3, June.

References

Le Courrier du Vietnam, 46 Tran Hung Dao, Hanoi.
4ᵉ année, Nos 101–2. 13–20 March 1967 and supplement, No. 102, 20 March 1967.
Association d'Amitié Franco-Vietnamienne, Paris 7ᵉ. 5 rue Las Cazes: No. 1 Colloque du 19 novembre 1966, 'La Guerre chimique au Vietnam'; No. 18, June 1967, 'Documents' on the war in Vietnam.

8
Spain: A Constant Preoccupation

La Passion du Général Franco. La Passion du Général Franco par les émigrés eux-mêmes

With *La Passion du Général Franco* there was a certain amount of purpose-building, particularly in the preliminary stages. But Spain was also a constant preoccupation of Gatti's and had been since before the time of his Cuban visit. His attempts to write on Spain were, however, long-drawn out. They began as early as 1963 when he was busy with the first production of *Chroniques d'une planète provisoire* in Toulouse. Toulouse was the headquarters of the CNT (Confederación nacional del Trabjo; the confederation of trade unions) in exile, and it was at the request of Spanish exiles in the town, labourers and floor-tiling specialists for the most part, that Gatti wrote a number of 'sequences' for performances in Spanish by Spanish amateur dramatic groups for audiences of Spanish refugees, with the proceeds going to the strikers in the Asturian coal-mines. The mobilization of a whole Spanish community around this common cause gave these sequences a sense of immediacy which was quite new in Gatti's work for the theatre so far. They could even be seen as a forerunner of the 1968 mini-plays.

The content and structure of the sequences were determined by the circumstances in which they were written. The diaspora of the Spanish refugees throughout the world was their experience, and Gatti dramatized this in four 'trajets' which were documented by his lengthy discussions with the exiles, as his personal contact with Spain had been of the briefest – in 1961, at Barcelona Airport, he and his Siamese cat, which his young son Stéphane, had brought along to welcome him after his success with *L'Enclos* at the Moscow Film Festival, were refused admittance to the country. Now, he says, he is better known in Spain than in France, because of the affair of *La Passion du Général Franco*. Each of the 'trajets' was to present a different form of emigration. Each was to consist of six sequences needing only three actors. Any of the 'trajets' or separate sequences could be performed by itself because each was self-contained. They could be put on anywhere, as little was required by way of sets.

Gatti subsequently decided to make a 'professional' play from this material. He kept the idea of the Spanish 'diaspora' and knitted the various itineraries together. In the play as published in 1968 before its proposed performance at the TNP – and doubtless much as it existed already on 2 November 1965, when Gatti gave the first of its many public readings to an audience of trade unionists at the Théâtre de Plaisance in Paris – each sequence in a particular 'trajet' marks a new stage in the itinerary of the three characters concerned. The Communist ex-combatants en route for Krasnoyarsk, for example, are seen first at Kiev Airport, later in a plane over the Urals, approaching Kazan, and finally at the airport in Krasnoyarsk. Gatti paints a vivid picture of this town and the surrounding gold- and copper-mines in his book *Sibérie − zéro + l'Infini*.

In between the six sequences of the Kiev–Krasnoyarsk itinerary representing exile, the six sequences of each of the three other itineraries, 'Madrid–Frankfurt' ('economic' emigration to the factories of the EEC), 'Toulouse–Madrid' (a mission, real or imagined), and 'Havana–Mexico' (exile) are intercalated. The Havana–Mexico (trajet) was inspired by Gatti's visit the previous year to Cuba to make the film *El otro Cristobal*, and it contains echoes of the Santiago Carnival, the aftermath of the Cuban Revolution, and the vigilance of the Cuban militia before the expected invasion at the Bay of Pigs on which is superimposed, as in a film, an image of the Durruti brigade during the defence of Madrid.

At times all the characters are brought together, despite the concrete fact of their geographical dispersal. Because Gatti's characters do not move about in real time and space but in 'mental time and space', this is possible. The first occasion comes at the end of the opening Kiev–Krasnoyarsk sequence when they all gather together to introduce themselves and explain their different predicaments, and intone together the 'lament' of the city of Madrid from which 'all its children are fleeing'. The 'lament' ends: 'Notre ville/par tant de peines/tant de gares/tant de neuvièmes mois mis bout à bout: comme les grains du rosaire se terminant toujours/sur la même croix.'

In the professional version a new dimension is thus added to the original idea of the Spanish 'diaspora', that of a 'passion' suffered not by Franco but by the emigrants themselves.[1] The extended title of the 1975 version, *La Passion du Général Franco par les émigrés eux-mêmes*, makes this clear. In the opening sequence of this version one of the emigrants, a new character called Carlos, states that any objective study of Franco would have led to the writing of a psychological play in line with usual theatre products. But Gatti was not interested in individual psychology; he was interested in Francoism; and it was through the prism of the exiles and emigrations which Franco's ascent to power had caused that he sought to examine this social phenomenon.

Spain: a Constant Preoccupation

The enigmatic title, *La Passion du Général Franco*, is explained at the beginning of the 1968 version, when the characters en route for Krasnoyarsk talk of the fight they intended to carry on at a distance against General Franco's 'crusade', a crusade which was an unending calvary with tens of thousands of crosses. 'This is a Passion, a Passion on the scale of a whole people', they declare. In the final sequence of their itinerary, they elaborate on their definition:

> It is not Franco who dies on this Calvary [...] Franco [...] was made by guns. Guns are inert matter. They kill but create nothing. It is not Franco who dies in this Passion, nor is it Franco who is resuscitated. It is us.

These final lines of the play are spoken by the Asturian miners, several thousands of whom had been 'shot in groups' by Franco's troops under the monarchy and later under the Republic. They rise from the dead with their spirit unbroken to welcome the exiles: 'Wherever you may be, it is your country [Republican Spain] which welcomes you.'

There is little action as such in the various sequences. Gatti sought to paint the past, not to imagine the future, so he built the play around the memories of the Spanish exiles with whom he had been in contact in Toulouse: in the absence of lived experience of his own, the lived experience of others was his subject matter. To present these memories Gatti uses a number of different techniques, including the materialization on stage of memories which haunt the characters. As Pancho dozes in the plane over the Urals, he relives the horror of the '*paseo*': that is, the summary execution of citizens at the gates of Seville, and the subsequent defiling of their corpses by fine ladies of the city.

Gatti also materializes stories told by the exiles, such as Gil's oft-repeated yarn of a sportsman who aims at a partridge and shoots down a plane. This yarn prepares Franco's entry on stage in a shooting jacket, and allows for allusions to be made to the opportune deaths in plane crashes of Franco's political rivals such as General Sanjurjo. Then there is the story told to Ricardo by Luis, a fellow-emigrant, on the train journey to Frankfurt. It is about his father, a Falangist who had disappeared fighting with the Blue Division on the Eastern front, and about his own hopeless 'mental' search for his father. This too is materialized on stage, as is the account later given by Luis (in Frankfurt) to his mother (in Madrid) of events leading up to Ricardo's suicide. Ricardo, a Republican, had been caught in possession of bombs when on a visit to Spain, and had been forced to act as a Francoist agent and spy on his fellow-workers in Frankfurt in order to save his life.

Play-acting by the characters is another of the techniques. Gatti uses it to illustrate the favourite topic of conversation of the Spanish exiles who gather on Sundays on Frankfurt Station, as though after church:

Colonel Eymar, the iniquitous judge of the military court and second to none in the whole history of Francoism as an inventor of 'terrorist activities against the army'. They mockingly take him off in imagined trial scenes. These mock trials then 'dissolve', as in a film, into 'genuine' trials, the final victim being Joaquin, a student of twenty-six who is too young to have fought in the Civil War and has been attracted to Cuba by the Cuban Revolution. Always a Spaniard at heart, however, he returns to Spain to play his part in the revolutionary movement of his own country. This means leaving Soledad, with whom he is in love. She also has played a part in the Cuban Revolution in the campaign against illiteracy, but she leaves Cuba for Mexico with her uncle Miguel, a former militant of the anarcho-syndicalist Partido Obrero de Unificación Marxista (POUM) He has remained a 'prisoner of the lost revolution' and hopes to join the Spanish revolutionary government in exile. On her arrival in Mexico Soledad scans the press for news about the Madrid trials. As she silently reads the papers the course of the trials of Joaquin and others, rigged by Eymar, is materialized on stage. She reads the sentence aloud – thirteen years' imprisonment. She murmurs: 'And when you come out of prison you will be old (yes!). We shall be old.'

A different technique is used in an earlier scene. Soledad is on board a ship for Mexico and Gatti imagines a conversation between her and her mother, Violetera, whom she has never known but whose image haunts her. She learns that only minutes after giving birth to her, her mother had been dragged out to be shot in place of Soledad's father, who was a member of the Durruti column but has escaped. 'Rejoice, your child is pardoned', her mother was told. In Toulouse, Marino, a member of an anarchist brigade, is haunted by a date, June 1937 – the date of the fall of Bilbao, the date when his daughter, aged eleven, was raped then bayoneted to death by four Moorish soldiers under the helpless gaze of the statue of Saint Francis of Assisi. This date, Marino says to Saint François, who calls on him like an old friend, is all that is left to him of his child.

The saint's reply further elucidates the word 'Passion' as used here by Gatti. In order to be canonized, the saint says, one had, in his time, to assume the Passion oneself even to its consummation. But things had changed under an almost canonized Franco; it was others who died, Christ and his cohort of saints alike. The scene turns into a strange corrida organized by anti-working-class Church dignitaries in which this 'reproduction' of Saint François, doing duty as the proletarian bull, is put to death by Falangist and Carlist red-bereted banderilleros. This ceremonial slaughter of a 'reproduction' of the saint is intended to underline the unending atrocities of the continued repression in Spain.

In *La Passion*, *all* the numerous characters are haunted by their past, but this past is no longer a closed personal past as in *La Deuxième Existence du Camp de Tatenberg* or even *Auguste Geai*; it is projected into the present and is the past-present of a whole people. At the same time the past – that is to say, the lived experience of the various emigrants, together with their reasons for leaving Spain or returning to it, their political outlook, their particular preoccupations – is all carefully detailed by Gatti. Their respective life stories are the most easily followed by a consecutive reading of the six sequences composing each itinerary in turn, but *La Passion du Général Franco* is more than a group of individual stories. It is an organic whole having as its central theme the conflict between Francoism on the one hand and the progressive forces of Spain on the other, both during the Civil War and under the Caudillo's regime.

It is through the interweaving, or montage, of these autonomous sequences – each built round the theme of revolt and repression, and each firmly rooted in Spanish history – that the overall picture of the conflict emerges. There are frequent references to historical events such as the formation of the 1934 October Commune and Franco's brutal repression of the Asturian miners. There are also references to historical persons like Grimau, who died from a Francoist bullet twenty-five years after the Civil War ended, and particularly to Durruti, whose role and that of his Column or brigade in the Battle of Madrid is conjured up visually in a scene between Soledad and Joaquin, who is mounting guard in Havana alongside Cuban soldiers. Even the monk Astigarabbia, who reads the sermon to the Blue Division in which he equates Franco with Christ, is a historical figure; he is a member of a *'junta de defensa'* for Bilbao.

The twofold aspect of the Spanish people's 'Passion', exile or death, is the theme of the 'Complainte de la frontière et des deux visages', sung after the arrival of the millionth emigrant on the Madrid–Frankfurt itinerary is greeted with flowers on the frontier at Irun, as if being the millionth was a matter for congratulation. This 'Lament' begins: 'Sur le positif/ le millionième émigré/ Sur le négatif/ le millionième fusillé/ Dix provinces en une seule image', and ends: 'Du positif au négatif/ dix provinces – tout un peuple/ en marche/ Vers quoi?' From her exile in Mexico, Soledad gives the answer to Joaquin across the space that divides them: 'I shall go to Madrid and I shall be at your side'. The only true revolution in the opinion of the emigrants, as in Durruti's, is the revolution you accomplish yourself in your own country; the revolutions of others, be they Cuban, Russian or any other, can be only distorting mirrors.

As might be expected, Gatti does not limit himself to dramatizing the ideas and memories of emigrants he had got to know, but himself offers direct comment on the Spanish situation. In one curious sequence he reviews the Spanish political scene in the years preceding Franco's rule by means of an assembly of antediluvian monsters – creatures of pre-[Franco] history preparing for a comeback in post-[Franco] history. The assembly which breaks up in violent recriminations presents a picture of the profound cleavage of the Left, the mutual antagonism of Anarchists, Republicans, Social Democrats, Trotskyists, Communists – in fact the civil war within the Civil War which resulted in the failure of those parties to present the united front alone capable of successfully combating the 'Francisco-Francosaure'. This sequence is packed so tight with precise historical references that without a detailed knowledge of events and attitudes during this war-within-a-war, its full significance goes over the head of the spectator. The type of presentation, with actors who represent the different political groupings masked as dinosaurs, pterodactyls, diplodocuses, is an added complication.

In a scene which is a materialization of one of the emigrants' thoughts, Gatti satirizes the Church and its relationship with Franco. The scene includes a 'mannequin parade' of a number of Christs for all the regions of Spain, proposed by the Generalissimo himself to 'mop up the terrible individualism of the Spanish people'. They are Christs 'for all tastes and all situations'. Each has a special role in the Franco regime, and is dressed accordingly. For example, the crown of thorns of the 'Christ économico-politique' has been 'modernized' and becomes a cap – Roman, German, American – and when necessary a Downing Street bowler or a Brigadier's *képi*.

The parade is broken up by the Christ for Asturian miners, who appears in the costume of a civil guard armed with a bludgeon and sets about the bishop and canon. A battle of bludgeon and croziers ensues until the miners' Christ is subdued. The Christs protest against the exploitation to which they have been subjected, and to the undermining of their teaching by the powers that be. They decide to come down from the cross and form a union; but, as only vertical unions with Franco at the head are tolerated, they opt for an all-out strike against the Fascist takeover of which they see themselves the victims. As always, revolt provokes repression, and in an ending which brings to mind Clovis Trouille's painting of hilarious Christs with which Gatti is familiar, the striking Christs are lined up with their hands above their heads, a target for laughing gas and tear-gas bombs hurled at them by the Civil Guards.

Two satirical scenes turn on Franco and his wife, Doña Carmen. The first pictures Franco as a balloon or windbag which gradually assumes the form of the Generalissimo when pumped up by the police. In the second scene Dolores, who lives in Toulouse, visits Madrid to rid herself of the picture of Spain during the Civil War which her father and his friend Marino, both Catalan anarchists, never stop recalling. There she finds herself in the midst of a demonstration by women carryng a banner with the words 'Soon, potatoes dearer than diamonds'. The police disperse the demonstrators and reveal Carmen at a prie-dieu with

Spain: a Constant Preoccupation

her rosary in her hands. She prays to the Virgin Mary to obtain Evita Perón's famous diamond necklace for her. True or false, this sequence, which takes the spectator back to the time of Evita Perón's death in 1952 and to Perón's overthrow in 1955, together with other grotesque sequences, provide a contrast with the lyrical sequences embodying the 'crucifixion' of the emigrants, and the choral passages (*cantilène, complainte, dit* – 'Le Dit de Madrid en guerre') which close the earlier sections.

Despite the absence of plot as generally understood, *La Passion du Général Franco*, with its great variety of tones and techniques, its sudden changes of register, is an exciting piece of dramatic writing. The fragmentation [*éclatement*] of the action in time and space suits the 'mental space' in which the characters live their lives. They are not 'circumscribed' by their present existence. They are often in the past and the present at the same time, in their memories and in their immediate experience. They are as much shaped as the other dramatic elements by the technique of *éclatement*. Another distinctive feature of the play is the synthesizing of fictitious characters and documentary background. Each 'traveller' in the four itineraries is a distinctive character and has a sum of very personal experience while representing at the same time a particular aspect of the historical conflict. When taken all together they give a picture of the 'passion' of a country which has been so fragmented as to be thrown to the four corners of the earth, but whose citizens continue to struggle to re-create a Spain without Franco and without Francoism.

The increase in complexity of this 'professional' version over the original four agitprop 'trajets' calls for a considerable increase in the number of actors and is a factor likely to deter an ordinary commercial theatre from contemplating a production. A further consideration for a commercial theatre manager is the possible withdrawal of tax concessions should any production offend the authorities. As a result, the ban suddenly imposed by the government on the performance billed for February 1969 by the Théâtre National Populaire in Paris – and afterwards, by extension, on its performance by any state-aided theatre in the whole of France – sealed the fate of the play for several years.[2] The ban was entirely unexpected as the season's programme had been submitted for approval to André Malraux, the Minister for Cultural Affairs, on 2 October 1968 by the Theatre's director Georges Wilson in accordance with the terms of his contract, and had been approved with the proviso that Gatti's play's title be changed, and all allusion by name to the General be suppressed. These changes were required by the government after objections had been raised to the production by the Spanish Embassy on 8 October.

On 15 October, with Gatti's consent, the play was re-entitled *La Passion en violet, jaune et rouge*, and the character in question renamed Général

Médaillas, although the reference to Franco's be-medalled uniforms was obvious. In November, sixty actors were engaged for the production. On 2 December rehearsals began and work was started on scenery and costumes. After renewed protests from the Spanish Embassy, an order was given on 18 December for the with-drawal of the play from the programme 'in accordance with international rules' – which rules? it was generally asked. The order was given officially by the Minister for Cultural Affairs, who was known to be in disagreement with it. It was given at the request of the Minister for Foreign Affairs, Michel Debré, with the support of General de Gaulle, because Debré was due to go to Spain to negotiate a commercial agreement at the date scheduled for the first performance.

A production of the play in Kassel at the Staatstheater, which is subsidized by both state and municipality, had, however, taken place the previous year on 6 November despite objections from the Spanish Embassy, which then proceeded to bring a civil action against the theatre 'for insult to the first lady of the regime'. The case was tried by Judge Bauer, who had been sentenced by Hitler to ten years in a concentration camp. His verdict was as follows: 'Not only do I refuse to ban the play, but I advise everyone to go and see it.'[3] The production ran there for a year.

In France the ban was imposed '*after* government acceptance of the season's programme, and *before* at least *one* performance which could be considered to have caused public disorder'. The ban therefore violated the charter of the National Theatres and was obviously a political sanction, the first ever to have been imposed on a national theatre. The political nature of the ban became even more obvious at the minister's subsequent refusal to allow the theatre building, which is open for bookings for occasions of all kinds, to be hired by an association wishing to arrange ten private performances for the 35,000 people who had already booked seats. The ticket money had to be refunded with serious implications for the TNP's finances, as actors had to be paid, or paid off if they did not belong to the regular company. Furthermore the theatre's programme for the year was completely disrupted.

Reaction against the suppression of 'freedom of expression' came from all sides: from professional groups of many kinds as well as the press. All feared an extension of repressive measures in other fields. All equated 'subsidy' with 'subservience'. There were individual protests as well. Jean-Paul Sartre addressed the TNP audience from the stage on 28 December, before the performance of his own play, *Le Diable et le bon Dieu*. He accused the authorities, 'who had already proved their dislike of the masses' (he was thinking back to May of that year), of trying to destroy the popular audience which had grown up around the plays of 'Brecht, Gorki, Gatti and Dürrenmatt'; they seemed to think that a true

Spain: a Constant Preoccupation

cultural revolution meant bringing popular theatre back to the Comédie Française! He urged the public to defend itself.

In defence of his play, Gatti gave a public reading on 23 January, at the Centre Dauphine in Paris 16e, and the next day an audio visual montage of the play was shown at the Jean-Jay University hostel at Antony. Before this, on 10 January, nine of the actors gave an acted reading of the text at Trappes near Paris, at the invitation of the Service cultural communal. It took place in the public hall [*salle des fêtes*] with, as the only setting, a table and four huge placards to group the characters of the four itineraries. A popular audience of four hundred filled the small hall to the doors. They listened in silence for two hours, then stayed on to discuss the play with the actors.

Gatti subsequently produced a new text entitled *L'Interdiction ou petite histoire de l'interdiction d'une pièce qui devait être représentée en violet, jaune et rouge dans un théâtre national*. This was performed on 25 April at the Cité Universitaire in Paris and afterwards widely in France and Germany. The text was drawn by Gatti from the collective reflections of the actors on the regimes of Franco and de Gaulle, and on the general situation arising out of the ban particularly as it affected the theatre. It took the form of a wildly extravagant burlesque of public figures concerned in the affair.

As a result of the ban there was subsequent evidence of autocensorship in the Centres Dramatiques and Maisons de la Culture. As far as Gatti is concerned, the ban was the final factor in his change of view on his position as a dramatist in the existing political and social system. May 1968 and Gatti's own participation in the events had prepared the change, and his activities during his self-imposed exile from France after the ban completed it. The results can be seen in the reworking of *La Passion* as published in 1975, and even more so in the style of the production when the play was at last put on in Paris on 20 March 1976.

La Passion du Général Franco par les émigrés eux-mêmes

This version was not performed in Paris theatre-land but at the Porte de la Chapelle in the Ney Calberson lorry warehouse. The production was undertaken by Gatti's personal group of actors called La Tribu with the help of Pierre Laville, director of Le Centre National de Création contemporaine, a non-profit making organization which came into being in June 1975 and received a state subsidy. There was apparently no longer any official objection to staging the play, as Franco was dead. Nevertheless the authorities seemed to think it best that no one should hear about it! No advertisement was allowed; there was none of the usual publicity in the Paris métro and, after the first performance, no arrows pointing the way to the 'theatre' as for the Théâtre du Soleil in the Bois de Vincennes. The reason? This was 'political theatre'. No placarding was allowed even outside the warehouse itself except at the actual time of the performance; it was alleged that placarding 'might disturb the neighbours', of which, in fact, there were none in that part of Boulevard Ney!

Finally a good part of the press, faced again, as at the production of *Le Crapaud buffle*, with a performance that bore no relation to drama as they knew it on the Paris boulevard, gave the production short shrift. Behind adverse criticism made apparently on aesthetic grounds, political prejudice was clearly visible. Marc Kravetz, however, wrote in *Libération* (26 April) an article entitled 'Un Spectacle à hauteur d'homme', where he says: 'This performance (one of the finest and most sincere to be seen in Paris) is also a remarkably well-constructed criticism of all show businesses. Hurry up and see it: it will be over in ten days' time.'

When Pierre Laville asked Gatti to stage his play Gatti wondered at first whether there was any point, but the nonstop executions in Spain and the prolonged imprisonment and torture of the founder of the Democratic Women's movement, Eva Forest, gave him his answer. Eva Forest had been arrested, along with others, following a bomb attack on 13 September 1974 on the Café Rolando in the Puerta del Sol in Madrid, in which twelve people lost their lives. She was further accused of complicity in the murder of the Prime Minister, Carrero Blanco, on 13 December 1973. Once again Gatti rewrote his play. He had also written versions for productions in Poland, Italy and the German Democratic Republic, but they had been banned for economic or political reasons. 'One of the rare privileges of political theatre is that it is not written once and for all', was Gatti's comment of 1972 in Berlin with reference to the version of the play staged in Kassel (Preface to the published version, 1975).

The text as performed at the Ney Calberson warehouse was published in *Avant-Scène* (1 May 1976) together with pictures taken during rehearsals. This version alludes several times to Franco's death, which had occurred shortly before, though Gatti said it did not affect his play. In this version a revolutionary fighter hopes to see the day when the disease which took the name of Franco and persisted despite Franco's death is rooted out, whereas the Minister of Health prophesies that Francoism will descend on the powers that be as the Holy Ghost descended on the Apostles on Whit Sunday. Given the circumstances, Gatti saw his production in terms of a demonstration, *une manifestation*, requiring the participation of everyone, but any spectator who disagreed with it would be free to leave.

The action, as in the 1968 version, proceeds by 'trajets', but there are several changes of detail. The itinerary 'Madrid–Frankfurt' becomes 'Barcelona–Frankfurt'. There is a redistribution of scenes, a change of name for some emigrants (as of their roles) and additional characters, two of whom play important parts. One, the historical figure of Admiral Carrero Blanco designated here as the Count of the Tower of Babel, represents the Establishment. The other, the political prisoner Alfonso, represents a new itinerary, 'le Trajet des Sans Trajet', 'internal exile' – that is to say, prison with (at the performance) the Republican flag as an emblem, and the expressed idea that each floor-stone of a prison is a piece of free Spain. In this version an emigrant's recurrent nightmare of the '*paseo*' becomes the nightmarish present and likely future of Alfonso, who for some forty years has expected his turn to come.

The sequence of the revolutionary Christs, which is a figment of Marino's imagination in the 1968 version, is moved in the new version into the 'Trajet des Sans Trajet' and is hinged on Alfonso, and it is with Alfonso's words that the play ends as he tells of Joseba Elosegui, a Basque revolutionary who set fire to himself in front of Franco at the Pelota championship in San Sebastian, exclaiming as he did so: 'Franco only exists in your minds'.

Certain scenes of the 1968 version are dropped, but after some hesitation Gatti retained the scene with Saint François because of the shooting of four workmen by Juan Carlos's police on the steps of Saint Francis's Church in Vittoria. This incident made of Saint Francis a ready symbol of working-class protest, and Gatti's retention of the scene underlines his continuous dialogue with Spain. So does a new scene, the Round-Spain Cycle Race managed by Blanco. It offers an amusing parody of the Spanish Bourbons' 'race' for the 'crown'.

Gatti's two published post-exile versions of *La Passion* do more, however, than bring the documentary aspect of the play up to date. They show clearly the radical change that had taken place in his whole approach to the theatre. With the banning of the original text of *La Passion*, what Gatti refers to as the 'long bourgeois period' of his career as a dramatist, characterized by committed political drama, had come to an end. Instead of speaking in the name of the exploited, as he had done in the plays which had provided high spots of the seasons of the various Centres Dramatiques, his new aim was to help them to speak for themselves and to help them to arrive at some creative action relating to their particular problems and struggles. The collective creation on the Durruti Column for Louvain University marks the actual turning point in Gatti's career, and it is in the context of his new career as a 'catalyst' that the revised versions of *La Passion* must be viewed. The two shows, *La Passion du Général Franco par les émigrés eux-mêmes* and *La Colonne Durruti* have much in common not only as regards the subject, the Spanish Civil War (the story of Durruti is extended in this second version of *La Passion* to include his frustration over Saragossa), but also as regards the structure of the texts and the style of the productions.

In an interview with Christian Binder at the time of the performance in the Ney Calberson warehouse, Gatti described himself as 'the animator of the collective creation of a "tribe" of variable size'.[4] Nevertheless, although the 'Tribe's' performance of the play gave it the appearance of a collective creation, the fact remains that the revised text is clearly the work of a single author. Its form is obviously inspired by the experiments Gatti had been engaged in during the three previous years for the University of Louvain.

The play begins with the cast setting the stage for the performance, and Jasmin, an Asturian miner on the Kiev–Krasnoyarsk itinerary, as director, starting up the action then criticizing the cast's first efforts. There follows an explanation of the title of the play, of the situation in Spain and of the personal predicament of each; also a discussion of some of the problems that had to be faced in certain itineraries such as the relevance of the scene with Saint François. At one point in the 'trajets réunis' the 'actors' even discuss whether the itineraries should continue, or be replaced by something else. To solve the performance crisis, one of them proposes 'not revolution' but 'auto-criticism' of the itineraries. The upshot of this discussion is the suggestion of a Cycle-Race. In the *Avant-Scène* edition the contestants for the 'throne' are reduced to a single starter, Juan Carlos, in view of the situation in Spain just after Franco's death.

This takeover of the action by the actor/emigrants makes of the play a mass action, unlike the theatrical action that would have been seen on the stage of the TNP had it been performed in 1968, and as it had been performed at Kassel the previous year. At the warehouse there was no question of a 'performance' in front of an audience with stage and auditorium constituting two separate areas. In the new version – and particularly with Gatti's new type of production – *La Passion* took on the form of a procession or parade, even of a political demonstration organized by the characters who are at the same time actors; these twenty-five actors performed indiscriminately the various roles. Freed from the constraining limits of a theatre-stage, the acting area extended, in the warehouse, over the whole expanse of the huge floor which was also the audience area, because the spectators had to remain on their feet and move around with the actors for two-and-a-half hours of the show instead of sitting comfortably on a fixed seat.

This was a much more radical approach than that of the Théâtre du Soleil in *1789* and *1793* when seats were provided, although the aim of the director, Ariane Mnouchkine, was to persuade the spectators to leave them and move around among the four or five small raised platforms some of which were bridged together. These platforms, however, never ceased to be purely acting areas with theatrical backcloths and lighting effects, and at no time was the convention of a performance for spectators breached. Mnouchkine's audience remained 'consumers', albeit voluntarily peripatetic, of a show directed at them from a number of fixed points, namely the fixed stages. Those who attended the performance of *La Passion*, on the other hand, were incorporated into a collective event which made of them an active element surveying the event from freely chosen angles. When some of the sequences ran simultaneously, the spectating element of this 'spectacle without spectators' which Gatti had declared to be the aim of his experiment in Brabant with *L'Arche d'Adelin* in 1973, had to commit itself to one or other of the itineraries and become as much a part of it as were its 'official' emigrants.

Unlike *1789* and *1793*, there was no decorative element or stage lighting to set the actors apart from the spectators. Gatti's aim and that of the 'Tribe', so he told Marc Kravetz, was to allow the spectator to establish a libertarian relationship with what was being performed, and also to abolish the usual authoritarian relationship between the show and those watching it. The action took place *alongside* the spectator, who stood on the warehouse floor surrounded by rough brick and cement walls and under strip lighting in the ceiling. With the idea of a 'Passion' in his mind, Gatti saw the warehouse almost as a cathedral with the centre of visibility in the main 'aisle' between the two rows of columns (supporting the ceiling) and the space between the columns as side chapels with spectators having to choose amongst them. Depending as it did on the spectator's choice, the play would be different for each of them.

The actors were at the same time makers of costumes, masks and 'scenery', and general hands. They built an enormous mobile cross in metal scaffolding six metres high. This cross of the Valley of Death, set in the central 'aisle', was called the Tower of Babel. It housed the forces of law and order ranging from the Army, the police, the Church, Opus Dei, to certain masked dignitaries such as Carrero Blanco, who declaimed 'Le Dit des étages du pouvoir' from the Tower where the guest of honour was Doña Carmen (Polo de Franco) masked, bejewelled and befurred. In addition to the Tower there were five tall, unadorned mobile stepladders, each representing an itinerary.

When the 'play' began, the emigrants, in black trousers and sweaters, each seated on a suitcase which was the symbol of his lived experience, rose to make their way towards their respective ladders carrying the suitcases with them. These suitcases played an active part in the action and formed what Roger Planchon calls 'working sets'. Set out in two rows, they suggested an avenue down which the parade of the 'Christs for all purposes' filed. When they were set out around the actors by

Alfonso, at the foot of the cross or Tower, they symbolized the prison into which Joseba Elosegui was thrown after his act of defiance in the presence of Franco. When the imprisoned actors kicked them aside, this created the final image of the play: 'the destruction of all the cells which continued to imprison freedom even after Franco's death' (Programme). As they burst out of the 'cell' the actors called out: 'Joseba Elosegui – it's us – Wherever you may be, Comrades in exile, welcome back to your country' (*Avant-Scène* text).

This type of presentation emphasized the move, already clear in the 1975 text, away from the drama of individual characters as in the 1968 version and towards the drama of a collective, of a vision of the whole Spanish people. 'The emigrants' vision', says Carlos of the Barcelona–Frankfurt itinerary in the opening sequence of the revised version, 'is a mass vision which tends to place the spectacle on a fighting footing.' This change of outlook, coupled with the style of the staging, greatly reduces the intimacy and the emotional appeal of some of the sequences of the 1968 version.

Instead of a lonely Soledad haunted by the image of the mother she had never known, in the new version five actresses, playing 'five possible Violeteras', re-enact in front of her the 'historic case' of her mother as reported in a number of newspapers. Instead of the private and pathetic parting of Soledad and Joaquin, the couple's words of farewell (*after* Soledad has returned to Cuba and Joaquin has been thrown into prison in Spain) are given almost choral treatment with two groups of actors lined up behind the two characters reciting the text. A choral effect is similarly obtained in the prison scene in which Joaquin is visited by his Francoist father, the Minister for Aviation, who has 'devoured Reds all his life' but has, in spite of himself, 'fathered and raised a Red' in his son. In these sequences, the formerly private tragedies of the individual emigrants take on the appearance of a debate on an issue of public importance.

The revised version is denser than that of 1968. This, together with the choice of site for the production, the amount of movement needed to bring it to life in such a vast setting, and the rapid pace of the performance, again made complete assimilation difficult in the space of a single performance. Richness is a weakness in the play as a stage play. With its fevered movement, its songs, its moments of fairground farce, its masks and antediluvian monsters, it inevtably invited comparison by the critics, – and, it must be said, often unfavourable – with Mnouchkine's *1789*, the street theatre of Peter Schumann's Bread and Puppet Company, and Luca Ronconi's *Roland Furieux* (in French), which had had an enthusiastic reception in Les Halles in Paris in 1970. With its simultaneous actions and chariots driven amongst the standing spectators, who created their own view of a show based on an original text that had

Spain: a Constant Preoccupation

been reconstructed, *Roland Furieux* was at that time the final stage of a search for an entirely new physical space. The notion of actors interpreting a text did not pertain in any way.

As against these productions, *La Passion* should not be seen in terms of picturesque popular theatre, as were the others. It has a different purpose and the choice of the site made this clear. So did Gatti himself when he said, as he perched on the top of a ladder at the beginning of the performance, 'What we are doing is political theatre; for those who are not interested in politics, the Way Out is the same as the Way In.' He was not, he declared, a militant of any political party or of any organization, nor was the play intended as a piece of propaganda of any political colour. The aim of the show was to induce the spectator to reflect on the action portrayed together with the facts on which it was based, and perhaps arrive through it at a keener awareness of the social and political problems that had to be faced by each and all.

The better to link the dramatic action with the reality of the time, Gatti arranged for the walls of the warehouse to be lined with political bookstalls where books and pamphlets could be bought or consulted before and during the performance; he had already adopted this procedure for *La Colonne Durruti*. 'The whole of exiled Spain will be there,' Gatti had said to Martin Even; 'rival groups on the losing side, reunited since the Civil War [One thinks here of the sequence with prehistoric monsters]. It is important for us to be the pretext for such a meeting, more important than the commercial sale'; but if, as it turned out, the stalls were only those of the extreme left such as the CNT, POUM, UHP (*Uniaos hermanos proletarios* – the slogan of the Asturian miners in 1934) the fault was not Gatti's, as he had no personal axe to grind.

With its origins in Gatti's 'bourgeois period' and its new form reflecting his post-1968 experimentation, *La Passion du Général Franco par les émigrés eux-mêmes* is a specially interesting work bridging two totally different approaches to the problem of what theatre is, and what its function is. Jean-Pierre Sarrazac makes an interesting evaluation of Gatti's work when he sees Gatti as trying out, with this production and other recent experiments, the theatre of the future which would allow the members of the public to intervene in the two decisive stages of a production: the first during the composition of a text, by telling the playwright of their own ideas and experiences as the Spanish emigrants in Toulouse had done in 1963, the second by following the actors who are their substitutes for the duration of the performance, to whom they may give even a silent hint of their agreement or disagreement.[5]

Armand Gatti in the Theatre

Notes

1. Martin Even, interview with Gatti, 'Les Exils de Gatti', *Le Monde* 30 March 1976.
2. 'To be banned or not to be banned', by Dorothy Knowles, *Drama*, Summer 1969.
3. *L'Humanité*, 2 March 1967, J.-P. Leonardini.
4. 'Gatti-le-visionnaire': *Politique hebdo*, No. 217.
5. 'Les Étapes de la Passion, une modification dramaturgique', *Travail Théâtral*, vol. 24–25, July–December 1976, p. 129.

9
Facets of Rosa Luxemburg: A Dramatic Character?

Rosaspartakus prend le pouvoir. Rosa Collective

The last of Gatti's plays to be written for the legitimate theatre is *Rosaspartakus prend le pouvoir*. It was written in Germany after his exile from the French theatre. To a certain extent it is a follow-up of *Chant public*, in both its subject and its technique. The subject of both plays is the martyrdom of well-known historical figures, although in neither play do these figures actually appear as dramatic characters on stage. Their presence, evoked by means of an invisible theatre performance in *Chant public*, is evoked by a television studio discussion group in the play on Rosa. In both works the technique of *éclatement* or fragmentation of the subject-character is used, but whereas in *Chant public* the fragmentation is the work of the imagination of individual members of the 'theatre audience' on stage and is always partial, in the play on Rosa there are from the very beginning as many Rosas as there are people who know her name. Between *Chant public* and *Rosaspartakus* Gatti had travelled a long way, and the latter play shows a technical mastery not wholly achieved in *Chant public*. Unfortunately neither *Rosaspartakus* nor *Rosa Collective*, as it was finally to be called in France, has yet been put to the test of a theatre performance in that country. *Rosa* was, however, staged under the title *Rosa Kollektiv* at the Staatstheater in Kassel on 3 April 1971, in a production by Kai Braak.

The play was actually written for the Staatstheater but was not purpose built, as was *V comme Vietnam* or *Les Treize Soleils*. It was the fulfilment of a project that Gatti had turned over in his mind for eight years and which the Staatstheater helped him to realize. He had collected a mass of documentation; the extent of this documentation, both historical and political, is set out on the first pages of the two published texts. Nevertheless *Rosa* is not a documentary play; it is a free theatrical creation. Since the period in question was not one with which the German public was generally familiar, the Staatstheater prepared a number of pamphlets for its audience. These contain information on the historical and political issues raised in the play and often give chapter

Armand Gatti in the Theatre

and verse for them, as in the case of the picture of Karl Liebknecht painted by one of the characters, Reinhardt, who had supposedly seen Karl a few days before his assassination. He was stretched out exhausted and unshaven at midday on a billiard table in a restaurant, with socks wet with snow from the Berlin streets and a gaping hole in the sole of his left shoe (*Rosa Collective* 70).

In 1968, when Gatti was in Berlin, he sent out a questionnaire asking 'What do you know of Rosa? Can her struggle help yours in any way? What would you do if she came and knocked at your door today?' Replies poured in from all over the Federal Republic and Gatti received permission from the Ministries of Culture and Production in the Democratic Republic to interview women belonging to Rosa Luxemburg associations in various factories. He was on the point of writing a play entitled *Qu'as-tu vu, Rosa?* in which two Rosas, one from East Germany and one from West Germany, come together, when Ulrike Meinhof (whom he had met cursorily just before the attack on Rudi Dutschke in April 1968) asked to see him because she had heard of his intended play. After a whole night of discussion with her, he realized that although he once boasted jokingly: 'I am the German who knows Rosa the best', he in fact knew very little about her.

In July 1969 when the run of his play *Die Geburt* (*La Naissance*) came to an end at the Staatstheater, Gatti was surprised to be asked by the theatre what he would be writing about next. It would be Rosa Luxemburg, he replied, but her image constantly eluded him. He would have to get to know the town of Berlin where Rosa had lived, fought, been imprisoned and murdered. Thereupon the theatre offered him a three-month stay at the Academy of Arts in Berlin to enable him to write the play, asking in return only the right to stage it. On 15 September 1969 Gatti went to Frankfurt to sign a contract with the Author's Publishing House. In March 1974 it put out a duplicated text in German (*Rosa Kollektiv*). Two French versions were earlier published in France: *Rosaspartakus prend le pouvoir* (*Travail Théâtral*, No. 3, April–June 1971) and *Rosa Collective* (Seuil, 1973).

These two are not identical. In the second version there are certain changes of structure, some redistribution of the contents and reallocation of lines. This second version is almost identical in structure with the German version apart from the fact that in the latter, because of the cease-fire in Vietnam in 1973, the proposed 'Possibilités en marche vers le Vietnam' is generalized to become in the German text –Möglichkeit auf dem Weg Überallhin, wo es etwas zu verteidigen gibt'. Furthermore the collective character, Rosa-Vietnam becomes Rosa-Kollektiv, and certain specifically American references are omitted. Although it was Gatti's usual practice to keep rewriting his plays in order to bring them into line with contemporary ideas and events, never before, as he

Facets of Rosa Luxemburg: a Dramatic Character?

admitted in 1971, had he worked over a text so many times and never had the final product seemed so short to him. There was, in fact, enough material for 'twenty-four possible plays', he said.

The historical figure of Rosa, one of the instigators of the Spartakist movement in 1914 and co-founder on 31 December 1918 of the German Communist Party, is of course the point from which the play starts, but Gatti sought to bring it into today's world, showing 'the thousand ways Rosa had of beating her wings through the history of my contemporaries', to quote one of the characters, Dr Ursula Koch, whom Gatti actually knew. The play ranges over the struggle against Hitler, the Vietnam War, and the Black Panther movement in America in addition to the Spartakist insurrection in Germany:

'But why mix Spartakists and Black Panthers?' 'Spartakists, whoever they may be, only exist through us (even the most cowardly of us).'

This exchange in the thirteenth scene, or rather 'Possibilité', sums up the theme and action admirably.

During the eight years of the play's gestation a number of dramatic forms, each with a different image of Rosa, had suggested themselves to Gatti, but it was not until his stay in Berlin in 1969 that he had the idea of opposing the various images dialectically to each other within a single dramatic action. In the Introduction to the play Gatti writes that the confrontation of the different conceptions of Rosa held by the various political factions provides the dramatic element, and the natural expression of these factions dictates the way the action develops. The problem arose as to whether the possible plays on Rosa should be presented in abstract dramatic conflict with each other or united in time and space by a story. The successful prosecution of Stuttgart Television for its programme 'The Case of Liebknecht and Luxemburg', in January 1968, conveniently supplied the 'story'. The prosecution had been brought by Captain Waldemar Pabst of the Auxiliary Guards Cavalry Division responsible for the brutal killing of Karl and Rosa, in official terminology: 'an execution in accordance with martial law.' A version of the event had in fact been published by Pabst in a German newspaper in January 1962. Gatti managed to obtain a three-day interview with Pabst, but only in the presence of Pabst's lawyer. Two days later Pabst died.

Given this framework and Gatti's obsession with the repressive role played in the world today by the mass media, the obvious setting for his play was a television studio. Gatti sees a television studio as presenting 'an image of the world', so it is not surprising that in his play the Stuttgart studio should become the Weltheim studio. In the second version, the studio takes on the authoritative status of Germany VII. In both versions the aggrieved television team plans a follow-up to the contested programme 'Rosa-la-Spartakiste' with 'Rosa Collective', and invites individuals and organizations having some connection with Rosa to participate. Amongst them is Major Waldemar of the Auxiliary Guards Cavalry Division. He is not a resurrection of the real Captain Waldemar Pabst but a dramatic character created by Gatti. In the play it is he who had brought the case against the television programme, and he made his acceptance of the invitation to take part in this second programme conditional on his being accompanied by his lawyer, Madame Metzger, who had pleaded his case against the previous broadcast. Rosa being a 'revolutionary', Waldemar's purpose was once again to be 'the first to shoot', for although Rosa was dead, she was still a threat (RC 35).

The guests are to offer suggestions for possible plays about Rosa. Each suggestion is called a 'Possibilité ...'. The final choice amongst the 'Possibilités' rests with the participants who are to vote on them. Votes by telephone are also to be accepted from viewers. The whole of the play is therefore a single 'possibility' – the possibility of resuscitating Rosa, of doing a performance on Rosa, of writing a play about Rosa. In the final moments of Gatti's stage play, the Presenter of the 'broadcast' announced to participants and viewers alike that the proposed programme on the great revolutionary Rosa Luxemburg 'cannot be given'. 'Why?' The answer comes from 'Rosa Collective' who says: 'Never look for the prophet'. The 'prophet' merely points to a path which has by now already been traced and consequently defuses any possible dynamic action. 'Militancy alone has the gift of prophecy.'

This statement defines the line adopted by Gatti throughout the play and announced by the title of the first published version, *Rosaspartakus prend le pouvoir*, which places Rosa in a historical perspective linking revolutionary struggles throughout the history of mankind. The six possible titles, discussed at Kassel and set out on the first page of the published editions, make up what Gatti calls the 'Global title' and further clarify his intention. Gatti's preference for the final title would have been 'Tsui! Tsui! Tsui!'; the song of the great tit which Rosa had wanted to have engraved on her tomb, and which could well 'proclaim on the town walls the permanence of the struggle of the poor and underprivileged'.

Another significant title which gives an idea of the political field covered in the play is formed by the integration vertically and horizontally of the two Rs of ROSA REV(olutionnaire) into PANTHÈRE NOIRE. The Black Panthers are represented by the Afro-American 'Red Alger', an unofficial 'guest', almost a gate-crasher in the studio, where he gives an impromptu reading of the ten-point programme of the Black Panther Party, and announces that he brings news of Karl and Rosa: 'They live in the United States, and are black like me' (RC 50). Once again the text states clearly Gatti's purpose of exploring the contemporary relevance of Rosa's struggle which, so he told Denis

Facets of Rosa Luxemburg: a Dramatic Character?

Bablet, would continue as long as the Soledad 'brothers' and Black Panthers remained in prison (*Travail Théâtral*, No. 3).

To put viewers who had not seen the supposed 'broadcast' of 'Rosa-la-Spartakiste' in possession of the facts, the Presenter interviews two veterans who 'knew Rosa when she was alive': Frieda Becker, Rosa's ex-typist on the newspaper *Rote Fahne*, and Peter Reinhardt, an ex-combatant of the Spartakist movement. These two are composite dramatic characters but are based on interviews with the two people themselves. In the 'broadcast' Frieda Becker is to speak about Rosa, and Peter Reinhardt is to outline the history of the Spartakist movement for the benefit of the 'less well informed'. To this end, both are asked to make use of huge photographs of historical characters such as Hindenburg, Ludendorff, Jogishes, Dieffenbach and Habersaath which line the walls of the studio. The interview with Frieda and Reinhardt and its transmission constitute the *Présentation* and immediately precede the *Émission*, in which the Presenter explains the reasons for the broadcast and introduces the guests.

In the interview, the frivolous questions put to Frieda by the Presenter's assistant, Gisela, concerning Rosa's frail appearance, her favourite colour, etc. – together with Gisela's suppression of all Frieda's references to Rosa's political activities as 'being of interest to specialists only' and her insistence on the story of Rosa's love life, her friendship with two women, Klara Zetkin and Louise Kautsky, her affection for her cat Mimi, and her letters from the Wronke prison (1916–17) which talk of birds and flowers – go to show, as Reinhardt bitterly remarks, that 'once out of the way', the one-time revolutionary heroine had been transformed into a cultural object, a museum piece, fit to be 'recouped' by the bourgeoisie – a representative, the assistant adds, of the historical past of the 'spiked helmet and maxi-skirt', a past long since dead and buried.

The anti-revolutionary outlook of the Germany VII team accounts for their deliberate devaluing of the character and importance of the heroine and their determination to impose on the viewers the image of a very ordinary feminine figure, a frail coquette having no relevance for the present. When the veteran Reinhardt asks why the team is attempting to 'recoup' Rosa since, in the class struggle, she is obviously not one of their number, the answer is: 'Rosa belongs to everyone'. As a final thrust a police file from Rosa's time containing uncomplimentary remarks made about Rosa by her contemporaries and even one-time friends such as the Kautskys is read out, but the accusation of terrorism made against her is indignantly refuted by the two veterans who then recite what they call the 'terrible poem' published by Arthur Zickler in the working-class paper *Vörwartz* itself on 13 January 1919, two days before Rosa's assassination. The Spartakist movement is subjected to the same devaluation by the Establishment which deems it a failed revolution fit only to be consigned to the dustbins of history. 'History had condemned it to death. God help the vanquished' (*RC* 145). It is an exemplary failure.

In the play mass-media methods once again come under attack by Gatti. Frieda and Reinhardt are invited by the cameraman to view their image as it has been fashioned by the television team during the interview. 'Manipulation is the only great art we still have today. It is a whole culture! We are its employees – here as elsewhere' (*RC* 33). Ironically, in this particular instance the Establishment proves unintentionally, by its manipulation of the witnesses' testimony, that it does after all believe that Rosa, the Spartakist, has an 'afterlife' – that is, a role to play in present-day struggles – and seeks to destroy it by 'recouping' her. Its methods are diplomatic. By their evident hostility the members of the right-wing group, consisting of Waldemar, his lawyer who threatens 'further action', and Dieter, who had already been involved in a symbolic *mise à mort* or 'putting to death' of the two Spartakists by publicly burning their portraits wrested from student demonstrators, testify despite themselves to Rosa's 'afterlife'. For them Rosa 'represents subversion' (*RC* 69).

A third group consisting of Rosa's political sympathizers is very varied and comes from Cologne, Munich and Dresden. Others from Strasbourg, North Africa and Brazil rank as 'foreigners'. They include Dr Ursula Koch, a former consul of the German Federal Republic in Rio de Janeiro who had been for a time a hostage of the 'Luxemburgist group' of the 'Brazilian Army of Liberation', and the Black Panther, Red Alger, a deserter from the Vietnam War. Gatti knew them both. All believe in a Rosa who continues to be operative in the struggles of our time, but in the context of the television programme they are caught up in a debate on a suitable mode of resurrection for the revolutionary heroine.

In the *Émission*, when the Presenter introduces the individual guests and the various groups who are to take part, he introduces them not in their own right as individuals but in respect of the roles they are expected to play in the broadcast-debate of which the framework has been fixed in advance by the television team. Structurally there is no break between the *Émission* and the *Présentation* which precedes it, since three characters who have no part in the *Présentation* – Red Alger, Waldemar and Dr Koch – make an unexpected entry into the studio while Frieda and Reinhardt are watching the transmission of their interview and technicians are preparing the set for the introduction of the guests at the beginning of the debate. The easy transition from the *Présentation* to the *Émission*, like that between the fourteen 'Possibilités' to follow, gives proof of a technical mastery which assures at the same time the unity of the whole.

Facets of Rosa Luxemburg: a Dramatic Character?

In the fourteen 'Possibilités' the action moves outside the framework as preconceived by the team, and apart from the officer of law and order who remains that throughout and nothing more, the characters escape from their predetermined roles and develop individual features productive of unforeseen situations which the Presenter cannot always handle.

The first proposition for a possible presentation of Rosa – the creation of a single archetypal figure which would 'be to everyone's taste' – comes from the television team. It would be programmed by a computer on data furnished by the guests about themselves; it would create a Rosa in whom everyone could 'recognize himself', a Rosa projected in a global image in which all divergences of outlook would be glossed over, a Rosa functioning as the projection of the self. The only thing that Waldemar and his like could recognize of themselves in Rosa is the bullet they lodged in her head! Reinhardt snaps. The computerized figure proposed by the television team, stripped of the historical significance of Rosa's existence and of the dynamism inherent in a revolutionary heroine engaged in a revolutionary action, could obviously have no further function in the future than the image of Rosa the innocuous cultural object which the Establishment has already tried to foist on to the guests. On the contrary, the fragmentation of the global image of a hero allows for it to be taken up in any existing situation.

In the ensuing 'Possibilité des deux Allemagnes' the two Germanies of today are shown to be re-enacting the drama of the two Germanies of Rosa's time, when Liebknecht the Spartakist chief thundered from the balcony of the deserted Imperial Palace as a declaration of intent, 'I proclaim the Socialist Republic of Germany', and the Social Democrat Philipp Scheidemann, one-time minister of the Imperial War Cabinet, countered in the Reichstag on the same day, 9 November 1918, with 'Long Live the German Republic'. The continued existence of the two German republics is underlined by the opportune arrival of the guests from the Democratic Republic, who declared themselves Rosa's 'heirs', 'descendants of Spartakism'. As they spread roses at the feet of one of the 'Rosa structures' (outlines of her figure) on stage, they chant a 'Hymn to Peace – a duo on the theme of Rosa's grief and distress in the Barnimstrasse prison'. The hymn ends with a plea for the 'universal brotherhood of workers' for which Rosa had fought all her life. This being a stage play, the East German proposal is made to get an angry reception from Rosa's enemy, Waldemar, which heightens the dramatic action. In fact throughout, every point that is made by any one guest or group is immediately countered by other participants in the television programme, ensuring that the dramatic tension never flags.

Militancy is the hallmark of the amateur dramatic group of students and workers from Strasbourg, and it proposes the 'Possibilité des conseils de personnages', on the model of the Workers and Soldiers

Councils of 1918. It would be a collective creation by councils which would take all decisions relative to the historical characters in the show and would thus do away with dramatic characters in the usual sense, with author and actors – in fact with traditional theatre itself, which in their eyes is part and parcel of a form of culture that has always signified oppression (*RC* 67). Their stance reiterates Gatti's own views of the post-1968 years when he reversed his former belief in culture as a useful weapon in the hands of the working class and saw mass culture as an additional means of repressing the working class.

The Strasbourg proposition further provokes Waldemar, along with Dieter and his followers, into creating an organization for the defence of 'traditional values' testified to by the 'military cemeteries all round Germany', but 'trampled underfoot' in the studio. The two veterans, Frieda and Reinhardt, also contest the Strasbourg proposition, but do so in the name of historical truth. They had an 'ankle boot with a hole in the sole' and even that was being taken from them. They oppose any reconstitution of Karl and Rosa by actors and see reconstitution as sheer caricature. The Strasbourg group is not, however, proposing an attempted resurrection, caricatural or otherwise, of 'what no longer exists', nor 'of being Rosa', but of 'continuing Rosa' by themselves taking part in the struggles of our time. 'What we shall put on will never be petrified, pre-established, but will be capable of engaging in any struggle' (*RC* 68). Much the same opinion is later expressed by a North African cinema attendant: 'It is not up to us to interpret Rosa (and other historical characters). It is up to them to graft themselves on to us and play their part in the struggles of our time' (*RC* 92). A living Rosa fighting on all fronts at all times. Such a view would also seem to be Gatti's own, judging from his introductory remarks to the published text.

The Strasbourg group are prepared, if need be, to adopt what they call 'active language' and are provoked into using it by 'elements' such as the discovery of a number of German generals' sabres among the stage props, 'much more numerous than proletarian caps'. Red Alger approves these 'cowboys from Strasbourg': 'If your Rosa cannot take part in our struggles, she is well and truly dead' (*RC* 112). It is significant that when he made his unheralded appearance in the studio before the *Émission*, he enquired of Frieda whether the 'Spartakus week' – the German Communists' paper – not the 'Spartakist week', was being held there. He obviously refuses to limit revolutionary action to a particular place, or a particular time, '191 ...'. What is more, he announces himself as 'Karl Liebnecht in the physical absence of Karl'.

For Reinhardt, the authentic Spartakist, the fate of the Spartakist movement, destined to wander through history in search of a place to take root in, is a sorry one. Frieda, the other authentic Spartakist, regards its 'exile' as its special way of engaging in the fight today, just as

Facets of Rosa Luxemburg: a Dramatic Character?

the death of Karl and Rosa at the hands of their enemies was their way of continuing the fight. Rosa's body was small and frail, but there burned within a fire that neither sickness nor prison could put out, and which continued to burn after her death. To dub the Spartakist movement an ex-revolution, as the Presenter does, is to fail to appreciate it as a revolution waiting to be carried through to a finish, and also to deny the possibility of any repercussions of the past on the present or the future. This negative view is countered by the Strasbourg group, who were inspired to adopt the name of Rosa Luxemburg by the events of May 1968, and by the Cologne University group, which painted her name over the university entrance, also in 1968.

The number and variety of the Rosa images, all of them combative, reflected by different countries and political parties, had convinced Gatti that to base his play solely on her personal history would have been a betrayal of what she signified. Echoing Rosa's wish to be 'the cry of the great tit for future generations' (*RC* 130), Gatti says in his Introduction: 'Rosa has existences throughout time and space', and in the play makes his characters attempt to establish these existences in the light of their own experience and by all the means in their power at the time.

Amongst the multiplicity of images of Rosa held by her friends and enemies, the Rosa of yesterday is the only valid one in Frieda's eyes, and the Karl of yesterday the only valid one in Reinhardt's, yet these two veterans allow themselves to be drawn by the Cologne group into a Collective Personage in which the different images of Rosa, while retaining their particular profiles, band together round a common cause – on this occasion Vietnam, where the war still waged ('Possibilités en marche vers le Vietnam'). Did not Rosa herself point the way to Vietnam when she wrote: 'We send our greetings to our comrades over there [in Bremen, where she had been asked to go and speak against revisionism]. But whatever happens, neither Karl nor I will let the Berlin workers down.' 'It is the Berlin workers' way of going to the Vietnam rendezvous', Reinhardt adds.

Graphic form is given to the Collective Personage when the dramatic characters climb on to a battered motorcar, a museum piece of the 1918 November Revolution. It serves as a focal point for the demonstration, and according to the stage directions, the flashes of light which sporadically pinpoint the different 'elements of the Collective Personage' on the car translate the 'harassment which in street after street, town after town, drives people on to the Vietnam rendezvous'. Any resemblance to a demonstration of the interwar years is precluded. To reply to the question by the West German Klaus as to what he would do if the Collective Personage came his way, Waldemar, who alone believes in a 'global' image of Rosa and considers that image to be dangerous, climbs on to the car to declare that all governments are united against Rosa, whatever she may be: Rosa 'represents subversion', and all the judges on earth will band together in another collective personage in order to condemn her. They will say: 'Judges of the world unite', and throughout the centuries 'rifles of the Auxiliary Cavalry Division will remain at the ready'.

This brings the reply from the Collective Personage: 'The violence of the bourgeois counter-revolution must be answered by revolutionary violence on the part of the proletariat.' A flash of light shows Red Alger on the car, armed with a sub-machine-gun from the stage props, declaring that in Texas, Alabama, Rosa is Mrs Rosa Parks, who defied the segregation rule in a Montgomery bus. Frieda's contribution is the historical image of Rosa declaring on the barricades after the defeat of the Spartakist uprising: 'The Revolution was, the Revolution is, the Revolution always will be'. The night before her assassination, Rosa had countered the triumphal cry of the bourgeois press, 'Order reigns in Berlin', with the words, 'You stupid lackeys! Your order is built on sand. Tomorrow the Revolution will raise its head again to your dismay, and proclaim to the blare of trumpets, I was, I am I will be!' 'Ich bin, ich war, ich werde sein' – With these last words, in German, of Rosa's, Gatti ends his introductory remarks to his text.

The dissolution of the Collective Personage is brought about not by those attempting to form it but by outside intervention which prevents the success of the enterprise, by the Presenter who breaks up the march to Vietnam and by the violence of the military organization, all convinced of the danger of a common action undertaken by the different images of Rosa together. The military organization builds an enormous scarecrow by attaching, to one of the three big structures which offer a silhouette of Rosa, placards attacking the Democratic Republic, and also inscriptions seen on the Berlin walls in 1918–19 calling for the death of Karl and Rosa and the suppression of the 'violent dictatorship of Spartakus'. However much the 'Lady Luxemburg may have changed', Waldeman declares, 'one thing that has not changed is Communism'.

Gatti's stage directions (*RC* 33) indicate that the three structures on the set are intended to give visible shape to the various images of Rosa and to facilitate the passage from one image to another. By making of Rosa a scarecrow, the right-wing organization gives tangible form to the bourgeoisie's fear of revolution, and in an attempted 'Possibilité (en suspens) de l'Opéra-Putsch des militaires' provokes the militant Strasbourg group to resort to their 'active language'. They take the three representatives of the extreme Right as hostages and add to them the two representatives of the Establishment before proceeding to demonstrate 'how to conduct a revolution'. They appropriately dress up the hostages as the *personae* of Capital (compliant judge, call girl, hit men) and order

Facets of Rosa Luxemburg: a Dramatic Character?

them, at the point of stage-prop swords, to dismantle the Fascist scarecrow in what Gatti describes as an 'acrobatic ballet'.

In the belief that the Revolution has taken place the hostages quickly opt for the Left and set to work to demolish the scarecrow, but their subsequent revolt causes the 'Revolution' to end in a punch-up engineered by Dieter, who calls for help from his supporters, a group of extras seated in the auditorium. The dramatic function of these extras, like that of the left-wingers' extras seated on stage near the official studio guests, is to provide a visual symbol of potential violence from factions outside the academic debate.

The fight is finally settled by the police, who are called in by all parties. During the scuffle the Rosa scarecrow is used as a 'tank' with 'troops' in the rear advancing on the Strasbourg 'tank' which is a realistic 'Rosa structure' with shoulders decorated with red and black flags like a general in the Peking Opera. The clash between the two structures is intended to offer the spectator a visual image of a clash between two monolithic parties, there being no trace of plurality in the Rosa of the Strasbourg group.

The physical confrontation, like the verbal confrontation arising out of the conflicting images of Rosa held by the assembled company, makes the play more dynamic still, and tension grows right up to the final five minutes, when the Presenter announces the failure of the proposed programme, expressing at the same time Gatti's own conclusion that the multiple images of Rosa cannot be focused in a single image through the refracting prisms of a theatrical performance. The several elements of the 'global' title on the front page of the three editions stress the divergence of the images present in the public's mind, and the structure of the play exteriorizes these images.

As might be expected, the various images of Rosa held by the different groups – Germany VII, the veterans Frieda and Reinhardt, Rosa's assassins, and Rosa's sympathizers – are antagonistic. But so too are those held *within* the body of her sympathizers, since they cover the whole political spectrum of the Left. The divergence of opinion emerges clearly in the section entitled 'A la recherche d'une possibilité qui les contiendrait toutes'. When the Presenter tries to continue with the programme, he finds himself faced with a demand by the Strasbourg group that the only image of Rosa that should be projected is that of 'Rosa the Revolutionary'. The Establishment considers this image too limited and rejects it in the name of 'humanism' – or, as the Strasbourg group puts it, in the name of 'demobilized man', of 'capitulation'.

The Presenter then suggests a 'parliamentary debate' on the person of Rosa, to be followed by a 'democratic vote' on the relevance of Rosa to the struggles of today. Klaus, from the Federal Republic, says his answer would be 'No', and hurriedly explains himself by saying that Rosa could be used by reformists and others who seek merely to collaborate in the government of a capitalist régime, alleging that she was opposed to organizational unity and did not see the necessity for the unity of theory and practice by means of a party. This criticism of Rosa is resented by Frieda and by the Strasbourg group, which scorns it as Soviet theorizing, as party talk, with an indirect reference to Vishnievski's *Optimistic Tragedy*. The Presenter's plea for language that a bourgeois audience can understand results in a free-for-all, with order being restored by the television technicians and with the police, at the Presenter's request, just looking on.

In a terrorist act of his own (Révolte [du Cameraman] qui aurait pu être une possibilité), the cameraman, in exasperation at the lack of guidance in the programme, seizes the life-size puppets of soldiers, sailors, workers, bourgeois, which were crowded round the car, and 'recycles' them into modern unheroic characters before throwing them, so much dead wood, to the guests. Since the puppets represented Rosa's immediate entourage, his gesture is as much a denial of Rosa's contemporary relevance as of the relevance of the puppets. They create a petrified image of Rosa which can only impede any march in the lived reality of today. Rosa is 'recycled' as the heroine of a strip cartoon for mass culture: 'Wonder Woman divested of her bullet-proof American-flag dress [...] militating in all the comics for the emancipation of women.' The East German 'Walter' argues that the only acceptable image of Rosa is as a member of the proletariat but the cameraman's final gibe is that women have been completely re-created by the media, that it is the media that decides what they are. 'And that goes for Rosa too', is the Presenter's opinion. The theme is more fully developed by the cameraman in the equivalent scene in the *Rosaspartakus* version where he flaunts the camera's ability to manipulate its material and the unlimited power of the media to arbitrate on a person's 'existence' or 'non-existence'.

Thirty-seven minutes are left for the programme after the cameraman's revolt. It is to be projected on a huge television 'screen' let down from the flies, and is to be entitled 'Rosa today – her life story – that of a Berlin proletarian'. Five possible Rosas: Ilse from Munich, Irene from a chemical factory in Dresden, Ursula Koch, Frieda and Gisela, the assistant Presenter, all mass-media Rosas – that is to say, 'set images' – are to represent her. However, when the 'screen' lights up, instead of Rosa, an officer of law and order makes his appearance in an unexpected 'Possibilité de l'uniforme policier' and announces an impending prosecution of the television team by Waldemar. 'Hats off to this Rosa of today', is the cameraman's comment. Reinhardt protests that Rosa had never worn such a uniform. The West German Klaus welcomes the image as God-given: on Germany VII such a Rosa could not be a mistake; it is a faithful image of revolutions of the past which became oppressive once invested with official ideology, and of revolutions of an unwanted kind in the future.

A further clash ensues between the guests before the story of 'Rosa today', the 'Berlin proletarian' as created by the media, can be told, or the great tit's cry reconstrued. In both Germanies it turns out to be a cry for better conditions of existence. But Walter, as an East German, protests against such an image, claiming that in his country at least the Revolution is still alive, and he quotes by name the many German women who met their end at the hands of the Nazis in continuing Rosa's fight. Ursula too pays homage to them in the name of the Brazilian Communist guerrilla Olga Benario, whose courage sustained the morale of her fellow-prisoners in the Ravensbruck camp before she herself died in the gas chamber alongside her child, whose sole experience of the world was the camp and the gas chamber.

The difficulty of finding an adequate dramatic language to present the German working-class woman of today as being closest to the authentic image of Rosa made Gatti shift his action from the Spartakists to the Black Panthers. Red Alger has had, of course, no part in German history, but his experience of American prisons has brought him to the rendezvous with Karl and Rosa, and in *Rosaspartakus* this experience is set in a dramatic action built round the case of George Jackson, then in the Soledad prison; it is omitted from *Rosa Collective*.

In both versions of the play, Red Alger founds a 'Spartakist Republic of a single evening' in which Rosa escapes from the history of the Whites to play her part in the history of the Blacks. The Presenter considers this resurrection of Rosa within the context of the Black American movement to be 'inverted racism'. Yesterday Jewish, today Black. But for Red Alger she is one and the same woman, living and fighting under different features. In *Rosaspartakus* the 'black woman' has a name; it is Angela Davis, officially proclaimed Public Enemy Number One by the FBI. The global image of Rosa which Red Alger tries to create symbolically in both versions of the play, by tying together the white mass-media Rosas of today with a long black band so as to form a single personage, is in fact not a single image but a 'monster' racked by internal dissensions which are given visual expression by its different 'elements' coming into conflict with each other.

The final disintegration of the global image is shown visually when the group divests itself of the black band and refuses Red Alger's call to man the barricades, 'save Angela Davis', who is in danger of being sent to the gas chamber, and 'free the Soledad brothers'. The group rejects the 'confusion of the times, that of the Spartakists and that of the Black Panthers'. These statements, which appear only in *Rosaspartakus,* make the sequence more explicit than does the monosyllabic 'No', in *Rosa Collective,* in reply to Red Alger's order: 'You too set the black people free'. By then Angela Davis had already been freed, and Gatti altered his text accordingly. At the end of the introduction to the earlier *Rosaspartakus*, written when Angela Davis's fate hung in the balance, one reads: 'When this fight is won (and it must be won) the play will turn to the fights which need to be fought at that moment.'

With Angela Davis freed, the Black Panther movement gets only summary treatment in *Rosa Collective*, whereas in the first version the history of the movement is acted out in a 'nine-round boxing match' with the studio guests in the parts of George and Jonathan Jackson, Angela Davis, two American 'Pigs', and the prosecuting judge at San Raphael. They do not, however, 'act' these parts; they 'recount' the actions of the figures they represent, using a technique which Gatti was developing in his dramatic experiments at that time. In *Rosa Collective*, Ursula implies that Red Alger is 'putting on a Nigger show for the Whites'. He retorts that it is a show that the Blacks themselves are putting on at that very time, and quotes names of black victims of the white US society. He symbolically shoots down each of the mass-media Rosas, then in discouragement tenders his resignation as 'Minister of Images for the constitution of the Spartakist Republic of one evening'.

The action in the studio comes to an end with with 'Possibilité de la prise de pouvoir' (*RC* 145) mimed by the historic figures of the Spartakist week. The guests surge on to the stage brandishing the puppets of soldiers and workers and carrying banners bearing Rosa's dictum for revolution: 'Dare', 'Dare to Think', 'Dare to Act', 'Dare to Create the Revolution'. They man the barricades built at Red Alger's behest with parts from the battered car. Unfortunately the puppets, mere images of a past revolution, can contribute nothing to the struggles of the living.

Red Alger makes a frantic call for action from the 'Spartakists of a single evening'. They respond with one of their Spartakist songs, described by the Presenter as a 'Hymn to Death'. It recalls for Ursula the fate of Rosa's friend Louise Kautsky, her prophecy of prison bars for her friends should they continue the fight and, ironically, her own end in the Ravensbruck camp which her very abandonment of the fight had helped to set up. Louise, says Ursula, died a victim like Rosa, but Frieda firmly draws the line: both victims indeed, but Louise did not die a combatant like Rosa, she died a rich Jewess at the hands of the Nazis. Ursula cannot dismiss the horrors of Ravensbruck from her mind and admits to having 'understood Louise'. This, according to the militant Red Alger, is defeatism, and he rejects her just as he rejects Martin Luther King for having gone down on his knees before the police on Pettus Bridge, with 1,500 black and white demonstrators at his back.

In the 'Five minutes' which remain for the programme, Frieda regrets the guests' persistent attempt to arrive at a modern Rosa; it would have

Facets of Rosa Luxemburg: a Dramatic Character?

been enough for the cry of the great tit to reach out from all the prisons in the world. To the Presenter's question: 'Why had they not been able to offer a programme on Rosa the Great Revolutionary?', the women of the programme give the answer: 'Never look for the prophet ... Militancy alone has the gift of prophecy.' According to the final stage directions, the women do not declare themselves to be a Rosa Collective because they are already a 'collective Rosa', albeit unconsciously. Gatti says in his conversation with Denis Bablet, published with the text of *Rosaspartakus*, that his play is not the 'negation' of the prophet, but the 'refusal' of the prophet. Any lesson to be drawn from the play would be that the fight has to be fought to the finish; that it is in the fight that a man finds his own truth and decides his line of action. The play is *la mise à mort*, or putting to death, of Rosa but the death of a hero does not signify the end of the fight; it signifies its continuation.

The set, composed of photos of historic figures and of the murderous inscriptions on the Berlin walls, of the puppets and the three 'Rosa structures', is not intended as a backcloth for a historical drama. All are active elements, each playing a special part in the action. Besides identifying the historical figures for the uninitiated, the dated photos materialize them and help to reconstruct the world of Rosa's activities. The wall inscriptions, particularly those putting a price on the heads of Karl and Rosa, recall the 'Red Terror' feared by the bourgeoisie of the time. The puppets function very much like the photos, but they have a stronger physical presence and can also actively collaborate with Rosa's sympathizers. The three 'Rosa structures' present the image of Rosa that those who use them seek to spread abroad.

The live characters are chosen according to the function they are to fulfil in the play. They are sociopolitical entities bearing the stamp of their country of origin and speaking the language of their profession or their social class. They are not characters in the literary sense. There is no examination of the psychology of the *dramatis personae*, nor any concern with their physical traits. Gatti is preoccupied, as always, with political issues and seeks to present them through the clash of *dramatis personae* who betray their political affinities by their attitudes, in this case at a round-table conference organized to discuss a specific subject, the possibility of a programme about Rosa. Each has his own view of Rosa and defends it as being the only authentic view. Each dismisses the views of others with a 'your Rosa' (*RC* 112, 125), never saying 'my Rosa'.

The idea of Rosa is therefore subjected to a fragmentation, or *éclatement*, which is the creation of others. 'There are as many possible Rosas as there are people in this studio', the Presenter tells the guests (*RC* 25). Gatti's experience as a journalist had taught him from an early date that the facets of an important public figure are as multiple as the points of view from which that figure is observed. His response, in the domain of art, is like that of Cubist painters, the facetization of the object and then its fragmentation. In this play the fragmentation technique consists of continually shelving the 'presentation' of the heroine until the final moment when it becomes clear that any 'presentation' is impossible. Rosa is not a 'subject' to be treated within the framework of a normal theatrical action. She cannot be reduced to the physical contours of a dramatic character; she can be apprehended only as a dynamic force behind revolutionary action in the world of today. Yet in seeking to find out how to write a play about Rosa, Gatti was in fact writing the play. The questioning and the writing were one and the same thing.

As regards the production, Gatti had to thank the Staatstheater in Kassel, a regular theatre for which the play had been commissioned. That very fact worried him. He had not sought to make a 'cultural object' to be admired by a bourgeois audience. As he said to Denis Bablet, he was the system's 'jester', to be retained or dismissed as it suited the system. The ambiguity of his situation lay in the fact that whilst attempting to fight the system with his political plays he had nevertheless remained within it, always at the service of an exploiting class. His one desire was to escape from this dilemma and take root in the real world, the world of the factory worker, in order to learn how to create an art form that would be a true expression of working-class reality. Gatti had been conscious of this dilemma for some time, especially since 1968 when he had made a first attempt to change direction through the series of scenarios for 'mini-plays' which he had written for the use of various action groups of students or trade unionists in 1968–9. His description of his state of mind while awaiting the first night of *Rosa* in 1971 shows that he had not found a solution and explains why, that same year, he accepted with alacrity the invitation of the University of Louvain to work with the students of its Institut des Arts de Diffusion. The last in line of the plays of Gatti's self-styled 'bourgeois' period was therefore to be *Rosa Collective*.

References

Peter Nettl, *Rosa Luxemburg* (Oxford University Press, 1964).

Section XII , 'Possibilité de la Rosa berlinoise (mass-médiatique)' contains a passing reference to Erika von Brockdorf, wife of the Expressionist painter Cay von Brockdorf. She reappears as a dramatic character under the name Erika Terwiel in Gatti's film/opera scenario *La Licorne* (see Chapter 15, 'The Archaeopteryx') and in his more recent play/opera, *Opéra avec Titre long*, based on the film/opera scenario and performed in Montreal in March 1986.

10
May 1968 and the Mini-Plays

Petit Manuel de guérilla urbaine.

Interdit à plus de trente ans. Le Chat sauvage

March 1968 had seen the production of Gatti's two new plays, *Les Treize Soleils de la rue Saint-Blaise* and *La Cigogne*, and November the production of his play of 1966, *La Naissance*. December saw the banning of *La Passion du Général Franco*. All Gatti's plays written for the legitimate stage, with the exception of *Rosaspartakus*, were therefore in existence by 1968. All had been written in the firm belief that through their performance and the contacts established by them with workers in the factories, they could help working people to equip themselves for their part in the class struggle which Gatti held to be the basic predicament in modern life. Their enriched intellectual culture would be a weapon in their hands. But already in *Les Treize Soleils* the customary view of human relationships, together with the meaning of the word culture, are challenged. What sort of culture should be fostered? With *V comme Vietnam* (1967) Gatti had already come up against the fact that without outside support from trade unions and specialized groups, the production of a political play would have been materially impossible. Moreover, to attempt to talk politics with the general theatre-going public was completely unrealistic.

The events of May 1968 convinced Gatti that he and his group had so far taken no serious step towards any real action. Not that the theatre could bring about a revolution, but at least it could provide information for serious reflection and debate. It was nevertheless clear that however much one sought to popularize the theatre, it could not be brought within the experience of working-class people – the 'non-public', as it has become known since 1968 – because of general working conditions, particularly long working hours. The full realization that one cannot work against a system whilst remaining within that system came only with the banning of his play on General Franco. This official ostracism was the last straw for Gatti and in 1969 he deliberately turned his back

Armand Gatti in the Theatre

on the cultural circuit of subsidized theatres (the only ones, in fact, where he had been played), just as he had turned his back on journalism ten years earlier. Traditional drama was, in his opinion, dead, and political drama, which alone interested him, could find no outlet in the theatres.

The month of May 1968, when factory work stopped and social and political questions were discussed in the street, had seemed to open up the way for street theatre. Gatti set to work to form twelve groups of actors to present the Commune to the people. The actors were to converge on the Hôtel de Ville from the rue Saint-Blaise, Belleville, the Porte d'Orléans, etc., and were to stage on the way different moments of the history of the Commune, using puppets up to four metres tall. Such puppets had, unknown to Gatti, been used by Peter Schumann's Bread and Puppet show the previous month at the Theatre Festival in Nancy. Gatti intended to use puppets to create centres round which a demonstration would form, but the street theatre never materialized because the actors were arrested beforehand. The audiovisual tapes which were to accompany the action were, however, projected on street walls until this was stopped by the police.

Except in circumstances such as those of May 1968, Gatti did not believe that street theatre could have an effective role, so he turned to writing a series of mini-plays which were directly related to a specific cause, or case. They were intended for performance by militant groups within the framework of their political action and constituted a deliberate attempt at *agitprop* theatre. Their collective title, *Petit Manuel de guérilla urbaine*, was meant as an ironic reply to the Chief of Police's declaration that in May the police had had to deal with specialists in urban guerrilla warfare. Since the mini-plays were designed for groups seeking to use the theatre as a weapon in the cause of the working class, the cast list is restricted and the staging reduced to spaces at cardinal points in a hall. This enabled the groups to be independent of subsidies and theatre managers, and safe from the arbitrary use of power by the authorities. The texts were not published in the ordinary way but appeared in a student leftist paper, *Action*. In 1976, however, offset copies from typescripts were issued by the Institut de Recherche des Mass-Média et des Arts de Diffusion (IRMMAD), German versions were published earlier in 1971 in Munich under Gatti's original ironic title, *Kleines Handbuch der Stadtguerilla*.

The first of these mini-plays was outlined in May 1968 at the request of militants of a Comité d'Action working with the local hospital staff, and is entitled *Pourquoi les animaux domestiques? ou La Journée d'une infirmière*. Gatti based it on discussions between the committee and the nurses. The title exactly describes the play's theme: the exhausting daily round of Louise, nurse and housewife, beginning at 5.15 a.m. – two hours getting to and from work, eight hours of intensive hospital routine, carefully minuted, and five hours of household chores, equally carefully minuted to prevent a complete collapse of the day's schedule. Years before, a chink was made in the walls of the social and moral prison in which Louise lived by a strange young man, but his violent death in Algeria closed the chink through which the outside world could have reached her and made her fight for a more human existence. This suggestion of drama was Gatti's personal contribution; the rest of the play is built on the recorded discussions. The suggestion gives a typical Gatti slant to the situation by implying that everybody is a creator and must assume the direction of his own life.

The text of this mini-play can be read in *Partisans* (No. 56, November–December 1970) alongside an article by the militant 'Group V' which undertook its performance. The article describes the violently conflicting attitudes adopted by the spectators, particularly during performances in hospitals. Groupe V also performed it in hostels and public halls, but this particular mini-play was subsequently performed widely throughout France in 1971–2 by the Théâtre permanent des Pyrénées after its success with it at the 1970 'Off-Avignon' Theatre Festival. In this production a single actress, Viviane Théophilidès, with no stage or barrier of any kind between herself and the public, succeeded in a series of 'confessions', which she made seated beside individual spectators as if they were the actual people in her life story, in building up the personality of Louise the harassed housewife and nurse, imprisoned in a soul-destroying existence which she herself helps to perpetuate by her very resignation to it. The setting suggested by Gatti in the text is eight clocks placed round the room in a circle, with chairs for spectators in front of each clock. In this way the spectators form part of the set and are also drawn into the action.

Les Hauts Plateaux, ou Cinq leçons à la recherche du Vietnam pour une lycéenne de mai which was performed in several towns in France, arose out of a day of protest staged by high-school pupils. The starting point of the play's action is the pupils' refusal to accept the dry bones of historical data served up by the history teacher without any account being taken of the human history behind the data. They therefore turn to those who actually *make* history, and in 1968–9 (the date of the play's composition) that meant the Vietnamese in their fight against the American attack. *Les Hauts Plateaux* is not, however, intended as a page of Vietnamese history; the Vietnamese struggle is taken as the symbol of class struggles the world over. No magical solutions are offered, but by its dialectical approach the play outlines the clash of two different views of society: a passive view in which the present is seen only in terms of the past, with the reality of today appearing as yet another repetition of history – 'all wars are cruel, no one denies the fact' – and a view which slowly gets to grips with concrete reality and leads on to efforts to bring about a transformation of the existing order of things. The two views are embodied in the persons of Ariane and her father, also a history teacher, and are presented in a dream sequence which traces the path trodden by Ariane in her attempt to situate herself in relation to history which is being made each day.

As a setting for the drama Gatti specifies three spaces on the east, north and west sides of a room or hall. In each is a blackboard, and in addition in the north space is a school desk. The spectators are seated in between the spaces and on the south side, where there are also two planks [*planches à tirer les images de nuit*] for Ariane and her father to sleep on. These form the realm of the Imaginary.

The three other characters are Vietnamese. One, Xuan, a Saigon lawyer and delegate from the National Liberation Front, is sent to enlist the mountain villagers of Sung-so in the fight against the attackers – that is to say, to persuade them to move from the policy of non-violence to a policy of violence-in-self-defence. Faced with the villagers' evident distrust of outsiders, as shown by their attitude to a couple who have come from Saigon to live there, Xuan decides to hide in a hole in the ground near the village until the single activist amongst the villagers manages to convert the others to the policy of active resistance. This takes three years. As if in a classroom, Xuan sketches on the blackboards the various holes he has constructed with the help of the activist. They constitute a veritable Maginot Line. The hole in which Gatti lived in the Corrèze maquis during the war until he was captured by the Gardes Mobiles is never far from his mind: it was there that for him, as for his dramatic character, 'everything began'.

As Ariane's father sees it, she has merely exchanged one lesson for another. She therefore goes (in imagination) to Vietnam to fight alongside the Vietnamese, only to find that the difference between their lived experience and that of a Paris high-school girl forms a gulf that is as difficult to bridge as that between the intellectual (the Saigon lawyer) and the worker (the Sung-so villagers). After her early compassionate-romantic approach – seen in her use of such words as 'suffering', 'justice' – and her participation in demonstration marches, she comes to realize that a solution has to be found to the existing separation of militants of different classes so as to achieve commitment to 'rebuilding the whole world' – the text specifically takes the spectator beyond the cause of the village of Sung-so. 'We' (Ariane and all the pupils of the high school) 'are the future', Ariane declares as the alarm clock wakens her from her dream.

The play does not feature a conflict of generations – the text specifies this – but the conflict of opposing views of society: one bourgeois (Ariane's father's), the other fired with a revolutionary purpose (Ariane's).

This makes it as topical today as it was in 1969. *Les Hauts Plateaux* is a study of attitudes put in a historical context, not a page of past history.

Gatti does not propose these mini-plays as finished works but as 'tools', as starting points for further research by the groups interested in them. When the play, then entitled *Cinq leçons à la recherche du Vietnam pour une lycéenne de mai*, was put on in a Strasbourg school with a member of staff in the role of the history teacher, the discussion between him and a pupil (in the role of Ariane) gave the impression that a class was being held. The Daniel Jacquin group used the text as a scenario which they developed according to their own ideas. Other groups preferred to underline, in their productions, the full import of the text. In every case the text was the source of much discussion. An analysis of the discussions which arose during rehearsals by the group *Comité Hauts Plateaux* was published by the *Comité* in *Partisans* (No. 47, April–May 1969) under the title 'une pièce outil de travail'. The discussions turned on the role of the theatre in present-day bourgeois society and the steps that need to be taken if the theatre is to have an effective revolutionary function, given the power of the dominant social class to silence any work, or to 'recoup' it in the sense of using it for its own purposes.

La Passion du Général Franco had provided a classic example of effective silencing, all the more significant as Jean Vilar's production in 1960 at the same theatre (the TNP), of *Arturo Ui*, on a related but more comfortably remote theme, illustrated the authorities' power to 'recoup'. By 1960 Brecht had become part of Western cultural heritage; this had not been the case in 1951 when Vilar produced the same author's *Mother Courage*, also at the TNP. Brecht's play was then considered by Rightists to be 'Communist' and caused a clamour for Vilar's instant dismissal from the management of the National Theatre, luckily unheeded by the Minister for Culture.

In *La Machine excavatrice pour entrer dans le plan de défrichement de la colonne d'invasion che Guevara* Gatti turns his attention away from the performers, to whom he had given full licence to do what they wished with his texts, and concentrates on the spectators, with the aim of achieving a solid actor–spectator synthesis. To this end he supplied only half a text, and this half is carried by characters who are just barely sketched. The challenge presented to actors and spectators alike is great. It was not taken up in France but was at Turn in the German Federal Republic, where audience participation was so keen that the performance, which began at 7.30 p.m., went on until midnight. Some of the spectators, however, complained that they had paid to see a play but had had to make the play themselves.

Apart from the technical experimentation, Gatti's purpose with this play was to provoke a discussion on the theme of revolution and the real nature of revolution. According to one of the characters, Marianne, 'A revolution changes with the times. It evolves by virtue of its own dynamism or it ceases to be a revolution.' It was therefore not enough for the Revolution to have succeeded in the small island of Cuba with Castro and Guevara. It had to pursue its drive forward; that meant into South America, where Guevara in fact carried it. Marianne refers with relief to Guevara's departure from Cuba, unaware of the consequences it will have for her.

The dramatic action turns on Totuy, officially Captain Diaz. He is a Cuban and a former revolutionary who went to Paris to study architecture, given the need for architects in the People's Republic of Cuba. Because of his earlier revolutionary contacts in South America Captain Diaz is recalled to Cuba, ostensibly to help the 'pacific revolution' with the use of excavating machines, but in reality to join the Guevara column in South America, where the 'excavation' is of a political and guerrilla kind. Marianne is kept in ignorance of her husband's final destination, and this deception weighs heavily on his mind. He also has a guilty conscience with regard to his companions who are completely committed to the Revolution, but he insists that he will make the 'romanticism which is his coexist with the Revolution at the service of which he had put himself'.

The dramatization (or a-dramatization according to one's point of view, as Gatti writes at the head of his text) is based on an exchange of letters. Except for a few necessary counterpoints, the characters do not speak directly to each other; they 'tell' of themselves. If necessary, the text can be performed by five actors speaking directly to the public, though Gatti sees this as a facile solution. He further seeks to open up perspectives in staging other than those traditionally accepted. Dispensing with the separation of stage and auditorium as in *Les Hauts Plateaux*, he envisages a room or hall in which four spaces to the north, south, east and west are marked out by a suitable accessory, in this instance parts of an excavator. In the centre a few instruments indicate the Paris meteorological station where Marianne works, whilst a household accessory placed between the meteorological station and the south space indicates her flat. This area is to be kept clear of spectators. Astride the north and east spaces Totuy and his three companions, who are training for the 'excavation' at the Minas del Frio in the Sierra Maestra where Castro had trained recruits for the Cuban Revolution, 'speak' his letter to Marianne. It tells about his companions. They stand motionless as though in a photograph, but say aloud their own words which Totuy is repeating in his letter. On the station in Paris, Marianne silently reads the letter but keeps stopping to consult the photograph Totuy has sent with it.

Gatti interrupts the text at this point. Assuming that 'everyone is himself a creator', he leaves it to the spectators to improvise the rest of

May 1968 and the Mini-Plays

the play. He states in the script: 'Everything the actors have said so far is merely a pre-text to serve as a pretext for discussion'. Possible leads are given to enable the spectators to fill in the dramatic 'structure' he has provided: for instance a young man disappears, leaving his wife without a word, and one day she learns that he is dead. Totuy's confession of a guilty conscience suggests a possible development of the action along sentimental lines, as in many boulevard plays. Alternatively it can provide the germ of a political drama highlighting South American problems. According to Gatti, a dozen plays can coexist on the theme, and the public which makes a choice never sees the same play.

Parallel with his treatment of the 'structure' is his treatment of the characters. They are as 'empty' as the 'structure' itself and need to be 'filled in by the spectators'. Marianne herself tells the audience so, saying: 'Marianne is no preordained character to be accepted or rejected by you. She will be born of you, the spectator', and she draws a parallel between the problems arising in a situation like Marianne's, not only for Marianne but also for the spectators. Marianne can become 'Louise, Dolores, Brigitte ... any woman in the Paris streets ... According to what you need to express, she will be what you want to say.'

Once the 'structure' is presented, the actors step out of their roles and address themselves directly to the audience to invite their participation. According to the response – or non-response – the actors have recourse to one or other of the 'possibilities' (possible lines of development) indicated by Gatti to stimulate the spectators' inventiveness. These may include the distribution of tracts for the audience to consult in the interval. One tract suggests several possible lines of action open to Marianne and Totuy; the other poses a number of pertinent questions in the South American context, the questions themselves containing much information on the situation there. If audience creativity is sufficiently stimulated, the actors can cease to be actors and take the place of the spectators, but should the spectators vote for the performance to be continued, the actors have been provided by Gatti with a text which takes up from where the first half-text left off.

Marianne is seen receiving letters from Cuba. These letters are typewritten and are composed in Totuy's name by two of his companions, since he himself has already left Cuba to join the Guevara column in South America. The letters are copied from newspaper reports on the progress of the peaceful revolutionary advance in Cuba in which Totuy is supposed to be engaged. Marianne discovers this when, in her anxiety, she takes the plane to Cuba and fails to find any trace of Totuy himself.

The third 'act', entitled 'Les Cités Solaires', follows the progress of the Guevara column, which has by now been joined by all Totuy's companions. This is revealed partly through an 'authentic' letter from Totuy to Marianne, and partly through the dramatic action presenting the guerrilla campaign in which the four men are engaged. The fate of the four is similar to that which Guevara and his column actually met in Bolivia in 1967. In Cuba, Marianne learns from a brief newspaper report that a Cuban captain and his guerrillas have been killed on the Brazilian frontier. It is for others to take up the challenge and pursue the Revolution in their place.

Given the experimental nature of this mini-play and the purpose behind its composition, one might have expected a down-to-earth approach to the problems raised. One is confronted instead with a piece of poetic writing. The image of Totuy as a cosmonaut, disappearing through the clouds to travel on eternally through space in pursuit of his mission, is ever present in the minds of all the characters. To Marianne this image affords some comfort as she follows Totuy in her imagination. Music, according to the stage directions, frequently 'punctuates' the action. The letters written about Cuba on Totuy's behalf are declaimed to a rhythmic beat.

The remaining panel of the *Petit Manuel, Ne pas perdre de temps sur un titre – Que mettez-vous à la place? – Une rose blanche*, is a dramatic text complete in itself. At no point do the actors propose to hand over the development of the action to the spectators, although involvement is sought by one of their number who enters by the same door as the audience and seats himself in their midst. As in the other mini-plays a system of 'spatial' settings, corresponding to the four cardinal points of the compass, is used and frontal staging is specifically excluded by a statement in the text. In one space, four chairs and an armchair accommodate the Disciplinary Council of the University of Munchenberg in Oderneissie: Gatti distances the historic action by playing on proper names, as he had done in *Chroniques d'une planète provisoire*. The armchair is transformed during the course of the action into a 'semi-electric' chair, alike in appearance to the 'chair for criminals' in 'Apaponasie'. A lie-detector called a 'polygraph', and a two-way mirror for the 'correct functioning' of the polygraph, occupy another space. In a third hang a number of animal masks modelled on 'Apaponète' strip cartoons.

Additional references to universities in 'Merlin', 'Bankfort', 'Tonn', and accusations against the students made by the 'Spring-und-Spring' press, identify the subject as being the anti-authoritarian revolt of German students led by Rudi Dutschke in 1968, although Dutschke's name does not figure in the text. The philosophy student called before the Disciplinary Council is named 'Hans Scholl'. Scholl comes in, obviously beaten up by the police and carrying a white rose which he claims to be the reason for his being summoned before the Council.

In this way the student revolt of 1968 is associated with anti-Nazi resistance in 1942 by the students of the 'White Rose', a group led by the twenty-five-year-old medical student Hans Scholl, on leave from the

May 1968 and the Mini-Plays

Eastern front. In a number of pamphlets, some of which Hans and his sister Sophie were seen to scatter from a balcony in the University of Munich, the group denounced the 'bestial murder' of 300,000 Jews in Poland 'as an example of what is happening', calling it a 'terrible crime against human dignity'. They urged the youth of Germany to rise in opposition. Hans and Sophie were denounced by a beadle of the university and brought before the dreaded 'People's Court'. They were executed on 22 November 1943, along with other members of the group including Kurt Huber, a professor of philosophy. In Gatti's play Hans is not executed; he is shot on the spot by a member of the Council, alarmed at the panic his final denunciation has provoked. The parallel with the attempted assassination of Dutschke by Josef Bachmann on 11 April 1968 reaffirms the association of the '68 movement with the White Rose.

During the greater part of the action Hans stands in dignified opposition to the university officials, pillars of the Establishment, each called 'Papa' because of the paternalism of universities and each with an accompanying adjective – 'Grand', 'Moyen', 'Petit' and 'Mini' – indicative of a pecking order.

A second theme, 'The passage of the characters from their Oderneissian nationality to the Apaponète nationality' – that is to say, the Americanization of their country – is worked into the play, and is given visual form through the Council members' assumption of various American strip-cartoon masks relative to their changing attitudes as they adapt themselves to the new order: when Moyen Papa shoots Hans he has become Grr, the Bulldog Policeman who had been sent to 'sniff' round the corridors. It is a world in which personal files 'pyramids high' are kept on everybody; a world of McCarthyite enquiries, of interrogations conducted on the 'semi-electric' chair wired up to the lie-detector, of infiltration by the FBI and the CIA, and of the ambivalent morale of the business community. The resulting dismay of the Councillors leads to indecent manoeuvring amongst their number; also to moments of broad comedy.

As for the 'man with the White Rose', the 'Apaponète' agents understandably fail to find any files in 1968. They conclude that he 'does not exist' despite the fact that he stands there in front of them; the conclusion of the computers is not to be gainsaid, and the computers say he does not exist. Faced with this Americanization of the society in which he lives and the uncertainty of his own future, Hans gives in and allows himself to be 'recouped' by the authorities. He hesitantly accepts the directorship offered by Grand Papa and, 'immediately adopting the Apaponète style as it is exported', assumes the mask of Niag the Tabby Cat. However, his experience of the working of this new society sickens him. He throws aside his mask and, standing on a chair in the midst of the audience, shouts:

> There comes a time when the operation of the Machine becomes so odious [...] that one can no longer take part, even tacitly, in it. At that moment one must lay one's body on the cogs, wheels and levers, and on the whole Machine, to bring it to a halt. We must make those who work it understand that even if we are not free, we will do all in our power to prevent it from functioning.

He could have added Dutschke's rejection of 'this society where man is not master of his destiny, where an inhuman bureaucracy, obeying rules established by the ruling classes, imposes his conduct on him in every walk of his life.'

The play closes with Hans's body stretched out in the 'semi-electric' chair, under a spotlight which gradually narrows until only the White Rose in his hand is visible.

The play would seem to have been written with German actors and audiences in mind. It was published in Germany and was performed in Bremen and elsewhere, but it was not taken up by any groups in France after the French students' own revolt of 1968, doubtless because of its exclusively German system of references.

A mini-play entitled *Interdit à plus de trente ans* was written in 1969. It follows in the tradition of the *Petit Manuel*, particularly *La Machine excavatrice*, where inventive participation of the public is sought, but it is not included in the *Manuel*. The student revolt in Paris, in Munich where two students were killed by the police, in Tokyo where two others were killed, and the troubles of the 'hot summers' in the Black ghettos of America are recalled, and this sets the stage for the action, which centres round Don Quixote, whose idealism and romanticism appealed to the whole of Gatti's generation. Did not Gatti himself take the name Don Quichotte when he joined the Maquis during the Occupation? Twenty years later, the public is asked by the actors, early on in the performance, whether they agree to the literary characters of Don Quixote and Sancho Panza being confronted by the events of the spectators' own times. In the event of a refusal it was to be left to the public to continue the action as they saw fit, and to the actors to take the place of the public. But should the public accept the proposal, a text was provided for the actors to perform.

In a number of 'selmaires', with 'characters' designated by numbers, not names, to avoid their being individualized, Don Quixote seeks a place in the new times. In each 'selmaire' the action is set in a different place. The 'selmaire of the Sorbonne to protest against the deluge' presents a satirical picture of the American student revolt against the ideology which was imposed on them and which they saw as being dispensed by the university. This attitude is essentially apolitical, romantic and quixotic, whether it is exasperated individualism or 'collective individualism' of the let's-get-together-and-communicate type. Gatti has them all set sail in Don Quixote's Ark on the 'deluge' which is coming.

In a 'selmaire' which recalls the Resisters of the war years, Don Quixote finds that their descendants have been incorporated into the forces of law and order. What sort of dialogue can he establish with the policemen-sons of Clarine, who was beheaded by the Nazis?

Yet another 'selmaire' suggests a criticism of 'I'm-all-right-Jack' trade unionism, and contrasts it with the militant trade unionism of earlier years. The 'selmaire' ends with the militant delegate apologetically declaring, 'I'm not Don Quixote. I am Georges Pompidou come to inaugurate your 14th July Ball'. 'Long live 14 July', is sung by the 'collective person who is trying to give a clear image of the present-day proletariat'.

The general butt of these sardonic satires, in whatever field, is acceptance not struggle, and Don Quixote finally gets back into the book. There is, however, one 'selmaire' – that of a 'remembered event' – which allows the play to 'fall back into unprocessed documentation' concerning young people capable of carrying an action through to the bitter end. It describes an event in June 1968 when Gilles Tautin, a college student, was shot by the CRS as he swam away in the Seine after demonstrating in support of the Renault workers at Flins-sur-Seine when they occupied their factory. The attempt to establish a dialogue between the literary character of Don Quixote and the young Gilles Tautin was, in Gatti's mind, the central point of the script.

Over the space of almost a year 'Groupe V' gave readings of the text to audiences of many kinds, and in the light of the discussions recorded during the readings Gatti rewrote the text completely. The new text is entitled *Le Chat sauvage,* and in it Gatti even inserted arguments, mainly political, with which he himself did not agree. To do otherwise would have invalidated the experiment, he said, since he was himself only the scribe. Don Quixote disappeared entirely from this version. The humanistic vision gave way to the strongly political attitudes of the generation of 1968. The reference to the 'wild-cat' strike at Flins with its fatal outcome leads, in the new version, to a consideration of the meaning of Tautin's gesture for today, and of how one can play a part in the cause for which Tautin died. Among those who will actively take part in politically motivated and lucid international struggles, the spirit of Don Quixote will live on.

Le Chat sauvage was staged in June 1970 in a tent pitched in a street; afterwards in the university building of Paris-Censier; and finally in a hall in the 20^e *arrondissement*. As with the other mini-plays, there was no question of *Le Chat sauvage*, a 'collective work written up [*mise en texte*] by Armand Gatti', being put on in the normal theatre circuit. In view of audience reaction to this version, Gatti went on to write a third and dubbed the series 'work in progress'. This experiment was brought to a halt by ideological differences arising within 'Groupe V', but Gatti found it 'enthralling'.

11
Belgium–Germany: Not a Theatre but a Human Community

I La Colonne Durruti. L'Arche d'Adelin

II Quatre schizophrénies à la recherche d'un pays dont l'existence est contestée. La Moitié du Ciel et nous

Given the boycott to which Gatti was subjected in France as far as the normal theatre circuit was concerned after the affair of *La Passion du Général Franco*, the invitation from the Staatstheater in Kassel in 1968 to stage *La Naissance* there did not come amiss. The unusual type of performance of the German version, *Die Geburt*, which began outside the theatre building and ended up in an impromptu political demonstration, made Gatti think that perhaps after all the legitimate theatre could be pressed into the service of political drama. Two years later, however, when his play on Rosa Luxemburg was ready to open, he expressed a fear that the audience would be a typical first-night audience prepared to pay five or ten times the price of a seat for the privilege of being present. The idea that they might claim ecstatically afterwards: 'That's our fight', filled him with horror and made him wonder what political theatre really was and whether its real venue was not the factory. This made him think that he had better go and work in a factory, not to do a bit of slumming but to get to know the thoughts, fears, hopes and reactions of working-class people, and so help himself to create a 'language' capable of expressing them.

Gatti put his idea into practice and, after the production in Kassel of his play on Rosa Luxemburg, took a job in a factory in West Berlin for six months. He told me an amusing tale of his experiences there. Because he was considered to have 'lady's hands' he was put to work amongst Turkish women in the weaving shed. To hide his humiliation he deliberately dirtied his hands on leaving the shed instead of washing them like the others. While he was at the factory Giorgio Strehler brought the Piccolo theatre to Berlin to play Gorki's *Lower Depths* and invited Gatti to the performance. After much hesitation Gatti accepted. The performance was followed by a visit to a restaurant with the cast, most of whom had played in *Auguste Geai* in Italy. The meal went on for some hours, and when all Gatti's attempts to get away failed, he finally had to admit at 4 a.m. that he was due at a factory at 5 a.m. All took this to be a joke and piled into three taxis which took them to the factory gates! Gatti confesses to having learnt in the factory that men left the place exhausted and with but one idea in their heads, namely sleep, and the Sunday 'rest' was indeed a day for sleep!

Gatti's origins, as he frequently recalls, were working-class, but he had finally come to feel himself in the same position as the workman who had told him that since he had been promoted to the works committee and was no longer engaged on the production belt, he had lost contact with the men on the shop floor and knew nothing of what was happening there. As an 'intellectual' Gatti was uncomfortably aware of his privileged position and of his minority culture, which was as much a closed book to the proletarian as the proletarian's was to him. It was clear that without the lived experience of the proletarian, any attempt to present working people would be made only from the outside or at best be based on his own personal and necessarily limited experience as a workman. To write for the people one had to live amongst the people, be 'implanted in a community'. This belief led him to take up residence in communities of all kinds and work with the people in them, no longer as a playwright but, to use his own word, as a 'catalyst' of the creative powers of the people of the community in question.

I *La Colonne Durruti*

The first of these experiments took place with the help of the Institut des Arts de Diffusion of the Catholic University of Louvain.[1] For some time the Institute, faced with the ever-widening scope and diversity of contemporary dramatic art and with the concrete evidence that the protean actor capable of switching from Grotowski to Planchon, of appearing in the Comédie Française and also in children's theatre, did not exist, had called foreign producers into the school to try to solve the problem of suitable training for the modern actor. One of these, Pierre Debauche, had staged Gatti's *La Cigogne* in Brussels in 1970 with students from the Institute, and Gatti had been a guest at the performance.

When he was invited to direct the students' work the following year, Gatti made it clear that he would not use conventional methods of training, nor undertake any formal theatrical performance. He proposed instead to involve the students in a 'project' of which the starting point would not be a written text already in existence, but a collective text and a collective production to be arrived at by the students working

Belgium – Germany: Not a Theatre But a Human Community

together under his guidance. He suggested as a subject the Spanish anarchist Buenaventura Durruti, and the mystery of his death on the Madrid front during the Civil War. This was the first the students had ever heard of Durruti, but when it came to their production – *Columna, Colonne, Κολλona, Kolonne Durruti*, – they presented seven different images of the man: the journalistic, the bureaucratic, the popular, the image of the family man, the political theorist, the guerrilla fighter, and the police image – Durruti had been sought by the police in many countries. The text on the mystery of his death was written up finally by Gatti, but each student chose the version he wished to perform. The question of how Durruti died was debated. Was he shot by Francoists – his enemies? By Communists – his allies? Or by some disillusioned member of his own brigade who saw his statement during the defence of Madrid: 'I am prepared to sacrifice everything, but not victory' as a betrayal of the basic anarchistic principle of revolution first and foremost?

Initial discussions about the project took place with the students in October 1971 when they divided into groups to collect relevant documentation under the supervision of their regular teachers during Gatti's absences in Germany.[2] Books, films, Spanish immigrants in Brussels were all consulted. On his periodic visits to Louvain from Germany, Gatti discussed their documentation with the students and the dramatic forms they proposed to use to present it. This was to be a real attempt at 'collective theatre' and if, as Gatti said, he was the scribe, theirs were the voices. The discussion also centred on the setting in which the project was to be realized, since the text, as well as the presentation of the text, would necessarily be dictated by the choice.

Durruti himself had never been to a theatre; the hours at which performances took place were a sufficient deterrent for three-shift workers; so to put 'Durruti' on a stage would have been a real assassination of the man. The scenes of his activities were the street, prisons the world over, and the factory. Incessant rain ruled out a street performance and no disused prison was available. There remained the factory; moreover it was to the factory that Durruti, disdainful of 'medals and portfolios', intended to return once the success of the Revolution was assured. The choice fell on the dilapidated Rasquinet factory in the rue Josaphat in the working-class Schaerbeek Commune of Brussels. In this setting it immediately became obvious that the text on Durruti's 'three deaths' first written by the students in the quiet confines of Louvain University was quite out of place. A new dramatic 'language' had to be invented, one that would be in keeping with the factory setting. The factory itself was in a bad state of repair; water and electricity had to be installed by the students; they also had to repair the roof, through which rain poured incessantly. Umbrellas were in constant use; they even became the symbol of the students' own struggle to fulfil their project – 'the umbrella is our dialectical materialism', was Gatti's comment.

27 April 1972 marked Gatti's permanent return to Brussels, and he camped out in the factory together with a number of the students. Shortly afterwards some of Gatti's 'comrades' arrived from Paris to take over practical tasks and leave the students free to prepare the production. These tasks included the distribution of tracts, the decoration of the factory walls, and the construction of massive puppets representing the international powers that confronted the revolutionaries: Hitler, Mussolini, Franco, Stalin, Blum, Chamberlain and Pacelli, who became Pope Pius XII in 1939. On their tunics were badges ironically thanking those powers said to patronize and finance both the puppet and the figure it represented; for the Pope it was the Opus Dei and the International Red Cross. Each puppet had hands capable of expressive gestures. Because of this and their great size – they were twelve feet tall – they needed three people to manipulate them. The 'comrades' also organized the final 'fête' for actors and public alike, who were joined after the performance, which was itself free, by people who invaded the factory from the street bringing provisions with them. They came to make merry, and in no time one could hear, as in May 1968, the rhythmic chanting *'Ce-n'est-qu'un-début-con-ti-nu-ons-le-combat'* 'This is only a beginning, the fight must go on'. If those who earned a living by the sweat of their brow could occupy official buildings in much the same way as the proletariat of Barcelona had made themselves masters of the street during their resistance to the military putsch of 1936, that was 'la fête au futur' for which Durruti had striven – 'the story of Durruti did not end with his death in 1936' (*Caheirs* p. 36). In this way the fête became a 'fourth version' of Durruti's 'death'.

The factory had a number of rooms of different shapes and sizes on the same floor, though on slightly different levels. The main rectangular hall was named for the occasion the Salle Makhno. On its walls was painted a plan of the layout of the factory with the programme of events scheduled to take place in the other sections, together with an invitation in Makhno's words to the working class to create its own truth. In this hall the students installed a number of old cars, fitting platforms for the performance of the three official versions of Durruti's death; Durruti was killed by a bullet from an unidentifid adversary as he stepped out of his car on the Madrid front.

A slope led up from the Salle Makhno to two long narrow adjoining rooms, the Salle Sacco-et-Vanzetti and the Salle Rosa-Luxemburg, which in turn led to the Salle Guérillero Solitaire where, as the barricades were put up during the performances, a link was forged between events of the Spanish tragedy and of tragedies as far afield as the New World. A

Belgium – Germany: Not a Theatre But a Human Community

further slope led from this room to the Salle Commune Asturienne. Through the dividing wall a cinemascope-shaped hole was cut to act as a 'screen' on which the actors could be seen from both sides. As none of the rooms was large enough to accommodate the spectators at any distance from the players, the decision was taken to perform among the spectators, who had to remain on their feet and move with the actors from room to room. In this way they became active participants in the drama, and this active role was allotted them from the outset by the simultaneous enactment of the seven 'images' of Durruti in different parts of the Salle Makhno; each spectator had therefore to choose the image that attracted him the most.

Durruti's name was linked with three towns – Barcelona, Madrid and Saragossa – which the lack of arms and munitions, promised by the Madrid government but never delivered, prevented him from taking. Saragossa represented the 'idea-programme' of the Durruti anarchists: 'to win the Revolution is to win all wars'. For the students it represented a 'rebirth' enabling them to get to grips with world events and, less exaltedly, it meant the successful conclusion of their 'project' with the use of the hammer, saw and pliers, and also the umbrella to shelter them from the incessant rain. Events in Barcelona and Madrid were seen as belonging to past history and were presented in different ways.

The struggle in Barcelona took the form of a bullfight with the proletariat as the bulls wearing huge masks and the Civil Guards as the toreadors urged on by the huge puppets. The sequence on Madrid presented, in the first instance, the front with the Garibaldi brigade winning a psychological victory over Mussolini's expeditionary force. This was followed by the story of the bombing of Madrid, the first deliberate bombing of a civilian population, related simultaneously in different rooms by four actresses each giving her own version of the horror it entailed. Their stories were followed up in the Salle Makhno by an active representation of the massacre of the civilians – actors and spectators alike – carried out by the puppets of 'Hitler', 'Mussolini' and 'Franco' who spread their arms like giant wings and swooped down on the crowd like death-dealing bombers to a deep-throated throbbing produced by the actors. 'One's thoughts went to Guernica, and when Stalin appeared preceded by a child's plane fluttering on the end of a stick, the disproportion between the forces facing each other needed no further commentary' (*Cahiers* p. 55). In the Salle Rosa-Luxemburg another aspect of Madrid life was represented: black marketeers, pimps and prostitutes all prospering.

For Durruti the Civil War was in reality the revolution of the proletariat, and as such was one part of an international struggle. For Gatti this means Vietnam, Quebec, Latin America, Germany, France – and it was this aspect of the theme that the students, under Gatti's guidance, sought to bring out, refusing to limit their production to the dramatization of a page of Spanish history. 'One of our reasons for making a play about Durruti was Vietnam,' said a student on the forty-fourth day of their collaboration, 'because no one carried the guerrilla movement further than Durruti, whether ideologically or in practice' (*Cahiers* p. 116).

In order to relive the Durruti saga through their personal experience, the students chose to represent those historic revolutionary figures who had most in common with their own experience. Amongst them were S. Lorenz, a former Spartakist who had joined the International Brigade, the English painter Felicia Browne, who was shot through the head in a street battle in Aragon on 25 August 1936, or Durruti's personal friend, Francisco Ascaso. A tiny actress playing the part of the printer Free Huey Arm, a huge Afro-American, 'the only Black in the Durruti column', made this point when she said that the problems of her native Quebec were very like those of the Blacks: 'We are a species of Negro: white Negroes'. Another student said: 'This experience helps me to continue May '68 and to carry on my own fight against the present system.'

This statement was written up along with many others on the walls of the Salle Rosa-Luxemburg where all were encouraged by Gatti to write up, in a sort of collective diary similar to the *da dzi baos*, or wall newspapers of the Chinese Cultural Revolution, not slogans but personal feelings and opinions with regard to the characters they chose to represent. In May 1968 wall-posters, handbills, the street where ideas grew and spread, were the true revolutionary medium of communication; they provided a real alternative to the mass media. Gatti wanted the walls of the Salle Rosa-Luxemburg to be alive with inscriptions, and himself wrote up on them the names of Rosa Luxemburg and Sacco and Vanzetti; he regretted that more recent fighters and victims – such as the Maoist worker Pierre Overney, who was killed while distributing tracts in front of the Renault works at Billancourt during the strikes after 1968; or Denis Gezmiz and his two compatriots, just executed in Turkey – were not written up as well. He urged the students to 'take possession' of their own times and not lag fifty years behind them (*Cahiers* p. 20). It was this establishment of a relationship between past and present, the consciousness of the present as continuing the past, that provided the vocabulary of the 'dramatic language' the students needed, just as the name Durruti had appeared spontaneously on the walls of the Black ghettos in California in 1966.

Gatti's rejection of traditional theatre was radical by this time. Character-acting, psychological analysis, lyricism were all repudiated. Instead of 'interpreting' a character, the actor was to approach the historical personage he had decided to play by starting from his own political experience – his own 'context', as Gatti was to put it later. The production itself was to be a combination of a show with song and dance, masks and puppets, and also a political meeting aimed at provoking discussion with the public, who were to be invited to follow the action from room to room. The involvement of the public ruled out any idea of 'finish' in the acting. What was offered the public was not a finished production but the rehearsal of a work still in progress and with spectators discussing with the actors. The evening ended with further discussions between the actors and separate groups of spectators held under the 'chairmanship' of the appropriate puppets – 'Hitler' on the question of the militarization of a nation, 'Franco' on collectivization as against landed ownership. The performance did not, however, conclude with any 'triumphalist' political eloquence. Durruti's column of the 1930s gave place to the IAD column of the '70s (the title of the students' venture although not of the show, said Gatti) which marched off at the end with their umbrellas on their shoulders to mark the continuity.

Gatti's other innovation was to invite political parties to set up stalls in the main hall so as to broaden the 'project' by taking in contemporary history. As was to be the case for the 1976 performance of *La Passion du Général Franco* at the Ney Calberson lorry depot in Paris, the stall-holders were left-wing in outlook, although the only condition imposed by Gatti was an interest in the group's work. The stalls also served as rest centres for spectators who opted out of active participation in the show, and created an atmosphere favourable to discussion for the political parties which wished to profit by it. The stall-holders even intervened in the show from time to time. The Trotskyites turned up with beer and sandwiches. The anarchists went one better, giving free drinks. Then stalls with black puddings and chips appeared. Some Spanish Communists who had refused to take part nevertheless came and argued frankly in a spirit of comradeship, while rejecting the way in which the events of the Civil War were portrayed.[3] An apparently extraneous element was thus completely integrated into the performance and became basic to it.

La Colonne Durruti was performed – or rather enacted – on 9, 10 and 11 June 1972, and three thousand people, largely from outside the normal cultural circuit, were admitted free. Because of this experience some participants acquired a new idea of the theatre's role and possibilities. But Gatti was still not satisfied. The Tribe, as his group was known by then, had not succeeded in breaking away completely from the notion of a 'performance' given before an audience; whereas Gatti's objective was theatre without an audience, 'un spectacle sans spectateurs', in which all those present were to be co-creators in a non-commercial event. The spectator-consumer who receives his ration of culture in exchange for money was to be replaced by an active assembly. With this in mind Gatti embarked on a new experiment, again with the co-operation of the IAD and the Drama Department of the University of Louvain. The experiment was entitled *L'Arche d'Adelin*[4] and was to be extended to a rural area of Walloon Brabant where theatre was non-existent.

L'Arche d'Adelin

In September 1972, the Tribe and those students of the two institutions who agreed to take part installed themselves in a country school, without the four resident teachers of the IAD. They divided into groups to contact schoolchildren, agricultural workers, housewives and others with the aim of stimulating their powers of inventiveness, of getting them to write scenes and sketches about experiences outside their own. In a word they sought to help people become creators of the theatrical act and not remain passive spectators of it. A number of lines of approach were tried out such as *pièces-enquêtes*, one of which concerned a celibate Breton peasant, Hervé, a former prisoner of war, then an industrial worker who returned to the land before hanging himself from a tree. In farm after farm the students asked about the possible motives for Hervé's suicide. The farmers were not politically minded and were not given to reading books or newspapers. They were interested in what concerned them the most closely, and that was the Common Market. Each imagined an explanation of Hervé's suicide in the light of his own experience of the Market.

Another case was that of an agricultural worker who had been shot dead on 23 March 1972 during a demonstration in Brussels. After days of research extending as far south as Dinant amongst demonstrators who had been questioned by the police, the students were left with two images of the dead man, the summer image and the winter image, each showing him as the prisoner of his daily and seasonal routine before his disquieting realization that pensions were so low that, at about fifty years of age, an agricultural worker had to go into industry in order to earn enough to live on as a pensioner. The peasantry saw itself as the unfairly exploited milch cow of the Common Market. Then again, since Esso and Nestlé were busy trying to make food products out of petrol, etc., what sense was there in sowing and reaping?

In a long scene giving several versions of the Brussels demonstration according to the police, the agricultural trade union, etc., a peasant declares: 'The peasants are the Indians of the New America that Belgium has become'. The complex reality of rural life formed the basis of these and other scenes written by local people or by the student-actors, with the guiding principle of individual experience being examined in relation to current affairs of national and world scope. A comparison with the Army Bureau of Current Affairs (ABCA) service in England during the last war springs to mind, with of course the differences implied by the Tribe's total commitment to theatrical execution.

The experiment, however, never really got off the ground until the affair of Omer Labarre, a Bousval smallholder who was expropriated to make way for a new motorway. Without a word to anyone Labarre took to the road with his flock and went straight ahead until he landed up in the Dordogne valley in France. The story caught the general imagination; for many it was the modern Belgian version of Noah and his ark. Children in the schools were asked to write about *L'Arche d'Adelin*. Adults began to embroider on the theme of the 'flood' that had caused Labarre to flee (motorway, Common Market regulations, Mansholt plan, new summer residences?) and to give different impressions of the man. Some had known him before his departure; others completely reinvented him and his wife Louise according to their own experiences or professions. At one point during the 'performance' these imaginary Adelins were confronted with the real 'Adelin' in an audiovisual recording made by the Tribe in the Dordogne.

The general public contributed twenty-two plays, student-actors seven, and there was a musical comedy, *Les Îles*, based on a confrontation between the Tribe and the young people of Bousval. Contributions by small children usually took the form of invented games such as hopscotch on a Noah's dove drawn on the ground, but one of their plays particularly impressed Gatti by its creativeness: it presented the clock as the force that had driven Adelin away. Another clock, however, awaited him on his arrival in the Dordogne. Then came the war, represented by lighted matches thrown right and left by the child until the box was emptied, when the child fell to the ground saying: 'I am dead'.

Posters advertised *L'Arche d'Adelin* as a 'spectacle où tous les âges de l'homme sont au rendezvous', and indeed the ages ranged from five to eighty-three. The scenography was established not in space but in time, the span of a human life, which was integrated into the history of Belgium, and even of the world. It passed from the lived experience of the Brabançon worker Théophile D, aged eighty, who had seen the first motorcar to appear in his village, through the lived experience of others in the region, the mechanization of agriculture, the struggles of the trade unions, the World War. The characters embodying these aspects of local life were presented in various versions – video, dramatic, even 'plastic', that is to say by giant puppets made from directly identifiable instruments of the character's work: farmer Cyril V, aged sixty-five, had a body made of pieces of a 1955 tractor, arms made of sacks of fertilizer from a local firm, and for a heart a heater from a pigsty. The aim was not to make an aesthetic object, but a version of the person that would be immediately recognizable by everyone. This was one of a number of *pièces-trajets*.

With such rich and varied material there remained the need to structure the 'collective spectacle'; this was Gatti's task. *L'Arche d'Adelin* was launched on 20 May 1973 and took the form of a motorized column of 145 tractors with trailers serving as stages for the numerous plays which were performed simultaneously over a period of twenty-eight hours as the column drove thirty-five kilometres from village to village. The vehicles were provided free of charge by the farmers and were driven by them. They stepped in when the Belgian Army, which was to have supplied lorries for the purpose as it had done in March for the Carnival arranged by the Tribe at Melin, suddenly changed its mind. As Gatti explained to K.D. Kaupp: 'French spies attempting to get the Walloon incorporated into France, carriers of arms for the IRA, traffickers in drugs and dropouts: this is how we were described in the Belgian press.' It was again very reminiscent of the outcry which had greeted Gatti fifteen years earlier when *Le Crapaud buffle* was staged in Paris.

In the Brabant the collective theatrical experiment, with its three thousand spectator-actors (all had participated in the creation of it in some way) and the women's supply of home-made dishes and tarts, had the air of a people's carnival. Gatti called it 'magnificent'. He was satisfied at having put three thousand people 'into a state of creativity during several months', at having enticed them out of the 'ghetto of their daily routine' into 'different territories', and at having made them realize that these different 'territories' could be occupied by them. He went so far as to declare that three thousand people coming to confront their various points of view by means of Adelin's motorized column was a more important event than the attendance of twenty thousand paying spectators at *Chant public devant deux chaises électriques*. In Belgium an event had been created which implied individual and collective activity in both time and space. It was an activity in which the participants had changed both their view of the world and of themselves, and that was the *essence* of the group's work according to Gatti, the 'catalyst'. Who can doubt that the activity was an enrichment for all concerned? Who can doubt that for the successful accomplishment of such socially useful work in our generation, what are called in English 'left-of-centre' tendencies are indispensable?

Gatti's own sympathies were now carrying him well to the left of centre. His interest as a theatrical creator was aroused more and more keenly by figures of the 'extreme left', 'gauchistes', 'terroristes', 'guerrilla fighters', anarchists, profoundly and passionately hostile to the social organization of our time. They fired his imagination as no cool analysis of the capitalist crisis and failure could ever do. For a detached observer the mere existence of guerrilla fighters or their equivalent in a score of countries would itself suffice to diagnose a profound disorder of modern society. But Gatti was not a 'detached' observer: he was an 'involved' observer. For Gatti, 'observation' *is* action, and a 'detached' position is one of tacit complicity with the existing order. It is for this reason that his attention was drawn to two figures, those of Michèle Firk and of Ulrike Meinhof. They appear in two 'collective' plays which he went to Germany to write in 1974.

II Quatre schizophrénies à la recherche d'un pays dont l'existence est contestée

Michèle Firk is the main figure in this play. The play itself continues the line of research followed in *La Colonne Durruti* and *L'Arche d'Adelin*, but the community in which it was carried out was the more restricted one of a theatrical company, that of the Forum Theatre in West Berlin. As in the Belgian experiments, Gatti brought no pre-existing text with him. His aim in the Berlin theatre was to involve the director, the actors *and* the author – that is to say, himself – in the creation of a 'collective work' or, as he was later to call such productions, *une écriture plurielle*. Work on the project began in mid-November 1973 and the performance – in German, under the title *Vier Schizophrenien auf der Suche nach einem Land, dessen Existenz umstritten ist* – was given on 14 February 1974. The German text was published by the Forum Theater, along with a description of the method used throughout the experiment. The volume includes several pages of historical documentation on the subject and a bibliography.[5] No French text exists, although the play is listed amongst Gatti's works under the French title.

For the experiment Gatti proposed, as a possible subject, the Central American country of Guatemala as seen through the eyes of Berlin actors. They accepted the proposal. They listened to Gatti's description of that country and sought further documentation in libraries. Discussions on the situation in Guatemala followed, and possible ways of presenting on stage the issues raised were tried out. Each day Gatti would arrive about noon with some fifteen pages of handwritten script based on the previous discussions. He would give a graphic interpretation of his script, which was then translated into German and subjected to further discussion. In the light of the criticisms and suggestions Gatti rewrote the day's text which was retranslated, amended or rejected, and then rewritten. The process was one of gradual textual creation and of inventive theatrical presentation. Gatti's final version (in French) was handed to Klaus Hoser and Christian Rateuke on 30 January for translation into German, and has not survived. The numerous lyrics were set to music by the French composer Jackie Moreau-Meynard. The reference in the title to four *schizophrénies* is simply to the four actors who followed the project the most closely.

Gatti's purpose in proposing Guatemala as a subject was to bring the actors to an intuitive understanding of a land in which everything, even death, has a different meaning. The Western categories of time, place and causality themselves cannot relate in any way to life in Guatemala, so only as a schizophrenic can one go to that land. What, for instance, can a European intellectual, with Marx in his European heart and Lenin in his European head, achieve in a struggle in Latin America? He can only become a new conquistador, unless he arrives at an intuitive understanding of those of Indian descent.

Any thought of a mimetic representation of historical characters such as the infamous General Ubico on the one hand, or Michèle Firk the revolutionary fighter on the other, was alien to Gatti, who sought to help his actors to an understanding of such figures starting from their own experiences. So the actors recount their own experiences in their own name, in front of the spectators at the beginning of the play, and these experiences decide the way they will present the various roles they assume.

Helmut, who has had experience of heavy portering in a fruit market and so can sympathize with porters, accepts to play Ubico, whose car is carried by Indians wherever there are no roads. Barbara, on the other hand, refuses to appear in a scene she considers as racist but accepts the part of Michèle Firk, and when asked why replies: 'Perhaps because I have three children, or because wherever Michèle Firk was, in her short life, Algeria, Cuba, Guatemala, something of Barbara is to be found.' Inge plays Michèle simultaneously with Barbara. Both express Michèle's feelings, often in Michèle's own words, about the *real* 'meaning of life' and about the need to fight for the oppressed, even to the deliberate sacrifice of one's own life, however dear one holds it.

Such a way of presenting a character, like the playing of Ubico by five actors successively, is of course outside normal dramatic practice. So, too, was the staging. To concentrate attention on the development of thought and action, stage effects were reduced to a minimum. The aim is to bring Guatemala nearer to us through each actor discovering himself. The performance in West Berlin took place in a darkened hall without a stage. Six podiums surrounded a central podium. Each actor had his podium but the central podium, only a stride away from the others, was for general use. The audience sat amongst the podiums.

The play proper begins with a 'Proletarian Opera' entitled 'How the quetzal [the national bird of Guatemala, which dies when in captivity] became a dollar bill'. The birth of a 'new Messiah', the dollar, in 1517 is presented in an unholy Nativity scene, and its progress through the world is followed by means of a continuous biblical parable ending with the crash on Wall Street when 'twelve Bank apostles sing: "My God, my God, why hast thou forsaken me?"'

The international situation in Guatemala, the oppression of the Indian people under General Ubico, the appalling torture and killing that went on, are revealed in an animated conversation with actors announcing from time to time that they are playing such and such a person. The discussions also reveal the deliberate corruption by the West of the Indians whose Maya culture goes back a thousand years, and the West's use of Indian men and women as guinea pigs in scientific experiments, such as the testing of the contraceptive pill. The picture is very different from that conjured up in the Western mind of a land heavy with tropical fruit, or a land 'dangerous for Whites' where a good-for-nothing indigenous people stretches out a begging hand for whisky or a dollar. Gatti's play *Le Quetzal* would seem to have been drawn on directly by the actors for this picture of the enslavement of the Indians, and of the plight of the imprisoned quetzal become no more than an emblem on a dollar bill.

From the internal situation, attention is moved to the border quarrel between Guatemala and Honduras which is presented as an international football match played in the capital city of Tegucigalpa, with running commentaries by a number of national radio stations. Radio Havana, Cuba, 'The First Free Land of America', implies that the border clash between the two countries is in fact a clash between two fruit companies, both American, United Fruit and Cuyamel Fruit. After arbitration involving people like Cabot Lodge, the dispute is settled by the cession to Guatemala by Honduras for ninety-nine years of a piece of land referred to here as the 'Procustean bed'.

The football match is followed by a number of interviews given to a group of 'journalists' by highly placed dignitaries such as the Papal Nuncio to Guatemala, or William Gill, White House spokesman. The 'journalists' seek information about the kidnapping and murder of the West German ambassador to Guatemala, Graf Von Spreti. To do this they assume various roles in turn and deploy maps, pictures and photos on the central podium. Why, they ask, had not 'friendly Latin American countries', United Fruit, the CIA or even President Nixon, been called in to save Von Spreti? They receive dusty answers. Von Spreti had been kidnapped by the guerrillas in the hope of forcing the Guatemalan authorities, in 'a horrible game of Patience', to reveal the fate of twenty-six of their number who had been taken prisoner. These included Camillo Sanchez. Sanchez was one of the men – along with César Montès, leader of the Armed Forces of Liberation, Yon Sosa, Commander of the Revolutionary Militants 13, and Otto René Castillo – whom Michèle had wanted to meet in Guatemala.

The final 'act' of the play is concerned with Michèle and her

Armand Gatti in the Theatre

relationship with Camillo Sanchez. It is suggested that there could well be a love story here, although 'not a hint of it appears in Michèle's writings'. Michèle's story is introduced by one of the 'journalists' reading aloud from the central podium a news item in *Le Monde* (September 1968). It announces the suicide of Michèle Firk, 'a member of the guerrillas who had been sought by the Guatemalan police in connection with the murder of the US ambassador'. She was thirty-one years old. When Michèle had learned of Camillo's capture, she planned to try to obtain his release by taking the US ambassador hostage. The ambassador attempted to escape, so she fired at him from her red Volkswagen. When the police caught up with her, rather than face capture and torture, she put a bullet through her own head. It was an eventuality for which she had been prepared from the beginning of her commitment to the cause of revolution in Guatemala.

The two actresses who play the part of Michèle express her hopes, fears and political stance in Michèle's own words. They also answer questions about her life, put by other actors. Why, for example, had she not stayed on in Cuba, where she was serving the Revolution and making films, which was, after all, her profession? From all this emerges the portrait of an intelligent, determined woman, totally committed to the cause for which she had fought in whatever country she had been, and also a woman who had become completely integrated into the Indian people, for whom she fought her last fight. 'It is shameful to be "objectively informed", that is to say from afar, without becoming actively involved', she said. The horrors to which these people were daily subjected are described in songs sung by the whole group during the course of these discussions. They could well be based on Michèle's own writings.

The play closes with a poem written by Otto René Castillo, who had been savagely done to death by an army patrol at Easter 1968 – at the same time, that is, as the attempt was made on Rudi Dutschke's life in Berlin, so Ulli recalls. The poem, which was unpublished, was discovered and translated by Michèle, along with other poems by Otto René. It was entitled 'Apolitical intellectuals', and asks what these intellectuals had done to alleviate the lot of the people. It ends with these words: 'Your meanness will eat into your souls, and you will hold your peace in shame'.

'Camillo is dead.' He was tortured, put into a sack and while still alive thrown from a helicopter on to rocks on the Atlantic coast. 'Michèle follows him. We must not take the American airline to Guatemala, but get to the land where such a love story exists, and become citizens of that land.' This piece of 'collective writing' is unashamedly political, and is as enlightening as it is moving. As drama, it has all the inventiveness of method that characterizes Gatti as a group leader.

La Moitié du Ciel et nous

In the autumn of that year the Forum Theatre was involved in the production of a play, *La Moitié du Ciel et nous*, written by Gatti in co-operation with the Forum actors and with the Baader-Meinhof group, then in the third year of their imprisonment in the Stammheim prison in Stuttgart. The 'prejudging' of the accused, not only on the Right but also on the Left, before the trial actually began in May 1975, in the temporarily reinforced courtroom of the prison, shocked Gatti. He returned to Germany from France convinced that an overt expression of solidarity with the prisoners was imperative.

When he first met Ulrike Meinhof in Berlin in 1968, during his discussions about a possible production of *V. comme Vietnam* in West Germany, she was working as a journalist for *Konkret*.[6] At that time she was for him no more than a 'face among the thousands of faces of the social opposition', a product of the students' revolt of the 1960s. 'There was nothing to suggest that she was to become a leader', but when he met her some months later in connection with his fact-finding activities on Rosa Luxemburg, he was struck by the forcefulness of her character and the singular lucidity of her mind. She kept on repeating: 'We must put an end to these fruitless discussions. We must act'. And act she did, in 1970, when she joined the Esslin-Baader couple. But why, Gatti asked, did she engage in illegal and clandestine action? Would it not have been possible to proceed otherwise?

The answer was forthcoming in May that year. Gatti was in East Germany on business and saw on television his own film *Übergang über den Ebro* (*The Crossing of the Ebro*),[7] made for Stuttgart Television the previous year. A programme by Ulrike, *Tumult*, which he expected to see shortly afterwards, also on West German television, was suppressed at the last minute, following Baader's escape from a Berlin prison. His escape had been engineered by Ulrike. Ulrike had become a militant. According to the right-wing Axel-Springer press, every militant was a 'criminal'. As early as 1967 Ulrike had publicly denounced the 'criminalization of all militants'. Seeing that it was not 'criminal' to drop napalm bombs on women, children and old people in Vietnam, why was being a militant in itself 'criminal'? It was 'criminal', apparently, to protest against the use of napalm. In the hysterical political climate of West Germany in the 1960s, did not such 'criminals' serve as 'God-sent scapegoats'?

So, says Gatti, Ulrike was 'criminalized' even before she had done anything illegal. Not that he agreed with the ideology of the Baader-Meinhof group, nor with their activities, but he recognized in them a 'political logic and a political identity', and Ulrike herself defined that identity in autumn 1974 in a letter from prison to President Gustav

Armand Gatti in the Theatre

Heinemann as that of 'revolutionary guerrillas and anti-imperialist fighters'. Gatti claimed[8] that the operations of the B52 in Vietnam were computerized at Heidelberg and that the group's bomb attack on the American headquarters there at Christmas 1971 was an act of war in a worldwide war, and that when this aspect was brought to light at the hearing by the defence, the trial was adjourned *sine die* to avoid repercussions that would have extended to Brandt, Scheel and the Pentagon. How far this claim is founded on fact cannot, of course, be established here. Ulrike's stance was very much like that of Michèle Firk, and she welcomed the information passed to her in prison that Michèle had figured so largely in the *Quatre schizophrénies* staged earlier that year at the Forum.

With the plight of the imprisoned group in mind – they had been on hunger-strike and Holger Meins was to die in November 1974 – Gatti went to Stuttgart with the idea of writing a play on 'politicized woman' based on an exchange of views between the imprisoned women of the Faction of the Red Army and himself. The title of the play was inspired by Mao Tse-tung's description of women as 'half of heaven', that is to say the equal of man, given to Gatti during an interview in China in 1959 by Mao himself, doubtless with the fate of his first wife in mind.

The co-operation of the group in the Stammheim prison was secured by the defence lawyers (some of whom were accused of complicity with the accused) and others, acting clandestinely as intermediaries between the prisoners and Gatti and his actors. In this way a dialogue was established which provided the substance of the play, *Die Hälfte des Himmels und wir*, to give it its German title; and a text by Ulrike herself on her position as a prisoner, likewise smuggled out of prison, was incorporated into the work. The experiment came to an abrupt end after a rooftop demonstration by some of the accused, equipped with loudspeakers. The demonstration had been organized by Gatti as a sort of New Year's Evening 'show' amid the lighted Christmas trees in the surrounding windows and a firework display in the heavens. 'Footlights' were unwittingly added by the Army's searchlights during the ensuing rooftop chase, while down in the streets the Forum actors handed the 'spectators' a printed scenario of the show. This 'brilliant spectacle', as Gatti called it, led to his arrest and the seizure of the text of the play by the police, so putting an end to the planned production at the theatre. But Gatti was satisfied; solidarity had been expressed with the 'Band' and everyone from the prisoners to the actors, public, and forces of law and order, had been caught up in the event.

The Social Democrat government followed up the event with a decree to the effect that anyone found supporting the 'Band' would be considered as belonging to it. So Gatti left Germany, but the day he had gone to Berlin he was, he said, at one with the prisoners' struggle. With the prospect of a life sentence for the accused, he considered all talk of ideology irrelevant. It was clearly no longer a matter of stifling dissidents but of stifling contestation itself through the complete isolation of the dissidents in their prison cells and, by extension, in the schools, universities and blocks of cheap flats. 'We are nothing but merchandise in the hands of the system. It is against this that we must mobilize our forces', Ulrike had said and, as Gatti saw it, that is where her fight became everybody's fight. Knowing her temperament he never believed in her 'suicide' in prison, on 8 May 1976, during the 103-week trial: it was the 'big lie' intended to decry her once and for all.

As one experiment followed another in Belgium and in Berlin the horizon of Gatti's work widened, although its aim was always to stimulate the creativity of others. From the first Belgian experiment in collective creation with amateur actors of the IAD in front of an audience encouraged to intervene in the creation and so escape the role of voyeur, or 'peeping Tom', as Gatti had come to think of the normal theatre audience, the move to the rural areas, where theatre was not part of the inhabitants' cultural life, turned the 3,000 prospective 'consumers' into 3,000 'producers' in Gatti's project of a 'spectacle without spectators'.

In the two German projects, although Gatti was back within the confines of a real theatre, with all that that implied, he still worked collectively with the company. In the first of the projects aimed at some understanding of the unimaginable repression and genocide in Guatemala, the actors had nevertheless been invited to start out from the context of their own lives. Gatti was more forthright in the project on the case that was being brought against Ulrike Meinhof: the work of the collective and the ongoing reality were identical at the point where Ulrike's statement, smuggled out of prison and later seized by the police in the theatre, was read out. Were Gatti and those working with him rehearsing a play? Or taking part in public life? It was hard to say. Gatti declared that this last Berlin experiment was the culmination of his search for a viable form of expression in the very heart of the event itself.

Notes

1. *Cahiers-Théâtre de Louvain*, Nos 14 and 15, contain an account of the experiment and of the text. See also *Travail Théâtral*, vol. X: 'La Colonne Durruti-Gatti', by Armand Delcamp, based on notes by Gatti.
2. In January–February 1972 Gatti gave a series of lectures on 'Street Theatre' in the Technische Universität in Berlin.
3. K.D. Kaupp, *Nouvel Observateur*, 9 September 1974.
4. 'Armand Gatti dans le Brabant Wallon', *Cahiers-Théâtre de Louvain*, Nos 26, 27, 28, 29.

5. Verlag der Autoren, 6 Frankfurt/Main, Staufenstrasse 46.
6. *Unité*, 'Témoignages', 4–10 June 1976 – Interview with Jean-Paul Liégeois. Gatti goes on to say that this first meeting was no more a 'great moment' than his first meeting with 'Che' in 1954 in Guatemala. One day United Fruit overturned the head of state, Arbenz. Some militants had to be saved quickly. It so happened that he helped an Argentine doctor to get to an embassy. 'I did not then know that I would come up against this doctor later in Cuba, "Che" Guevara. I did not know that this was "Che".'
7. *Übergang über den Ebro* was shown on 12 May 1970, on Stuttgart Television, and was subsequently chosen to represent the Federal Republic at the Prague Film Festival. It is a militant work and was considered by French critics to be one that would certainly not appear on official French circuits. This film sees society through the eyes of a Spanish immigrant worker in Germany and has its source in Gatti's scenario of 1963, *Joseph Continet ou le Combat contre l'Ange*, which had found no backers in France. In it Joseph is jolted by the death of his son, a volunteer in the Vietnam War, into an awareness of the meaninglessness of his own existence: that is, of his twenty years spent underground as a sewer worker, symbolic of the restricted vision of the world resulting from menial work.

In the German version Joseph becomes Manuel Aguirre, also a sewer worker, but in Stuttgart. He sends money back to his family in Spain every month until such time as his son can come to work alongside him. The son is killed on his first descent into the sewer along with the German worker who tried to save him. At the double funeral the German's widow and children ignore the hand of friendship stretched out by Manuel, making it clear that it is because he is a foreigner and as such is the cause of the husband's death. It is Christmas, and Manuel buys toys for the children as a gesture of reconciliation, but ends by throwing them on to the sewer water as one scatters flowers on the sea after a drowning. Manuel comes to realize that there is only one issue for him: to get out of the 'Affluent Society' in which he has become a sort of circus animal – fed, clothed and housed, condemned to perform his act every day, always the same act. He decides to go back to Spain where, by force if need be, he must try to build the country he might have built for his son.

C. Mathon and J.-L.Pays (*Revue du Cinéma* No. 240, June–July 1970), who saw the German version along with 'millions of German telespectators', described it as an unprecedented cultural enterprise, because it synthesizes objective information on the West German workers' predicament and the daily life of a member of the proletariat as felt in his consciousness. They saw it as a film which makes one want to change the world, and concluded that the film owed its existence to a certain cultural liberalism in the Federal Republic resulting from less tense political relations than elsewhere, with a proletariat better integrated into the current economic expansion and sharing its rewards.

The film gets its title from the last battle of the Civil War that the Republicans won before retreating into France. Images of the war Manuel had not 'lived' are frequently projected on to the windows of shops and the fronts of city buildings and serve as a counterpoint to the main theme. Images

of what is to be seen behind the windows – refrigerators, cars and the like, all representing hours of labour in excess of a worker's life span – provide a counter-attack by the dominant ideology.
8. *Unité*, 4–10 June 1976.

References

Hans Magnus Enzenberger, *Le bref été de l'anarchie. La vie et la mort de Buenaventura Durruti* (Paris: NRF Gallimard, 1975).

Michèle Firk, 'Écrits réunis par ses camarades', ed. Eric Losfeld (14 and 16 rue de Verneuil, Paris 7ᵉ).

12
France: an Official Challenge

Avignon – *La Tribu des Carcana en guerre contre quoi?*

The experiments undertaken since 1968, and particularly during his three years in Belgium and Germany, convinced Gatti that he had at last discovered his real bent as well as the true function of theatre. To go back to the formulas of traditional theatre that he had followed previously would automatically change him, like Lot's wife, into a pillar of salt. But France was the country towards which it was natural for him to look, and the condemnation of 'la contre-culture' by the Minister of Information, Philippe Malaud, at Tourcoin early in 1973, along with the warning in May by Maurice Druon, Minister for Cultural Affairs, of his determination to refuse subsidies to cultural enterprises considered by him to be subversive – 'those who come to the door of the Ministry with a begging bowl in one hand and a Molotov cocktail in the other, will have to make their choice' – presented a challenge which Gatti could not ignore. He returned to Paris. His first action there was to give a showing in June 1973 of the videotapes made in Belgium with the IAD along with a running commentary by himself. The following year he reappeared as an active creator at the Théâtre Ouvert in Avignon on the invitation of Lucien Attoun and France-Culture, with an equally politically conscious work.

La Tribu des Carcana en guerre contre quoi?

The Théâtre Ouvert ran parallel with the main programme at the Avignon Theatre Festival, and aimed at bringing new works and new playwrights to public notice. It operated without costumes or sets; what was called a *mise en espace* or 'blocking' was all that was required. Gatti arrived at Avignon for the Twenty-eighth Festival with his Tribe and, in the space of two weeks, transformed *La Colonne Durruti* into *La Tribu des Carcana*, 'a mirror-play' which interrogates as well as reflecting the earlier play.[1] This was not Gatti's first appearance at the Festival.

France: an Official Challenge

Already in July 1971 he had given a solo reading at Attoun's request of *Rosaspartakus prend le pouvoir*, the play currently in production at Kassel. The reading marked the inauguration of the Chapelle des Pénitents blancs as a 'theatre', and in it Gatti proved himself a prodigious one-man orchestra with the inflections of his voice and the expressiveness of his gestures. He seemed to be creating the work spontaneously in front of the spectators, and clearly the text was his own.

Such might not seem to be the case with *La Tribu des Carcana*, but on this question Gatti stated categorically to me that while *Durruti* was a collective adventure *Carcana*, based as it is on that adventure, is his own dramatic composition which, in the course of writing, opened up for him a deeper understanding of the Spanish problem. A text exists, and is published in the same volume as the 1975 version of *La Passion du Général Franco*. It was performed at Avignon by the Tribe which had carried through the *Durruti* project and was therefore conversant with the subject matter and technically well prepared to 'concretize' the text at short notice.

In this text, however, there is a bonus not present in *La Colonne Durruti* and it proves Gatti's claim to authorship. It is his dramatized analysis of the political struggle between the Communist Party and the anarchists with their rejection of hierarchical structures of every kind, their faith in self-discipline and direct action, their refusal of militarization and their purpose, after victory, to return to the land, the factory, the mines: 'That's the only army we have' (p.162). The clash between the two political attitudes is made explicit at the very beginning of the play when the Tribe are assembling the limbs of the Carcana puppet. The head is referred to as the

> Residence of the Trinity, the Father, Son and Holy Ghost. The father is the Party; it identifies itself with its militants in times of repression (bouquets of flowers, speeches, petitions); it points the way to be followed ... Get on with the job ... As for me, I'll see to the rest [...] The son is the militant. He is always sacrificed, and what's more he doesn't come back to life'. (pp.155–6)

Parallel with the conflicting theories of political revolution are conflicting theories of theatre: that of traditional theatre and that of a new more militant theatre put forward by Gatti. The parallelism is pointed out by one of the characters: 'Can't you see that the army against which you rebel in playing Carcana is exactly the same thing, the same ideology, as the theatre which you so staunchly defend?' (p.226). Gatti's theatrical revolution implies the rejection of theatre as a show, 'of the theatre of words and actors', of the theatre 'of reconstitution' – 'I don't care a damn for that [particular] reality. If I write theatre it is to put another reality in its place' (p.209). It also implies a 'reading of a character's possibilities' and not the 'supposed psychology of a character' (p.218). It implies, as in his play on Rosa Luxemburg, 'the destruction of the chronicle (that of the revolutionary militant Carcana) in order to get back to the purpose and driving force behind it' (pp.147, 210).

A further bonus is the introduction of the now extinct archaeopteryx which was to become the emblem of Gatti's Toulouse venture. Reported, in the play, to have been stolen from the Berlin Natural History Museum by Carcana and his comrade, Teodoro Pichardo, this extinct bird had refused to accept its extinction and had laid an egg in defiance of all the laws of history. Carcana's non-militarized column had disintegrated in Madrid, and Carcana had been shot dead: the bird's message is persistence even beyond all reason; for man it means 'exemplary revolts', but these revolts must be reinvented in terms of his daily existence. Revolution is action. History is written afterwards (p.248).

As for the egg supposedly carried off with the bird, it was the 'giant egg' of a pterodactyl, the symbol for the libertarians of a world where everything is possible, and on it Carcana painted the words *la justice des errants*, the justice of the Errantry. The fact behind this seeming poetic invention was the theft of the egg from the museum at the time of the rise of Nazism by two libertarians, hunted by the police, who had taken it to their hide-out in a bakery in Lehrterstrasse. Gatti retains the mistake about the egg's size because, like the image of the archaeopteryx, it serves his purpose. Both come very much to the fore towards the end of the play. Saragossa or Madrid, revolution or war, these had been the impossible alternatives open to Durruti, and either way he could not win. Carcana, a fictitious character, refuses the alternatives and defines the enemy as not only the enemy which faces him, but also 'whoever attacks the achievements of the Revolution. If he is among us he will be crushed' (p. 237). A Tribe member, Jonathan, referring to the Berlin archaeopteryx and its significance for their future struggle, says: 'The struggle going on throughout the cities of the world is a reality. It has a name: "the justice of the Errantry". It began in Berlin the day it [and its giant egg] was carried off' (p. 240).

In a short pamphlet distributed to the public at the Avignon Festival, Gatti described his Tribe as the *ensemble* of the roles of those who had led the real struggles of their times, or would lead them in the future: Louis Michel, Ulrike Meinhof, Gramsci, Auguste Sandion, Nguyen Van Troy. The final choice fell on Roman Carcana, the fictitious character supposed to have 'died in Madrid along with the Spanish Revolution'. 'We', Gatti writes in the play's Preface, with an obvious reference to the Tribe, 'started out with the libertarian Durruti killed with his column in Madrid' in 1936. There was no intention of staging a play, but of expressing solidarity with Salvador Puig Antich, who was executed by the Fascists in Barcelona on 2 March 1974. The 'trajectory' from Durruti to Puig Antich was made through the person of the revolutionary militant Carcana, whom the Tribe 'dissected', 'constructed', 'reconstructed', in the light of their own degree of consciousness, as of their own 'context', until, at the end of the 'trajectory', it became clear that Durruti, 'Carcana' and Puig Antich were one and the same 'integral' person – namely the 'revolutionary militant'.

This revolutionary militant whose life it was the Tribe's business to retrace is represented by the massive puppet whose scattered limbs covered with slogans were assembled by the Tribe in the presence of the spectators. Underlining the 'integrality' or oneness of all revolutionary militants, the early part of the text repeats whole sections of *La Colonne Durruti*, suitably modified to be applied to Carcana. As in *Durruti*, there are several different versions of his life – that is to say, 'several different ways of envisaging him today' – and, as in *Durruti*, these versions are recounted simultaneously to force each spectator to make his own choice.

Then come the REPLIES – Catholic, Anarchist, Fascist, Communist, to the question: 'Who killed the man whose death spelled the end of the Revolution?' Each makes of the man and manner of his death what he wills. All 'recoup' him. The COMMUNIST REPLY reclaims the anarchist for the Party by hinting at some flaw in his character which prevented him from 'being a Communist from the start' and by putting into his mouth Durruti's fateful words, for which his men never forgave him: 'I am prepared to sacrifice everything, but not victory'. The REPLY is presented as a film which is being shot using a sequence from *Le journal de guerre de Mikhaïl K* from the Mosfilm studios in Moscow. The 'director's' unashamed intercalation into the story of Carcana's life of extraneous historical documentary sequences of the time, his judicious cutting and mounting of the Carcana film, together with the twists in the scenario itself, allow Gatti to denounce once again manipulation by the media, particularly when funded by the Establishment.

Amongst other details designed to identify one militant with another is the name 'La Colonne Carcana', invented by the Tribe for Carcana's followers. In this way dramatic form is used to demonstrate a fundamental principle of Gatti's dramatic theory: his refusal to countenance any reconstruction of a page of history or of a historical person. For Gatti, the page or person, be it Durruti or 'Carcana', exists only as a means of putting a question to the spectator for him to answer. The principle itself comes under discussion on stage by the members of the Tribe: 'If we are to be a reply (good or bad, it matters little) to Carcana, and not a reconstitution of his life, his context is no longer Spain ... His context is us ourselves' (p. 188); it is pointless to live a revolution with the words and gestures of a revolution that is spent; revolution must be in the here and now.

This idea runs through the whole of Gatti's dramatic work, and one of the Tribe confirms this, saying that the 'battle which did not take place [the reference is to Saragossa] begins in every political prison that revolution leaves behind it and is still being fought' (p. 247). The Tribe argue too, as in the 1975 version of *La Passion du Général Franco*, about the propriety of incorporating in their performance the unedifying episode of Carcana's desecration of the statue of the Virgin of Pilar whom the Francoists claimed as their supreme leader.

How to present characters is another problem debated on stage by the Tribe. They put forward suggestions on the lines indicated by Gatti when he directed *La Colonne Durruti*. They go even further in the 'filmed' COMMUNIST REPLY: the direct 'je joue' claim to play such and such a part becomes twice removed: 'I [a Tribe member] am playing the actor who plays Mikhaïl K'; 'I [a Tribe member] am playing the actress who plays Passionnaria', etc.

At Avignon, in the second half of the show in which the Carcana files are reconstituted in front of the audience, the Tribe, faithful to their motto 'Pour un spectacle sans spectateurs: rien que des créateurs', seemed to be performing for themselves alone, oblivious to any audience, but the production was part of the Festival and the Festival had to be commercially viable, so spectators did exist at the Tribe's performances and they had to pay to see them. In principle, according to the published text, the performance takes place in the street – four streets, to be exact. The prospect of being able to stage Carcana's activities where they would normally have taken place – in the street – seemed to be good at Avignon in the month of July, whereas in Belgium incessant rain had driven *Durruti* into the factory, an acceptable venue in the circumstances; but the 'street' in Avignon was a little closed square in front of the Pénitents blancs to which admission was by ticket!

There the Tribe set up two structures, the one to support the puppet as it was being assembled, the other to suggest a cinema screen for the COMMUNIST REPLY. From these vantage points the actors harangued the spectators standing around them. They also moved round amongst them, causing groups to form to listen to one or other of the versions of Carcana's life as they recounted them simultaneously. At the same time they distributed photocopies, on huge poster-like sheets, of the manuscript text of this part of the show – or was it a 'meeting'? At this point, rain – at the performance I attended, at least – drove Gatti, his Tribe and the spectators into the Chapel, where the Tribe proceeded to reconstitute in front of the audience, now seated on benches lining the walls, the Carcana files on the Saragossa, Barcelona and Madrid fronts, with Carcana's existence being viewed from different angles.

The verbal recomposition was accompanied by a fast-moving physical and ballet-like transcription which the Tribe created before the spectator's eyes by their imaginative use of the several *disjecta membra* of the Carcana puppet. With these they made all the sets – a car, barricades, a tribune, and even Malraux's plane with 'Malraux' in the cockpit arguing about the shortcomings of non-militarized troops on the battlefield as he ferried 'Carcana' from Barcelona to Madrid. This was no mere *mise en espace* but a show with complete mastery of all the dramatic and scenic elements by a group of singers, mimes and acrobats playing one character after another as they carried the dramatic action along at a furious pace using the puppet to give visual expression to their revolutionary purpose.

This is stated in the closing lines:

> Keep alive this revolution which was never based on any dogma – the new man has long been in the street already. He is created each day by the struggle he pursues. Afterwards he is called Durruti, Carcana, Lumumba, Mulé Lé, Puig Antich, but he is always there.

An embarrassment to all while alive, these heroes are 'recouped' by history once they have been disposed of. But since, to quote the text, revolution is achieved only by what is outsize in man, the play closes on the bold exhortation: 'Soyons tous démesurés' ('Let us all be outsize') – larger than life.

The dramatic technique, as against the theme, caused the production to be hailed by several critics as 'the most striking event of the Festival'. Nevertheless it seemed to me to fall between two stools. The second part, by the very perfection of its presentation, became undeniably a performance for spectators despite Gatti's statement in the Preface that the Tribe's aim was not a show but a political act. It was 'theatre' as generally understood. The first part is quite different. Enacted, as it was, on the public square amid a standing audience whom it incorporated into its own movement, it was in line with Gatti's new conception of the function of theatre and, as played at Avignon, was more original and more arresting than the performance within the Chapel walls.

Notes

1. *Gatti: Journal illustré d'une écriture*, p.128.

13
In Search of a New Creative 'Language'

I Montbéliard – *Le Lion, sa cage et ses ailes*

Gatti went to Montbéliard at the invitation of Jean Hurstel, director of the Centre d'Animation culturelle. Hurstel was familiar with Gatti's work and ideas, as he had already produced *La Deuxième Existence du Camp de Tatenberg* and *La Cigogne*. Furthermore, he had invited Gatti to the Alsthom-Bull-Belfort works in October 1968, to help to form a workers' theatrical group since reduced-price tickets had not enticed Peugeot workers into the theatre.

Gatti arrived at the factory, as he himself said, 'with *Auguste Geai* under his arm', only to find interested workers opposed to the idea of staging a play that was already written, yet somewhat apprehensive at the idea of writing one themselves. Gatti gave a reading of his play, and shortly afterwards the new group met for the first time and declared their intention of preparing an improvised spectacle based on their own experience. 'I believe', Gatti said, 'they must be left to speak for themselves. We professionals must recede into the background, though not disappear.' His own role should be to provide the equipment and the technical know how, and this is what Gatti proceeded to do.

At Montbéliard it was the custom each year to invite an artist to create a work in collaboration with the population of the town and to give him a completely free hand. The form Gatti's contribution was to take was determined by the attitude of the Commission of the National Film Centre, which had just rejected unanimously – this was unusual – his 1973 scenario, *Les Katangais*, which he had very much at heart. So at Montbéliard, he would make a film.

One might be surprised to see Gatti concerned (in the refused scenario) with the gang of young thugs with their iron bars and bicycle chains who occupied the Sorbonne along with the students in May 1968 and had to be thrown out by them. However, a meeting with two of them five years later, on their release from prison, provided the spark for Gatti's 'reflection on the event'. Nicknamed the 'Katangais' by the press because one of them, a mercenary, had belonged to the Katanga police, they were a news item during the May protests, but according to one of the characters in the film script, a news item is 'the way the dominant ideology of the time writes history'. Gatti presents the press image of the gang in the opening shots by means of a huge marionette wearing a helmet, a nail-studded leather jacket, and the white-and-red-striped breeches of the Sansculottes.

In his discussion with the two men who had been serving a sentence for the murder of one of their number, the leader of one of the two rival factions in the gang, Gatti sought to reach beyond the news item and arrive at the 'totality' of the event. The technique of a film in the making, within the film, is the technique used to present the 'reflection', and a further dimension was added to it during the preparation of the scenario by the suicide of a former 'Katangais', Pierre Meynard, who set himself on fire on a Paris racecourse. This young man had refused to accompany the gang in their flight to Normandy after being turned out of the Sorbonne. There they intended to continue the May '68 movement. In the film the gang sees itself as an 'Army of Liberation'. The young 'dissident' sees Liberation in terms of a new mental attitude outside all party politics. His hero is Nestor Makhno, whose silhouette had already appeared in the *Durruti* 'play'. A more detailed portrait of the Ukrainian anarchist appears in Gatti's long dramatic text of 1977, *Le Cheval qui se suicide par le feu*, which makes it clear that no revolt is valid in his eyes outside the context of working-class struggles.

Shortly after arriving in Montbéliard in January 1975 Gatti discovered that it was not a single town but a conurbation, 'urban nebula', containing France's second largest working-class population all engaged in the Peugeot enterprises. He describes Montbéliard as composed of 'schizophrenic' communities – Polish, Yugoslav, Turkish, Italian, Georgian, Maghrebin, Spanish, Portuguese – living side by side yet having no contact with each other. For two months he attempted to secure suitable contacts but made little headway, so he changed his method entirely and began a poster campaign directed at the inhabitants in which he proposed 'A Film'. 'Your Own.'

The campaign brought responses from various quarters, including people who saw it as the first rung on the ladder to Hollywood, but it was the ten thousand immigrant workers and a French group of unemployed and part-time workers who saw the project through. To each of the immigrant communities Gatti extended an invitation to write a scenario tracing the story of their emigration from their own countries and of their new work in the area. Gatti's role would be to translate the scenarios into filmic images, not to make a film himself about immigrant workers. He directed his appeal to individuals: an Italian, Gian Luca, whom he met in the street; two Georgians encountered in a post office near the telephones. Individuals proved to be the moving spirit of national groups, and they appear under their own names in the final films. He did not address himself to collective organizations since he considered them to be the very negation of creativity.

The town's walls were soon covered with placards which the immigrants prepared, suggesting lines of approach for scenarios. One, by a Moroccan worker, ran as follows:

> We must write a letter for King Hassan. He must be told what is wrong in Morocco. Those who surround him hide it from him. If we write it well, it will reach him no matter in what language, he understands them all.

Scenarios followed the placards, their different versions becoming more and more expressive of the culture of the groups – a phenomenon which Gatti realized had to be taken into account when he wrote up the final texts, more or less like a public scribe, after consulting with them. He rejected some scenarios outright, such as that of the Yugoslav called Radovan who had worked at Peugeot's to pay for his studies but had been sacked for venting his frustration on a car on the assembly line. Radovan wanted a film to be made on this theme with a star actor playing his part. Weeks later, after seeing a film on the Yugoslav maquis with Richard Burton in the role of Tito, he realized that Richard Burton was Richard Burton, not Tito, and that such films are aimed at making money, 'just like the factory'. This discovery inspired a new scenario called *La Bataille des 3 P.* in which there is a more general theme which is that a Yugoslav is made up of Poet, Peasant and Partisan, and that at Montbéliard the immigrant worker found only Peugeot, Power and Production. That was the source of conflict.

From the Maghrebin immigrants Gatti received thirty-one scenarios. *Le Ramadan* was chosen. It is based on the laws of religious festivals coming into conflict with the non-Moslem demands of work. Two workers are torn between the sound of the sirens of the Peugeot factory calling them to work, and the Orchestra of the Prophet Mohammed installed on the hilltops of Montbéliard. Because the unemployed did not agree entirely with the religious and fantastic element in the film, *Le Ramadan* became *Arakha* (Forward), and a day of fasting alternated with a day of employment. All 350 of the Maghrebin immigrants took part in the film.

The cast of the Spanish film, *El Tio Salvador*, which recalls nearly a century of Spanish history, includes a famous matador from Bouriana, Vincente Jipolies, who had refused to do military service under Franco. He preferred to work at Peugeot's, where he became a C G T militant. The film is centred on his Uncle Salvador, who was the most representative of them all. As a member of the Republican forces, Salvador had been condemned to death by the Fascists during the Spanish Civil War.

In Search of a New Creative 'Language'

Salvador would not work at Peugeot's but grew fruit for sale, and every tree in his orchard bore the name of a fallen comrade.

From their abortive struggle to be allowed to put posters about Antonio Gramsci on the walls of their hostel bedrooms as a starting point, together with their experience of Peugeot enterprises, the Peugeot hostel, Peugeot canteen, Peugeot factory, the Italians drew the conclusion: 'Montbéliard is a wineglass out of which no one can climb'. After the glass of wine drunk on the train from Italy to exile, the solitary glass offered on arrival at Montbéliard, the glass in which friends' health is drunk, the glass broken in a brawl, there is Peugeot, the glass in which they are trapped. *Montbéliard est un verre* – such is the title of their film.

The scenario which impressed Gatti most was that of a Georgian aged forty, Charles Zedguinidze. It was sculptured on a beam from a house that was being demolished. Zedguinidze modestly set it up in front of Gatti, saying that he did not know how a scenario should be written but that he had written it in the only way he knew how. This was the first scenario to be written, or rather sculptured, scene by scene, on a tree trunk. It told the story of Georgia with its invasions and massacres, and was entitled by Gatti *La Difficulté pour un Géorgien de ne pas être du douzième siècle*. A young Pole's personal contribution was in a similar vein: he made the film titles in wrought iron. Gatti wondered whether he, writer that he was, could have invented a better 'language'.

Le Premier mai by the Polish community has, as its starting point, a street in Montbéliard on 1 May, surprisingly silent and empty, with none of the flags and processions one is accustomed to see on that day. The Polish workers were not interested in images of social struggles; after their day of numbing mechanical work they sought to re-create a Poland of song and dance. They wanted to change *their* world, not *the* world. This is stated at the end of the film.

All the films which were shot at Montbéliard-Sochaux were put together under the collective title *Le Lion, sa cage et ses ailes*: that is, the lion of the Peugeot badge, Montbéliard as its cage, its immigrant workers as its wings. *Le Premier mai* heads the series of films. Gatti left the imagining of the world to the people he was with. He came to the conclusion that the political language he had used in his plays did not work 'on the job'. To try to line people up in a 'working class' which existed only in his mind, and to try to impose a 'language' on them, had been a grave mistake. In any case Montbéliard was not a 'working class' in the abstract, to be helped along towards the 'Hugolian' culture that the schools sought to inculcate. Montbéliard was a conglomerate of cultures, half-forgotten but real, and paradoxically, perhaps, the most 'subversive' leftist activity was to help to develop the creativity of the individual members of these heterogeneous communities. In Montbéliard, the young were in much the same position as the immigrants. They were caught between the world of their elders, which had little relevance to the new times, and the existing world, which was little concerned with them. Being at Peugeot's alone provided them with an identity; they were 'Peugeot workers'.

As everything was filmed on videotape, the five hundred who had taken part were able to see their own contributions and also those of other immigrant groups, and during the discussions which followed the showings a mutual respect or appreciation of the work of others emerged. Singing and dancing helped to establish togetherness in the 'schizophrenic towns'; so did the local television station, which put out a documentary on 'Gatti at Montbéliard' with a song sung by Chérif, a character in the Moroccan film. The next day Chérif was addressed by his real name for the first time on the shop floor. It was no longer 'Good morning, Mohammed'. Chérif had an identity. At Montbéliard all the Turks were 'Mustapha', the Italians 'Gigi', or 'Salami' and the Spaniards 'Chorizo'. As a child Gatti had been 'Macaroni' or 'Pastasciutta'.

During the filming Gatti had his problems with the company. Peugeot looked with disfavour on the experiment and at their request in June, Poniatowski withdrew the 30,000 francs grant made by the Fonds d'Intervention Culturelle. The grant was restored, curiously enough, at the prompting of Jacques Chirac, who feared the political capital that could be made out of the incident. Additional money had nevertheless to be found to meet the cost of the eight months' work from January to August (1975), which rose to 120,000 francs. It was obtained from the Fonds d'Action Sociale, the Institut National de l'Audiovisuel, and the Société de Production 'Les Voyelles',[1] which undertook the editing and montage of the film. This took over a year and was done by Hélène Chatelain and Stéphane Gatti, who made six films of an hour each out of a hundred hours of shooting.

Four of the films were shown on 21, 22 and 23 January 1977 at the Atelier des Môles in Montbéliard to those who had taken part in them. The remaining films were ready in June. Gatti was at the Atelier to receive the groups. The Polish film was shown on the first night and was followed by merrymaking with chicken, cakes, wine and vodka brought by the participants. The second night was more subdued because of the death of two of the Georgians since the filming. The complete series was presented by the Institut National de l'Audiovisuel in a run of six television programmes for the Anjou Festival in June 1978. On 15, 16 and 17 September they were shown by the Bibliothèque Publique d'Information at the Centre Pompidou and were followed by a debate with Gatti and his team.

What had been achieved by these video films could not have been achieved either by television or by the cinema proper. Memories of the 'historic' past, as in the film of the Spanish group, or a flight into the

In Search of a New Creative 'Language'

legendary past of the country of their dreams, as in the Georgian film, were woven into the lived experience of the immigrants. By allowing the 'schizophrenic towns' to speak for themselves a lively creative filmic language had come into being. Gatti's hope was that although the video films the immigrants had made would not solve their problems for them, they would give a lead for professional films in which the oppressed of all countries, races and ages would have their rightful place. Films that would no longer be commercial straitjackets. Was it not time to stop creating consumers, buyers of tickets, and think of people as creative minds?

II Ris-Orangis – *Le Joint* (a school project)

The Montbéliard video films were still being processed when Gatti agreed to work on a production for the Palace Theatre in Paris, in March 1976, of a play of which he was the sole author. This was his new version of *La Passion du Général Franco*. He accepted, although it meant a return to 'popular' theatre, which he now looked upon as a pillar of the Establishment. However, lives were at stake in Spain and only in this way could he, Gatti, protest against the wave of executions. The saving of lives took precedence over theoretical preoccupations concerning collective creativity, so he agreed to go back into the 'system' for a time.

The experience at Montbéliard had led him to reject the idea of a dramatist working alone, and to believe in 'collective writing' understood as expression in terms of social background and interests, but with no encroachment by any one interest that would establish constant domination.

The 1975 Autumn Theatre Festival, organized by Michel Guy, Secretary of State for Cultural Affairs, provided Gatti with the opportunity to continue to work in the field of his choice. For some time previously, he and his Tribe had been preoccupied with the situation in America following the emergence of a new absolute opposition attitude represented by the Symbionese Army of Liberation which had assassinated – or, as they put it, 'executed' – Marcus Foster, Director of Education for Oakland, California. Foster had decreed that schoolchildren should carry identity cards to keep 'foreign elements of disorder out of the schools'. The SLA's reply was 'Death to the Fascist insect which attacks the lives of others'. They followed this up with the kidnapping on 4 February 1974 of Patricia Hearst, daughter of the multimillionaire Randolph Hearst and granddaughter of W.R. Hearst, the 'Citizen Kane' of Orson Welles's film.

Starting from the sententious pronouncements of the F B I Inspector and the Attorney General and the 'jargon of the so-called well-informed circles' Gatti worked on what he called 'the death of a language', or the stereotyping of linguistic expression. He planned for the Festival three simultaneous actions in three different institutions, all equally formal and standardizing, all run by 'codified' language: first the school, which moulds the individual and his future, 'the mother-prison of all the others' (*Le Joint*); then the theatre, which inculcates the cultural values of the dominant class; then the press, which manipulates its readers' minds. Like these three deforming prisms created by ourselves and freely accepted by us, these three cultural stresses provided the three planned events: a play by students at Vincennes, another by actors in the Bouffes du Nord theatre which was put at the disposal of all participants in the Festival, and a session directed by professional journalists.

For two of his proposed events, Gatti was unable to secure suitable premises. To accept the limitation of his project to the single site of the Bouffes would have entailed changing its whole nature, so the offer made by M. Charles Fontanat, director of the Collège d'Enseignement Secondaire named after Jean-Lurçat at Ris-Orangis, to place the school at his disposal was readily accepted. All three aspects of his project could be worked out there. Moreover, the college provided Gatti with a community in which to 'implant' his Tribe. It was a 'living cell' with a collective life of its own, and the newcomers were to play their part in it on the same footing as the teachers, the pupils, whose ages ranged from eleven to nineteen, and their parents. The experiment was intended to be conducted during the 10 per cent of school time allocated by law to extra-curricula activities.

The expected cultural subsidy was reduced from two million francs to a 'paltry' hundred thousand, but Gatti was not deterred. The sum was used not to put on a single production, as was expected, but to finance, over a period of three months, the 'creative agitation' of a collectivity as a protest against 'codification' in school or elsewhere. This aspect of Gatti's project was not appreciated by the authorities, and M. Fontanat, already known for his interest in advanced pedagogical research, was summoned before a special Consultative Committee which was to meet on 22 June the following year. On 21 June the meeting was postponed *sine die*. Sixty-one of the sixty-five teachers had signed a motion of support for the director of the college.

The day after Gatti settled in with his Tribe at the C E S – 19 September 1975 – Patricia Hearst and two survivors of the S L A were arrested. Since neither the S L A nor the 'death of a language' as such was a subject likely to appeal to the members of the college, Gatti proposed as a theme 'le chat guérillero' after telling the staff the story of Patricia Soltysik's pet Siamese cat, which 'chose' to die with her and four other members of the S L A when the police set fire to their hide-out in 54th Street in Los Angeles. On the story of this cat was grafted the

In Search of a New Creative 'Language'

legend of a cat's seven lives mentioned by Che Guevara in a letter to his mother. Guevara had twice been reported dead but, like the cat, he 'still had five lives left.' The cat of 54th Street was to live its second life at Ris-Orangis, and the pupils of the college were invited to imagine what that life would be, and what would be the 'thoughts' of a cat which agreed to die in a fire in a house besieged by the police under the bright lights of the Columbia Broadcasting System cameras.

The final count of the three months of work ending at Christmas was twenty-eight scenarios by the pupils, one by the teaching staff, and the thirtieth, a production by the Tribe of *Le Joint*,[2] a text written by Gatti during the actual experiment, synthesizing all the themes which had emerged. The scenarios and *Le Joint* constituted a 'play with thirty "facettes"' created by the school and the Tribe working as a single unit. Each 'facette' of this *spectacle éclaté* was the complement of all the others. It was not just a play translating a single author's vision enriched by the contributions of a group; nor was it a composite creation in which the *subject* was provided by the one, the *verb* by the other, the *object* by a third. Round a single theme, a great many true ideas had come to the surface according to the age, social class and position of the participants. All had found their own expression without any direction from above.

Gatti refused to be considered an 'animator'. He was a 'catalyst' whose aim was to provide opportunities for people to express themselves on their own behalf, in the language that was their own and not in a codified language learnt at school or elsewhere. For some children 'language' took the form of 'theatre'. For others, the pupils of the Section d'Enseignement Spécialisé, the S E S – that is to say, the less academically able pupils who were directed towards a basic technical training and consequently towards lower-paid jobs – their 'language' was practical. It was the work of their hands. These pupils were very conscious of the social stratification in the school, and Gatti's project was a golden opportunity for them to step out of the ranks and assert themselves as persons with particular practical skills. The lie of the equal-opportunities school was exposed by the experiment.

The pupils of the S E S were actually the first to enter the field. They built a gigantic cat, five metres high. Its metal skeleton was covered with multicoloured strips of cloth, and they set it up not on their own territory but in the confines of the C E S. This was their first victory. Four smaller cats followed, and soon there were cats everywhere, made in workshops specially set up for the experiment. The S E S played the biggest part in the venture, making most of the accessories for the scenarios: cat-masks of all kinds, puppets, pieces of sculpture, strip cartoons, scenery and 'cat-lorries' for the final procession in the streets in December.

The scenarios showed considerable variety of approach to the proposed theme. For the youngest pupils the word 'guérillero' had little meaning, and they saw in the cat a pretext for all kinds of flights of fancy. Older pupils seized upon the notion of 'guérillero' to attack the adult world, often violently, for its 'repressive attitude.' One of the classes took 'streaming' as the theme of their scenario and pitted rooftop cats against pedigree cats. Another scenario, 'L'Invasion des chats', from pupils hostile to the experiment, showed that they had been caught up in the spirit of the project in spite of themselves. Two-thirds of the nine hundred pupils, however, stuck almost completely to the school programme, and although the teachers agreed in principle with the project, some were aggrieved when pupils absented themselves from classes to work on it.

Nevertheless fifteen of the staff, teachers of literature, the sciences and gymnastics, made a contribution to the collective creation of the community. Their play, *La Solitude du professeur de fond*, reflected their uneasiness at their own enforced acquiescence in the stratification implicit in a modern school's business of turning out specialists, a business that requires the inculcation of principles and precepts to the exclusion of real concern for the development of the individual's creative ability. Little was left of the old radical outlook according to which school was the revolutionary ferment for changing society. Their theme was pessimistic. Resignation, in one or other of the senses of the word, was their lot.

In the meantime the bare walls of the college became wall-newspapers emulating the *da dzi baos* of Peking with their placards, drawings, slogans and criticisms. One of the first of the placards by the pupils announced that the 'chat guérillero' would come at the same time as Father Christmas, laden with their inventions, constructions, dreams and hopes. Christmas was the time when the college was opened up for performances of a number of cat-scenarios. Others were staged on the lorries, or in the old marketplace, or on the Commercial Centre's car park. The climax of the venture was the performance in the school's canteen of Gatti's new play *Le Joint ou 24 heures de la vie d'une page*, that is to say Page 5 of an imaginary newspaper, the page of miscellaneous news items. The performances were authorized by the Committee for Public Safety only at the last minute and with the proviso of a maximum of two hundred spectators, under threat of banning for 'security reasons'. Entry was to be by ticket, costing 10 francs.

Le Joint was performed on 18, 22, 23, 26, 27, 29 and 30 December. Gatti made no attempt to transform the canteen into any semblance of a theatre. The canteen was one of the centres of activity of the 'living cell' in which he was 'implanted', and he chose to use it exactly as it was. The spectators sat at tables, as if for a meal. The actors performed on other tables arranged to represent the eight-column layout of Page 5 of *Le*

Joint, where the action takes place. The main concern is the elucidation of the relationship between the several elements of a newspaper: the journalists and readers, the articles, and the individuals who are the subjects of the articles. The action does not proceed by abstract discussion. Gatti 'theatricalizes', as he says, the Articles by embodying them in live actors, and these argue with both Readers and Journalists on behalf of the *reality* of the Individual behind the *persona* of the Article.

In the first edition of the paper the items range from the advertisement of a big store in the form of a standardized saleswoman to a 'personalized' Stock Exchange, an elderly policeman on trial for having shot an inebriated Algerian in the police station, a young delinquent arrested after a smash-and-grab raid, and two musicians arraigned in the Music column for having played in an anti-military rally. In front of them, on a small platform, a Committee of Readers from different walks of life bring up their chairs to read the news.

At the side are seated, in person, two professional journalists, Marc Kravetz of the left-wing paper *Libération*, and Pierre Joffroy of the right-wing weekly *Paris-Match*. Both had accepted Gatti's proposal to take part in a journalistic experiment in an imaginary newspaper called *Le Joint*. Their contributions point the way for the discussion of subjects set out by Gatti. Each explains how, according to his own background and also the colour of the paper for which he works, a journalist shapes the material he handles. He also shapes it to suit the taste of the paper's readers. Each of the four elements of a paper is shown to be a prisoner of the other three; each owes its existence to the others. How, then, is one to distinguish between the reality of a person and the *persona* created in the newspaper article? For example, did the policeman (on the verge of retirement) who shot the Algerian do it in 'legitimate self-defence', or is he a 'fanatical racist'?

The problem of 'translation' is presented in the form of a game of 'tennis' played by the two Journalists with imaginary rackets of different makes, 'news item' and 'history'. The game demonstrates how journalists can colour, blow up or kill the events they are reporting. Another game is later played between the journalists and the Articles with the S L A as the ball. The Articles' racket is 'truth', the Journalists' 'verisimilitude' – of the Right or of the Left. As one Journalist states, it is pointless to expect journalists to be 'roadmen keeping a road open through the shapeless maquis of reality. There should be no shadows on the road, alone the sun of reality should be let shine on it. Completely decoded' (IRMMAD, p.102).

The demystification of journalism is radical and is done by one (Gatti) who had had wide experience of the profession. The young delinquent learns from one of the Journalists that he and his smash-and-grab raid are of no interest to the paper; he is 'publishable' only if he appears as a helmeted motorcyclist, acid-thrower, etc. But as this would give him a Fascist *persona* he 'refuses' it. Fascism forms no part of his life story, so he withdraws from the column, saying: 'I have the impression in this paper of being a product (like a washing powder or a detergent) of what you say. You make it look as though what you say is the truth. But it is not the truth.'

Action is engaged in the newsroom of *Le Joint* when a despatch arrives from Los Angeles announcing the arrest of Patricia Hearst and her two companions. This raises the question of the contents and layout of Page 5 of the paper. The despatch comes in the form of three militants who burst in and recount the full story of the SLA. According to the Journalist of *Libération*, official despatches are not self-evident truths: they are like pictures given to children to colour. *Le Joint*, however, like *Le Point* in real life, claims to be unbiased. The Journalists were faced not with one despatch but with several which, put end to end, would measure three metres. Also they were in a language which no one spoke, especially Patricia Hearst. To make room for this news item one of the Articls had to be cut, and the Articles argue about which of them it is to be. How is the hierarchy of news to be established? In what light is a news item to be presented, given the colour of the paper and the tastes of its readers?

The contributions of the two Journalists provide a demystification of the ways of the press. Their reference to the 'literature' of repentance put into Patricia's mouth by the press, and their deliberate suppression of her defiant description of herself at her first appearance before the magistrate as an 'urban guerrilla' – considered too subversive by the editors for their readers' peace of mind – goes right to the heart of Gatti's preoccupation with the deadening effect of institutionalized language, whether in the family, school, works, political parties or the state.

From being a short news item the SLA takes on, in the second edition, the proportions of a full-length article. It becomes the forces of the mass media which penetrate into every home. Reduced from twenty fighters to a mere three, the SLA is multiplied by the media into millions. The play theatricalizes the event in the form of an attempt by the three members of the SLA at a forcible takeover of *Le Joint* with a view to carrying out their programme of 'changing the world' and 'securing the well-being of man, against his will if need be'. In dramatic terms this means changing the layout of the paper. The attempt fails because of the SLA's 'graphic dictatorship', which puts Articles and Readers alike to flight. No third edition comes out, but press and television reports condemning Patricia for joining the SLA, and implying 'brainwashing' and the like, bring the realization that they are all living 'the death of a language'. In this way *Le Joint* links up with Gatti's aim stated at the

In Search of a New Creative 'Language'

outset of the project: that he would confront the reactions of the pupils of the CES with the story of Patricia Hearst, who suddenly realized the terrifying role that her father, the press magnate, played in America and elsewhere. At the same time she was accused by the media of uttering nothing but shibboleths, whereas her real language would have been that of frustration.

III Saint-Nazaire – *Le Canard sauvage*

Gatti's next 'implantation' was in Saint-Nazaire where, on 15 October 1976, he and his Tribe began on another project. It was undertaken at the Maison des Jeunes et de l'Éducation Permanente at the invitation of its director, M. Gilles Durupt. The invitation was given in June, when M. Durupt had the idea of introducing the man he considered to be 'amongst the foremost creative minds of his time' to the working-class population of the shipyard-town of Saint-Nazaire through a production of one of Gatti's plays by Gatti himself. However, a debate on the subject of justice at the Maison led instead to a plan for a collective creation on the theme 'Are psychiatric wards not a battlefield of all the civil wars we have not waged?', with Gatti to supervise it.

The starting point was the plea of Vladimir Bukovsky's mother for the release of her son from a psychiatric hospital in the USSR where he was detained. The programme suggested by Gatti, with the approval of the Maison's committee, stated that in his opinion the appeal should be answered by the people of a French town using the medium of the theatre, although not theatre in the traditional sense. The collective creation would be the work of people of all ages, trades and professions, and be pursued over a period of four months.

The first phase was to be concerned with the Bukovsky affair, Bukovsky being the author of a manifesto, 'A New Mental Illness in the USSR: Opposition', and also co-author with a fellow-detainee, the psychiatrist Semion Gluzman, of *A Psychiatric Guide for the Use of Dissidents*. This book was dedicated to another detainee, the Ukrainian mathematician Leonid Pliutch. A second phase was to bear on psychiatric hospitals in general, and was documented by the Tribe's visit to an important asylum in Dinan. The third phase would seek to bring the subject nearer to each one personally with an enquiry into the 'personal psychiatric ward' of the ordinary 'normalized' citizen – Bukovsky's words. The symbolic title of the venture, *Le Canard sauvage*, relates to the life story of the wild duck which must fly at 300 kilometres an hour against the wind in order to survive, because to fly with the wind means freezing to death in flight. Gatti tells of their flight in his book on Siberia.

To draw in as many of the townsfolk as possible, tracts and posters were to be designed by the Tribe and those local people already engaged in the venture. Everyone was to be encouraged, with the help of the Tribe if need be, to write sketches within the terms of the subject set, to make video films and strip cartoons, to arrange exhibitions of photos, drawings and other objects of their work which had made them 'prisoners of the system' or would-be dissidents.[3] Parallel with the creative activity, group discussions and public debates were to be organized on the problem of psychiatric treatment or related topics, with or without specialist speakers. The high spot of the venture was to be a visit by Leonid Pliutch advertized for 5, 6 and 7 November. Meanwhile, Bukovsky had been exchanged for the Chilean Communist Party Secretary Luis Corvalan, and had arrived in Zurich on 18 December 1976. Gatti went there to meet him. Bukovsky then moved to France. In the light of his release, changes had to be made to the original project. With Bukovsky freed, the problem, according to Gatti, became more urgent still. It was no longer a question of conducting a campaign for a particular 'silhouette', for an 'exotic Russia'. The campaign was 'our own', in everyday life.

Even before Gatti set foot in Saint-Nazaire, opposition to the proposed programme had arisen. The government subsidy normally given to a theatrical experiment approved by a municipality – in this case twelve thousand pounds – had been withdrawn. As a result, the financing of the enterprise fell entirely on the Maison des Jeunes and the socialist local authority. On 31 August 1976 the mayor and the secretary of the local Socialist Party published a communiqué to the effect that the programme could well be used as a pretext by reactionary elements to foster anti-socialism, and they pointedly recalled the fact that they had already asked the Maison in July to reduce the Bukovsky affair to a single element in a 'global creation'. In September the executive of the local Confédération du Travail protested to the mayor that reference to the internments in the USSR, which 'of course were to be deplored', would give rise to anti-Communism as well as anti-Sovietism and so be disruptive of the Left.

This action was followed up by the local branch of the Communist Party (though not by the Central Committee, where it met with the approval of Georges Marchais) with the distribution of a tract deploring the cost to the taxpayer of an experiment which had 'no relevance for the worker', for whom the immediate 'realities of daily life' were unemployment, inflation, and heavy taxation. Individual opposition led to such graffiti on the walls round the Maison as 'Let's scalp the Tribe', 'To blazes with Bukovsky', 'Death to Gatti-Cohn-Bendit' – Cohn-Bendit's brother was a teacher in Saint-Nazaire. The thirty-foot-high wild duck that had been erected outside the Maison was also set on fire.

Despite the opposition, a number of institutions including the Institut

Universitaire de Technologie and two secondary schools, workers from an aeroplane-component factory, groups of peasants and a number of private individuals took part in the venture, relating their personal contribution to the subject set. One play, *La Solitude du gardien de phare*, by Mohammed, a dockyard worker in Saint-Nazaire who had been orphaned during the Algerian War, told the story of his life. It was the same story as that of the wild duck, always flying against the wind. Another was by a group of farmers who wished to recall the case of Lucien Pinel and his wife Denise, evicted from their farm by the landlord, a veterinary surgeon who wanted the land for his son to rear goats and birds on. They were dissuaded by the Tribe from distributing a tract in dialogue form and from demonstrating. The use of puppets was suggested as a more suitable form of 'dramatic language' for the occasion and for criticizing the vet's power over peasants who were obliged to make use of his services. With the promptings of the Tribe there was no lack of inventiveness, but most of it expressed private feelings and could not be used publicly.

There were moving moments in the course of the experiment, as at the reading in the marquee of a tragic letter addressed by Nadedja Mandelstam to Osip Mandelstam, although she did not know whether he was alive or dead, or as when Pliutch and Victor Feinberg listened with emotion to *Le Voyage du centre du Goulag*, a concerto for two guitars and a solo voice speaking words by Solzhenitsyn set to music by Michel Arbatz and Kirinhel. Feinberg had been sent to a mental hospital after demonstrating on the Red Square over the occupation in 1968. He wanted a photograph of himself holding the string of a kite in the 'battle of the kites' in Saint-Nazaire arranged by the pupils of the CES, to send to Barissov, who was in the hospital.

The experiment came to an end in February 1977 in the marquee, with an exhibition entitled *La Loire salue le Kolyma* linking the Loire with the North Siberian river of Varlam Shalamov's *Kolyma Tales*. It was opened by Bukovsky and Pliutch.

During their visit the dissidents were invited into many homes. Gatti's purpose was to create a 'territory for a possible dialogue' between the dissidents and the population of an area composed essentially of workers and peasants. Bukovsky spoke of life in the USSR and made the point that neither the French people nor the Russian people had a realistic view of each other. Pliutch warned of a common threat of totalitarianism to be resisted wherever it was installed and nipped in the bud wherever it gave signs of developing: 'All wild ducks from wherever they come and wherever they go have no other course than to fly together against the wind', he said.[4]

Some of the statements they made were, however, very tendentious, and Gatti was a worried man. The worst shock came when Victor

Nekrassov, who had written a novel on the stand made at Stalingrad for which he had been awarded the Stalin Prize, addressed an audience of workers and dockers in a factory. He made it seem that Gatti, the libertarian, had gone over to the Right by his sponsorship of the debate. Gatti gave me a graphic description of the meeting. In front of his factory audience, where every Left tendency was represented, Nekrassov – who spoke French fluently, having spent his early childhood in Paris – began by replying to the opening question about the level of Soviet workers' pay that the Soviet worker earned ten million French francs and had five dachas, a main one and four others! It took the audience some time to realize that Nekrassov was making fun of them. To a question about his opinion of Lenin and Stalin, he was loud in his condemnation. This brought applause from the Trotskyists, but some Communists got up and left the hall. To a Trotskyist's question on his opinion of Trotsky he answered: 'He was an assassin, a butcher', at which some anarchists shouted 'Bravo!'. An anarchist then asked his opinion of Makhno, and got the reply: 'He was a brigand'. Nekrassov added later: 'I'm an anarchist, as I was before!'

Gatti, nonplussed and 'sweating blood', so he said, told Nekrassov that this was not what was expected at a political discussion in France. Nekrassov now appeared to him as a reactionary. He had thought of the dissidents as anarcho-syndicalists, libertarians like himself, but now saw them as individuals who were completely alienated from their own people – though not for political reasons – and once out of their country they easily went over to the extreme Right and became anarchists of the Right. Of Bukovsky Gatti said that he was discreet, and at least waited until he got to England before declaring his admiration for Margaret Thatcher. Later, in 1979 in Cambridge, where he was studying, Bukovsky declared that all socialism leads to Stalinism, that all the Communist leaders were 'little Stalins', and that Mao himself was just a copy of Stalin. This was in an interview with Françoise Favier for France Culture on 21 September, concerning the publication of his memoires *Et le Vent reprend ses tours*. Lenin, said Bukovsky, was the instigator of the 'Red Terror' in 1918, the 'first to give legal recognition to concentration camps', and he accused every one of us of 'complicity in the crimes committed by totalitarian states'.[5]

Pliutch had assured Gatti in private that he was a Marxist, but in a programme on the second French channel in 1982, of which Gatti has a video copy, he denied this. The programme began with the presenter relating the history of several Czech dissidents including Vaclav Havel, and Gatti was supposed to follow this up with a discussion with Pliutch on the question of dissidents. Instead, Pliutch produced a paper from his pocket and read a declaration on Ukrainian Nationalist literature, referring particularly to the poet Chernichevski, whose statue may be seen in front of the Ukraine Hotel in Moscow. Pliutch may in fact not have realized that his ideas were really the same as those of the most reactionary Ukrainians who came West with the German armies. An obviously discomfited Gatti was unable to get a single word in, and the presenter drew the failed interview to a close. One wild duck had not found a following mind in the West.

The most violent of the incidents at Saint-Nazaire came at the end of the experiment when an American television crew arrived from the Voice of America in Germany and set up their apparatus in the marquee for an interview with Gatti on the Soviet dissidents. What had made Gatti treat the subject? Obviously, they implied, he supported them, and they asked him for a statement to this effect. It was equally obvious, Gatti says, that they were completely mistaken about his (Gatti's) attitude to the dissidents. He was far from approving of them *en bloc*, and even further from identifying 'dissidence' with the Bakunin tradition. He refused to discuss the matter, and said that he was prepared to discuss Ulrike Meinhof instead. Whereupon they shouted that Ulrike was a criminal etc., and the interview came to an abrupt end.

Incidents of this sort, coupled with the attacks to which they had been subjected from the beginning from all sides, made Gatti and the Tribe feel that they had put themselves in a false position. So far it had been their belief that political dialogue was not dead and that there was still some 'oxygen' in extreme 'gauchiste' views, at least in the anarchist variant. The Saint-Nazaire experiment had seemed to belie this, but they came to realize that the pro-dissident stance they had adopted at Saint-Nazaire had little in common with the traditional libertarian ideal, their own tradition. The Russian dissidents were not anarchists – that is to say, anarcho-syndicalists such as Gatti approved of – and the point is made by a character in *Le Cheval qui se suicide par le feu*, which has its origin in the Saint-Nazaire affair. The character says: 'Once one strays from the path traced by working-class struggles, one becomes (even if one thinks one is not) a reactionary' (Typescript, p. 15). With this new text Gatti sought to open up political discussion by getting back to anarchism in the tradition of Bakunin, and he based it on Nestor Makhno, the Ukrainian peasant leader who fought against the Whites and then against the Red Army.

IV Avignon – *Le Cheval qui se suicide par le feu*

With *Le Cheval* Gatti did not pursue the line adopted so far by himself and the Tribe working within a particular community. The text was written in the privacy of his retreat in Piedmont, and when Gatti arrived at the Thirty-first Theatre Festival at Avignon (1977), all that had been divulged of his text was its title. The text was then 'concretized' in the Cordeliers' Chapel with the collaboration of the Tribe. The starting point of the text as announced in the *Cahiers du Festival*, No. 18, was 'the cavalcade of Nestor Makhno (the damned soul of the Revolution of '17) whose autonomous movement of the poor peasants of the Ukraine attempted to realize the dream of a libertarian society freed from all political authority'.

The play follows the fortunes of anarchism through many countries up to the the present day. It recalls a hundred years of world history and some ten years of the history of the work of Gatti, the nomad. The horse which commits suicide by fire is Makhno's horse, and Makhno's horse is the Revolution which begins with the establishment of a libertarian commune at Gulyai-Polye, Makhno's birthplace, and ends with his wretched final years in Paris before his death in 1934 when he used to stake each week his meagre earnings on a racehorse always an outsider, as if in a re-run of his career in the Ukraine. But the play is bravely optimistic. 'We have been marching towards the Promised Land since the Commune and have already got a foothold in it', says one of the characters (p. 13).

The theme of fire is first stated when a revolutionary named Bondarenko, who shared Makhno's cell (cell 23) in the Tzarist prison of Butyrka, pours the lamp oil over himself to commit suicide. The last is when the young disillusioned 'Katangais' of May 1969, Pierre Meynard, burns himself to death in front of the Tote on the Saint-Cloud racecourse in memory of Makhno. With reference to his play, Gatti recalls his rejected scenario of 1973, *Les Katangais*, in his interview with Marc Kravetz (*Libération*, 21–22 July 1979). He notes the recurrence of the theme and the extra light shed on themes by such recurrences. In 1984, in Gatti's first *stage de réinsertion sociale* at the Archéoptéryx, the two themes of Makhno and Pierre Meynard came suddenly together when a video film, *L'Émission de Pierre Meynard*, was made from the *stagiaires*' collective play, *La Colonne Makhno*.

In *Le Cheval qui se suicide par le feu* Gatti makes no attempt to reconstitute Makhno's life story, nor the libertarian saga of the Makhnovshchina, in which thousands of peasants died between 1917 and 1921. Using his 'selmaire' technique, he rewrites the saga 'as it is written in the gaze of Makhno's horse', Outsider. In this remake of Makhno's history, Bondarenko does not commit suicide by fire but lives to continue the march towards the Promised Land. Such is the theme of the first 'selmaire'. In the second an aeroplane takes off for the Promised Land with Svetlana Stalin, Georges Pompidou, Liou Shao Chi and later 'the outsider' Dr Andrew Young, President Carter's black counsellor, as passengers, all going in search of his or her Promised Land. The aeroplane's 'flight' is watched from the auditorium by Makhno's horse, which prefers to die by fire rather than be thrown out of the plane – the plane is twice hijacked by a passenger who would have thrown the horse out.

These two 'selmaires', together with a third, that of the 'Cheval d'arçons [a vaulting horse] qui se croyait la ville de Berlin' and a fourth, the 'Cheval de frise [barbed-wire obstacle] qui ne voulait pas mourir de bonheur', constitute stages which extend from Makhno's libertarian revolt to modern psychiatric wards, passing on the way through a pig factory in Chicago [Gatti remembers his father's misfortunes there], a factory where everything is transformed into 'normalized' products [kilometres of identical sausages, thousands of identical chops] and finishing at the shop window in West Berlin in front of which he met Ulrike Meinhof. Gatti sums up his work in this way. In this 'selmaire' he looks forward to the student revolt of 1968, and backwards to the Nazi prison of Plötzensee where 'the whole German Revolution which had a woman's face' went to the guillotine, nicknamed the White Horse by the prisoners to make it less fearsome. In this way Makhno's horse is at the nexus of a complex structure of revolutionary dreams and hopes, concretized visually. Such is the dramatic function of the Chinese 'selmaire' in the work.

However, the event which acted as a catalyst for Gatti's dramatization of the Makhno theme was nearer home. It was the sight of a horse at the Frankfurt theatrical fair in 1969, where he presented *L'Interdiction de la Passion du Général Franco* alongside other *avant-garde* shows. The horse, to quote the script, was not a 'real' horse but a 'naturalist' horse on a covered stage in the open air, with a 'naturalist' bucket of hay and a 'naturalist' bucket of water, performing its 'naturalist' functions each day in front of three hundred spectators sheltering under three hundred umbrellas. The municipal 'stagehands' were incorporated, without realizing it, into a show in which the elements of dramatization were the horse's 'freedom of expression' and a German preoccupation with cleanliness. The Frankfurt horse is the example of what Gatti was anxious not to do. 'Natural' is a synonym neither of 'artistic' nor of 'free'.

In the play the horse provides transport to the Promised Land. For different people the Promised Land means different things, and the roads leading to it diverge. So *Chevalet le constructeur*, the master of ceremonies, decides to auction the parts of the horse – feet, legs, head and so on – according to whether the purchaser chooses the paths of Babeuf, Bakunin, Durruti, etc. To acquire his part each one has to assume a name which is one of the uses of the word *cheval*, such as *cheval d'arçons* or related words such as *licorne*. Gatti called it dramatization by semantics. The characters also perish in divers uses of the word *feu: feu follet, feu d'artifice*. However, the only material body in the play is that of Makhno's horse, fragmented and scattered but to be found taking the lead again in every clash with 'programmed' society. This horse, which fire cannot devour, is reconstituted in the final 'selmaire' and will continue the journey towards a land which Gatti does not describe, but which is obviously neither that of 'natural' 'neo-liberalism' nor that of rationally ordered socialism, but a land where justice, and therefore equality, is reconciled with freedom. For the moment, however, the journey and the struggle alone count.

Le Cheval was listed in the Festival's *Cahiers* as a 'free confrontation between the written text and its actors, in the presence of a public invited to come and watch the work in progress every day at 2 o'clock', a 'work in progress' being understood as the discovery of a text made simultaneously by actors and spectators alike. The confrontation extended over a period of eighteen days as part of Lucien Attoun's experiment in the 'Cellule de Création', formerly his 'Théâtre Ouvert'. Gatti considered the conditions of work ideal, as Attoun had agreed that the public should have free access to the sessions and that no 'finished performance' would be required at the end. Before each session, Gatti told the gathered public: 'There will be no performance here. Those who wish to leave may do so now.' The 'confrontation' was followed enthusiastically by people who queued up each day from 10 a.m. to be sure of getting in.

In Gatti's mind the Cordeliers' Chapel *was* the horse, and spectators were *inside*. As in 1974, when the Tribe performed the play on Carcana in the Chapelle des Pénitents blancs in Avignon and created the sets with the *disjecta membra* of a huge Carcana puppet, the sets here were created by the positioning of the 'horse's' limbs. Supposed spectators became actors and gave their reasons for the parts they wanted to play. Discussion turned on the matter of the play rather than on its performance, though passages were acted in such a way as to take account of observations made by a number of people who had known Makhno and who attended the sessions. Amongst those who had known him in Paris was a man of ninety-eight who was still translating the works of Bakunin. There were two Russians who had been in contact with him. One had been at the International Congress along with Kamenev and Sinoviev; the other was a woman who had written about him. All gave their opinions on his character and his appearance – which did not square with Gatti's mental image of the man. Then there was the question of the big scar on Makhno's face. Did he get it in battle, or was it inflicted by his second wife? A few questions were put by the general public; they concerned the Korean anarchist party, the Palestinians, Saint-Nazaire. Madame Pliutch attended the 'selmaire' on the psychiatric hospital, and the poet and musician Galitch brought his guitar for the songs, which were composed on the spot.

This confrontation with the audience made Gatti feel the need to re-establish a connection with the evolution of political and social ideas in

France during and since the war. In this evolution the movement of the Resistance was all-important, so not surprisingly it became the subject of his next experiment.

V L'Isle d'Abeau – *La Première Lettre*

While at Saint-Nazaire Gatti had received an invitation from Jean Perret, the director of L'Isle d'Abeau Animation, to undertake an experiment in the new town that had been formed out of a regrouping of some twenty communes in the Isère *département*. Perret had followed Gatti's activities in Montbéliard with interest, and teachers in the area knew of Gatti's experiment at Ris-Orangis. All felt that he had a contribution to make to the new town's cultural life. Gatti had doubts. He and his Tribe did not 'sell culture to populations', nor 'practise creation to order'; nor was he an 'animateur'. On this point he expressed himself firmly. He was opposed to the very principle of 'cultural animation', believing that if a state or a local authority engaged an 'animateur' it was with a view to securing support for its policies. Culture did not come into it. The principle on which he and his Tribe worked was 'contestation'; they aimed at flying against the wind. It was not a question of seeking unanimity, but of sharpening contradictions. It was not a question of taking people in hand but of giving them the means to express themselves if they really had something to say, of encouraging them to follow paths they would never have dared to follow alone. That, he explained, is how the films at Montbéliard had been made.

Gatti decided, however, to accept Perret's invitation and make a film with the inhabitants of the new town on the theme of the Resistance, even though L'Isle d'Abeau itself had not been particularly active in it. Indeed, the clergy there had condemned the men of the Resistance as 'terrorists', 'children of the Devil', until they discovered, much to their discomfiture, that amongst the 'outsiders' who had been shot there was a young priest.

Gatti had become involved in a project for a film on the Resistance as early as 1965 when Louis Daquin asked him to provide a scenario on 'L'Affiche rouge', as the Red Poster put up by the Propagandastaffel on the walls of Paris in February 1944 was known to the French. The company had in mind a film for large audiences, with well-known actors to reassure them. Gatti did not see things in that light but finally went ahead with a telling scenario called *Le Temps des cerises*.

A question, 'Liberators?', had headed the Red Poster. Underneath were photographs of ten members of the Manouchian–Boczov Resistance cell, 'Judaeo-Bolshevik aliens', together with pictures of derailed trains and bullet-riddled bodies. At the bottom of the poster was the German reply to the rhetorical question, 'Liberation by the army of crime'. The Manouchian cell is the best-known of the Resistance cells organized amongst immigrant workers in Paris in 1943. Misaak Manouchian, an Armenian who had been orphaned at the age of three in the Turkish massacres of 1915, was a metallurgist and a poet. Joseph Boczov, a Romanian Jew, was a chemical engineer.

Because of the group's experience of racial and political persecution in their native lands, Gatti decided to concentrate on the immigrant workers, but the mere idea of Jews as Resistance fighters, together with Gatti's insistence on the dominant role played by the working class in the Resistance, dismayed the film companies. They lost interest, despite the 300,000 francs allocated to the project by the Commission Nationale du Cinéma. A semi-official agency even intimated that it would not handle a film in which the only names were those of immigrant workers.

The title, *Le Temps des cerises*, comes from the name of the traditional air whistled by the group as a signal but Gatti's script, as might be expected, is not limited to the events in question. Whatever their date or place, he always incorporates into the events the experience of his spectators at the time of composition of his script – in this case 1965. He represents the spectators – that is to say, 'us' – as the 'survivors of the Manouchian group', and the question put by the scenario concerns our way of continuing the struggle of those who died for it.

The 'spectators' watch a film-within-the-film depicting the real Manouchians. This gives rise to a confrontation between the comfortable notion of them as martyrs and the original definition of them as criminals. The action of the film-within-the-film, in which the 'actors' are helped in the interpretation of their roles by the 'spectators' – that is to say, the 'survivors' – describes the attacks made by the group, then their betrayal, their capture, torture, trial and execution.

On reliving the painful events of the past, the 'survivors' raise the question of the why and wherefore of their efforts in a war in which, as always, 'the outcome is decided by economic factors'. The final sequence presents the last moments and attitudes of the men as they separately await execution; these shots alternate with shots of the film-production team, 'survivors' and 'witnesses' (a collaborationist journalist and various police officers) wending their way up Mont Valérien on 21 February, on the twentieth anniversary of the men's execution in a clearing there. The last shot is that of the firing squad, rifles at the ready, as seen face-on by the condemned men, with the comment: 'Have we taken the meaning out of the last image engraved on their eyes?', and with Manouchian's reply, taken from his last letter to his wife, Méliné: 'Today [the day of execution] the sun is shining'. But on what does it shine? is Gatti's last question.

In May 1968 it was proposed to use the scenario as matter for discussion at the 'People's University' which was planned by the students for the summer at the Sorbonne. The events of May had given the scenario a new significance. The relevance of the situation faced by the men of the Resistance group to the situation of 1968 called for comment, and Gatti considered modifying his scenario within this framework. Film units, feeling the change of wind, considered making the film, but the subsequent evolution of the political situation put paid to these projects.

Gatti had, however, 're-entered the Resistance' and began to live, as it were, day after day with every member of the group, getting to know each one personally. This is apparent in the 1970 scenario which contains detailed portraits of the condemned men. This scenario, entitled *L'Affiche rouge*, seeks also to answer the question whether the fight in which they gave their all is as remote as that of the three Horaces and the three Curiaces, or does it form part of the struggles of today? Boczov, the cell's specialist in the technique of train derailment who had made his way on foot from Romania to Spain to join the International Brigade, getting rough personal experience of Fascist prison cells on the way before joining the Resistance movement in France, gives the answer: 'We began the fight in Spain, we went on with it in Paris. It will continue after us throughout the whole world' – Prague, Algeria, the maquis of Columbia, Vietnam, the prison in Saint Quentin on the day of Jackson's assassination, Germany with the Baader-Meinhof group, Paris in May 1968 – all to be illustrated by sequences from newsreels.

The scenario ends on a reaffirmation of the main intention of the film, with the Polish Jew Marcel Rayman facing the firing squad on Mont Valérien with a smile on his lips. In the film-within-the-film Rayman looks at the firing squad and at the fifteenth coffin intended for him near the execution wall, then, stepping out of his role, refuses to be shot. Instead he makes his way towards the camera crew, saying: 'I have fought to change history. I shall go on fighting to change it.' At this the Basque group and the Spaniards flock into the studio to the accompaniment of a soundtrack of the real trials at Burgos where the ETA group 'sang much more than the Basque anthem; they sang the birth of a fighting mass movement'. Significantly, the scenario concludes: 'The End and the Beginning'.

Gatti's series of scenarios came to an end when Frank Cassenti and René Richou, with whom he had been associated, made another film which they entitled *L'Affiche rouge* (1976) in the Cartoucherie in Vincennes. It presents a group of actors reconstructing the story of the Manouchian group with the help of the survivors. The film won a prize at the Cannes Festival. Gatti shelved his own project, but when he and the Tribe received an invitation to lead a discussion on the Resistance in a factory near Rouen, he proposed as an opening gambit for the discussion: 'Yesterday, Today, You, the Resistance, the Immigrants', and was taken aback when he was accused by some workers of implying that the men who were killed in the Resistance were heroes, whereas they themselves were 'poor mugs'. One of the Resistance men, however – a young Frenchman, Roger Rouxel, executed with the Manouchians – caught the imagination of the shop floor because of his last letter[6] written in Fresnes prison to a girl, three hours before his execution on Mont Valérien. It was Roger's last letter and also his first and only love letter to Mathilde, whom he had never told of his affection. The letter appears in the 1970 scenario, *L'Affiche rouge*.

Mathilde was sixteen years old, the daughter of immigrant Italian workers living near the Rouxels, in shanties in the old zone of the Paris fortifications at Vitry. Roger, who was executed shortly before his eighteenth birthday, was a metalworker at the Texier-Dufort factory. He did not belong to the Manouchian group but his portrait appeared along with theirs on the 'Red Poster'. His 'acts of terrorism' had been the derailment of trains, and reprisals on the occupying troops in Paris for the shooting of the fifty French hostages at Chateaubriand in Brittany, designated Communists by Pétain himself. Some of the young metalworkers in the factory readily identified themselves with Roger, and Gatti listened attentively to them. Gatti himself identified easily with Roger, seeing that he too had been sentenced to death as a Resistance fighter at about the same age as Roger, and could quite well have suffered Roger's fate.

On 10 June 1977 the trade-union committee of L'Isle d'Abeau voted by thirty-two votes to two for a project of audiovisual animation by Gatti lasting nine months. The Giscardian mayor of Saint-Alban, one of the associated communes, declared, however, that a Gatti enterprise would be an 'enterprise of intellectual pollution' and that Gatti would not be allowed to 'set foot in his commune'. The experiment went ahead regardless, and in October 1977 Gatti and his Tribe, together with their cats, dogs and cameras, settled down in a mansion by the lake of St-Quentin Fallavier, and for nine months L'Isle d'Abeau and a vast area around it, extending as far as Le Pont de Chéruy, Bourgoin-Jallieu, Chambéry and even the Cistercian Abbaye de Tamié in the mountains near Albertville in Savoy, were a hive of activity.

To introduce the people of these areas to Roger Rouxel, Gatti and his Tribe made a preparatory film entitled *La Première Lettre* which told the life story of Roger, the son of a Breton who had gone to work in Paris as a sewerman. it showed the squalor of the 'zone' of Vitry, which was, however, being cleared to make way for blocks of cheap flats when the film was being made. It records the memories of Roger's brother Paul, of Roger's capture and the words of Mathilde, of his workmate Arsène Tchakarian, and of Méliné Manouchian, who recalls the mocking laughter of the men as they were being shot.

In Search of a New Creative 'Language'

The Tribe showed the film more than two hundred times to trade and professional groups, to peasants and workers, and in institutions of all kinds. They made no attempt to force themselves or the film on the spectators, and on one occasion in a school when a child made fun of Mathilde and other children laughed, Gatti and his Tribe just left the hall. They did not seek 'unanimity'. Gatti's aim was to approach the Resistance not as it had been but as the Resistance had come to be imagined – namely, a sort of Pétainism, 'attentisme' or passive resistance which all claimed for themselves, and which was all the more absurd because it was Pétainism that had made him, Gatti, take to the maquis during the Occupation, and join those of the insurrection. The Resistance had been a very different experience for Gatti; it was the Pétainistes who had condemned him to death.

In the new town of L'Isle d'Abeau, Gatti sought to bring Roger back from Mont Valérien and give him 'one more year of life'. The problem was how to resurrect the past in a film without making of the film a historical reconstruction 'more lethal than the firing squad's rifles'. Gatti's solution was to name, to any person wishing to take part in the project, five places which could provide a possible meeting-ground between those who lived in them today and Roger, who had died thirty-five years before: places like the 'zone', a school, a factory, a Resistance group, a prison. Each one would choose the place in which he might have been along with Roger.

Prison was chosen by six ex-convicts, but they abandoned the idea and the 'prison' featured only as a model made by schoolchildren. Roger's day as an apprentice was mimed by a hundred apprentices using huge stuffed cloth puppets. These also expressed the apprentices' dreams and the collapse of those dreams. Others looked to the Resistance and represented it with articles of daily life such as baths, which the occupying authorities had turned into instruments of torture. Roger was tortured and, as he said in his letter to Mathilde, could write only with difficulty. Through the linking of contemporary images with the places in which Roger had lived his life and carried out his acts of resistance, the railway for example, the picture that emerged of him was not that of a dead youth but of one living on into the present.

Sixty-three groups became involved in the project, which began with the offer by a pupil from the local technical school (CES) to make Mathilde's wedding dress 'because had Roger lived he would have married Mathilde'. The offer also pointed the way forward for the venture; it was to be in the use of one's own experience. Student seamstresses made the dress, a diaphanous dress ten metres long, needing a crane to hold it up. Apprentice cooks engaged a dialogue with Roger in the only way they knew how, by cooking a meal. They prepared a 'banquet of life for Roger', and reserved his place at a long table set out on the banks of the Fallavier lake, together with places for the twenty-two who died with him. Wine came by boat, and a huge three-tiered cake arrived on a tractor with the wedding dress held high by the crane.

In the Technical College (CET) in Bourgoin, Michel Dalla, an apprentice turner like Roger, saw the 'trajectory' of Roger's life in terms of a pin-table ball being driven from pillar to post. He made a huge ball 1.60 metres in diameter, with sixteen facets, each representing a stage in Roger's life, and propelled it through the streets of Bourgoin where arrows on the road or on the walls showed the way it was to go, and traffic lights, No Stopping and No Access signs kept it rolling or held it up. On the waste ground of Champfleury it encountered a young girl on a moped – Mathilde, perhaps? It finally came to rest in the 'zone' where it had started, and lay abandoned in a car-breaker's yard like the unsung Resistance fighter, prisoner Number 10247, in the cemetery at Ivry.

The different forms of expression used by the groups were all recorded on video film by the Tribe. A particularly touching contribution came from primary-school children at Villefontaine. They refused to accept the cruel story, and reinvented it by reversing the legend of Orpheus and Eurydice. At the end of Eurydice/Mathilde's groping descent into the kingdom of the dead, she is met by the men of the Manouchian group who died with Roger. They decide, in council, that he is too young to die and should return to earth to continue the fight against racism and for justice and peace. Frédéric's scenario also contains a moving extract from Roger's letter to Mathilde: 'Dear beloved Mathilde ... I must tell you something. No one can live with the dead. I had fine plans for you and me, but fate decided otherwise.' The whole text was turned into song sung by the children themselves. Meanwhile Cerberus, Gatti's big black spaniel, mounts dignified guard at the entrance to Hades and at one moment rises to inspect it.

A slightly mischievous text by Gatti, sung on the lakeside by a chorus of teachers from different schools, describes their role as 'disseminators of pedagogical learning dressed up by them in frills' to make the learning more saleable. For the child Roger, school was his apprenticeship for the factory and subsequently for prison.

The scenario for the military tribunal was the brainchild of Christophe Gérard, a young pupil at the CES at La Verpillière. Starting from the idea that each person in the trial is cast in a role from which he cannot escape, Christophe concluded that any musical response to the situation must be made through mechanical instruments. The construction of suitable 'instruments' was undertaken in collaboration with a member of the Tribe, and they were named 'planquophone', 'celestofuel', 'contrefuel', 'cavernon', 'ogalu'. With this stridently grating collection of 'instruments' made entirely out of old oil drums, car engine blocks, metal fish-boxes, old piano strings and pieces of polystyrene collected

In Search of a New Creative 'Language'

from rubbish dumps, the tribunal took on a curious aspect. These 'instruments' represent the different protagonists in the drama, and make the clash between judges and accused a 'duel of decibels'. The instruments also do duty as puppets; by their appearance the four resonance cones of the 'cavernon' which represent the military tribunal also bring to mind the loudspeakers in German prison camps. Christophe himself introduces the different 'instruments' and relates them to the respective participants in the drama that had been played out in the sumptuous setting of the Hôtel Continental in Paris, used by the Germans as the courtroom. The music recurs – for example in the final film, *La Dernière Nuit* – and is a kind of leitmotiv.

Roger's letter is another leitmotiv. It is stated early in school, where children count the vowels and consonants in it. They number 1,327, and the letters lay siege to the town and countryside. They float on the five channels of the river Bourbre, on the yellow waters of the lake and ponds, are blown by the wind across fields and roads, or are caught on stone walls or house balconies where they form the words JE, TU, and the sinister word MORTS. The letter itself does duty as a dictation exercise in school.

All this is a far cry, Gatti insists, from the procedure adopted by official animators who impose their 'language' on others, and from a belief in a superior language used in the name of culture. It is for each to express himself through the objects and tools used by him in daily life. Gatti admits to having learnt at Montbéliard and Saint-Nazaire not to seek to impose his ideas or means of expression on others, but to help them to find their own.

Out of two hundred hours of shooting and several kilometres of film, Gatti made a series of one-hour films having as their starting point the several possible meeting-places between Roger and those living today. The films were shown locally in June 1979, then on six evenings between 22 July and 26 August they were put out on French television, Channel 3, along with Gatti's original preparatory film on Roger's story. In 1983, at the request of the Ministry for Foreign Affairs, Gatti made up a further film, *L'Usine*, from unused footage. In it the opening shots in the Dolbeau cloth factory – which had been shut down on 30 June 1976 even though it was in perfect working order – provide a parallel with the life story of Roger, cut off in his youth; this is just one example of a technique that is in frequent use throughout the series.

The most artistically satisfying of the films, *La Dernière Nuit*, begins also with a parallel: a Spitfire shot down in battle, 'the reality of our past', and a hijacked plane, 'the reality of our present'. On Pétain's France is superimposed France of the Resistance. On the death of a *maquisard*, René Travers, on a mountainside in Savoy on 14 August 1944, in a running fight with German soldiers and French militia, is superimposed

Armand Gatti in the Theatre

Roger's tortured last night in the Fresnes prison six months earlier. He was to die in a few hours' time, he wrote to his parents, but he had done his duty as a volunteer soldier in the Army of Liberation which fought to bring peace to all. People from all walks of life had sought a rendezvous with Roger on their home ground, but in prison there was no one to do so. This last rendezvous was, however, kept by the Cistercian monks of Tamié Abbey. Monks who live their lives *dans l'attente*, in the expectancy of death, and rise to pray in the middle of each night, alone could assume the agony of the last night of those condemned men in the Fresnes prison.

The Tamié Community had been brought into Gatti's venture by a member of the Tribe, Jean-Pierre Duret, a native of the region. A member of the same family, Louis Duret, a priest in Chambéry, wrote a meditation on Mathilde's reaction after Roger's arrest, as of the twelve apostles' after Christ's: three years of adventures for nothing – was it really worth it? The monks were shown the preparatory film, and in response themselves composed a series of poetic texts, one of which, *Dialogue de la dernière nuit*, moves from the human love of Roger for Mathilde to the consoling love of Christ. In the passage beginning 'Roger – Enfant debout dans la muraille', there is also a social connotation; *la muraille* is the 'wall built up by society, the walls of hatred, discrimination, injustice, violence – the wall each builds around himself which blurs his vision and restrains gestures of love.' The monks later composed a 'Petition to those responsible for the administration of Justice', pleading for the Rogers of today whose names are José, Djamel, John, Ivan or Claudio. The Petition is dated April 1978, and is published along with the poems in Volume 2, *Opéra*, printed by the press of Isle d'Abeau Animation. This volume and the next[7] also contain letters from people of the region on the impact of Gatti's venture upon them. All this lies outside the scope of the filmed scenarios but is considered by Gatti as an integral part of the project.

The Community in Tamié had to decide whether it should involve itself in the project. It is not surprising that it finally opted to do so. Its wartime record pointed the way. At considerable risk it had helped people to escape across the border into Switzerland, and when this was not possible, even conferred on them the 'honorary identity' of member of the Community. When the decision was taken to participate in the project, the youngest member was detailed to see it through. He admitted to me his initial reluctance, but after reading the long poem, *La Dernière Nuit*, composed by Gatti for the final phase of the film, he felt so deeply moved that he was more than happy to obey. Being a musician,[8] he set to work to compose liturgical music for the poem, and this was sung within the Abbey precincts by the white-robed monks in front of the lights and cameras of the Tribe, and under their professional guidance.

In Search of a New Creative 'Language'

The poem gives moving expression to Gatti's own feelings on the night when, like Roger, he had looked death in the face, condemned by the Vichy authorities. He had shared the experience of the Armenian poet who wrote: 'Life is not in time, but in the use one makes of it', the Garibaldian who 'said to the light of dawn, "Tell my father I shall keep his woolly on so as not to tremble with cold in front of the firing squad"'. Roger, 'the only one to believe in heaven, was the eighteenth to be executed, between the Garibaldian who said "Mother" in Piedmontese, and the Romanian Jew [Boczov] who said nothing.'

The opening lines set the agony of the condemned men in a Christian context:

> Jardin des oliviers, chaque nuit
> Recommencé: la prison de Fresnes.
> Le meurtre avait lieu hors les murs
> Mais pas l'agonie et ses sentences.

The music takes the poem over and it becomes a choral work sung by the monks, together, or intoned by a single voice accompanied on a zither, or by a second voice in a different register accompanied by a guitar. Each of the individual singers, together with his accompanist, performs full face to the cameras, in the meadow amid the stones of the old ruins. The choir of white-robed Cistercians officiates inside the church, but in the final shots of the film the monks sing in the sunlight of the meadow, spaced out, motionless in a square, all with their backs to the cameras. Clad in white or in white and black, according to their hierarchy, they sing the last verse:

> Devant la mitrailleuse, ils sont devenus
> Rose des vents et cri de l'enfance
> Seule l'enfance peut déchiffrer
> Les derniers moments du partisan
> Et sait répondre aux lieux où il s'abat
> Débuts de mots, restants de gestes
> En chacun, une solitude qui
> Ne sait pas en quelle langue mourir.

The beauty of the Abbey's church with the bare stone of its walls now stripped of disfiguring plaster, the long corridors with the golden light of the sun slanting through the windows and falling on the monks as their procession passed slowly along them, the peace of the meadow with the brothers walking in silent prayer amid the stones of the old ruins, so impressed Gatti that he sought to compose a symphony of images to accompany the symphony of sound, with the voices, organ and other instruments contributed by the monks themselves.

The sequence in the monastery is the superb high spot of the whole collective work hinged on the life and death of Roger Rouxel. It is self-contained and highly professional, and can be shown separately as an exquisite work of art. The poster made by the Community of the Abbey is also the most striking of them all. It contains the suggestion of a mangled body thrown against a prison wall, but the manacles on the bloodstained hand are broken. From the centre of a large heart, taking the place of the head, flies a bird carrying the letter to Mathilde in its beak.

Opera – there are ten choirs of various kinds and some local bands – poetry, cinema, theatre: *La première Lettre* in its final form is all of that. Part fictional history, part documentary, it re-creates a period of time still near, yet far enough away to be a closed book to many of the new generation. Memory and imagination had given rise to sixty-three scenarios at L'Isle d'Abeau, but as far as Gatti was concerned they were not an end product of the experiment. The experiment was complete in itself and for itself. It had provided not only a common meeting-ground with Roger, but a meeting-ground for people from widely different walks of life, different trades, different professions. Through Roger they had come to know each other and work alongside each other. When some, like René Lallement, a wartime *gendarme* turned *maquisard*, revisited the site of his exploits, he not only met former comrades but met for the first time in the flesh a comrade known to him in the Resistance only as a number. Survivors of the Manouchian group – among them the brother of Marcel Rayman, the condemned Polish Jew – joined the project in increasing numbers as it went ahead, and came to situate their fallen companions not only in the struggle of yesteryear but also in their present daily life.

Gatti sees the six films (now seven) of his 'opera in six parts' as a single song sung by many ordinary people who had become involved in the life of a young man of the Resistance. To ask 'how a death such as his could have happened' was to examine history through the life story of an individual. Gatti does not see the Resistance as belonging only to history, but as belonging to a state of mind to be found in each of us at all times.

Notes

1. The name 'Les Voyelles' was substituted for the longer title, Institut de Recherche des Mass Média et des Arts de Diffusion – IRMMAD – by the newly appointed director and co-director of the Institut, Armand Gatti and Jean-Jacques Hocquard: the presence of the five vowels in the title inspired the new name (address: 20 bis, rue Hippolyte Maindron, 75014 Paris).
2. *Le Joint* was issued (Roneoed) by the Institut de Recherche des Mass Média et des Arts de Diffusion (1977). Jean-Louis Pays, who played a part in it,

published an account of the text and of the whole project in *Travail Théâtral* No. 24–25, July–December 1976, under the title 'Le Combat contre l'ange (*Le Chat guérillero*, d'Armand Gatti, à Ris-Orangis)'.
3. Illustrations appear in C. Campos's article, 'What Gatti did next: The Wild Ducks of Saint-Nazaire' (*Theatre Quarterly*, VIII, 31, 1978).
4. *Unité*, 11–17 February: 'Les canards sauvages de Saint-Nazaire', by Jean-Paul Liégeois.
5. *Le Monde*, 23–24 September 1979: 'Le Stalinisme n'est pas un incident de parcours', déclare Vladimir Boukovski.
6. The text of the 'Letter to Mathilde' is reproduced in *Armand Gatti*, published by the Ministère des Relations Extérieures – Cellule d'Animation Audio-visuelle (Paris, 1981).
7. Volume 3, *Le Temps de la Mésange*. Volume 2, *Opéra*, contains drawings of the 'musical instruments', planquophone, etc.
8. Later (1982) named as Philippe Hermon Tamié.

References

Ida Mett, *Souvenirs sur Nestor Makhno* (Paris: Éditions Allia, 1983).
Bruno-Jean Martin, *Histoire des moines de Tamié et de quelques autres* (Saint-Étienne: Le Hénaff, 1982).

The affair of *L'Affiche rouge* resurfaced in 1985 when a documentary – *Terroristes à la retraite* by M. Mosco, dating from 1983 – was to have been shown on Antenne 2. It was withdrawn after a campaign by *L'Humanité* accusing it of being 'defamatory' to the French Communist Party. The issue at stake was the film's treatment of the question of the responsibility for the fate of the Manouchian Resistance Group, who furthermore were not 'terrorists' but 'freedom fighters'. The film was finally shown on 2 July 1985 in the programme 'Dossiers de l'Écran', and was followed by a lengthy debate aimed at discovering the truth. The speakers included some former members of the Resistance. Seven cars full of CRS were stationed near the television station.

14
Northern Ireland: a Blind, Imperative Rendezvous

Nous étions tous des noms d'arbres
Le Labyrinthe

Gatti's starting point, he explains with regard to the film *Nous étions tous des noms d'arbres*, shown at the Edinburgh Film Festival in August–September 1982 and in the London Film Festival in November under the title *The Writing on the Wall*, is always some event to which he reacts, and within the bounds of which he remains contained. The event comes first. He had, he recalls, reacted strongly to the 'birth of China' – *Le Poisson noir* and *Un Homme seul* are there to prove it; and did not the events in Guatemala inspire his first piece of dramatic writing, *Le Quetzal*? He was a 'vibratile' animal: incapable of writing without having reality to prompt him to invent. The reality of his film on Ireland is the town of Derry, with its singsongs in the pubs and its daily tragedies.

Gatti's 'discovery of Ireland' started with an invitation to Dublin to see a production of *La Cigogne*, and a further invitation to follow a company taking its production of a play by John Arden into the pubs of Belfast, the Belfast 'ghettos'. The warmth of the welcome, the music and song, amid the photographs on the walls of those killed by the Protestants or by British soldiers, made a deep impression on Gatti. He felt the need to make a fraternal gesture, and set out to meet the people of Northern Ireland. Everywhere he heard of Derry – a name meaning oak-grove in Gaelic. But in the seventeenth century the town was chosen for settlers from London and given the 'none sense' name of Londonderry, which at the same time pointed to its 'colonization'. It was given back its original name of Derry in 1984. In Derry Gatti found a town at war: its centre destroyed, armed patrols in the streets, checkpoints everywhere, electronic surveillance devices on a pylon reaching up into the sky as high as the church steeple, and cameras on circling helicopters. Computers installed in a disused psychiatric hospital stored all the information. This surveillance by invisible cameras with their 'hundred eyes' 'continually undermines a person's identity because this threat is always present, always imminent, always round the corner'. Nevertheless Derry said of itself, with typical Irish humour, that it was the 'wisest city' in the world because it had 'locked up its police in a lunatic asylum'.

In Derry Gatti came into contact with the Youth and Community Workshop installed in a derelict military establishment by Paddy Doherty, a Catholic who had been summarily dismissed by his Protestant employer after twenty-five years' service for taking part in a Civil Rights demonstration. Paddy's Workshop was the 'only non-denominational school in Northern Ireland'. It took in boys and girls of all ages, Catholic and Protestant, mainly Catholic because the majority of the poor were Catholics. It was immaterial to Paddy whether they belonged to the IRA or not. His aim was to get the children of large families off the streets. Most of them were unemployed, had relatives in prison, or mourned others killed by Protestants or by British rifles. He sought to give them some sort of education, as nearly half of them could neither read nor write.

The school was not only tolerated by the British authorities but was also given some financial assistance in the hope of stifling 'militants in the bud'. For the well-off in Derry, whatever their denomination, this training school with its rudimentary teaching of trades was a 'zoo', and the press attached the names of carnivorous animals to the members of the 'bestiary'. In the film the Catholics of Bogside are 'Piranhas', the Protestants of Waterside 'Tsetse Flies', and those from mixed areas 'Weasels'. From the Creggan district come the 'Cannibals', as Father O'Donnell explains to the Irish American Eamon Kelly (a fictitious character) who has come to Derry to 'find his roots' and 'get back to the time when our names were names of trees': 'In the old days the letters of the [ogham] alphabet were the names of trees, and Derry was one.'[1] Eamon has come to the Workshop to teach writing and printing on the invitation of its director, 'Seamus Doherty'.

The workshop was started with the watchword 'Build your own knowledge'. It was to be more than a place for learning a trade – it was to be a 'place of awareness', and what mattered was for everyone to become aware of the world around his world and of the history in which he lived. Little wonder that Gatti saw in the Workshop, and even more so in Derry, 'The Promised Land' – a curious name, as he admitted, for a land where civil war had become part of the very nature of the town. It was as much part of the day as the shopping basket or the supermarket, is Eamon's comment. Gatti had even thought of 'The Promised Land' as a title for his film.

Nearly three years passed before he was able to make a start on the actual filming. He had been unable to obtain financial backing for the film and so had to 'fall back into the system' – to apply to the Commission for Advances on Receipts. His application was turned down, but was later allowed on condition that he made changes in his project. Gatti resubmitted the same project and received the subsidy! He went to Ireland and was working on a co-production with Belgian friends, one of whom was in the Ministry of Culture, when the Socialists took office in France and doubled his subsidy. He was given 300,000 dollars, the maximum at the time. But it was the people of Derry who earned Gatti's admiration. They 'paid for their film' by housing and feeding the team, supplying petrol and their other needs. Faced with their outstanding generosity, Gatti felt ashamed. These people were not just making a film; total solidarity existed between them and the film-makers.

The film is situated at the crossroads of three stories retailing three events. There is the story of Paddy Doherty (his real name) and his 'Libertarian' Workshop, with Noel McCloskey, a deaf-mute appointed by Paddy as master of communications who taught the pupils his sign language; it became a code language in the Workshop. He also sought to teach them Gaelic to re-establish their lost 'identity'. Noel told Gatti of one of his friends, a deaf-mute like himself, who had been shot by a British patrol because he did not hear the patrol's warning, and he came into the film to play the part of his dead friend as well as his own. In Gatti's eyes Noel was the most 'precious gift' the Workshop made him.

A second story, contributed by boys of the Workshop and played by two of them, is also a real story. It tells of two youths, Gerald Craig and Paul Russell, one Catholic, the other Protestant, friends and both members of the IRA, who were blown up while delivering explosives in the region. Their names are engraved together on the statue of the mythical hero of Ulster, Cuchulainn, with his raven, which marks the Catholic section of the cemetery, but their bodies were buried in different cemeteries by their families. Paul's father disowned his son, and this fact is retained in the film. In the film the youths are called Hugh and Wesley (Cha for short) and are Catholic and Protestant and IRA, like Craig and Russell. They meet their death while driving a van full of flowers potted in the explosive powder in an attempt to get it past the soldiers at the checkpoints. When the film was shown in Derry at the Rialto on 13 December 1982, the father of the Protestant boy-actor locked his son in his room to prevent him from seeing it. History repeated itself.

The third story was contributed by Gatti. An incident in Derry stirred the memory of it. The story is that of Gatti's 'death' as a British SAS paratrooper, a death which might have been his during the Second World War in a corps in which an 80 per cent casualty rate was not unexpected. The incident was the invitation given to Gatti by an inhabitant of the Catholic Creggan, on the edge of Bogside, to see the spot in front of his door where an English soldier had been shot shortly before. He told him how, a few days after the soldier's death, his father had called to find out how his son had died, and the two men had recognized each other as former fellow-labourers on the Liverpool motorways. The son, out of work, had joined the Green Jackets. He had been killed on duty in Ireland, and this dead soldier could well have been Gatti himself, a former SAS in the British Army, 'a self, fighting Nazism to liberate subject peoples [...] who came and died on the doorstep of this house in the course of the occupation of a country and the repression of its people.' Gatti asks:

> How could a regiment which had set out to free Europe, and which had lost so many of its young men in the cause, become this repressive force [...] the Gestapo of Ireland? ... I had come to Ireland to face up to my own 'death'.

This incident was the embryo of the film's scenario.

At the same time – pure coincidence or miracle? Gatti wondered which – Paddy Doherty suggested to the pupils in the Workshop that as the overriding problem of their time was the death of British soldiers, they should discuss the subject and, to avoid any clashes, should take the case of an exemplary British soldier who had lost his life trying to save a Catholic family in a fire – a real incident. They should 'live to the full all the implications of this death'. In the film, the 'soldier' is Private Hobson, killed by a shot coming from the Workshop during an accidental alert, and his father and sister travel to Derry to enquire into the circumstances of his death. The surveillance authorities, however, see the proposed discussion in the Workshop 'on the death of an English soldier' as a 'six-month rehearsal for the killing of Private Hobson', and the electronic memories in the Anti-Terrorist Centre set to work to count all the clues time and time again on its screens. One of these is the misspelling of a Catholic girl's name, Maeve (the name of a Celtic queen) as Mave by the boy Wesley whose family were Loyalists. But as this is not a 'who dunit', all that is established in the film is that Hobson was shot by a bullet of a certain calibre.

However, 'according to what they are saying in Derry, it is the cannon which came up out of the sea four hundred years later [to avenge the luckless Spaniards] that killed Major Hovendan's symbolic soldier outside the Workshop.' Gatti tells Pierre Lavoie and Michel Vaïs in an interview[2] of an invitation from Sir Brook to Stormont to discuss the film, and Sir Brook's denial of the presence of the English in Derry at the time. This was a shock for Gatti:

> Everything depended on the legend: the English treachery, the cannon which came out of the sea [to kill an English soldier]. The legend was to a certain degree the mirror in which topicality was reflected.

It would mean rewriting the scenario, but before doing so Gatti consulted documents in a Belfast library. He found Sir Brook's statement to be incorrect, but his visit to Stormont almost cost him two bullets in his kneecaps from the IRA!

The salvaging of the cannon from the Spanish galleon *Trinidad Valencera*, wrecked in Kinnagoe Bay in 1588, is one of two historic facts presented in the film. The O'Doherty clan had negotiated a safe-conduct for the Spanish crew with Major Hovendan of the English garrison in Derry. The crew were nevertheless massacred on his orders when they came ashore unarmed, as arranged. The film shows a mock-up of the cannon made by the boys of the Workshop, and shows them bringing the cannon ashore. One of them hides an American 7.65 pistol which had mysteriously appeared on the beach inside the cannon to get it through the checkpoints.

The other historical fact is the arrival and welcome of the British troops in Ulster in 1969. 'Eleven years ago,' says Una, a member of the Derry community,

> Catholics were giving the soldiers cups of tea in the street, along the peace line set up by the British with barbed-wire fencing. Nowadays when a soldier is killed they cheer. That's something we should at least talk about.

These two historical facts are viewed, in typical Gatti fashion, as it were from the centre.

A fourth element made a dramatic entry into the project and into the scenario the very day filming was due to begin. That morning, 5 May, the death of Bobby Sands was announced. Was that to be the end of the project? The Workshop voted to continue with the film. On 7 May, the day of Bobby Sands's funeral, the cameras went with the mourners to Belfast to follow the coffin, and these shots, together with shots of the rioting in Derry and the Bogside after his death and after that of the next hunger-strikers, are worked into the film with many of the Workshop pupils actively participating in the riots. Reality and fiction merged of themselves completely. The two had already been intentionally merged in the scenario in the person of Paddy Doherty, who plays his own part as founder and director of the Workshop under the 'stage name' of Seamus Doherty. Reality and fiction merged accidentally during the filming of the kidnapping of the Workshop's Protestant deputy director, Paul, who was actually injured in the heat of the 'game'.

Like Paddy, the other participants in the film were members of the Derry community – apart from the 'foreigners': that is to say, the English, whose roles were part of a function and not part of the Irish struggle itself. These characters and that of Eamon, the American, were acted by professionals. Real British soldiers were at the checkpoints. The

Northern Ireland: a Blind, Imperative Rendezvous

Derry community is 'living in history' which goes back '2,400 years'; it is not just living in a town, Seamus tells the English anti-terrorist squad on the old Ring Fort where he had promised to reveal who killed the English soldier. To catch the person who shot to kill would merely scratch at the surface of the problem and not affect the march of history in any way. His version of history runs contrary to that of the English soldiers who are hunting down the deaf-mute. History, for them, is made by the power of the bullet: they reply to a child's question in the church cemetery, 'Who are they after now?' 'You'll learn that at school.'

The scenario is based on the opposition to each other, in the struggle of the century, of the computers in the Anti-Terrorist Centre and the graffiti on the walls of Derry, particularly of the Workshop, itself 'the temple of graffiti'. 'And between the computers and the graffiti there is a town trying to regain control over the tree-name that had been its own.' Often the graffiti become the language of the resistance and give a lead to the development of the script. Some play an active part in the action, as when the oldest of the graffiti, 'Is there a life before death?' comes in for a stoning by Workshop boys: What life? What prospect of life is there for them? Then there is the incident of the callous shooting of the deaf-mute on the flimsiest of 'circumstantial evidence'; he is spray-painting a 'Letter to the dead soldier's father' on Craigavon Bridge. 'He is deaf. There will be warnings', Mayor Bond cynically says, happy to have tracked down not necessarily the criminal, but a suspect who 'fits into the logic of his reasoning'. Bond is Quadrature of *V comme Vietnam* all over again.

The shooting of the deaf-mute brings the film back to its starting point, the Spanish wreck. Along with the cannon, an organ in mahogany casing had been salvaged from the wreck and installed in the Protestant cathedral of Saint Columb's in Derry. It was intended for use at services for soldiers who had died there. Like Noel, however, it had been 'dumb', 'because history', according to Noel, 'has no room for the deaf'. But after the shooting, the organ takes up from the deaf-mute and begins to 'speak'. As its voice swells up drowning all other sounds, a phantom flower-bedecked van drives on and on, in slow motion, amongst the hills of the Derry countryside. The film comes to an end with this image and this music.

The organ music was specially composed in France by Philippe Hermon Tamié, who had already composed for Gatti's films. An Irish piper playing 'Four Green Fields' accompanies the funeral in the 'Cuchulainn Domain' of the cemetery of the two boys who had died in the flower-bedecked van, just as each week he piped others to their final resting place. The singing of 'Roishin Dubh', the song of the clandestine Irish Resistance, is a reminder in another scene of Cromwell's attempt to suppress the Gaelic language, and with it Gaelic identity. But the Gaelic spirit lives on, despite the American's accusation of the 'colonization' of the Irish, not only of their land but also of their language. As far as Gatti was himself personally concerned, this 'colonized country fighting to establish its identity, fighting for its freedom', was an experience such as he had not had since his days in the maquis and the concentration camp. It vividly recalled the Resistance and the maquis in its fight against Nazism and Fascism.

In making the film Gatti came up against a problem he had never met before: he was asking a whole population to become actors of a piece of fiction. That meant preparing them in drama sessions in the Workshop. These began on 27 April 1979. The sessions had nothing to do with actor-training as such, but were devised to help people to 'play' their lives with the spontaneity of real life, improvising their words and gestures as they went along. The next problem was how to get beyond the pre-established framework of the script, and make improvisation and discussion the basis for film-writing. A pamphlet (No. 3) printed in the Workshop explains how this was done, so also does a video film, *Irlande Terre Promise*, made by Hélène Chatelain, in 1982. The film contains discussions of events and themes by the future participants in the film, and shows them in improvised studios learning the various arts required for the *écriture plurielle* that constitutes a film. There is also the statement by Gatti that the words uttered by Seamus Doherty are indeed Paddy Doherty's own words and not his, Gatti's. Gatti insists on the authenticity of the matter in the film.

In some scenes, such as the discussion on the death of the British soldier, certain parts of the discussion were written down and remained like demarcation lines in a playing field. The space between had to be filled in spontaneously by the pupils and tutors of the Workshop. There resulted a constant toing and froing between fiction and reality. Fiction – the written texts; Reality – everyone's reactions to these texts. Fiction – the incorporation of these reactions into the words of the film characters. In this way various 'meetings', as seen in the film, could well have been 'real', even though the text was by then fully written out. The line between lived history and acted history was very thin indeed for the people of Bogside. Adults and young alike improvised on themes suggested by their own lives: explosives that had to be hidden at whatever cost, a brother or father imprisoned in Long Kesh, the Maze itself, a Protestant friend being brought for the first time into a Catholic household.

It is significant that Paddy asked Catholics in the Workshop to play the part of Protestants, Protestants to play the part of the IRA, and those whom he knew to belong to the IRA to play the part of the Army. Each should adopt the 'language', in its broadest sense, of his opposite number. Perhaps in this way they would arrive at an understanding of

Northern Ireland: a Blind, Imperative Rendezvous

the reasoning of the other. Each cast aside the role he was born into in order to take over the opposite role, and they did it with all the violence that was the key to everything in Derry, like the unintentional harming in the kidnapping sequence of the deputy head of the Workshop, who was playing the 'coroner'. His task was to decide on the burial place of the 'dead English soldier' who was claimed by Catholics, Protestants, the IRA and the British alike. He had to be made to disappear!

On leaving Ireland, Gatti felt that he was swimming against the tide of all the explanations of the Northern Irish problem that had been given by the media and others – an archaic war, a religious war – but that he had established common ground with those Irish who had taken him in: Paddy Doherty, the people of the Workshop, the community of Derry. In the film the deaf-mute says: 'In Derry there are Catholics, Protestants and the deaf. But all are not deaf in the same way.' Gatti, for his part, says:

> When speaking of Northern Ireland one must not forget that there is no rivalry between well-off Catholics and well-off Protestants, unless it is a commercial or social rivalry such as one finds everywhere else. It is the poor quarters that do the fighting; [...] No one is nearer to a well-off Protestant than a well-off Catholic [...] both are on the side of the British authorities. They have the means to live, and to live well, on this earth. Why should they change their way of life in the name of a mythical Ireland which, according to them, ceased to exist a long time ago? That is where Paddy Doherty, the mason, comes in.

This analysis by Gatti of the Northern Ireland situation is to be read in the retranscription of a press interview prepared for the Cannes Film Festival in May 1982 (in the section Perspectives du Cinéma français), as Gatti was unable to present the film himself. By a unanimous vote the film was awarded the 1982 Jean Delmas Prize.

Preparation for filming began in April 1979. The text of the first scenario was ready in January 1980. It is written in French and approaches the tragedy of Derry somewhat from the outside with its opening shots of a fictitious camera crew making careful 'takes' of various quarters of Derry and of hooded men, in order to set the scene for the 'film proper'. The text ends with a meeting in the Workshop where all who took part in the film are asked to vote on two suggestions for possible endings, one by Major Bond, the other by Seamus. Bond's version ends with the shooting of Noel on Craigavon Bridge and Bond's triumphal announcement to his suspected accomplice that 'Ireland has just lost another bad poet'. This is a reference to the shooting of the Irish writers Pearse and Plunkett, the 'bad poets' mentioned by Noel in his lessons. Seamus's version shows the wounded Noel fleeing towards the cathedral, from which now comes the voice of the organ. Round the cathedral crouch patrols, their rifles at the ready, as they give their reply to the child's question, 'Who are you hunting now?'

The version on which filming began was translated into English by Joseph B. Long of University College Dublin and reduces to very little the role of the fictitious camera crew. It dispenses with the alternative endings proposed in the French text, and keeps near to Seamus's. It closes directly on the child's question. In neither text is there any real reference to what was happening in Long Kesh, but with the death of Bobby Sands on the first day of filming, the hunger-strikers burst into the film, almost taking it over. The hunger-strikers, said Gatti, 'were at every street corner' in the riots which 'gave them a few more days of life amongst their own – the kids of the district'. On the last day of filming, 20 August, the tenth hunger-striker, Micky Devine, died, so while the Workshop people were trying to *record* history, they were *making* history, as Paddy Doherty says at the end of *Irlande Terre Promise*.

Perhaps it would have been better to make a film on the hunger-strikes, but a decision had been taken to make one on the Workshop, and with all that was happening around them it was a challenge. Yet they had a feeling of guilt; men were dying not only in the hunger-strikes but at the hands of the police; meanwhile their film was a film on the past, albeit a not very distant past, two years old. The intrusion of the present into that past had, however, made a balance between the story of the Workshop and the daily tragedies difficult to achieve in the filming. Such is Paddy's judgement on the project which they had undertaken.

Gatti insists that the film was entirely the creation of the people of Derry, and to those who said that certain elements in it were 'pure Gatti' he replied that this was not so; they were the spontaneous contribution of the community, whereas he, Gatti, was the public scribe. The context of the film was the daily life of a 'town at war'. A number of sequences in the film were contemporary newsreel material without any reconstruction; the part played in them by his 'film actors' was actually real. There was no separating town and film, life and art.

The filming in Derry ended on the day the sixth hunger-striker died, but the film was not finished because the parallel scenes showing the computers at work in the Anti-Terrorist Surveillance Centre had not been shot. Gatti and his team had failed to gain admittance to the Centre, although there had been no formal refusal. The scenes had to be shot in a mock-up of the Centre in a disused prison in St Léonard de Liège, Belgium. Filming there ended on the day of the death of Mickey Devine.

The background theme of men slowly starving to death, and Gatti's contacts with many of their families who showed him minute pieces of cigarette paper and toilet paper on which was written an account of life in the Maze and which had been hidden by the men inside their own bodies, left Gatti with an uneasy conscience about his film. He felt he had not kept faith with the subject. He could not admit that men were living naked amid their own excreta and that this had gone on for four years and his film had ignored it. On the one hand the action itself ran counter to the golden rule of the French Resistance fighter who was required to keep his body healthy, ready for any contingency. The slow degradation of human beings that was taking place in the H-Blocks was alien to his fundamental optimism. But seeing the return of some corpses to their families in Derry, Gatti came to feel that their appalling clashes of will had been brought about by people who, like himself, had sought to remain aloof and detached. He had filmed from his scenario on the Workshop, but the filming had been done 'under the gaze of the ten blanket-men' whose real situation had not been and could not be re-created in it. The consciousness of this drove Gatti to begin work on a play – even before starting to cut and mount the Workshop film. He lacked the means to make another film. The death of Bobby Sands had made him warm to the Republican cause, just as the knowledge that two million Irish had died in the potato famine of 1845, amongst barns stocked with grain, had moved him when he had first learnt of it.

As he himself has confided to the present author, his heart leads him to the Irish, although not to the Catholic cause. Perhaps the best definition of his position is to be found in his comment to Jacques Siclier on audience reaction to his film in Edinburgh: 'The English realized that they did not understand the Irish language of the North, that that country belonged to a different culture. I am proud at having succeeded in showing that.'[3] How far, one may wonder, is such a position from that of James Connolly?

> Believing that the British government has no right in Ireland, never had any right in Ireland, and never can have any right in Ireland, the presence, in any one generation of Irishmen, of even a respectable minority, ready to die to affirm that truth, makes that government for ever a usurpation and a crime against human progress.

Or that of Karl Marx? 'I used to think the separation of Ireland from England impossible. I now think it inevitable.'

To write a play on the hunger-strikes was to face up to four years of Irish history, the four years of the 'three strikes': the refusal to wear the clothes of common-law criminals; the No Wash, No Slop-out Protest after the hardening of prison conditions; and finally the hunger-strikes. Gatti's repeated efforts to find a dramatic form that could contain the three strikes ended in failure. The Northern Irish gaols, like the Nazi camps, defied every approach. Reality as lived by the blanket-men in their 'concrete tombs' amid 'the urine, the excreta, the putrefaction, the worms', passed all description.

Confronted with the impossibility of reconciling this experience with his own culture, Gatti finally realized that the impossibility of dramatizing such a subject was itself dramatic, and alone worthy of the ten dead men's predicament. He had thought first of writing a dramatic poem which would have the title *Lorsque les femmes du Bogside frappent sur les poubelles*. The sight of the women banging on the pavements with their dustbin lids amid the smoke of the riots was a 'violent image', true matter for a poem, but the more complex reality which eventually provided the starting point for a dramatic composition was the name 'the Maze', given to the internment camps at Long Kesh by the English. With the myth of the labyrinth behind it, this name, 'the Maze', suggested the structure of Gatti's dramatic composition and also its title: *Le Labyrinthe*.

Le Labyrinthe

The original version, which ran from 20 May to 4 June 1982, in Genoa, was translated into Italian and published under the title *Il Labirinto*. It was produced at the Teatro Dell'Archivolte by its director, Gino Zampieri. A second version in French was put on by Gatti at the Avignon Theatre Festival in the Cloître des Carmes from 1 to 6 August the same year, and a third version was given a reading or 'one-man show' by Gatti on 30 March 1983 in Toulouse at the Archéoptéryx, the Atelier de Création Populaire. This, Gatti says, is the definitive version.

The first version is unknown to the present writer but the duplicated copy of the second version (the version for Avignon), put out by IRMMAD allows for a comparison to be made between the second and the third version, written in Toulouse and published there at the Archéoptéryx in 1983 in the volume *Notes de Travail en Ulster* (editions Pierres Hérétiques). This volume contains the story of Bobby Sands, his political and literary education when in prison, and long excerpts from what he wrote there. It also contains an outline of Irish legend and history; from 1960 the history is presented in some detail. The changes in legislation affecting the position of imprisoned Republicans are noted: the Special Category Status granted by William Whitelaw in 1972; its withdrawal in 1976 by Merlyn Rees; the subsequent application, in accordance with the Diplock Report of 1972, of Internment by Preventive Detention even in the absence of specific charges (Bobby Sands spent eleven months in Preventive Detention in Crumlin Gaol while awaiting trial); the 'confessions' obtained allegedly by force at Castlereagh and described in detail by Bobby Sands in October 1976.

Interviews with Republicans and families of the hunger-strikers figure in the *Notes*, and Gatti draws freely on them in his text. But it was the interview with Patrick Ward, whom he had gone to see in Donegal before beginning to write, that he found the most instructive, also the most profoundly disturbing. Patrick Ward had been imprisoned twice in Eire in 1972–3 and had gone on hunger-strike three times; the third strike ended in a military camp at Curragh with Patrick in a coma, 'the antechamber of eternal cold'. He was saved by the Eire government's last-minute acceptance of the prisoners' demands. The strike left Ward a permanent wreck but 'he alone', Gatti explains, 'could help us approach, from inside, what the hunger-strikes in Long Kesh meant for the ten men who went through them and died of them.' Gatti obtained from Patrick Ward a detailed description of what Ward calls 'the anatomy of a hunger-strike', the slow disintegration of the body, and the mental torture that accompanies it. It was easier, Ward maintained, to face up to death than to face life of this kind, a life of slow self-destruction. He expressed his anger at the silence of Southern Ireland.

Gatti also drew on the testimony of Tony O'Hara of Derry, brother of Patsy, the third hunger-striker to die. Tony was arrested in 1976 and spent five years as a blanket-man in the Maze. He said to Gatti: 'I had read a lot about the Maze and thought I knew all about it. In fact I knew nothing. Nothing I had read bore any relation to what I found there.' He added, with regard to the No Wash, No Slop-out Protest:

> I do not know how I lived in those conditions, and for so long ... Living with someone in a cell with the walls covered with human excreta ... Now the smell has gone (it was a long time going) I don't know how to find words to describe it.

'Impossible' sums up what O'Hara had to say to the dramatist.

Interviews with families of two of the dead hunger-strikers find echoes in the play. They are the McElwee family and the Doherty family, both of whom resisted pressure from the Church to persuade their sons to break their fast. 'I could not ask my son to return to his cell and relive what he had already gone through [...] He was fighting for his country, and was dying for it', said Mrs Doherty. Long Kesh was 'impossible'.

The play also contains echoes of the document published on 3 October 1981 by the Republican prisoners of the H-Blocks after the repeated intervention of the strikers' families had succeeded in bringing the hunger-strike to an end. The document describes the attitude of the prisoners *inside* the Maze, and that of the IRA Command *outside*. The Command *outside* advised the men to refuse to wear prison clothes and so reject the 'criminalization' of their acts, but it was opposed to the unlimited hunger-strike which those *inside* understood to be the only possible action, given the failure of the fifty-three-day hunger-strike of 27 October 1980 by seven men – seven in memory of the seven shot in Dublin in 1916. Once that strike was ended the Secretary of State for Ireland, Humphrey Atkins, reneged on his promise and required the men to put on prison clothes as a precondition for getting their civilian clothes back.

Bobby Sands, who had been refused permission by the Command *inside* the Maze to take part in the first strike, had foreseen action of the sort by the government, so when as leader he inaugurated the second strike on 1 March 1981, it was with a clear realization that he would have to die, with perhaps two or three others as well, before their claim of political prisoner status was recognized. A solution was impossible. The men were betrayed. The document further castigates 'the true face of the present Irish establishment: the Catholic Church, the Dublin government, the SDLP':

> We believe that the Dublin block (Fianna Fáil, Fine Gael, Labour) has been an instrument of the legal assassination of ten Irish men [...] who died heroically in the long tradition of Republican resistance in Ireland against the British occupation, oppression and injustice [...] They did nothing, and in this way have encouraged the British to pursue their policy of death. (pp. 110–11)

Such was the historical material on the impossible drama of Long Kesh, of ten men brutally crushed by a feelingless world of the Thatcher era – the women of Derry might well bang their dustbin lids. Such was the 'labyrinth' in which Gatti had to find Ariadne's 'guiding thread', to quote the programme-document *Le Labyrinthe: L'Irlande et une pièce*, subtitled 'guide pour *Le Labyrinthe* en forme de glossaire', issued for the 1982 Avignon Festival and published in Toulouse by L'Action Coopérative pour le théâtre working for the production in conjunction with Gatti's Atelier. Gatti has referred several times to the difficulties encountered in trying to find Ariadne's guiding thread, through the labyrinth of the three strikes. The fact that the three strikes had no place at all in his experience, in his culture, explains the existence of his three attempts at giving them dramatic form. In the first version of the play Malachi, an actor taking the part of a hunger-striker, vainly seeks (it would seem) to give expression to the reality of the strikes using one or other of the traditional forms of theatre. The second version inverts the procedure, and seeks to make the different forms of theatre themselves attempt to re-create the whole experience of the strikers by putting forward one aspect of it, then another. The resulting picture is fragmentary.

In this second version, Malachi McLocchlainn, a fictitious blanket-man in the H-Blocks, is the central character. Grouped around him are a number of characters: his family, members of the IRA, fellow-prisoners, an MP, a Church dignitary and representatives of the British occupying force. All have names: Kieran, a fellow-hunger-striker; Pauline, Malachi's mother; Father Liam O'Seoigh, the chaplain; the 'Brit' Richard 'Cœur de Lion'. Existing dramatic forms – tragedy, romantic drama, psychological drama, militant theatre, the political play – attempt in turn to express the hunger-striker's way of living and dying, and the pressures put upon him. But the three strikes find no place in any of them, although a partial truth emerges from each attempt. Together, these partial truths make up the long history of oppression of the 'Island of Birds', as it is known in the Gaelic tradition, and the perennial nature of the blanket-men's struggle. Malachi eventually declares that he is 'all the birds' of the island. Through him the struggle of the men locked up in the Maze to achieve a Catholic, socialist, 'Gaelic' republic will be brought to the notice of the world in the form of the only image the British have to offer it: a concrete box with an iron door, a little table, a chair, a warder's loudspeaker, a bowl of water and a packet of salt.

As performed at Avignon within the prison-like walls of the cloister, the 'island of birds' and the 'cages' of Long Kesh were re-created, as it were, by a huge bird-cage filled with stuffed birds of prey at one end of the cloister, and a number of other cages, rusty and sinister-looking, standing between tiered benches on two sides for a public which faced one another like two opposing factions. The actors, wrapped in blankets, crouched in the cages, or hoisted blankets bearing in succession the name of the particular dramatic form that was being tried out. Sets were constructed with the cages themselves. For this production of *Le Labyrinthe*, Gatti called on professional actors from Paris and from Toulouse, and on the remaining members of the Tribe.

In Toulouse only the core of the Tribe remained. Many of the members, including Jean-Pierre Duret, had found work 'within the system' – in state or commercial theatres. When Gatti had made the film in Derry he made it not with the Tribe, but with the town's people. The Tribe's technicians had shot the film, that was all. This was a new departure, and Gatti came to terms with the fact that the 'Revolution' as motivation had weakened. In this context, he quoted to me Mao Tse-tung's advice to his wife during the Cultural Revolution: that one should not push the pendulum too much to the left, or it would swing far back to the right. In the ranks of the Tribe, enthusiastic discussions as at Ris-Orangis, Montbéliard and elsewhere about subject and dramatic presentation had come to an end. *Le Labyrinthe* was Gatti's own play, but this did not mean that Gatti himself had 'gone back into the system'. Before presenting his play at Avignon he had made a point of pursuing a 'dialogue with the event', and did precisely this during rehearsals in Toulouse six months before the inauguration there of his Atelier de Création Populaire. He was working collectively, but no longer with the Tribe as such.

His 'dialogue with the event' was conducted during the rehearsals, to which Gatti had invited various people with whom he had been in

Armand Gatti in the Theatre

contact in Ireland when making his film, amongst them Paddy Doherty, the director of the Workshop in Derry, and Benedict McElwee, who had just been freed from the Maze and was the brother of Thomas, one of the dead hunger-strikers. There was also a priest who talked about the role of Catholicism in the Irish struggle, and Mary Nellis, who was President of the Committee for Aid for the hunger-strikers of Long Kesh. In conversation with me Gatti repeatedly referred to her as a remarkable woman. She had had two sons in Long Kesh, one an ordinary political prisoner, the other a blanket-man, the distinction being determined by the date of his arrest.

The guests sat round a table with the actors and described their personal experience as mother, brother, fiancée, priest, etc., when discussing the various possible characters and the way their parts should be played. The part of Malachi, the fictional hunger-striker, was based directly on McElwee's experience. Gatti had also invited Protestant friends from Ireland, but at the last minute they decided not to accept his invitation. During these sessions Gatti applied the method of *pré-écriture* already used in the Derry film and also in *Le Cheval qui se suicide par le feu* and *La Moitié du Ciel et nous*. So these sessions were as valid as the performances – in fact more so than the straight performances at Avignon.

Several directors of Centres Dramatiques who attended the performances at Avignon were impressed by the show and booked it for the following season. What was sent to them was not, however, Gatti's Avignon production but the production by Gatti's Toulouse assistant, Jean-Claude Bastos, of Gatti's new third text rehearsed in Gatti's absence, mainly with Bastos's Toulouse cast. It would seem that the production as seen in the Centres in Grenoble and Besançon bore little relation to Irish reality, even though the text itself had not been tampered with. But although Gatti himself sees his texts in terms of their production on stage, it must be said that for another director this particular text would present a difficult challenge. As it was, strong exception was taken to the production as given in both Centres. One of Gatti's Tribe who performed in it described it to me as 'un massacre'. Gatti immediately cancelled the performances scheduled for Toulouse, Béziers, etc., despite his keen desire to be instrumental in providing a French public with some insight into the Irish problem through this drama in which the various possible characters and their roles are discussed. Not that he wished to make political tracts of theatrical performances, but an increased understanding of the issues at stake in contemporary controversy is a valid aesthetic experience.

No specific setting is required for the Avignon version, but Gatti's dialogue during rehearsals for Avignon with the people of the Derry Workshop and Derry itself, for whom the events of Long Kesh were an integral part of their lives, led him to consider writing a new version (the third) in a 'real' setting, that of the Workshop. Its title was to be *Le Labyrinthe tel qu'il a été décrit par les habitants de l'Histoire de Derry*, 'Lieu: l'Histoire de Derry. Personnages: Les habitants de cette Histoire'. This would not be theatrical fiction but a real dialogue with history, with the 'inhabitants of history, and at the same time of a town [Derry]' taking charge themselves of the script and the production in their own words, without him (Gatti) – to his exclusion, even.

The cast of the supposed Workshop is given as consisting of four teachers, four apprentices and a visiting Irish-American woman. The play begins in four of the institution's specialist workrooms with everybody busy making mock-ups of the statue of the legendary Cuchulainn and the wire cages of Long Kesh which are to serve as sets. Ten *gigantographies*, huge cardboard cut-outs representing the ten hunger-strikers, are being put up by two of the teachers in a long corridor linking the four workrooms. Nigel, one of the teachers, explains to another teacher, Martin, that the figures are to provide the starting point for a discussion by pupils and teachers on the three strikes of the H-Blocks in Long Kesh during which ten blanket-men died, several of whom came from Derry. The discussions are dramatized and are also very dramatic. They range over issues raised by the strikes within the Maze and also for people outside the Maze.

The only character as such (all the others being 'Workshop members') is the 'First Volunteer' as a hunger-striker, but he never appears on the stage. In an opening scene Nigel describes him as a 'kaleidoscopic character (Bobby Sands in the first place, but with all the nine others always present)'. Martin declares that he is 'likely to be made up of the whole of Ireland'. Nigel asks: 'Which Ireland? There are two: the new united Ireland which cannot yet be born, and the old united Ireland which has become a myth.' The whole play is a quest for the 'First Volunteer'. Various members of the Workshop opt to play him, and each announces that he is about to take on the part. A circle of functional figures forms round him: mother, sister, fiancée, MP, chaplain, cellmate, British soldier, British Intelligence Officer (a woman pretending to be a laundress in order to report back to the authorities suspect washing of unusual size, blood-stained, etc.). The parts are taken indiscriminately by the Workshop 'cast' who likewise announce their assumed identities.

Between the Avignon version and this new one there is a clear difference of dramatic technique. At Avignon the discussion on the possibility of dramatizing an impossible subject determines the structure of the work, but the 'selmaire' technique is chosen by Gatti for this third version because it allows the strikes to be looked at from various opposing points of view. In the 'glossary' appended to the *Notes*, the 'selmaire' is defined as a creation by a character, with the other characters following the lead given by the point of view adopted in the 'selmaire'. This falling in step might seem like a Commedia dell'Arte technique, but is of course 'one of the forms of Chinese theatre still in use on the Bridge of the Sky in Peking'. It locates the dramatic conflict in a clash of views on the situation, not in a clash of characters. There are eleven 'selmaires' in all, and they symbolize the labyrinth.

The action begins with the Workshop actors' attempt to reconstruct what happened on the night of 31 December (Saint Sylvester) 1980–1 in Block 3 in Long Kesh when the hunger-strike 'to the finish' was decided on, and a warning was given to volunteers for the strike of its likely fearful outcome. The 'selmaire' ends with the agonizing question of whether this third strike, undertaken to back up the other two, would remain, like them, buried in the Maze. The Irish-American visitor argues in another 'selmaire' that if the three strikes are to be brought out into the open, it can be done only through a straight fight between the 'First Volunteer' and a British Occupying Soldier. Everyone would then understand.

The fight is presented as a 'boxing match in ten rounds', and is to take place in a ring formed by the wire cages of Long Kesh. Malachi, as the 'First Volunteer', has for 'seconds' his family and friends from the Bogside, and James Connelly's citizen army of 1916. The English soldier has as his 'seconds' the whole apparatus of military surveillance, the training of the Camberley military college and the Union Jack, which always flies on the winning side. But the match does not take place because of the refusal of one of the apprentices to countenance the 'martyrdom' of his companions: 'Freedom is in living. It is not won by dying.' His outburst, coming from a Gael and even more so from a Provisional, surprises the others.

In another 'selmaire' a teacher, Eugeen, who plays a Social Democrat and Labour MP, attempts to take the tragedy out of the strike by arguing during a visit to the Maze, to see the 'First Volunteer', that his strike is old-fashioned and that the only intervention of fate in modern life is the road accident. During his visit a violent disagreement breaks out between those *inside*, for whom the hunger-strike is the only possible policy after the failure of the two others to produce any result, and those *outside*, family and Church, who oppose it. 'Rather than die they should live for Ireland.' Later, in Eugeen's 'Selmaire détourné', the death of the Londonderry MP in a 'road accident' raises the matter of Downing Street's reaction to the election of an IRA member (Bobby Sands) in his place: 'They can change the law'.

The appalling degradation of the hunger-strikers and the physical disintegration of their bodies, which has already been vividly pictured by the Workshop cast, leads up, in the apprentice Géraldine's 'heroic "selmaire" for a round-the-world trip', to the question of whether indeed the strikes were worth it all. It is a question which haunts the 'First Volunteer' during the last five minutes of consciousness before he sinks into a final coma. He is spared the anguish of replying to the question through his imagined flight with 'his first love' into life – a commonplace, even trite existence – in which, as in reality, the 'cup of tea' forbidden to the dedicated faster looms high.

In the 'Selmaire de la Libération de l'Ulster' – also proposed by Géraldine, this time in the role of the British Intelligence Officer who announces 'the withdrawal of the British troops' – the issues are presented in very graphic form. The action reflects first the violent internal divisions in Ulster even among Catholics, secondly the political, social, religious, financial problems that would result from a withdrawal, and finally the end of the illusion that the people of Ulster can achieve liberation by their own efforts.

In an interview with Jean-Claude Lévy in July 1982[4] where he discussed both his film on Derry and his play, Gatti made a statement which is echoed in the 'selmaire' of 'L'Oiseau-Lyre répondant à l'Oiseau-Roi'. He said: 'This march towards death is organized throughout the prison block in Gaelic, a language unknown to their English gaolers. A free territory is sometimes a language.' In Irish legend the song of the Lyre Bird transforms the defeats of the King Bird into victories, as does the fiddler in the pub today.

In the play this 'selmaire' is an optimistic one because it turns defeat into victory, a victory won by the prisoners over their gaolers through their use of Gaelic, which they learned in the 'university of Long Kesh' in language sessions called out from behind the locked cell doors and written up with their excreta on the walls. With this they took their first steps towards 'decolonization'. Each word remembered is an extension of the territory which is theirs alone and which the 'Brits' cannot enter: a linguistic territory, not a topographical one. The prisoners 'marked out the first free territory of Ulster, and it was a language'. 'With Gaelic on the walls we are no longer imprisoned.' This aspect of the prisoners' fight brought Gatti back to the days of his arrest in the maquis when he erected a protective barrier of language between himself and the interrogators, replying with lines of remembered or improvised verse.

The play ends with a reference to the loud cheering which echoed from the cells each time a hunger-striker started on his last journey from the concrete tombs of the H-Block to the sickbay. It is a triumph over death. Kieran then takes up his stand alone in front of the statue of Cuchulainn and declares that in baroque Italian comedy, when the mask is taken off, there is no face underneath, only another mask. He will take over from the 'First Volunteer' and play the 'Second Volunteer'. The struggle goes on.

Armand Gatti in the Theatre

The play thus ends on an optimistic note, but the impossibility of treating the subject adequately is never forgotten; one of the cast remarks: 'We pervert and misrepresent the hunger-strikers by the very act of forcing them into a dramatic action in which they cannot have any place.'

Notes

1. 'Daur', a Gaelic word for oak-tree. 'Derry' is the English transcription of 'doire', meaning oak-grove.
2. *Jeu*. Cahiers de Théâtre, 1891, 1 (Canada, Montreal-Quebec, p. 77).
3. *Le Monde*, 17 August 1983: 'Rencontre avec Armand Gatti à Toulouse. Sous le signe de l'archéoptéryx légendaire', by Jacques Siclier.
4. *Révolution*, 30 July–5 August 1982: 'La Parole errante'.

15
Toulouse: The Archaeopteryx: the Wild Duck Continues its Flight Against the Wind

In March 1983 Gatti, the itinerant public scribe, became a resident public scribe in university premises in Toulouse, for a period of three years. He was appointed by Robert Abirached, who was responsible for theatrical matters in the Ministry of Culture, to set up an 'Atelier de création populaire pour la région, Midi-Pyrénées'. This also takes in Albi, Montauban, Foix and Pailhès. It was understood that Gatti would continue the work he had been doing for fifteen years in the various communities where he had previously been 'implanted' on the invitation of some local authority or some specific body. The Atelier was to be funded by the government. The Archaeopteryx – a fossil bird with feathers, jaws with teeth, reptilian bones and skull which provided a connecting link between sea, land and air – was chosen to symbolize the Atelier's 'adventure in the different spheres of creative activity'. These embraced theatre, poetry, video films, music, radio, silk-screen printing, exhibitions and informative publications under the title 'Pierres hérétiques'. By August 1983 the five technicians with Gatti, remnants of his erstwhile Tribe, had grown to a hundred in the region. The small egg was on its way to becoming the 'giant egg' of the symbol.

Twenty years earlier Gatti had got to know Toulouse well. He had almost become the 'resident dramatist' of the Grenier theatre because of the enthusiasm of its director, Maurice Sarrazin, for his work. At that time Toulouse had been a town full of Spanish immigrants and a centre for the CNT. By 1983, however, the Toulouse–Barcelona axis of *La Passion du Général Franco* no longer existed. The Spanish immigrants at whose request Gatti had written a number of playlets in order to put their experiences into dramatic form had returned to Spain or been integrated into French society, and he found himself approached instead by immigrants of a very different kind.

There was a Yao community, some of whom he had known in China, and it was this community which in 1984 made at the Archéoptéryx the first Yao film, *Les Enfants de Li Ta-Hou*, on the history of the Yao people.

A dialogue with the Hmong community, which was of Chinese origin and only in contact with social workers, led to Gatti's discovery of the Hmong culture and the consequent making of a film, *Ceux dont le pays est l'exil. Les Hmongs*, by the community in October 1983. It depicted a traditional ceremony dedicated to the memory of their ancestors and included the ritual sacrifice of a calf. Eyebrows were raised in Toulouse, but because of the film, broadcasts and published texts, the language of these people, handed down by oral tradition alone and in danger of dying out in their exile, was written down and so preserved. Then there was the group of young Kabyle women of whom Gatti was particularly proud. On their own initiative they were making a film, *Les Tisserandes*, which reflected the culture of the country from which they had come and the loss of this culture in exile.

To the obvious question of where Gatti stood in all this, he replied that 'without any false modesty, Gatti is an element which helps certain people to be themselves'. They it was who did the inventing, not he. He brought his influence to bear on the invention. However, these experiments, he insists, would be impossible without the presence of the poet who goes to meet them, armed with their own words. Language is not part of these people's world. Theirs is the world of work and exploitation. It is for the poet to bridge this gap, and his task is even more difficult when there is a language barrier. With Gatti everything is thrown open for discussion by all and is then carefully worked out. He is in complete disagreement with the schools which believe in spontaneity and tell their groups to 'Go to it, work it out for yourselves'.

In Toulouse the new dimension that Gatti had sought to add to his work so far, by adopting the role of catalyst and public scribe, was introduced during the first year of the Atelier's existence in what is termed a *stage de réinsertion sociale*, or social reintegration scheme. The *stage* lasted from January to June 1984 and was intentionally remedial. It was undertaken by Gatti for fifteen ex-delinquents, drug addicts, immigrants, unemployed, illiterates, who sought him out of their own accord. In setting up this *stage* Gatti had no intention of adding to the already lengthy list of existing *stages* for vocational training, blind-alley training, or general training possibly leading to some sort of job. He sought to use the six months in such a way as to help the group members to find it in themselves to break with the chain of events in which they had been caught up so far and to choose, not suffer, their destiny – to secure for themselves an identity. Without his proviso – 'minimal and immense' at the same time – all *réinsertion* would be bound to fail.

The method adopted at the beginning of the *stage* was that of question and answer. 'You need to know', Gatti said, 'who is going to give you your dignity: it is you yourselves. So then – who am I?' Question One: 'Who am I?' – 'A sheep among so many others'; 'A tightrope walker on the umbilical cord of life.' Question Two: 'To whom do I address myself?' – 'My family'; 'Society, which daily humiliates me'; 'The judges' ... With these questions Gatti sought to help each member of the group to arrive at a better understanding of himself, to rid himself of the problem which had beset him so far. He asked for answers to be written down, the better to promote a pact of confidence between the two sides, given the disquieting private history of many of them.

Then, to make a dialogue of equals possible, Gatti suggested Nestor Makhno as a subject to write about. 'Who is Makhno?' 'A historical person.' 'What is a historical person?' 'What have we to do with history?' 'What has Russian history to do with us?' There was some dissension about the suggestion, but it was finally adopted and the writing of a play with the evocative title *La Colonne Makhno: La Rencontre historique* went ahead. It was, as one of the group significantly puts it in the text, 'the story of all those who arrive in France believing they will find a free country, but find only poverty, despair and death'. As Gatti put it, it was a meeting of society's rejects from France and elsewhere. The *stage* did not keep to fixed hours. So caught up in the experiment were these 'rejects' of society that even after long hours of rehearsal with Gatti they would stay on in the Atelier of their own accord to practise their parts, eagerly accepting the guidance of anyone prepared to offer it. They performed the play under the title *L'Émission de Pierre Meynard*.

A further reason for suggesting Makhno as a possible subject for his intentionally 'therapeutic' (the word is his) dramatic experiment was that the story of the Ukrainian libertarian would fit into the Atelier's month's programme entitled 'Russie 1905–URSS 1930 ou Comment la révolution a mangé ses enfants'. Gatti did not, however, seek to evaluate a period in purely historical or military terms. The role played by its artists had to be taken into account, and for this reason the poet Velimir Khlebnikov and the painter Kazimir Malevitch became the focal point of the programme. Also included was the presentation by Gatti, for the first time since its original performance in St Petersburg in 1913, of the provocative text of the futurist Vladimir Maiakovski, *La Révolte des objets*.

If events such as these were reserved for the public of the Midi-Pyrénées, an international public in Paris was given the opportunity of judging for itself the outcome of the 'therapeutic' experiment through the video film *Nous ne sommes pas des personnages historiques* (drawn by Hélène Chatelain from the earlier *L'Émission de Pierre Meynard*) and it was shown at the Centre Georges Pompidou on 28 June 1985, in the context of the Théâtre International de Langue française organized by Gabriel Garran under the patronage of the Minister for Culture, Jack Lang. The forum presented mainly a joust between two 'public scribes', Armand Gatti from Toulouse and Michel Garneau from Quebec – a joust won, in my opinion, by Gatti. Garneau's starting point for collective composition was a 'literary game' in which the players (future writers) had to 'do battle' against words taken at random out of a hat. For Gatti, collective writing presents a completely different image. It emerges at the point where the two paths of history and creative intent come together, and though in all the experiments the final text is Gatti's and Gatti's alone (he maintains this passionately), the material and its provenance are not.

The fruits of Gatti's second *stage de réinsertion sociale*, just then completed in Toulouse, were to be seen at the Centre Pompidou on the same occasion, but this time directly on the stage and not – as it were at second hand – through the medium of film. In his introductory speech to the subsequent showing of the film, Gatti thanked the 'actors' of the second *stage* for having stayed on in Paris on their own account in order to see what their predecessors had achieved. The film, Gatti explained, gave a general idea of the sort of theatre he was attempting, at this stage, to create. It was not 'théâtre nouveau' in the generally accepted sense of the term. Comparisons should not be made with the contemporary theatre, but rather with Greek theatre as created in their allotted 'day of free expression' for society's rejects, by those who were marginal and whose starting point was the march of history, what was happening in the 'city'.

'The sources of our inspiration are very simple,' Gatti said; 'they are to be found in the world of society's rejects, and in their various attempts to survive.' His 'actors' were better informed on the drug problem than any 'specialist', and the same was true of the racial problem with which many of his 'actors' were 'condemned to live'. The grimness of the Bagatelle quarter of Toulouse, the bleak outlook for its inhabitants, their exclusion from any form of culture, of personal expression, were vividly recalled by Gatti. But, he insisted, these rejects of society *were* capable, as the *stagiaires* had proved, of arriving at a new awareness of issues at stake: 'If theatre is to exist, it can only have as its starting point the dramas, hopes, joys of the community [*la cité*], what is happening there, what is all around them. That is the source of language.' Such was the final position adopted by Gatti at the international forum in Paris.

'Who am I?' 'To whom do I address myself?' This was Gatti's approach in his second experiment, as in his first, but on this occasion there was no reference to the personal history of the 'actors' – immigrants, ex-delinquents and the like. The small television screens hung round the main screen for the Makhno film presented the 'actors' and their particular background. Not so the television screens hung round the stage for the second experiment. On these were to be seen Spanish guérilleros whose life stories did not appear in the history books but were about to be told by the *stagiaires* under the title *Le Dernier Maquis*, a 'historical term' used by the international press at the death of the last of the guérilleros, the three Sabater brothers, to carry on the anti-Franco resistance campaign of the post-Civil War years, 1944–60.

The choice of the Spanish guérilleros from among the subjects suggested by Gatti was almost a foregone conclusion seeing that most of the *stagiaires* were themselves from the Toulouse–Barcelona area. One of them, a Portuguese immigrant in Toulouse, had had personal experience of Spanish prisons, allegedly for 'irresponsible youthful pranks'. There was therefore a ready-made bond between these outcasts of society and the unsung heroes of the Resistance movement. Three of them – Francisco Sabater, José Luis Facerias and Roman Vila – were taken up by the *stagiaires*, who formed themselves into three groups for the purpose. The lesson learnt from their life stories was that the decisive weapon of revolution is 'the word' – the pamphlet – and the printing presses that carry 'the word'. Clandestine presses, or spare parts for them, were carted by the guérilleros on their backs for some ten days at a time from Perpignan to Barcelona over the Pyrenees.

Whereas in the Makhno film the distance of time and place had made some reconstitution of style necessary – in clothes, for example – and certain sequences representing the Ukraine were shot at La Paluche, no such reconstitution was needed in Toulouse; reality was at hand in the form of immigrant ex-guérilleros. They were mistrustful of Gatti's venture at first until El Mano, one of the best-known of *les passeurs*, or Resistance mountain-guides, then living in retirement in Toulouse, volunteered, although well on in his seventies, to undertake once again the 'passage' of the Pyrenees which he had conducted so frequently right into the 1960s. During the performance, a small television screen at the side of the stage continuously showed him wending his way over the mountains.

Unlike El Mano, Sabater, known as El Quico, did not survive. His last journey ended in December 1959 when he was caught on the frontier and shot, but not before he had succeeded in discarding the portable press he was taking over the Pyrenees to help 'the struggle for the dignity of our ideas and our movement', to quote the words of a fellow-resister, Esteban, who managed to retrieve the precious press. But there are presses and presses, and the Atelier's *Journal* makes the point: 'In our democracies the press is a democratic guarantee, yet more often than not it acts as the mouthpiece of the Establishment.'

How far participation in these *stages* will awaken their members to a new and lasting awareness of the possibilities offered by life remains to be seen. New horizons were certainly opened up during each of the experiments, and Gatti has a strong conviction that some at least of the *stagiaires* will continue to pursue their course, as will a certain budding poet amongst them. But time alone will tell whether others may fall by the wayside.

Another of Gatti's projects was a show to be performed entirely by handicapped people – people without an arm, a leg, etc. One had only to see what the proposal meant to them, was Gatti's proud comment. But what about spectator reaction? Given his opinion of the spectator-consumer, he (Gatti) would not be put off by any reaction, was his reply. His type of theatre was not that of other theatres. He sought to make of an author a 'meeting-place', not a place for 'the consumer'.

The experiment unfortunately never got off the ground. The ages of the handicapped who were in special schools ranged from seventeen to twenty-six and the instructors, who mistakenly saw Gatti and his helpers as rivals, argued that their charges 'were not like other people' and should not therefore be subjected to any additional fatigue. Gatti maintained that they *were* like other people and should be given the chance to act the classics, Shakespeare for example, just like other people. It would be too delicate for them to write plays that were based on their personal experiences as the other *stagiaires* had done. The question, however, was clinched for Gatti by the impossibility of securing regular transport for the handicapped to the Atelier, the only suitable place for rehearsals.

Such activities had not been foreseen by the local authorities, who were clearly under a complete misapprehension as to what to expect from the newly arrived 'national figure', the 'Parisian', the poet-dramatist and film-maker. Gatti, it was soon realized, was not another Jean Vilar: he was not going to make of the Capitole Theatre the Théâtre régional populaire. He was not going to organize 'Parisian' debates for FR3, nor was he going to conform to establishment 'culture', whether of the Right or the Left. It was not by chance that those who came of their own accord to take part in Gatti's activities were the immigrants, the disadvantaged, and not the worthy citizens of the town. But this situation was not peculiar to Toulouse. Everywhere Gatti and his Tribe had been invited to work, they had come up against establishment culture.

Gatti sets out his own definition of culture in the monthly *Journal* of the Archéoptéryx announcing the performance of *La Colonne Makhno*. He describes culture as first and foremost an act of creation, a fundamental act through which one achieves a new awareness capable of initiating a new considered line of conduct. It is, however, with the disadvantaged who are possessed of little culture, with immigrants faced with a culture that is foreign to them and which reduces them to silence, with those who have never had the right to speak out, those who have never attempted to – it is with them in the first place that a dialogue must be most urgently sought. The *Journal* itself is a large sheet of fine white paper beautifully illustrated with designs in black by Ronald Curchod, presenting poems, texts of all kinds, and information relative to the

Toulouse: The Archaeopteryx: The Wild Duck Continues its Flight Against the Wind

month's programme, such as the outline of the history of the Hmong people. Specific events like *La Colonne Makhno* or the Yao film are also announced on colourful posters made in the Archéoptéryx's silk-screen printing workshop.

Despite his multiple activities in Toulouse, Gatti never forgot his obligations to Albi, Foix and the rest of the region, and already for the first of the July Festivals – that of 1983, which had chosen the situation in Guatemala as its main theme – he had provided on request, within a fortnight, the texts of two plays supposedly written by two Guatemalans whose names he adopted for the occasion without, however, attempting any deception. His first poetic script had not appealed to the authorities of Albi and Foix, who wanted more documented texts. Gatti had kept in touch with Guatemala and was in a position to supply such texts, and he did so without sacrificing the poetic element he considered so important.[1]

Gatti's final objective at the Toulouse Atelier, which he stated at the outset, was to be a filmed opera, *La Licorne*, on the fate of 117 German writers, painters, historians, many of them Expressionists and consequently classed as 'cultural Bolsheviks' under the Hitler regime. They were rounded up and put in Plötzensee prison in Berlin, and all were executed between January and April 1943 on a trumped-up police charge of belonging to an imagined 'Black Orchestra' or 'information network'. This work, Gatti has said several times, was to be his 'testament': 'It had everything in it that I would want theatre to be, that is to say, the song which rises out of the struggle and which confers on man a dimension on the scale of the universe.'[2] It is also his 'testament' in the sense that it is a symbolic representation of his own life story. 'I am not writing an opera,' he declared, 'I have carried this opera with me for a long time, since I was in prison with life defying death.' Here again Gatti restates his inability, like that of so many other camp survivors, ever to get out from under the shadow of the camps.

Gatti's permanent camp is Hamburg, the Baltic Sea. 'From the time of the diving-bells', he told Marc Kravetz in *Multilogues* (p. 75),

> my entry into the concave world ['as a pioneer of this world', he was to discover] has become for me a sort of garment, and sometimes I have the feeling – because the wind from the Baltic has never stopped blowing – that I have never divested myself of it. Sometimes this garment sets out alone. It does a world tour in a single night, and it is always a concentration-camp night.

The first play Gatti wrote after his return from the camp, *L'Enfant rat*, is part of that 'concentration-camp night' with its persistent, destructive memory of the camp's salt-mine which gave birth to a 'rat-child' in the mine's tip-truck. Between this play and the scenario *La Licorne*, dedicated to Ernst Bloch, who 'gave the century Hope as a principle', is a

Armand Gatti in the Theatre

line of works directly reflecting Gatti's experience of the maquis and the camps: *La Naissance* and *Les Hauts Plateaux* re-create the 'hole' of the maquis and its significance; in *Un Homme seul* the 'hole' is a mountain cave; *La Première Lettre* re-creates the cells of the condemned Resistance fighters and *Le Labyrinthe* those of the dying hunger-strikers in Northern Ireland. But the outlook in these plays is not that of *L'Enfant rat* or *La Deuxième Existence du Camp de Tatenberg*. Rather it is that of his film *L'Enclos*. Gatti defines that outlook with the four words 'with life defying death'.

The filmed opera was to be made in the Toulouse area by local people supported by some professionals. To prepare the ground – that is to say, the public as well as the local participants in the film – Gatti planned a series of *Rencontres* and *Créations* drawing on many of his previous sources. Makhno was one of them. But from the story of Makhno to that of the executed 117 in Plötzensee prison there is a change of emphasis. *Makhno* is a tragedy of the lack of togetherness or solidarity which allows Makhno, one of society's rejects, to die alone. *La Licorne* – to be so named after the book which the Munich Communist Eric Mühsam, hanged at Oranienburg in 1934, had planned to write in the prison camp but could not because his torturers broke both his wrists – is, in its final stages, a poem to togetherness and solidarity in the most desperate of circumstances.

Gatti's social consciousness is profoundly disturbed by the absurd individualistic doctrines put about in our time by what he sees as the so-called neo-liberals. He maintains that these doctrines strike at the very roots of human society, and he is struggling in his own way to prevent future social disintegration. In Plötzensee prison, where suspicion that each had been denounced by the other had bred mistrust and hatred, Erika, the wife of the Expressionist painter Cay von Brockdorf (Cay Terwiel in Gatti's scenario) – himself a militant of the extreme Left who escaped execution as a hero of the Russian front, also as a protégé of General von Paulus – reawakened the spirit of fraternity and solidarity by getting the last survivors to show their defiance of death, to which they knew they were condemned, by means of an 'opera of silence'. They composed the opera using deaf-and-dumb sign-language from window to window of the parallel lines of the triangular-shaped high-security cells. After a few unsuccessful attempts to give free voice to their 'Hymn to Life' based on the theme of the marriage of two of their number, representative of two social classes, the last airs were sung by Erika and by Lieselotte Kuntz as they stood facing the guillotine on 27 April 1943. 'Think, tomorrow I may well be a bar of soap', Erika joked to Eckhart, the fainting almoner, just as she had retorted to the judge at her trial, when he asked her what she was laughing about, that it was his face and that even on the scaffold she would double up with laughter were she to see it again. Some years later Gatti was able to interview the two remaining actors of the drama, von Brockdorf and the prison's almoner.

Gatti had hoped to film his opera in four castles in the Cathar country, a fitting setting – with its sombre history of massacres of religious dissidents – for the twentieth-century massacre of political dissidents. The 'orchestra' for this 'opera' was to consist of instruments made from local plants and from the historic stones that had witnessed the massacres and live 'cremations' of former times. These instruments were to reproduce the sound of whining winds, rushing waters, the crackle of fires and the crashes of bombardments by the Allies. Some of the 'instruments' have been made, and a number of bells have been cast in the Carcassonne area and christened by Gatti with the words 'My name is Erika', 'My name is Lieselotte', and other names of women victims in Plötzensee prison. These bells were to create a background of sonority worthy of the Sicilian Vespers. Despite the work already done, the film is being held in abeyance as funds are not as yet forthcoming from the Commission responsible for promoting films of this kind.

Gatti considers the play *Opéra avec Titre long*, which he took from the scenario, to be his major work: its subject reflects the crucial experience of his life, the concentration camp, and here technically Gatti breaks what is for him new ground by transforming contemporary history into song. He agrees that the work is not an opera in the accepted sense, and says: 'It is an attempted reconstruction of an opera as it succeeded in existing in the midst of the war in the triangular prison in Berlin where the executions took place.'[3] As performed in Montreal in March 1986 the *Opéra* lasted five-and-a-half hours – a daunting prospect, and some of the audience showed it, particularly those not specially interested in historical or political theatre, or those for whom the historical event, as with Gatti's play on Sacco and Vanzetti, had not come within the scope of their own experience. But the second half of the production, Act V, presenting the sung opera invented by the still-surviving members of the 'orchestra' round the 'marriage' of the two youngest of the group, got an enthusiastic reception.

Le Poème cinématographique et ses pronoms personnels, of which Gatti gave a reading at the Centre Pompidou on 24 June 1985, relates even more directly to Gatti's political outlook, starting as it did as an interview, then several interviews, with Pascal Gallet of the Ministry for Foreign Affairs. It ranges through the whole of Gatti's life and takes up the basic themes of his works. The word 'bataille' rings continuously through the text because it has always been the same struggle in which Gatti is engaged within the framework of what he has done; Gatti identified from the outset the 'battle', or *prise de conscience*, with the Spanish Civil War. Was that a battle lost or won? One must look to the Resistance movements for the reply. The answer is the concentration camps – again a battle lost or won? The conclusion: the century had died on the horrific stairway of Mauthausen. Ironically, this century, which began for Gatti with the Spanish Civil War, ends for him with the image of General Franco dead but refusing to lie down, a 'corpse' kept artificially alive by medical care. But what does political language become in a dead century? Does it die? Can it renew itself? Will it follow in the traces of Ulrike Meinhof? These are his questions as he looks towards the year 2000.

The visit of Peter Watkins, who was in France in 1984 working on a follow-up to his 1965 film on the A-bomb, *The War-Game*, brought Gatti back abruptly to the last of the three essential points of reference of his lifetime, the RESISTANCE, the DEPORTATION, and the BOMB, with the 'inevitability' of its use again. Watkins's purpose in his new film was to alert the people of the whole world to the horrific danger of global destruction under which we are at present living, and, significantly, Gatti sought to help by arranging public discussions with Watkins at the Atelier. After the discussions a reading of Gatti's 1968 play on the bomb, *La Cigogne*, was given by members of the Centre on Radio Canal Sud.

With reference to the reading, the Atelier's *Journal* (April 1984) wrote of the engineer Kawaguchi, one of the main characters in the play and also a real person:

> Kawaguchi, the only person to have been in two atomic bomb explosions (those of Hiroshima and Nagasaki) and survived. But at what price! To be eaten up by an atomic cancer. Gatti met him in Nagasaki wandering listlessly about, a month before he died. He wrote this play on the bomb and dedicated it to the memory of Kawaguchi.

Nagasaki, like immigrants' shanty towns or Central American dictatorships as in Guatemala, appear to Gatti to be as far removed from the norms of civilization as were the concentration camps themselves. Throughout, he stands as a witness of his times, an uncomfortable witness whose testimony is set out in open-ended plays directed towards a *prise de conscience* by the spectator in the light of issues raised by their action.

Gatti does not seek to impose his views, which are those of a libertarian. He denies adherence to any political party and has even described himself as an anarchist of the Left in reply to accusations that he was an anarchist of the Right. The critic Guy Demur sees Gatti as the last of the anarchists wholly committed to the cause of *le monde humilié*, the deprived and rejected, a cause he has served throughout without any demagoguery, and using complex artistic forms not always accessible to the general public. Demur's description of the fine exhibition *Cinquante Ans de Théâtre vus par les trois chats d'Armand Gatti*, put on at Montreuil in January 1987 and subsequently at the Avignon Theatre Festival in July, which vividly illustrated the life and work of this provocative man and artist, ends with the pertinent remark: 'His real Christian name is not Armand but Dante. Has he sought to write "The Divine Comedy" of our times?' (*Observateur*, 16 January 1987).

Gatti never inspires indifference. There are those who admire and support him and even attempt to keep up with *la parole errante*, whatever its destination. There are others who have attacked him violently, mainly on political grounds although some of these attacks have been made under the guise of artistic criticism. Gatti's technique – or rather techniques, so great is the variety of the means he employs – result from his oft-repeated belief that a revolutionary subject needs a revolutionary form to present it. It is a belief he shares with Meyerhold, whom he quotes as saying a revolutionary theme treated in a petty-bourgeois frame struggles like a rat in a trap and drops dead, asphyxiated.

Wherever there is a creative spark and Gatti passes by, the spark becomes a glow. The dynamism of the man is limitless, the creative activities he inspires manifold. What the 'Atelier de création populaire pour la région Midi-Pyrénées' must become after Gatti had 'passed by' (he is essentially a nomad), was not hard to imagine. Gatti modestly gave his answer, saying: 'The works will remain, the books, the broadcasts, the journals, the films – the first Yao film on the history of the Yao people made by the Yaos.'

So through flood, fire and high water, Gatti maintains his old traditions: those of his father, the Italian anarchist, even though in many respects, on the political plane, these attitudes no longer apply. However, they enable him to cherish a libertarian conception of man's destiny in a highly developed technological society. Gatti is not only a poet; he is also a moralist in the oldest French tradition, and all his work can be seen in this perspective.

Notes

1. *Crucifixion métisse, Retour à la douleur de Tous ou La Route de Zacapa*
2. *Gatti: Journal illustré d'une écriture*, p. 69.
3. Ibid., p. 138.

Writing political plays is for me a way of remaining faithful to the child I was at seven to ten years of age. My world is the world of road-sweepers, deportations and escapes. Shakespeare's universe, with its kings and princes, rings hollow for me. My kings lived in shanty towns. They are of more consequence for me than the kings in great literary works.

Gatti

Approches, No. 8, September–October 1968

The Nomad Moves On

1985 VIENNA October: At the Dramatische Zentrum. Gatti was to produce *La Deuxième Existence du Camp de Tatenberg* but official French opposition, alleging that the production was likely to affect adversely relations between France and Austria, caused the project to be abandoned. There would instead be a collective production on a subject proposed by the theatre group: the life of Ulrike Meinhof's two daughters, who were living in Hamburg. Rehearsals were interrupted by a police raid. Gatti neatly turned the tables on the police sent to 'make a report'. He invited them to play the part of the actors while the actors played the part of the police and to write their report on the experiment, so saving the situation.

1986 MONTREAL January–March: *Opéra avec Titre long*, production directed by Gatti at the Monument National at the invitation of the École Nationale de Théâtre du Canada. The work was performed by senior students of the Drama Section to music by the Quebec composer Joël Bienvenue, who also conducted the small orchestra of conventional instruments. This was Gatti's first incursion into opera.
Rosa Collective: A dramatic reading by Gatti of his play for the Theatre Section of the University of Quebec at Montreal on 20 March.
PARIS 13 September: *La Fête de l'Humanité*, Lecture by Gatti on the Spanish Civil War.
TOULOUSE September–December: *Les Arches de Noé*, the third of Gatti's *stages de réinsertion* undertaken at the Centre Cultural in the Mirail area. The subject: a train carrying deportees from Auschwitz which went from country to country without being allowed to stop, and finally disappeared.

1987 MONTREUIL January: 'Cinquante Ans de Théâtre vus par les trois chats d'Armand Gatti'. Exhibition on the life and work of Gatti, ending on 31 January with a performance of *Les Arches* *de Noé* at the Studio Berthelet by the *stagiaires* from Toulouse.

VIENNA January–March: at the Dramatische Zentrum. *Le Train*, a collective work on the theme of *Les Arches de Noé*, with a performance.

USA 1–10 April: Lectures by Gatti with a showing of *Nous étions tous des noms d'arbres*, at La Maison Française, Columbia University; The University of Rochester, New York; The Graduate Centre (CUNY).

AVIGNON July: The Exhibition 'Cinquante Ans de Théâtre vus par les trois chats d'Armand Gatti', with Gatti's presence.

MONTREAL 15 September–21 November: *Le Passage des oiseaux dans le ciel*, a new version of *Le Poème cinématographique et ses pronoms personnels*, produced by Gatti at the University of Quebec in Montreal and written by him in Montreal to adapt it to the circumstances of a pedagogical experiment. The twelve Pronoms/ Caractères of the original version became twenty-two in order to accommodate the twenty-two students of theatre studies who had signed up for the project. Montreal becomes the site of the action, and account is taken of the problems facing the French language in the province of Quebec. At the production each 'Pronom' was characterized by a karate movement providing a sort of physical grammar: each performed the movement before speaking his lines. This gave each 'Pronom' an identity without individualizing him as scriptwriter, camera man, sound engineer, etc.

1988 USA The University of Rochester, 15–23 January: *Train 713. A short title for a shortened work*, The Todd Theater, 19–23 April. *Train 713* is a new version of *Les 7 possibilités du Train 713 en partance d'Auschwitz* prepared for performance at the May 1988 Vienna Theatre Festival but then cancelled: 'From the American context [including exchanges with student/actors] came a new text rewritten from and for the participants in the project' (Teresa L. Jillson, producer). First production of a Gatti play in the USA.

PARIS 22–23 April: *Salut Armand Gatti*, International Colloquium organized by the University of Paris VIII, Vincennes à Saint-Denis, in the presence of Gatti and set in the context of the year's study at its Atelier Théâtre de IIe Cycle, concluding on 23 June with a '*Manifestation Culturelle* à Paris VIII' lasting over a period of seven hours and offering performances of scenes from Gatti's plays, together with original compositions by staff and/or students with Gatti's writings as the starting point of their creations. The programme concluded with the performance of an opera with *Le Quetzal* as the libretto and music by Jean-Paul Olive. A *Fond-mémoire GATTI* is to be inaugurated in the University Library of

The Noman Moves On

Paris VIII in 1989, providing access to Gatti's theatrical, poetic and cinematographic work.

Projects for 1988–9

1988 *L'homme qui volait avec des plumes de coque*, poem by Gatti about his father and his experiences in Chicago. Video film to be made in Chicago by Stéphane Gatti.
July: *stage de réinsertion* at Toulouse, a collective work on the theme of the French Revolution.
VENICE 30 September–3 October: an Oratorio (poems by Gatti, music by the Département Théâtre de l'Université de Paris VIII) in the presence of Gatti.
MARSEILLE October: a projection of all Gatti films.

1989 **FLEURY-MÉROGIS** (Essonne) January–15 March: on the initiative of the Ministère de la Justice and co-financed by the EEC, a project of work by Gatti in the prison, for a play and video film on the theme of the French Revolution, with insistence on the creative role of language and on the problem of "les Droits de l'Homme".
ITALY April–June: composition of a dramatic text on *The Book of Job* in collaboration with Michelle Kokosowski.
PARIS 15–30 October: performances of *Le Métro Robespierre répète la Révolution (Française)*, a production to be undertaken by Gatti at the request of the Centre d'Action Culturelle de Montreuil, which wishes to participate in a 'Concours d'idées' entitled *Inventez 89* proposed by la Grande Halle de la Villette to celebrate the bicentenary of the French Revolution. On the station 'Robespierre' of the Paris métro line 9 – the first to link two strongly working-class suburbs of the Capital, Montreuil and Billancourt – performances are to be given each evening by Gatti and the *stagiaires* from Toulouse to an invited audience of 70, on the theme of the real nature of the *Révolution (Française)*. 'Par quels chemins ... les exclus de la société, chacun à leur façon, ... vont-ils se retrouver à la station de métropolitain "Robespierre" pour en réinventer les droits de l'homme?' On this station, the trial of *Babeuf's Conspiracy of the Equals* will once again be held, but with the 'exclus de la société' as the 'éléments à conviction'. Armand Gatti's scenario (La Parole Errante).

Further Projects

Proposal by Pierre Vial, Professeur au Conservatoire de l'art dramatique, to direct an Atelier at the Conservatoire for a year.

Armand Gatti in the Theatre

Proposition by the Municipality of Casale in Lombardy to stage a play for the reopening of its nineteenth-century theatre after its restoration. Invitation from the region of Umbria to undertake a collective creation at Perugia to celebrate the renovation of its theatre. Avignon – Theatre Festival Proposal for 1990 or 1991 of the performance by professional actors with Gatti as director, of a new play of his on the Italian anarchist, Cafiero, a friend of Bakunin, also the first translator of Marx into Italian.

Selective Bibliography

Gatti — Theatre

1958 *Le Poisson noir* (Seuil [Théâtre I]).
1959 *Le Crapaud buffle* (Paris: L'Arche) (TNP repertoire).
1960 *Le Quetzal, Europe*, No. 372 (June 1960).
1960 *L'Enfant rat, Le Voyage du Grand Tchou* (Seuil [Théâtre II]).
  L'Enfant rat, re-edited 1968 (IRMMAD).
1962 *La Vie imaginaire de l'éboueur Auguste Geai; La Deuxième Existence du Camp de Tatenberg; Chroniques d'une planète provisoire* (Seuil [Théâtre III]).
1962 *La Vie imaginaire de l'éboueur Auguste Geai*, Avant-Scène, No. 272 (15 September 1962).
1963 *Notre Tranchée de chaque jour* (typescript).
1964 *Chant public devant deux chaises électriques* (Seuil [Théâtre IV]); 1966 (TNP repertoire).
1967 *V. comme Vietnam* (Seuil).
1968 *Les Treize Soleils de la rue Saint-Blaise* (Seuil).
1968 *La Naissance* (Seuil); 1969, new version in French of *Die Geburt* written for Kassel, IRMMAD).
1969 *La Passion du Général Franco* (Seuil).
1969 *Un Homme seul* (Seuil).
1970 *Pourquoi les animaux domestiques? ou La Journée d'une infirmière (Partisans, No. 56, November–December 1970).
1970 *Petit Manuel de guérilla urbaine: Les Hauts Plateaux, ou Cinq leçons à la recherche du Vietnam* (IRMMAD); *La Machine excavatrice pour entrer dans le plan de défrichement de la colonne d'invasion Che Guevara* (IRMMAD); *Ne pas perdre du temps sur un titre — Que mettez-vous à la place? — Une rose blanche* (IRMMAD).
1971 *La Cigogne* (Seuil).
1971 *Rosaspartakus prend le pouvoir, Travail Théâtral*, No. 111 (June 1971).
1973 *Rosa Collective* (Seuil).
1973 *La Colonne Durruti, Cahiers-Théâtre de Louvain*, Nos 14–17, Belgium (collective creation with twenty students of the Institut des Arts de Diffusion in Brussels).
1974 *Vier Schizophrenien auf der Suche nach einem Land, dessen Existenz umstritten ist. (Quatre schizophrénies à la recherche d'un pays dont l'existence est contestée).* (Berlin, Forum Theater).

Armand Gatti in the Theatre

1974 *Das Hälfte des Himmels und wir* (*La Moitié du Ciel et nous*) (Berlin, Forum Theater).

1975 *La Passion du Général Franco par les émigrés eux-mêmes*; *La Tribu des Carcana en guerre contre quoi?* (Seuil).

1976 *La Passion du Général Franco par les émigrés eux-mêmes* (Avant-Scène, 1 May).

1977 *Armand Gatti dans le Brabant Wallon: L'Arche d'Adelin*, Cahiers-Théâtre de Louvain, Nos 26–29 (nine months of creative work with students of IAD).
Le Cheval qui se suicide par le feu (IRMMAD).
Le Joint (IRMMAD).

1982 *Le Labyrinthe* (typescript).
Le Labyrinthe tel qu'il a été écrit par les habitants de l'Histoire de Derry, Notes de travail en Ulster, Toulouse, Archéoptéryx (Terres Hérétiques).

1983 *Crucifixion métisse*, by Genitive Rancun (i.e. Gatti) for Foix and Montauban, Archéoptéryx (typescript).
Retour à la douleur de Tous ou La Route de Zacapa (montage à partir des textes de poètes, dont Otto Rene Costello), by Blas Tojonabales (i.e. Gatti) for Albi and Montauban, Archéoptéryx (typescript).

1983 *La Colonne Makhno: La Rencontre historique*, Archéoptéryx (typescript); (1984 as video film, *Nous ne sommes pas des personnages historiques*).

1984 *La Licorne* (provisional title), Archéoptéryx (manuscript of film scenario; video film of Gatti reading the scenario).

1986 *Opéra avec Titre long* (play based on *La Licorne*) (duplicated text, La Parole Errante; 1987 L'Ether Vague, Toulouse).

1986 *Le poème cinématographique et ses pronoms personnels* (duplicated text, La Parole Errante).

1987 *Le Passage des oiseaux dans le ciel* (new version of *Le poème cinématographique* written in Montreal for the Département de théâtre, Université du Quebec à Montréal, with twenty-two roles instead of the original twelve) (manuscript, Montreal); revised version for thirteen actors (duplicated text, La Parole Errante).

1987 *Les 7 possibilités du train 713 en partance d'Auschwitz* (duplicated text, La Parole Errante).

1988 *Les 7 possibilités du Train 713 en partance d'Auschwitz* (Comp'Act, l'Ain), text prepared for performance at the University of Rochester, USA, translated there into English as *Train 713* for the performance.

IRMMAD, Institut de Recherche des Mass Média et des Arts de Diffusion, 20 bis, rue Hippolyte Maindron, Paris, 75014 (duplicated texts).

LA PAROLE ERRANTE, Esplanade Benoît Franchon, 93100 Montreuil, will supply all works by Gatti.

Gatti – Other Published Works

1954 *La Vie de Churchill*, A. Gatti, P. Joffroy, K. Yacine (Seuil).
1954 *Envoyé spécial dans la cage aux fauves* (Seuil).
1956 *Chine* (Seuil, 'Petite Planète').
1958 *Sibérie – Zéro + l'Infini* (Seuil).
1974 *Les Analogues du réel, Cahiers du Dragon*, No. 5 (October).
1986 *Creare per Crea*, text by A. Gatti, illustrations by Piero Rambaudi (Italy: Crea, December).
1988 *Les Analogues du réel* and *Le (?), Un tableau de Bernard Saby* (Toulouse: L'Ether Vague).
1989 *Écrits sur le théâtre*: texts by A. Gatti with interviews, Gallimard, Collection 'Théâtre', edited by André Veinstein.

Gatti – Films

1958 *Morambong*, directed by J. C. Bonnardot; scenario and dialogues by A. Gatti (shot in North Korea).
1960 *L'Enclos*, directed by A. Gatti; scenario and dialogues by A. Gatti and P. Joffroy (1 hr 50 mins) (Shot in Yugoslavia). (Avant-Scène du Cinéma No. 5, 1961); 1962 by Jean Michaud (Fayard).
1962 *El otro Cristobal*, scenario, dialogues and direction by A. Gatti (2 hrs 30 mins) (shot in Cuba).
1970 *Übergang über den Ebro*, scenario, dialogues and direction by A. Gatti for Stuttgart Television (1 hr 20 mins).
1975–7 *Le Lion, sa cage et ses ailes*, a series of six video films, shot in collaboration with nine immigrant communities in Montbéliard under the direction of A. Gatti (6 × 55 mins) (co-produced by l'INA).
1978–84 *La Première Lettre*, a series of seven films for television, shot in collaboration with the inhabitants of L'Isle d'Abeau, under the direction of A. Gatti (co-produced by l'INA).
1981 *Nous étions tous des noms d'arbres*, scenario, dialogues and direction by A. Gatti (90 mins) (co-produced by Tricontinental/Dérives, RTBF) (shot in Northern Ireland).
1987 *Il tuo nome era Letizia, Ton Nom était Joie*, poem and scenario by A. Gatti; video film shot by Stéphane Gatti (35 mins). Italian text spoken by Gatti; French text spoken by André Wilms for the Exhibition Creare per Crea at Turin, May–June 1987 (La Parole Errante).

Scenarios (Manuscripts and Typescripts) of Films not Made

1960 *Le Château de Kafka*.
1963 *Joseph Cotinet ou le Combat contre l'Ange*.
1965 *Le Parcours du combattant* (la guerre d'Algérie).
1965 *Clara* ('ma déstalinisation').

Armand Gatti in the Theatre

1966 *Le Temps des cerises* (la Résistance).
1966 *Les Frères Kreistos* (la guerre du Vietnam).
1968 *Les jours de la Commune* (la Commune de Paris).
1970 *L'Affiche rouge* (la Résistance).
1974 *Les Katangais*.
1984 *La Licorne*.

Critical Works on Gatti

1970 Gozlan, G. and Pays, J.-L., *Gatti aujourd'hui* (Seuil).
1973 *Cahiers-Théâtre de Louvain*, Nos 14–17 (*La Colonne Durruti*).
1975 Peter-Jurgen Klein, *Theater für den Zuschauer – Theater mit dem Zuschauer. Die Dramen Armand Gattis als Mittel zur Initiierung humanen Verhaltens* (Germany, Wiesbaden: Studienreihe Humanitas Athenaion [with bibliography]).
1977 *Cahiers-Théâtre de Louvain*, Nos 26–29 (*Armand Gatti dans le Brabant wallon*).
1978 *Armand Gatti et le théâtre ouvert*, Organon 78, recherches dramaturgiques et cinématographiques (University of Lyon 11).
1979 Séonnet, M., *Le Canard sauvage. Expériences d'écriture collective de la Tribu, A. Gatti à Saint-Nazaire*: October 1976–February 1977 (IRMMAD).
1981 *Armand Gatti – Une rétrospective*, Ministère des Relations Extérieures, Cellule d'Animation Audio-Visuelle (with bibliography, some dates inexact, illustrations).
1986 Kravetz, Marc, *L'Aventure de la Parole Errante: Multilogues avec Armand Gatti* (Toulouse: L'Ether Vague [curriculum vitae and bibliography]).
1987 *Gatti, le journal illustré d'une écriture*. Catalogue for the Exhibition 'Cinquante Ans de Théâtre vus par les trois chats d'Armand Gatti', with curriculum vitae and bibliography (by Stéphane Gatti and Michel Séonnet).
1989 *Théâtre sur parole*, papers read at the Colloque international 'Salut Armand Gatti' at the Université de Paris VIII, 22–23 April, edited by Philippe Tancelin and Michelle Kokosowski: Bibliothèque de l'Université de Paris VIII.

General studies

1984 Bradby, David, *Modern French Drama 1940–80* (Cambridge University Press).
1984 Champagne, Lenora, *French Theatre Experiment since 1968* (Ann Arbor, Michigan: UMI Research Press).

Theses on Gatti

1966–7 Dargent, Elizabeth, *L'Expression scénique du temps et de l'espace dans les mises en scène de Gatti*. Paris University, Censier, 'Gaston Baty Collection' (D 19).
1971 Duryée, A., *Armand Gatti: un théâtre nouveau pour un public nouveau*. Columbia University.
1972–4 Blanc, Dominique, *Rosa Collective et l'analyse dramaturgique*. Paris University, Censier, 'Gaston Baty Collection' (D 287).

Selective Bibliography

1973 Youens, A., *Romance and Anarchy: The Epic Vision of Armand Gatti*. Carnegie-Mellon University.
1973 Ward, P., *The Interaction between Intent, Content and Form in Contemporary Political Drama: Peter Weiss, Rolf Hochhuth, Armand Gatti*. Indiana University.
1976 Webb, Richard Charles, *Experimental Theatre in France, 1945–75*. (Chapter, 'An exploded theatre at the Service of the People') Hull University.
1977 Fléché, Marie France, *Figure mythique et héros révolutionnaire, Rosa Luxemburg*, Paris University, Censier, 'Gaston Baty Collection' (D 347).
1982 Pytlinski, Bonnie Lauri, *Armand Gatti and Political Trends in French Theatre under de Gaulle (1958–79)*. University of Florida.
1984 Hutchinson, J. Wesley, *Towards Creativity in the Theatre of Armand Gatti* (extensive bibliography of articles, interviews, and lists of foreign productions). Trinity College, Dublin 2.

Published Translations of Gatti's Plays

1961 *Der Schwarze Fisch* (Frankfurt am Main: Fischer Verlag).
1962 *Die zweite Existenz des Lagers Tatenberg* (S. Fischer Verlag, Deutsch von Eugen Helmle).
1963 *Das imaginäre Leban des Straszenkehrer Auguste G.* (Theatre Heute No. 11).
1964 *Die zweite Existenz des Lagers Tatenburg* (Fischer Verlag).
1965 *Auguste G.* (Italy: Parma).
1966 *Das imaginäre Leben des Straszenkehrer Auguste G., Die Schlacht der Sieben Tage und der Sieben Nächte*, in 'Zwei Bühnenstücke' (Fischer Verlag).
1967 *Öffentlicher Gesang vor 2 elektrischen Stühlen* (Fischer Verlag).
1969 *Das Hochland* (Frankfurt am Main: Verlag der Autoren).
1969 *General Francos Leidenswege, V. wie Vietnam*, 'Zwei Stücke' (Fischer Verlag).
1970 *Maschine, mit der die Arbeit zur Erschliessung neuen Landes durch die Brigade Che Guevara begonnen wird* (Frankfurt am Main: Verlag der Autoren).
1971 *Kleines Handbuch der Stadtguerilla. Vier Stücke* (Munich: Deutscher Taschenbuch Verlag: *Das Hochland*; *Weisse Rose*; *Maschine, mit der die Arbeit zur Erschliessung neuen Landes durch die Brigade Cher Guevara begonnen wird*; *Warum Haustiere?*).
1982 *Il Labirinto* (Collection du Teatro Dell'Archivolto de Gènes).

Index

Abbaye de Tamié, L' 16, 248, **252–254**
Abirached, Robert 275
Aboyeuse et l'automate, L' 62
Absurdists, The (with Eugène Ionesco and Samuel Beckett) 12, 26, 61, 63, 113, 114
Adamov, Arthur 12, 115, 127
Affiche rouge, L' 245, **247–248**
Allio, René 110, 112
Analogues du réel, Les and *Un tableau de Bernard Saby* 8, 283
Arche d'Adelin, L' 155, 169, 201, **208–210**, 211
Arches de Noé, Les 287–288
Archéoptéryx, 16, 222, 242, 266, **275–285**
Arturo Ui 193
Atlan, Liliane 83
Attoun, Lucien 220, 221, 244
Avignon 14, 15, 138, 155, 191, 220, 221, 222, **224–225**, **241–244**, 266, 268, **269–271**, 284, 288, 289, 290

Baader-Meinhof group, The 12, 215, 247
Barba, Eugenio (The Odin Theatre) 14
Barrault, Jean-Louis 26
Bas-relief pour un décapité 68
Bastos, Jean-Claude 270
Benedetto, André 21, 138, 146, **155–156**
Bienvenue, Joël, 287
Bouise, Jean 94, 95, 99, 110, 111
Boulevard Durand 115
Boulez, Pierre 8
Bourgeade, Pierre 21

Brecht, Bertold 11, 13, 27, 28, 29, 54, 79, 115, 155, 164, 193
Brig, The 14
Brook, Peter and François Darbon 83, 138
Brown, Kenneth, 14
Bukovi, William 128

Cage, John 8
Canard sauvage, Le **237–241**
Castle, The 89
Castro, Fidel 31, 38, 51, 93, 94, 99, 100, 101, 103, 104, 106, 194
Chaikin, Joseph (The Open Theatre) 14
Chantecler 65
Chant funèbre pour un soldat américain 138
Chant public devant deux chaises électriques 28, 59, 85, 104, 107, **116–129**, 132, 173, 210, 283
Charbonnier, C-L, and G Felhandler 138
Chatelain, Hélène 230, 262, 277
Chat sauvage, Le 189, **199–200**
Chaussat, Pierre 122
Che Guevara 18, 38, 193, 194, 195, 218, 233
Cheval qui se suicide par le feu, Le 119, 227, **241–245**, 270
Chiang Kai-shek 51, 55, 56, 58
Chine 42, 44, 54
Chine entre à l'ONU, La 138
Chroniques d'une planète provisoire 43, 67, 69, **78–89**, 118, 137, 142, 147, 157, 196

Cigogne, La 107, **129–135**, 189, 202, 226, 256, 284
Cinquante Ans de Théâtre vus par les trois chats d'Armand Gatti 284
Claudel, Paul 26
Cocteau, Jean 11
Cohn-Bendit 238
Colonne Durruti, La 155, 167, 171, 201, **202–208**, 211, 220, 221, 223, 224, 227
Colonne Makhno: La Rencontre historique, La 17, 242, 277, 280, 281, 282
Connection, The 14
Connolly, James 265, 272
Copeau, Jacques 27, 59
Corneille, Pierre 147
Cousin, Gabriel 62, 115, 135
Crapeau buffle Le 11, 18, 20, **21–29**, 40, 43, 44, 62, 69, 79, 93, 98, 111, 154, 166, 210
Cuba 12, 29, 31, 51, **93–106**, 116, 120, 122, 157, 158, 160, 161, 170, **194–196**, 212, 214, 218

Dasté, Jean 59, 61, 83
Davis, Angela 185, 186
Debauche, Pierre 134, 202
Dernier Maquis, Le 278
Deuxième Existence du camp de Tatenberg, La 55, 65, 67, 68, **73–78**, 94, 130, 134, 160, 226, 282, 287
Diable et le Bon Dieu, Le 164
Doherty, Paddy (and the Workshop) 257, 258, 259, 260, 262, 263, 264, 270
Don Quixote 5, **198–199**
Dossier Oppenheimer, Le 135
Drame du Fukuru-Maru, Le 135
Dürrenmatt Friedrich 164
Durupt, Gilles (Saint-Nazaire) 237
Durutti, Buenaventura 99, 158, 160, 161, 167, **202–207**, 222, 243
Dutschke, Rudi 174, 196, 197, 198, 214

El otro Cristobal 29, 31, 59, **93–98**, 103, 116, 158
Eluard, Paul 127

Emballage **155–156**
Émission de Pierre Meynard, L' 242, 277
Enclos, L' 12, 67, 68, **89–91**, 94, 157, 282
Enfant rat, L' 38, 55, 62, 67, 68, **69–73**, 85, 119, 128, 281, 282
Envie de tuer, L' 113
Envoyé spécial dans la cage aux fauves 9, 65
Et le vent reprend ses tours 240

Fast, Howard 121
Feinberg, Victor 239
Felipe 18, 19, 31
Firk, Michèle 16, 38, 39, 40, 98, 211, 212, **213–214**, 216
Fleury-Mérogis (Essonne), The prison 289
Fontanat, Charles (Ris-Orangis, CES) 232
Forest, Eva 166
France pleure son Gérard Philipe, La 11

Galitch, Alexander 244
Garran, Gabriel 119, 127, 277
Garson, Barbara 138
Gatti Stéphane 157, 230, 289, 292
Geburt, Die 38, 174, 201
Gelas, Gérard 21
Gelber, Jack 14
Gerbal, Raymond 117
Gerstein, Kurt 83
Gesang vom lusitanishen Popanz 21
Gide, André 54
Gilda appelle Maë West 134, 135
Gorki, Maxim 164, 201
Grotowski, Jerzy (The Wroclaw Laboratory Theatre) 14, 202
Guerre entre parenthèses, La 138

Halet, Pierre 135
Hälfe des Himmels und wir, Die 216
Hauts plateaux, ou Cinq leçons à la recherche du Vietnam pour une lycéenne de mai, Les **191–193**, 194, 282
Havel, Vaclav 240
Hearst, Patricia 231, 232, 236, 237
Hitler m'a dit 86
Hochhuth, Rolf 83
Hölderlin, Friedrich 4

Armand Gatti in the Theatre

*Homme qui volait avec des plumes de coq,
L'* 289
Homme seul, Un 11, 32, 42, **53–61**, 151, 153, 256, 282
Hörbiger, Hans **85–87**
Hurstel, Jean 77, 130, 134, 226

Ici et Maintenant, 12
Illusion comique L' 147
Il tuo nome era Letizia, Ton nom était Joie 293
Interdiction de la Passion du Général Franco 243
Interdiction ou petite histoire de l'interdiction d'une pièce qui devait être représentée en violet, jaune et rouge dans un théâtre national, L' 165
Interdit à plus de trente ans 189, **198–199**
Irish Hunger Strikers, The (Patrick Ward, Bobby Sands, Micky Devine, Benedict and Thomas McElwee, Tony O'Hara) 260, 264, 265, **266–267**, 268, 270, 271, 272
Irlande Terre Promise 262, 264
Isle d'Abeau, L' (Jean Perret) **245–253**

Joël Brand, die Geschichte eines Geschäfts **83–84**
Joffroy, Pierre 9, 25, 26, 235
Joint, ou 24 heures de la vie d'une page, Le 231, 232, 233, **234–237**
Joseph Cotinet ou le Combat contre l'ange **218–219**
Journal de guerre de Mikhaïl K 223

Kafka, Franz 89
Katangais, Les **226–227**, 242
Khlebnikov, Velimir 277
Khrushchev, Nikita 10, 44
Kipphardt, Heinar **83–84**
Kleines Handbuch de Stadguerilla 190
Kolyma Tales 239
Kravetz, Marc 4, 17, 69, 166, 169, 235, 242, 281

Labirinto, Il 266
Labyrinthe, Le 256, **266–274**, 282
Labyrinthe tel qu'il a été écrit par les habitants de l'histoire de Derry, Le 271
Lenin 240
Lettres de Sibérie 10
Licorne, La 188, 281–282
Liebknecht, Karl 174, 175, 179, 180, 181, 182, 187
Lion, sa cage et ses ailes, Le **226–231**
Little Boy 135
'Living Theatre, The' (Julian Beck, Judith Malina) 14, 15
Lochy, Claude 112
Loire salue le Kolyma, La 239
Lower Depths, The 201

Mac Bird 138
MacCoy, Horace 109
Machine excavatrice pour entrer dans le plan de défrichement de la colonne d'invasion Che Guevara, La **193–196**, 198
Maiakovski, Vladimir 277
Makhno, Nestor 17, 227, 240, **241–244**, 277, 278, 279, 282
Malevitch, Kazimir 277
Malheur aux sans-patrie. Le drame des personnes déplacées à vie 68
Mallarmé, Stéphane 4
Manet, Edouardo 93, 94, 95
Mann ohne Eisenchaften, Der 77
Mao Tse-tung 12, 44, **45–46**, 51, 54, 55, **57–58**, 146, 216, 240, 269
Maréchal, Marcel (Théâtre du 8e in Lyon) **29–30**
Marker, Chris 9, 10, 42, 51, 63, 127
Matin des Magiciens, Le 86
Medina, Rúben 93, 95
Meinhof, Ulrike 174, 211, **215–217**, 222, 241, 243, 284, 287
Meyerhold, Vsevelod 285
Meynard, Pierre 227, 242
Michaud, Henri 4, 8, 65
Mnouchkine, Ariane (*1789, 1793*), **168–169**, 170
Moitié du ciel et nous, La 201, **215–217**, 270
Monloup, Hubert 33, 60, 78, 94, 111, 119, 126
Monod, Roland 29, 32, **37–38**, 62

298

Index

Monsieur Fugue ou le mal de terre 83
Montagne Ixtaccyhuatl, La 19
Montbéliard (Peugeot) 16, **226–231**, 245, 251, 269
Montreal 283, 287, 288
Montreuil 284, 287, 289
Morambong **10–11**, 54
Moreau-Meynard, Jackie 211
Mother, The 54
Mother Courage 27, 193
Morts sans Sépulture 102
Mühsam, Erich 282
Musil, Robert 77
Mysteries and Smaller Pieces 14

Naissance, La 18, 28, **29–41**, 53, 189, 201, 282
Napalm 138, 146
Nellis, Mary 270
Ne pas perdre de temps sur un titre – Que mettez-vous à la place? – Une rose blanche **196–198**
Nerval, Gérard de 5, 7
Nombre ci-gît, Le 67
Notes de Travail en Ulster 266, 271
Notre Tranchée de chaque jour 30, 93, 94, **98–106**
Nous étions tous des noms d'arbres **256–266**, 288
Nous ne sommes pas des personnages historiques 277

O'Casey, Sean 28
Oiseau-dollar, L' 21
Olive, Jean-Paul 288
Opéra avec Titre Long 91, 188, 283, 287

Paolo Paoli, 12, 127
Paradise Now 15
Parent, Michel 134, 135
Paris 289
Passage des oiseaux dans le ciel, Le 288
Passion du Général Franco, La 29, 134, **157–165**, 167, 189, 193, 201, 207, 275
Passion du Général Franco par les émigrés eux-mêmes, La 157, 158, **165–171**, 207, 221, 224, 231
Passion of Sacco and Vanzetti, The 121
Pauwels, Louis and Jacques Bergier 86

Peking Opera, The 14, 42, 53, 183
Petit Manuel de Guérilla urbaine 189, 190, 196, 198
Peugeot 16, 226, 227, 229, 230
Pirandello, 26, 120
Piscator, Erwin 15, 60, 85, 111
Planchon, Roger 11, 12, 59, 62, 85, 99, 110, 111, 115, 119, 127, 169, 202
Poème cinématographique et ses pronoms personnels, Le **283–284**, 288
Poisson noir, Le 11, 21, 27, 29, 42, **43–53**, 54, 59, 62, 256
Pourquoi les animaux domestiques? ou la journée d'une infirmière **190–191**
Première Lettre, La 5, 245, **248–254**, 282
Prose pour Pékin 42, 54
Prost, Charles 29
Psychiatric Guide for the Use of Dissidents, A 237
Quatre schizophrénies à la recherche d'un pays dont l'existence est contestée 201, **211–214**, 216
Quetzal, Le 18, **19–21**, 35, 107, **212–213**, 256, 288

Rauschning, Hermann 86
Rétoré, Guy 149, 154, 155–156
Révolte des objets, La 277
Rimbaud, Arthur 4, 8
Ris-Orangis **231–237**, 245, 269
Roland Furieux **170–171**
Roli, Mino and Luciano Vincenzoni 117
Ronconi, Luca 170
Rosa Collective **173–188**, 201, 287
Rosa Kollektiv 173, 174
Rosa Luxemburg 174, 175, 201, 215, 222
Rosaspartakus prend le pouvoir **173–188**, 189, 221, 222
Rosner, Jacques 43, 98–99, **110–113**, 126
Rostand, Edmond 65
Rouxel, Roger 6, **248–254**
Rozier, Danièle 134

Sacco and Vanzetti 117
Saint-Nazaire 16, **237–241**, 244, 245, 251

Salacrou, Armand 115
Sarrazin, Maurice 11, 12, 43, 45, 50, 52, 53, 79, 99, 118, 137, 138, 145, 156, 275
Sartre, Jean-Paul 54, 102, 164
Scheidemann, Philipp 179
Scholl, Hans and Sophie 196–197
'selmaire' 42, 119, 120, 124, 125, 126, 128, **198–199**, 242, 243, 244, 271–273
7 possibilités du train 713 en partance d'Auschwitz, Les 288
Serreau, Jean-Marie 134
Shalamov, Varlam 239
Schlacht der Sieben Tage und der Sieben Nächte, Die 60
Schumann, Peter (Bread and Puppet Theatre) 14, 170, 190
Sibérie – zéro + l'infini 9–10, 158, 237
Sollers, Philippe 43
Solzhenitsyn 239
Somoza, Anastasio 12, **22–23**, 95
Soviet Dissidents (Vladimir Bukovsky; Semion Gluzman; Victor Nekrassov; Leonid Pliutch) 12, 16, 237, 238, 239, 240, 241, 244
'stages de réinsertion sociale' 242, **276–279**, 280, 287, 288
Stalin 10, 44, 45, 51, 240
Stellvertreter, Der 83
Strehler, Giorgio 201
Surrealists, The (Andre Breton; Robert Desnos; Philippe Soupault) **7–8**, 11

Tamié, Philippe, Hermon 255, 261
Tautin, Gilles 199
Tavet, Gisèle (Théâtre actuel) 77
Temps des cerises, Le **245–247**
Terminal 14
Tête d'or 26
Théâtre du Soleil, Le (*1789, 1793*), 166, 168, 169, 170
Théâtre Ouvert, Le 220, 244
They Shoot Horses, Don't They? 109
Train 713. A short title for a shortened work 288
Treize Soleils de la rue Saint-Blaise, Les 137, **149–155**, 173, 189
Tribu, La (The Tribe) 165, 168, 169, 207, **208–210**, 220, 221, 222, 223, 224, 225, 231, 232, 233, 237, 238, 239, 241, 242, 244, 245, 247, 248, 249, 250, 252, 269, 270, 275, 280
Tribu des Carcana en guerre contre quoi? La **220–225**, 244
Trotsky, Leon 240

Übergang über den Ebros 215, **218–219**
University of Louvain, The 15, 135, 155, 167, 168, 188, 202, 203, 208, 221
Université de Paris VIII, L' 288–289
University of Rochester, The (USA) 288
US 138

V comme Vietnam **137–149**, 173, 189, 215, 261
Valdés, Eriberto 97
Valdez, Luis (Teatro Campesino) **14–15**
Valéry, Paul, 17, 64
Venice 29, 289
Vicaire, Le 83
Vie de Churchill, La 9
Vienna 73, 287, 288
Vie imaginaire de l'éboueur Auguste Geai, La 3, 11, 28, 34, 35, 43, 66, 77, 79, 94, 98, **107–115**, 126, 128, 129, 134, 135, 143, 155, 161, 202, 226
Vier Schizophrenien auf der Suche nach einem Land, dessen Existenz umstritten ist 211
Vilar, Jean 11, 15, 21, **27–28**, 79, 93, 94, 111, 135, 137, 193, 280
Vinaver, Michel 115
von Brockdorf, Cay and Erika 188, **282–283**
Voyage du centre du Goulag, Le 239
Voyage du Grand Tchou, Le **62–66**

War-Game, The 284
Watkins, Peter 284
Weiss, Peter 21
Wilson, Georges (Théâtre National Populaire in Paris) 118, 163
Writing on the Wall, The 256

Yacine, Kateb 9

Zampieri, Gino 266